WHITE COLLAR CRIME: CASES, MATERIALS, AND PROBLEMS

WHITE COLLAR CRIME: CASES, MATERIALS, AND PROBLEMS

THIRD EDITION

DOCUMENT SUPPLEMENT

J. KELLY STRADER
Professor of Law
Southwestern Law School

SANDRA D. JORDAN
Professor of Law
Charlotte School of Law

2015

 LexisNexis®

Editorial Offices
630 Central Ave., New Providence, NJ 07974 (908) 464-6800
201 Mission St., San Francisco, CA 94105-1831 (415) 908-3200
www.lexisnexis.com

MATTHEW◆BENDER

Acknowledgments

Thanks to my research assistant, Kyle Leonhardt, and Neil Bautista, Southwestern Law School Faculty Support Assistant, for their invaluable help in the preparation of this Supplement.— JKS

Table of Contents

Table of Contents

Table of Contents

Table of Contents

Table of Contents

Table of Contents

Table of Contents

Chapter 1

UNITED STATES CODE

TITLE 14. COAST GUARD

§ 88. Saving Life and Property

(a) In order to render aid to distressed persons, vessels, and aircraft on and under the high seas and on and under the waters over which the United States has jurisdiction and in order to render aid to persons and property imperiled by flood, the Coast Guard may:

(1) perform any and all acts necessary to rescue and aid persons and protect and save property;

(2) take charge of and protect all property saved from marine or aircraft disasters, or floods, at which the Coast Guard is present, until such property is claimed by persons legally authorized to receive it or until otherwise disposed of in accordance with law or applicable regulations, and care for bodies of those who may have perished in such catastrophes;

(3) furnish clothing, food, lodging, medicines, and other necessary supplies and services to persons succored by the Coast Guard; and

(4) destroy or tow into port sunken or floating dangers to navigation.

(b)

(1) Subject to paragraph (2), the Coast Guard may render aid to persons and protect and save property at any time and at any place at which Coast Guard facilities and personnel are available and can be effectively utilized.

(2) The Commandant shall make full use of all available and qualified resources, including the Coast Guard Auxiliary and individuals licensed by the Secretary pursuant to section 8904(b) of title 46, United States Code, in rendering aid under this subsection in nonemergency cases.

(c) An individual who knowingly and willfully communicates a false distress message to the Coast Guard or causes the Coast Guard to attempt to save lives and property when no help is needed is—

(1) guilty of a class D felony;

(2) subject to a civil penalty of not more than $10,000; and

(3) liable for all costs the Coast Guard incurs as a result of the individual's action.

(d) The Secretary shall establish a helicopter rescue swimming program for the purpose of training selected Coast Guard personnel in rescue swimming skills, which may include rescue diver training.

(e) An individual who knowingly and willfully operates a device with the intention of interfering with the broadcast or reception of a radio, microwave, or other signal (including a signal from a global positioning system) transmitted, retransmitted, or augmented by the Coast Guard for the purpose of maritime safety is—

(1) guilty of a class E felony; and

(2) subject to a civil penalty of not more than $1,000 per day for each violation.

TITLE 15.　COMMERCE AND TRADE

§ 1.　Trusts, etc., in restraint of trade illegal; penalty

Every contract, combination in the form of trust or otherwise, or conspiracy, in restraint of trade or commerce among the several States, or with foreign nations, is declared to be illegal. Every person who shall make any contract or engage in any combination or conspiracy hereby declared to be illegal shall be deemed guilty of a felony, and, on conviction thereof, shall be punished by fine not exceeding $100,000,000 if a corporation, or, if any other person, $1,000,000, or by imprisonment not exceeding 10 years, or by both said punishments, in the discretion of the court.

§ 2.　Monopolizing trade a felony; penalty

Every person who shall monopolize, or attempt to monopolize, or combine or conspire with any other person or persons, to monopolize any part of the trade or commerce among the several States, or with foreign nations, shall be deemed guilty of a felony, and, on conviction thereof, shall be punished by fine not exceeding $100,000,000 if a corporation, or, if any other person, $1,000,000, or by imprisonment not exceeding 10 years, or by both said punishments, in the discretion of the court.

§ 77ff.　Accounts and annual balance sheet of Corporation; audits

The board of directors shall cause accounts to be kept of all matters relating to or connected with the transactions and business of the Corporation, and cause a general account and balance sheet of the Corporation to be made out in each year, and cause all accounts to be audited by one or more auditors who shall examine the same and report thereon to the board of directors.

§ 77q.　Fraudulent interstate transactions

(a) Use of interstate commerce for purpose of fraud or deceit

It shall be unlawful for any person in the offer or sale of any securities (including security-based swaps) or any security-based swap agreement (as defined in section 78c(a)(78) of this title) by the use of any means or instruments of transportation or communication in interstate commerce or by use of the mails, directly or indirectly

(1) to employ any device, scheme, or artifice to defraud, or

(2) to obtain money or property by means of any untrue statement of a material fact or any omission to state a material fact necessary in order to make the statements made, in light of the circumstances under which they were made, not misleading; or

(3) to engage in any transaction, practice, or course of business which operates or would operate as a fraud or deceit upon the purchaser.

(b) Use of interstate commerce for purpose of offering for sale

It shall be unlawful for any person, by the use of any means or instruments of transportation or communication in interstate commerce or by the use of the mails, to publish, give publicity to, or circulate any notice, circular, advertisement, newspaper, article, letter, investment service, or communication which, though not purporting to offer a security for sale, describes such security for a consideration received or to be received, directly or indirectly, from an issuer, underwriter, or dealer, without fully disclosing the receipt, whether past or prospective, of such consideration and the amount thereof.

(c) Exemptions, of section 77c not applicable to this section

The exemptions provided in section 77c of this title shall not apply to the provisions of this section.

(d) Limitation

The authority of the Commission under this section with respect to security-based swap agreements (as defined in section 78c(a)(78) of this title) shall be subject to the restrictions and limitations of section 77b-1(b) of this title.

§ 77x.   Penalties

Any person who willfully violates any of the provisions of this subchapter, or the rules and regulations promulgated by the Commission under authority thereof, or any person who willfully, in a registration statement filed under this subchapter, makes any untrue statement of a material fact or omits to state any material fact required to be stated therein or necessary to make the statements therein not misleading, shall upon conviction be fined not more than $10,000 or imprisoned not more than five years, or both.

§ 78b.   Necessity for regulation

For the reasons hereinafter enumerated, transactions in securities as commonly conducted upon securities exchanges and over-the-counter markets are effected with a national public interest which makes it necessary to provide for regulation and control of such transactions and of practices and matters related thereto, including transactions by officers, directors, and principal security holders, to require appropriate reports to remove impediments to and perfect the mechanisms of a national market system for securities and a national system for the clearance and settlement of securities transactions and the safeguarding of securities and funds related thereto, and to impose requirements necessary to make such regulation and control reasonably complete and effective, in order to protect interstate commerce, the national credit, the Federal taxing power, to protect and make more effective the national banking system and Federal Reserve System, and to insure the maintenance of fair and honest markets in such transactions:

(1) Such transactions (a) are carried on in large volume by the public generally and in large part originate outside the States in which the exchanges and over-the-counter markets are located and/or are effected by means of the mails and instrumentalities of interstate commerce; (b) constitute an important part of the current of interstate commerce; (c) involve in large part the securities of issuers engaged in interstate commerce; (d) involve the use of credit, directly

affect the financing of trade, industry, and transportation in interstate commerce, and directly affect and influence the volume of interstate commerce; and affect the national credit.

(2) The prices established and offered in such transactions are generally disseminated and quoted throughout the United States and foreign countries and constitute a basis for determining and establishing the prices at which securities are bought and sold, the amount of certain taxes owing to the United States and to the several States by owners, buyers, and sellers of securities, and the value of collateral for bank loans.

(3) Frequently the prices of securities on such exchanges and markets are susceptible to manipulation and control, and the dissemination of such prices gives rise to excessive speculation, resulting in sudden and unreasonable fluctuations in the prices of securities which (a) cause alternately unreasonable expansion and unreasonable contraction of the volume of credit available for trade, transportation, and industry in interstate commerce, (b) hinder the proper appraisal of the value of securities and thus prevent a fair calculation of taxes owing to the United States and to the several States by owners, buyers, and sellers of securities, and (c) prevent the fair valuation of collateral for bank loans and/or obstruct the effective operation of the national banking system and Federal Reserve System.

(4) National emergencies, which produce widespread unemployment and the dislocation of trade, transportation, and industry, and which burden interstate commerce and adversely affect the general welfare, are precipitated, intensified, and prolonged by manipulation and sudden and unreasonable fluctuations of security prices and by excessive speculation on such exchanges and markets, and to meet such emergencies the Federal Government is put to such great expense as to burden the national credit.

§ 78dd. Foreign Securities Exchange

(a) It shall be unlawful for any broker or dealer, directly or indirectly, to make use of the mails or of any means or instrumentality of interstate commerce for the purpose of effecting on an exchange not within or subject to the jurisdiction of the United States, any transaction in any security the issuer of which is a resident of, or is organized under the laws of, or has its principal place of business in, a place within or subject to the jurisdiction of the United States, in contravention of such rules and regulations as the Commission may prescribe as necessary or appropriate in the public interest or for the protection of investors or to prevent the evasion of this chapter.

(b) The provisions of this chapter or of any rule or regulation thereunder shall not apply to any person insofar as he transacts a business in securities without the jurisdiction of the United States, unless he transacts such business in contravention of such rules and regulations as the Commission may prescribe as necessary or appropriate to prevent the evasion of this chapter.

(c) Rule of construction

No provision of this chapter that was added by the Wall Street Transparency and Accountability Act of 2010, or any rule or regulation thereunder, shall apply to any person insofar as such person transacts a business in security-based swaps without the jurisdiction of the United States, unless such person transacts such business in contravention of such rules and regulations as the Commission may prescribe as necessary or appropriate to prevent the evasion of any provision of this chapter that was added by the Wall Street Transparency and Accountability Act of 2010. This subsection shall not be construed to limit the jurisdiction of the Commission under any provision of this chapter, as in effect prior to July 21, 2010.

§ 78dd-1. Prohibited foreign trade practices by issuers

(a) Prohibition

It shall be unlawful for any issuer which has a class of securities registered pursuant to section 78*l* of this title or which is required to file reports under section 78o(d) of this title, or for any officer, director, employee, or agent of such issuer or any stockholder thereof acting on behalf of such issuer, to make use of the mails or any means or instrumentality of interstate commerce corruptly in furtherance of an offer, payment, promise to pay, or authorization of the payment of any money, or offer, gift, promise to give, or authorization of the giving of anything of value to—

(1) any foreign official for purposes of—

(A)

(i) influencing any act or decision of such foreign official in his official capacity,

(ii) inducing such foreign official to do or omit to do any act in violation of the lawful duty of such official, or

(iii) securing any improper advantage; or

(B) inducing such foreign official to use his influence with a foreign government or instrumentality thereof to affect or influence any act or decision of such government or instrumentality,

in order to assist such issuer in obtaining or retaining business for or with, or directing business to, any person;

(2) any foreign political party or official thereof or any candidate for foreign political office for purposes of—

(A)

(i) influencing any act or decision of such party, official, or candidate in its or his official capacity,

(ii) inducing such party, official, or candidate to do or omit to do an act in violation of the lawful duty of such party, official, or candidate, or

(iii) securing any improper advantage; or

(B) inducing such party, official, or candidate to use its or his influence with a foreign government or instrumentality thereof to affect or influence any act or decision of such government or instrumentality.

in order to assist such issuer in obtaining or retaining business for or with, or directing business to, any person; or

(3) any person, while knowing that all or a portion of such money or thing of value will be offered, given, or promised, directly or indirectly, to any foreign official, to any foreign political party or official thereof, or to any candidate for foreign political office, for purposes of—

    (A)

        (i) influencing any act or decision of such foreign official, political party, party official, or candidate in his or its official capacity,

        (ii) inducing such foreign official, political party, party official, or candidate to do or omit to do any act in violation of the lawful duty of such foreign official, political party, party official, or candidate, or

        (iii) securing any improper advantage; or

    (B) inducing such foreign official, political party, party official, or candidate to use his or its influence with a foreign government or instrumentality thereof to affect or influence any act or decision of such government or instrumentality,

in order to assist such issuer in obtaining or retaining business for or with, or directing business to, any person.

(b) Exception for routine governmental action

Subsections (a) and (g) of this section shall not apply to any facilitating or expediting payment to a foreign official, political party, or party official the purpose of which is to expedite or to secure the performance of a routine governmental action by a foreign official, political party, or party official.

(c) Affirmative defenses

It shall be an affirmative defense to actions under subsection (a) or (g) of this section that—

(1) the payment, gift, offer, or promise of anything of value that was made, was lawful under the written laws and regulations of the foreign official's, political party's, party official's, or candidate's country; or

(2) the payment, gift, offer, or promise of anything of value that was made, was a reasonable and bona fide expenditure, such as travel and lodging expenses, incurred by or on behalf of a foreign official, party, party official, or candidate and was directly related to—

    (A) the promotion, demonstration, or explanation of products or services; or

    (B) the execution or performance of a contract with a foreign government or agency thereof.

(d) Guidelines by Attorney General

Not later than one year after August 23, 1988, the Attorney General, after consultation with the Commission, the Secretary of Commerce, the United States Trade Representative, the Secretary of State, and the Secretary of the Treasury, and after obtaining the views of all interested persons through public notice and comment procedures, shall determine to what extent compliance with this section would be enhanced and the business community would be assisted by further clarification of the preceding provisions of this section and may, based on such determination and to the extent necessary and appropriate, issue—

(1) guidelines describing specific types of conduct, associated with common types of export sales arrangements and business contracts, which for purposes of the Department of Justice's present enforcement policy, the Attorney General determines would be in conformance with the preceding provisions of this section; and

(2) general precautionary procedures which issuers may use on a voluntary basis to conform their conduct to the Department of Justice's present enforcement policy regarding the preceding provisions of this section.

The Attorney General shall issue the guidelines and procedures referred to in the preceding sentence in accordance with the provisions of subchapter II of chapter 5 of Title 5 and those guidelines and procedures shall be subject to the provisions of chapter 7 of that title.

(e) Opinions of Attorney General

(1) The Attorney General, after consultation with appropriate departments and agencies of the United States and after obtaining the views of all interested persons through public notice and comment procedures, shall establish a procedure to provide responses to specific inquiries by issuers concerning conformance of their conduct with the Department of Justice's present enforcement policy regarding the preceding provisions of this section. The Attorney General shall, within 30 days after receiving such a request, issue an opinion in response to that request. The opinion shall state whether or not certain specified prospective conduct would, for purposes of the Department of Justice's present enforcement policy, violate the preceding provisions of this section. Additional requests for opinions may be filed with the Attorney General regarding other specified prospective conduct that is beyond the scope of conduct specified in previous requests. In any action brought under the applicable provisions of this section, there shall be a rebuttable presumption that conduct, which is specified in a request by an issuer and for which the Attorney General has issued an opinion that such conduct is in conformity with the Department of Justice's present enforcement policy, is in compliance with the preceding provisions of this section. Such a presumption may be rebutted by a preponderance of the evidence. In considering the presumption for purposes of this paragraph, a court shall weight all relevant factors, including but not limited to whether the information submitted to the Attorney General was accurate and complete and whether it was within the scope of the conduct specified in any request received by the Attorney General. The Attorney General shall establish the procedure required by this paragraph in accordance with the provisions of subchapter II of chapter 5 of Title 5 and that procedure shall be subject to the provisions of chapter 7 of that title.

(2) Any document or other material which is provided to, received by, or prepared in the Department of Justice or any other department or agency of the United States in connection with a request by an issuer under the procedure established under paragraph (1), shall be exempt from disclosure under section 552 of Title 5 and shall not, except with the consent of the issuer, be made publicly available, regardless of whether the Attorney General responds to such a request or the issuer withdraws such request before receiving a response.

(3) Any issuer who has made a request to the Attorney General under paragraph (1) may withdraw such request prior to the time the Attorney General issues an opinion in response to such request. Any request so withdrawn shall have no force or effect.

(4) The Attorney General shall, to the maximum extent practicable, provide timely guidance concerning the Department of Justice's present enforcement policy with respect to the preceding provisions of this section to potential exporters and small businesses that are unable to obtain specialized counsel on issues pertaining to such provisions. Such guidance shall be limited to responses to requests under paragraph (1) concerning conformity of specified prospective conduct with the Department of Justice's present enforcement policy regarding the preceding provisions of this section and general explanations of compliance responsibilities and of potential liabilities under the preceding provisions of this section.

(f) Definitions

For purposes of this section:

(1)

(A) The term "foreign official" means any officer or employee of a foreign government or any department, agency, or instrumentality thereof, or of a public international organization, or any person acting in an official capacity for or on behalf of any such government or department, agency, or instrumentality, or for or on behalf of any such public international organization.

(B) For purposes of subparagraph (A), the term "public international organization" means—

(i) an organization that is designated by Executive order pursuant to section 1 of the International Organizations Immunities Act (22 U.S.C. 288); or

(ii) any other international organization that is designated by the President by Executive order for the purposes of this section, effective as of the date of publication of such order in the Federal Register.

(2)

(A) A person's state of mind is "knowing" with respect to conduct, a circumstance, or a result if—

(i) such person is aware that such person is engaging in such conduct, that such circumstance exists, or that such result is substantially certain to occur; or

(ii) such person has a firm belief that such circumstance exists or that such result is substantially certain to occur.

(B) When knowledge of the existence of a particular circumstance is required for an offense, such knowledge is established if a person is aware of a high probability of the existence of such circumstance, unless the person actually believes that such circumstance does not exist.

(3)

(A) The term "routine governmental action" means only an action which is ordinarily and commonly performed by a foreign official in—

(i) obtaining permits, licenses, or other official documents to qualify a person to do business in a foreign country;

(ii) processing governmental papers, such as visas and work orders;

(iii) providing police protection, mail pick-up and delivery, or scheduling inspections associated with contract performance or inspections related to transit of goods across country;

(iv) providing phone service, power and water supply, loading and unloading cargo, or protecting perishable products or commodities from deterioration; or

(v) actions of a similar nature.

(B) The term "routine governmental action" does not include any decision by a foreign official whether, or on what terms, to award new business to or to continue business with a particular party, or any action taken by a foreign official involved in the decision-making process to encourage a decision to award new business to or continue business with a particular party.

(g) Alternative jurisdiction

(1) It shall also be unlawful for any issuer organized under the laws of the United States, or a State, territory, possession, or commonwealth of the United States or a political subdivision thereof and which has a class of securities registered pursuant to section 78*l* of this title or which is required to file reports under section 78*o*(d) of this title, or for any United States person that is an officer, director, employee, or agent of such issuer or a stockholder thereof acting on behalf of such issuer, to corruptly do any act outside the United States in furtherance of an offer, payment, promise to pay, or authorization of the payment of any money, or offer, gift, promise to give, or authorization of the giving of anything of value to any of the persons or entities set forth in paragraphs (1), (2), and (3) of subsection (a) of this section for the purposes set forth therein, irrespective of whether such issuer or such officer, director, employee, agent, or stockholder makes use of the mails or any means or instrumentality of interstate commerce in furtherance of such offer, gift, payment, promise, or authorization.

(2) As used in this subsection, the term "United States person" means a national of the United States (as defined in section 101 of the Immigration and

Nationality Act (8 U.S.C. 1101)) or any corporation, partnership, association, joint-stock company, business trust, unincorporated organization, or sole proprietorship organized under the laws of the United States or any State, territory, possession, or commonwealth of the United States, or any political subdivision thereof.

§ 78dd-2. Prohibited foreign trade practices by domestic concerns

(a) Prohibition

It shall be unlawful for any domestic concern, other than an issuer which is subject to section 78dd-1 of this title, or for any officer, director, employee, or agent of such domestic concern or any stockholder thereof acting on behalf of such domestic concern, to make use of the mails or any means or instrumentality of interstate commerce corruptly in furtherance of an offer, payment, promise to pay, or authorization of the payment of any money, or offer, gift, promise to give, or authorization of the giving of anything of value to—

(1) any foreign official for purposes of—

(A)

(i) influencing any act or decision of such foreign official in his official capacity,

(ii) inducing such foreign official to do or omit to do any act in violation of the lawful duty of such official, or

(iii) securing any improper advantage; or

(B) inducing such foreign official to use his influence with a foreign government or instrumentality thereof to affect or influence any act or decision of such government or instrumentality,

in order to assist such domestic concern in obtaining or retaining business for or with, or directing business to, any person;

(2) any foreign political party or official thereof or any candidate for foreign political office for purposes of—

(A)

(i) influencing any act or decision of such party, official, or candidate in its or his official capacity,

(ii) inducing such party, official, or candidate to do or omit to do an act in violation of the lawful duty of such party, official, or candidate, or

(iii) securing any improper advantage; or

(B) inducing such party, official, or candidate to use its or his influence with a foreign government or instrumentality thereof to affect or influence any act or decision of such government or instrumentality,

in order to assist such domestic concern in obtaining or retaining business for or with, or directing business to, any person; or

(3) any person, while knowing that all or a portion of such money or thing of

value will be offered, given, or promised, directly or indirectly, to any foreign official, to any foreign political party or official thereof, or to any candidate for foreign political office, for purposes of—

(A)

    (i) influencing any act or decision of such foreign official, political party, party official, or candidate in his or its official capacity,

    (ii) inducing such foreign official, political party, party official, or candidate to do or omit to do any act in violation of the lawful duty of such foreign official, political party, party official, or candidate, or

    (iii) securing any improper advantage; or

(B) inducing such foreign official, political party, party official, or candidate to use his or its influence with a foreign government or instrumentality thereof to affect or influence any act or decision of such government or instrumentality,

in order to assist such domestic concern in obtaining or retaining business for or with, or directing business to, any person.

(b) Exception for routine governmental action

Subsections (a) and (i) of this section shall not apply to any facilitating or expediting payment to a foreign official, political party, or party official the purpose of which is to expedite or to secure the performance of a routine governmental action by a foreign official, political party, or party official.

(c) Affirmative defenses

It shall be an affirmative defense to actions under subsection (a) or (i) of this section that—

(1) the payment, gift, offer, or promise of anything of value that was made, was lawful under the written laws and regulations of the foreign official's, political party's, party official's, or candidate's country; or

(2) the payment, gift, offer, or promise of anything of value that was made, was a reasonable and bona fide expenditure, such as travel and lodging expenses, incurred by or on behalf of a foreign official, party, party official, or candidate and was directly related to—

    (A) the promotion, demonstration, or explanation of products or services; or

    (B) the execution or performance of a contract with a foreign government or agency thereof.

(d) Injunctive relief

(1) When it appears to the Attorney General that any domestic concern to which this section applies, or officer, director, employee, agent, or stockholder thereof, is engaged, or about to engage, in any act or practice constituting a violation of subsection (a) or (i) of this section, the Attorney General may, in his discretion, bring a civil action in an appropriate district court of the United States to enjoin such act or practice, and upon a proper showing, a permanent injunction or a temporary restraining order shall be granted without bond.

(2) For the purpose of any civil investigation which, in the opinion of the Attorney General, is necessary and proper to enforce this section, the Attorney General or his designee are empowered to administer oaths and affirmations, subpoena witnesses, take evidence, and require the production of any books, papers, or other documents which the Attorney General deems relevant or material to such investigation. The attendance of witnesses and the production of documentary evidence may be required from any place in the United States, or any territory, possession, or commonwealth of the United States, at any designated place of hearing.

(3) In case of contumacy by, or refusal to obey a subpoena issued to, any person, the Attorney General may invoke the aid of any court of the United States within the jurisdiction of which such investigation or proceeding is carried on, or where such person resides or carries on business, in requiring the attendance and testimony of witnesses and the production of books, papers, or other documents. Any such court may issue an order requiring such person to appear before the Attorney General or his designee, there to produce records, if so ordered, or to give testimony touching the matter under investigation. Any failure to obey such order of the court may be punished by such court as a contempt thereof.

All process in any such case may be served in the judicial district in which such person resides or may be found. The Attorney General may make such rules relating to civil investigations as may be necessary or appropriate to implement the provisions of this subsection.

(e) Guidelines by Attorney General

Not later than 6 months after August 23, 1988, the Attorney General, after consultation with the Securities and Exchange Commission, the Secretary of Commerce, the United States Trade Representative, the Secretary of State, and the Secretary of the Treasury, and after obtaining the views of all interested persons through public notice and comment procedures, shall determine to what extent compliance with this section would be enhanced and the business community would be assisted by further clarification of the preceding provisions of this section and may, based on such determination and to the extent necessary and appropriate, issue—

(1) guidelines describing specific types of conduct, associated with common types of export sales arrangements and business contracts, which for purposes of the Department of Justice's present enforcement policy, the Attorney General determines would be in conformance with the preceding provisions of this section; and

(2) general precautionary procedures which domestic concerns may use on a voluntary basis to conform their conduct to the Department of Justice's present enforcement policy regarding the preceding provisions of this section.

The Attorney General shall issue the guidelines and procedures referred to in the preceding sentence in accordance with the provisions of subchapter II of chapter 5 of Title 5 and those guidelines and procedures shall be subject to the provisions of chapter 7 of that title.

(f) Opinions of Attorney General

(1) The Attorney General, after consultation with appropriate departments and agencies of the United States and after obtaining the views of all interested persons through public notice and comment procedures, shall establish a procedure to provide responses to specific inquiries by domestic concerns concerning conformance of their conduct with the Department of Justice's present enforcement policy regarding the preceding provisions of this section. The Attorney General shall, within 30 days after receiving such a request, issue an opinion in response to that request. The opinion shall state whether or not certain specified prospective conduct would, for purposes of the Department of Justice's present enforcement policy, violate the preceding provisions of this section. Additional requests for opinions may be filed with the Attorney General regarding other specified prospective conduct that is beyond the scope of conduct specified in previous requests. In any action brought under the applicable provisions of this section, there shall be a rebuttable presumption that conduct, which is specified in a request by a domestic concern and for which the Attorney General has issued an opinion that such conduct is in conformity with the Department of Justice's present enforcement policy, is in compliance with the preceding provisions of this section. Such a presumption may be rebutted by a preponderance of the evidence. In considering the presumption for purposes of this paragraph, a court shall weigh all relevant factors, including but not limited to whether the information submitted to the Attorney General was accurate and complete and whether it was within the scope of the conduct specified in any request received by the Attorney General. The Attorney General shall establish the procedure required by this paragraph in accordance with the provisions of subchapter II of chapter 5 of Title 5 and that procedure shall be subject to the provisions of chapter 7 of that title.

(2) Any document or other material which is provided to, received by, or prepared in the Department of Justice or any other department or agency of the United States in connection with a request by a domestic concern under the procedure established under paragraph (1), shall be exempt from disclosure under section 552 of Title 5 and shall not, except with the consent of the domestic concern, by made publicly available, regardless of whether the Attorney General response to such a request or the domestic concern withdraws such request before receiving a response.

(3) Any domestic concern who has made a request to the Attorney General under paragraph (1) may withdraw such request prior to the time the Attorney General issues an opinion in response to such request. Any request so withdrawn shall have no force or effect.

(4) The Attorney General shall, to the maximum extent practicable, provide timely guidance concerning the Department of Justice's present enforcement policy with respect to the preceding provisions of this section to potential exporters and small businesses that are unable to obtain specialized counsel on issues pertaining to such provisions. Such guidance shall be limited to responses to requests under paragraph (1) concerning conformity of specified prospective conduct with the Department of Justice's present enforcement policy regarding the preceding provisions of this section and general explanations of compliance responsibilities and of potential liabilities under the preceding provisions of this

section.

(g) Penalties

(1)

(A) Any domestic concern that is not a natural person and that violates subsection (a) or (i) of this section shall be fined not more than $2,000,000.

(B) Any domestic concern that is not a natural person and that violates subsection (a) or (i) of this section shall be subject to a civil penalty of not more than $10,000 imposed in an action brought by the Attorney General.

(2)

(A) Any natural person that is an officer, director, employee, or agent of a domestic concern, or stockholder acting on behalf of such domestic concern, who willfully violates subsection (a) or (i) of this section shall be fined not more than $100,000 or imprisoned not more than 5 years, or both.

(B) Any natural person that is an officer, director, employee, or agent of a domestic concern, or stockholder acting on behalf of such domestic concern, who violates subsection (a) or (i) of this section shall be subject to a civil penalty of not more than $10,000 imposed in an action brought by the Attorney General.

(3) Whenever a fine is imposed under paragraph (2) upon any officer, director, employee, agent, or stockholder of a domestic concern, such fine may not be paid, directly or indirectly, by such domestic concern.

(h) Definitions

For purposes of this section:

(1) The term "domestic concern" means—

(A) any individual who is a citizen, national, or resident of the United States; and

(B) any corporation, partnership, association, joint-stock company, business trust, unincorporated organization, or sole proprietorship which has its principal place of business in the United States, or which is organized under the laws of a State of the United States or a territory, possession, or commonwealth of the United States.

(2)

(A) The term "foreign official" means any officer or employee of a foreign government or any department, agency, or instrumentality thereof, or of a public international organization, or any person acting in an official capacity for or on behalf of any such government or department, agency, or instrumentality, or for or on behalf of any such public international organization.

(B) For purposes of subparagraph (A), the term "public international organization" means—

(i) an organization that is designated by Executive order pursuant to section 1 of the International Organizations Immunities Act (22 U.S.C. 288); or

(ii) any other international organization that is designated by the President by Executive order for the purposes of this section, effective as of the date of publication of such order in the Federal Register.

(3)

(A) A person's state of mind is "knowing" with respect to conduct, a circumstance, or a result if—

(i) such person is aware that such person is engaging in such conduct, that such circumstance exists, or that such result is substantially certain to occur; or

(ii) such person has a firm belief that such circumstance exists or that such result is substantially certain to occur.

(B) When knowledge of the existence of a particular circumstance is required for an offense, such knowledge is established if a person is aware of a high probability of the existence of such circumstance, unless the person actually believes that such circumstance does not exist.

(4)

(A) The term "routine governmental action" means only an action which is ordinarily and commonly performed by a foreign official in—

(i) obtaining permits, licenses, or other official documents to qualify a person to do business in a foreign country;

(ii) processing governmental papers, such as visas and work orders;

(iii) providing police protection, mail pick-up and delivery, or scheduling inspections associated with contract performance or inspections related to transit of goods across country;

(iv) providing phone service, power and water supply, loading and unloading cargo, or protecting perishable products or commodities from deterioration; or

(v) actions of a similar nature.

(B) The term "routine governmental action" does not include any decision by a foreign official whether, or on what terms, to award new business to or to continue business with a particular party, or any action taken by a foreign official involved in the decision-making process to encourage a decision to award new business to or continue business with a particular party.

(5) The term "interstate commerce" means trade, commerce, transportation, or communication among the several States, or between any foreign country and any State or between any State and any place or ship outside thereof, and such term includes the intrastate use of—

(A) a telephone or other interstate means of communication, or

(B) any other interstate instrumentality.

(i) Alternative jurisdiction

(1) It shall also be unlawful for any United States person to corruptly do any act outside the United States in furtherance of an offer, payment, promise to pay, or authorization of the payment of any money, or offer, gift, promise to give, or authorization of the giving of anything of value to any of the persons or entities set forth in paragraphs (1), (2), and (3) of subsection (a), for the purposes set forth therein, irrespective of whether such United States person makes use of the mails or any means or instrumentality of interstate commerce in furtherance of such offer, gift, payment, promise, or authorization.

(2) As used in this subsection, the term "United States person" means a national of the United States (as defined in section 101 of the Immigration and Nationality Act (8 U.S.C. 1101)) or any corporation, partnership, association, joint-stock company, business trust, unincorporated organization, or sole proprietorship organized under the laws of the United States or any State, territory, possession, or commonwealth of the United States, or any political subdivision thereof.

§ 78dd-3. Prohibited foreign trade practices by persons other than issuers or domestic concerns

(a) Prohibition

It shall be unlawful for any person other than an issuer that is subject to section 78dd-1 of this title or a domestic concern (as defined in section 78dd-2 of this title), or for any officer, director, employee, or agent of such person or any stockholder thereof acting on behalf of such person, while in the territory of the United States, corruptly to make use of the mails or any means or instrumentality of interstate commerce or to do any other act in furtherance of an offer, payment, promise to pay, or authorization of the payment of any money, or offer, gift, promise to give, or authorization of the giving of anything of value to—

(1) any foreign official for purposes of—

(A)

(i) influencing any act or decision of such foreign official in his official capacity,

(ii) inducing such foreign official to do or omit to do any act in violation of the lawful duty of such official, or

(iii) securing any improper advantage; or

(B) inducing such foreign official to use his influence with a foreign government or instrumentality thereof to affect or influence any act or decision of such government or instrumentality,

in order to assist such person in obtaining or retaining business for or with, or directing business to, any person;

(2) any foreign political party or official thereof or any candidate for foreign

political office for purposes of—

(A)

(i) influencing any act or decision of such party, official, or candidate in its or his official capacity,

(ii) inducing such party, official, or candidate to do or omit to do an act in violation of the lawful duty of such party, official, or candidate, or

(iii) securing any improper advantage; or

(B) inducing such party, official, or candidate to use its or his influence with a foreign government or instrumentality thereof to affect or influence any act or decision of such government or instrumentality,

in order to assist such person in obtaining or retaining business for or with, or directing business to, any person; or

(3) any person, while knowing that all or a portion of such money or thing of value will be offered, given, or promised, directly or indirectly, to any foreign official, to any foreign political party or official thereof, or to any candidate for foreign political office, for purposes of—

(A)

(i) influencing any act or decision of such foreign official, political party, party official, or candidate in his or its official capacity,

(ii) inducing such foreign official, political party, party official, or candidate to do or omit to do any act in violation of the lawful duty of such foreign official, political party, party official, or candidate, or

(iii) securing any improper advantage; or

(B) inducing such foreign official, political party, party official, or candidate to use his or its influence with a foreign government or instrumentality thereof to affect or influence any act or decision of such government or instrumentality,

in order to assist such person in obtaining or retaining business for or with, or directing business to, any person.

(b) Exception for routine governmental action

Subsection (a) of this section shall not apply to any facilitating or expediting payment to a foreign official, political party, or party official the purpose of which is to expedite or to secure the performance of a routine governmental action by a foreign official, political party, or party official.

(c) Affirmative defenses

It shall be an affirmative defense to actions under subsection (a) of this section that—

(1) the payment, gift, offer, or promise of anything of value that was made, was lawful under the written laws and regulations of the foreign official's, political party's, party official's, or candidate's country; or

(2) the payment, gift, offer, or promise of anything of value that was made, was a reasonable and bona fide expenditure, such as travel and lodging expenses, incurred by or on behalf of a foreign official, party, party official, or candidate and was directly related to—

(A) the promotion, demonstration, or explanation of products or services; or

(B) the execution or performance of a contract with a foreign government or agency thereof.

(d) Injunctive relief

(1) When it appears to the Attorney General that any person to which this section applies, or officer, director, employee, agent, or stockholder thereof, is engaged, or about to engage, in any act or practice constituting a violation of subsection (a) of this section, the Attorney General may, in his discretion, bring a civil action in an appropriate district court of the United States to enjoin such act or practice, and upon a proper showing, a permanent injunction or a temporary restraining order shall be granted without bond.

(2) For the purpose of any civil investigation which, in the opinion of the Attorney General, is necessary and proper to enforce this section, the Attorney General or his designee are empowered to administer oaths and affirmations, subpoena witnesses, take evidence, and require the production of any books, papers, or other documents which the Attorney General deems relevant or material to such investigation. The attendance of witnesses and the production of documentary evidence may be required from any place in the United States, or any territory, possession, or commonwealth of the United States, at any designated place of hearing.

(3) In case of contumacy by, or refusal to obey a subpoena issued to, any person, the Attorney General may invoke the aid of any court of the United States within the jurisdiction of which such investigation or proceeding is carried on, or where such person resides or carries on business, in requiring the attendance and testimony of witnesses and the production of books, papers, or other documents. Any such court may issue an order requiring such person to appear before the Attorney General or his designee, there to produce records, if so ordered, or to give testimony touching the matter under investigation. Any failure to obey such order of the court may be punished by such court as a contempt thereof.

(4) All process in any such case may be served in the judicial district in which such person resides or may be found. The Attorney General may make such rules relating to civil investigations as may be necessary or appropriate to implement the provisions of this subsection.

(e) Penalties

(1)

(A) Any juridical person that violates subsection (a) of this section shall be fined not more than $2,000,000.

(B) Any juridical person that violates subsection (a) of this section shall be subject to a civil penalty of not more than $10,000 imposed in an action brought by the Attorney General.

(2)

(A) Any natural person who willfully violates subsection (a) of this section shall be fined not more than $100,000 or imprisoned not more than 5 years, or both.

(B) Any natural person who violates subsection (a) of this section shall be subject to a civil penalty of not more than $10,000 imposed in an action brought by the Attorney General.

(3) Whenever a fine is imposed under paragraph (2) upon any officer, director, employee, agent, or stockholder of a person, such fine may not be paid, directly or indirectly, by such person.

(f) Definitions

For purposes of this section:

(1) The term "person", when referring to an offender, means any natural person other than a national of the United States (as defined in section 101 of the Immigration and Nationality Act (8 U.S.C. 1101) or any corporation, partnership, association, joint-stock company, business trust, unincorporated organization, or sole proprietorship organized under the law of a foreign nation or a political subdivision thereof.

(2)

(A) The term "foreign official" means any officer or employee of a foreign government or any department, agency, or instrumentality thereof, or of a public international organization, or any person acting in an official capacity for or on behalf of any such government or department, agency, or instrumentality, or for or on behalf of any such public international organization.

(B) For purposes of subparagraph (A), the term "public international organization" means—

(i) an organization that is designated by Executive order pursuant to section 1 of the International Organizations Immunities Act (22 U.S.C. 288); or

(ii) any other international organization that is designated by the President by Executive order for the purposes of this section, effective as of the date of publication of such order in the Federal Register.

(3)

(A) A person's state of mind is knowing, with respect to conduct, a circumstance or a result if—

(i) such person is aware that such person is engaging in such conduct, that such circumstance exists, or that such result is substantially certain to occur; or

(ii) such person has a firm belief that such circumstance exists or that such result is substantially certain to occur.

(B) When knowledge of the existence of a particular circumstance is required for an offense, such knowledge is established if a person is aware of a high probability of the existence of such circumstance, unless the person actually believes that such circumstance does not exist.

(4)

(A) The term "routine governmental action" means only an action which is ordinarily and commonly performed by a foreign official in—

(i) obtaining permits, licenses, or other official documents to qualify a person to do business in a foreign country;

(ii) processing governmental papers, such as visas and work orders;

(iii) providing police protection, mail pick-up and delivery, or scheduling inspections associated with contract performance or inspections related to transit of goods across country;

(iv) providing phone service, power and water supply, loading and unloading cargo, or protecting perishable products or commodities from deterioration; or

(v) actions of a similar nature.

(B) The term "routine governmental action" does not include any decision by a foreign official whether, or on what terms, to award new business to or to continue business with a particular party, or any action taken by a foreign official involved in the decision-making process to encourage a decision to award new business to or continue business with a particular party.

(5) The term "interstate commerce" means trade, commerce, transportation, or communication among the several States, or between any foreign country and any State or between any State and any place or ship outside thereof, and such term includes the intrastate use of—

(A) a telephone or other interstate means of communication, or

(B) any other interstate instrumentality.

§ 78j.   Manipulative and deceptive devices

It shall be unlawful for any person, directly or indirectly, by the use of any means or instrumentality of interstate commerce or of the mails, or of any facility of any national securities exchange—

(a)

(1) To effect a short sale, or to use or employ any stop-loss order in connection with the purchase or sale, of any security other than a government security, in contravention of such rules and regulations as the Commission may prescribe as necessary or appropriate in the public interest or for the protection of investors.

(2) Paragraph (1) of this subsection shall not apply to security futures products.

(b) To use or employ, in connection with the purchase or sale of any security registered on a national securities exchange or any security not so registered, or any securities-based swap agreement any manipulative or deceptive device or contrivance in contravention of such rules and regulations as the Commission may prescribe as necessary or appropriate in the public interest or for the protection of investors.

(c)

(1) To effect, accept, or facilitate a transaction involving the loan or borrowing of securities in contravention of such rules and regulations as the Commission may prescribe as necessary or appropriate in the public interest or for the protection of investors.

(2) Nothing in paragraph (1) may be construed to limit the authority of the appropriate Federal banking agency (as defined in section 1813(q) of Title 12), the National Credit Union Administration, or any other Federal department or agency having a responsibility under Federal law to prescribe rules or regulations restricting transactions involving the loan or borrowing of securities in order to protect the safety and soundness of a financial institution or to protect the financial system from systemic risk.

Rules promulgated under subsection (b) of this section that prohibit fraud, manipulation, or insider trading (but not rules imposing or specifying reporting or recordkeeping requirements, procedures, or standards as prophylactic measures against fraud, manipulation, or insider trading), and judicial precedents decided under subsection (b) of this section and rules promulgated thereunder that prohibit fraud, manipulation, or insider trading, shall apply to security-based swap agreements to the same extent as they apply to securities. Judicial precedents decided under section 77q(a) of this title and sections 78i, 78*o*, 78p, 78t, and 78u-1 of this title, and judicial precedents decided under applicable rules promulgated under such sections, shall apply to security-based swap agreements to the same extent as they apply to securities.

§ 78m. Periodical and other reports

(a) Reports by issuer of security; contents

Every issuer of a security registered pursuant to section 78l of this title shall file with the Commission, in accordance with such rules and regulations as the Commission may prescribe as necessary or appropriate for the proper protection of investors and to insure fair dealing in the security

(1) such information and documents (and such copies thereof) as the Commission shall require to keep reasonably current the information and documents required to be included in or filed with an application or registration statement filed pursuant to section 78l of this title, except that the Commission may not require the filing of any material contract wholly executed before July 1, 1962.

(2) such annual reports (and such copies thereof), certified if required by the rules and regulations of the Commission by independent public accountants, and such quarterly reports (and such copies thereof), as the Commission may prescribe.

Every issuer of a security registered on a national securities exchange shall also file a duplicate original of such information, documents, and reports with the exchange. In any registration statement, periodic report, or other reports to be filed with the Commission, an emerging growth company need not present selected financial data in accordance with section 229.301 of title 17, Code of Federal Regulations, for any period prior to the earliest audited period presented in connection with its first registration statement that became effective under this chapter or the Securities Act of 1933 and, with respect to any such statement or reports, an emerging growth company may not be required to comply with any new or revised financial accounting standard until such date that a company that is not an issuer (as defined under section 7201 of this title) is required to comply with such new or revised accounting standard, if such standard applies to companies that are not issuers.

(b) Form of report; books, records, and internal accounting; directives

(1) The Commission may prescribe, in regard to reports made pursuant to this chapter, the form or forms in which the required information shall be set forth, the items or details to be shown in the balance sheet and the earnings statement, and the methods to be followed in the preparation of reports, in the appraisal or valuation of assets and liabilities, in the determination of depreciation and depletion, in the differentiation of recurring and nonrecurring income, in the differentiation of investment and operating income, and in the preparation, where the Commission deems it necessary or desirable, of separate and/or consolidated balance sheets or income accounts of any person directly or indirectly controlling or controlled by the issuer, or any person under direct or indirect common control with the issuer; but in the case of the reports of any person whose methods of accounting are prescribed under the provisions of any law of the United States, or any rule or regulation thereunder, the rules and regulations of the Commission with respect to reports shall not be inconsistent with the requirements imposed by such law or rule or regulation in respect of the same subject matter (except that such rules and regulations of the Commission may be inconsistent with such requirements to the extent that the Commission determines that the public interest or the protection of investors so requires).

(2) Every issuer which has a class of securities registered pursuant to section 78*l* of this title and every issuer which is required to file reports pursuant to section 78*o*(d) of this title shall—

(A) make and keep books, records, and accounts, which, in reasonable detail, accurately and fairly reflect the transactions and dispositions of the assets of the issuer;

(B) devise and maintain a system of internal accounting controls sufficient to provide reasonable assurances that—

(i) transactions are executed in accordance with management's general or specific authorization;

(ii) transactions are recorded as necessary

(I) to permit preparation of financial statements in conformity with generally accepted accounting principles or any other criteria applicable to such statements, and

(II) to maintain accountability for assets;

(iii) access to assets is permitted only in accordance with management's general or specific authorization; and

(iv) the recorded accountability for assets is compared with the existing assets at reasonable intervals and appropriate action is taken with respect to any differences; and

(C) notwithstanding any other provision of law, pay the allocable share of such issuer of a reasonable annual accounting support fee or fees, determined in accordance with section 7219 of this title.

(3)

(A) With respect to matters concerning the national security of the United States, no duty or liability under paragraph (2) of this subsection shall be imposed upon any person acting in cooperation with the head of any Federal department or agency responsible for such matters if such act in cooperation with such head of a department or agency was done upon the specific, written directive of the head of such department or agency pursuant to Presidential authority to issue such directives. Each directive issued under this paragraph shall set forth the specific facts and circumstances with respect to which the provisions of this paragraph are to be invoked. Each such directive shall, unless renewed in writing, expire one year after the date of issuance.

(B) Each head of a Federal department or agency of the United States who issues a directive pursuant to this paragraph shall maintain a complete file of all such directives and shall, on October 1 of each year, transmit a summary of matters covered by such directives in force at any time during the previous year to the Permanent Select Committee on Intelligence of the House of Representatives and the Select Committee on Intelligence of the Senate.

(4) No criminal liability shall be imposed for failing to comply with the requirements of paragraph (2) of this subsection except as provided in paragraph (5) of this subsection.

(5) No person shall knowingly circumvent or knowingly fail to implement a system of internal accounting controls or knowingly falsify any book, record, or account described in paragraph (2).

(6) Where an issuer which has a class of securities registered pursuant to section 78l of this title or an issuer which is required to file reports pursuant to section 78o(d) of this title holds 50 per centum or less of the voting power with respect to a domestic or foreign firm, the provisions of paragraph (2) require only that the issuer proceed in good faith to use its influence, to the extent reasonable under the issuer's circumstances, to cause such domestic or foreign firm to devise and maintain a system of internal accounting controls consistent with paragraph (2). Such circumstances include the relative degree of the issuer's ownership of the domestic or foreign firm and the laws and practices governing the business

operations of the country in which such firm is located. An issuer which demonstrates good faith efforts to use such influence shall be conclusively presumed to have complied with the requirements of paragraph (2).

(7) For the purpose of paragraph (2) of this subsection, the terms "reasonable assurances" and "reasonable detail" mean such level of detail and degree of assurance as would satisfy prudent officials in the conduct of their own affairs.

(c) Alternative reports

If in the judgment of the Commission any report required under subsection (a) of this section is inapplicable to any specified class or classes of issuers, the Commission shall require in lieu thereof the submission of such reports of comparable character as it may deem applicable to such class or classes of issuers.

(d) Reports by persons acquiring more than five per centum of certain classes of securities

(1) Any person who, after acquiring directly or indirectly the beneficial ownership of any equity security of a class which is registered pursuant to section 78*l* of this title, or any equity security of an insurance company which would have been required to be so registered except for the exemption contained in section 78*l*(g)(2)(G) of this title, or any equity security issued by a closed-end investment company registered under the Investment Company Act of 1940 [15 U.S.C.A. § 80a-1 et seq.] or any equity security issued by a Native Corporation pursuant to section 1629c(d)(6) of Title 43, or otherwise becomes or is deemed to become a beneficial owner of any of the foregoing upon the purchase or sale of a security-based swap that the Commission may define by rule, and is directly or indirectly the beneficial owner of more than 5 per centum of such class shall, within ten days after such acquisition or within such shorter time as the Commission may establish by rule, file with the Commission, a statement containing such of the following information, and such additional information, as the Commission may by rules and regulations, prescribe as necessary or appropriate in the public interest or for the protection of investors—

(A) the background, and identity, residence, and citizenship of, and the nature of such beneficial ownership by, such person and all other persons by whom or on whose behalf the purchases have been or are to be effected;

(B) the source and amount of the funds or other consideration used or to be used in making the purchases, and if any part of the purchase price is represented or is to be represented by funds or other consideration borrowed or otherwise obtained for the purpose of acquiring, holding, or trading such security, a description of the transaction and the names of the parties thereto, except that where a source of funds is a loan made in the ordinary course of business by a bank, as defined in section 78c(a)(6) of this title, if the person filing such statement so requests, the name of the bank shall not be made available to the public;

(C) if the purpose of the purchases or prospective purchases is to acquire control of the business of the issuer of the securities, any plans or proposals which such persons may have to liquidate such issuer, to sell its assets to or merge it with any other persons, or to make any other major change in its business or corporate structure;

(D) the number of shares of such security which are beneficially owned, and the number of shares concerning which there is a right to acquire, directly or indirectly, by (i) such person, and (ii) by each associate of such person, giving the background, identity, residence, and citizenship of each such associate; and

(E) information as to any contracts, arrangements, or understandings with any person with respect to any securities of the issuer, including but not limited to transfer of any of the securities, joint ventures, loan or option arrangements, puts or calls, guaranties of loans, guaranties against loss or guaranties of profits, division of losses or profits, or the giving or withholding of proxies, naming the persons with whom such contracts, arrangements, or understandings have been entered into, and giving the details thereof.

(2) If any material change occurs in the facts set forth in the statement filed with the Commission, an amendment shall be filed with the Commission, in accordance with such rules and regulations as the Commission may prescribe as necessary or appropriate in the public interest or for the protection of investors.

(3) When two or more persons act as a partnership, limited partnership, syndicate, or other group for the purpose of acquiring, holding, or disposing of securities of an issuer, such syndicate or group shall be deemed a "person" for the purposes of this subsection.

(4) In determining, for purposes of this subsection, any percentage of a class of any security, such class shall be deemed to consist of the amount of the outstanding securities of such class, exclusive of any securities of such class held by or for the account of the issuer or a subsidiary of the issuer.

(5) The Commission, by rule or regulation or by order, may permit any person to file in lieu of the statement required by paragraph (1) of this subsection or the rules and regulations thereunder, a notice stating the name of such person, the number of shares of any equity securities subject to paragraph (1) which are owned by him, the date of their acquisition and such other information as the Commission may specify, if it appears to the Commission that such securities were acquired by such person in the ordinary course of his business and were not acquired for the purpose of and do not have the effect of changing or influencing the control of the issuer nor in connection with or as a participant in any transaction having such purpose or effect.

(6) The provisions of this subsection shall not apply to—

(A) any acquisition or offer to acquire securities made or proposed to be made by means of a registration statement under the Securities Act of 1933 [15 U.S.C.A. 77a et seq.];

(B) any acquisition of the beneficial ownership of a security which, together with all other acquisitions by the same person of securities of the same class during the preceding twelve months, does not exceed 2 per centum of that class;

(C) any acquisition of an equity security by the issuer of such security;

(D) any acquisition or proposed acquisition of a security which the Commission, by rules or regulations or by order, shall exempt from the provisions of this subsection as not entered into for the purpose of, and not having the effect of, changing or influencing the control of the issuer or otherwise as not comprehended within the purposes of this subsection.

(e) Purchase of securities by issuer

(1) It shall be unlawful for an issuer which has a class of equity securities registered pursuant to section 78*l* of this title, or which is a closed-end investment company registered under the Investment Company Act of 1940 [15 U.S.C.A. § 80a-1 et seq.], to purchase any equity security issued by it if such purchase is in contravention of such rules and regulations as the Commission, in the public interest or for the protection of investors, may adopt

(A) to define acts and practices which are fraudulent, deceptive, or manipulative, and

(B) to prescribe means reasonably designed to prevent such acts and practices. Such rules and regulations may require such issuer to provide holders of equity securities of such class with such information relating to the reasons for such purchase, the source of funds, the number of shares to be purchased, the price to be paid for such securities, the method of purchase, and such additional information, as the Commission deems necessary or appropriate in the public interest or for the protection of investors, or which the Commission deems to be material to a determination whether such security should be sold.

(2) For the purpose of this subsection, a purchase by or for the issuer or any person controlling, controlled by, or under common control with the issuer, or a purchase subject to control of the issuer or any such person, shall be deemed to be a purchase by the issuer. The Commission shall have power to make rules and regulations implementing this paragraph in the public interest and for the protection of investors, including exemptive rules and regulations covering situations in which the Commission deems it unnecessary or inappropriate that a purchase of the type described in this paragraph shall be deemed to be a purchase by the issuer for purposes of some or all of the provisions of paragraph (1) of this subsection.

(3) At the time of filing such statement as the Commission may require by rule pursuant to paragraph (1) of this subsection, the person making the filing shall pay to the Commission a fee at a rate that, subject to paragraph (4), is equal to $92 per $1,000,000 of the value of securities proposed to be purchased. The fee shall be reduced with respect to securities in an amount equal to any fee paid with respect to any securities issued in connection with the proposed transaction under section 77f(b) of this title, or the fee paid under that section shall be reduced in an amount equal to the fee paid to the Commission in connection with such transaction under this paragraph.

(4) Annual adjustment

For each fiscal year, the Commission shall by order adjust the rate required by paragraph (3) for such fiscal year to a rate that is equal to the rate (expressed in dollars per million) that is applicable under section 6(b) of the Securities Act of 1933 for such fiscal year.

(5) Fee collections

Fees collected pursuant to this subsection for fiscal year 2012 and each fiscal year thereafter shall be deposited and credited as general revenue of the Treasury and shall not be available for obligation. (6) Annual adjustment

(6) Effective date; publication

In exercising its authority under this subsection, the Commission shall not be required to comply with the provisions of section 553 of Title 5. An adjusted rate prescribed under paragraph (4) shall be published and take effect in accordance with section 6(b) of the Securities Act of 1933 (15 U.S.C. 77f(b)).

(7) Pro rata application

The rates per $1,000,000 required by this subsection shall be applied pro rata to amounts and balances of less than $1,000,000.

(8) to (10) Repealed. Pub.L. 111-203, Title IX, § 991(b)(2), July 21, 2010, 124 Stat. 1952

(f) Reports by institutional investment managers

(1) Every institutional investment manager which uses the mails, or any means or instrumentality of interstate commerce in the course of its business as an institutional investment manager and which exercises investment discretion with respect to accounts holding equity securities of a class described in subsection (d)(1) of this section or otherwise becomes or is deemed to become a beneficial owner of any security of a class described in subsection (d)(1) upon the purchase or sale of a security-based swap that the Commission may define by rule, having an aggregate fair market value on the last trading day in any of the preceding twelve months of at least $100,000,000 or such lesser amount (but in no case less than $10,000,000) as the Commission, by rule, may determine, shall file reports with the Commission in such form, for such periods, and at such times after the end of such periods as the Commission, by rule, may prescribe, but in no event shall such reports be filed for periods longer than one year or shorter than one quarter. Such reports shall include for each such equity security held on the last day of the reporting period by accounts (in aggregate or by type as the Commission, by rule, may prescribe) with respect to which the institutional investment manager exercises investment discretion (other than securities held in amounts which the Commission, by rule, determines to be insignificant for purposes of this subsection), the name of the issuer and the title, class, CUSIP number, number of shares or principal amount, and aggregate fair market value of each such security. Such reports may also include for accounts (in aggregate or by type) with respect to which the institutional investment manager exercises investment discretion such of the following information as the Commission, by rule, prescribes—

(A) the name of the issuer and the title, class, CUSIP number, number of shares or principal amount, and aggregate fair market value or cost or amortized cost of each other security (other than an exempted security) held on the last day of the reporting period by such accounts;

(B) the aggregate fair market value or cost or amortized cost of exempted securities (in aggregate or by class) held on the last day of the reporting period by such accounts;

(C) the number of shares of each equity security of a class described in subsection (d)(1) of this section held on the last day of the reporting period by such accounts with respect to which the institutional investment manager possesses sole or shared authority to exercise the voting rights evidenced by such securities;

(D) the aggregate purchases and aggregate sales during the reporting period of each security (other than an exempted security) effected by or for such accounts; and

(E) with respect to any transaction or series of transactions having a market value of at least $500,000 or such other amount as the Commission, by rule, may determine, effected during the reporting period by or for such accounts in any equity security of a class described in subsection (d)(1) of this section—

(i) the name of the issuer and the title, class, and CUSIP number of the security;

(ii) the number of shares or principal amount of the security involved in the transaction;

(iii) whether the transaction was a purchase or sale;

(iv) the per share price or prices at which the transaction was effected;

(v) the date or dates of the transaction;

(vi) the date or dates of the settlement of the transaction;

(vii) the broker or dealer through whom the transaction was effected;

(viii) the market or markets in which the transaction was effected; and

(ix) such other related information as the Commission, by rule, may prescribe.

(2) The Commission shall prescribe rules providing for the public disclosure of the name of the issuer and the title, class, CUSIP number, aggregate amount of the number of short sales of each security, and any additional information determined by the Commission following the end of the reporting period. At a minimum, such public disclosure shall occur every month.

(3) The Commission, by rule, or order, may exempt, conditionally or unconditionally, any institutional investment manager or security or any class of institutional investment managers or securities from any or all of the provisions of this subsection or the rules thereunder.

(4) The Commission shall make available to the public for a reasonable fee a list

of all equity securities of a class described in subsection (d)(1) of this section, updated no less frequently than reports are required to be filed pursuant to paragraph (1) of this subsection. The Commission shall tabulate the information contained in any report filed pursuant to this subsection in a manner which will, in the view of the Commission, maximize the usefulness of the information to other Federal and State authorities and the public. Promptly after the filing of any such report, the Commission shall make the information contained therein conveniently available to the public for a reasonable fee in such form as the Commission, by rule, may prescribe, except that the Commission, as it determines to be necessary or appropriate in the public interest or for the protection of investors, may delay or prevent public disclosure of any such information in accordance with section 552 of Title 5. Notwithstanding the preceding sentence, any such information identifying the securities held by the account of a natural person or an estate or trust (other than a business trust or investment company) shall not be disclosed to the public.

(5) In exercising its authority under this subsection, the Commission shall determine (and so state) that its action is necessary or appropriate in the public interest and for the protection of investors or to maintain fair and orderly markets or, in granting an exemption, that its action is consistent with the protection of investors and the purposes of this subsection. In exercising such authority the Commission shall take such steps as are within its power, including consulting with the Comptroller General of the United States, the Director of the Office of Management and Budget, the appropriate regulatory agencies, Federal and State authorities which, directly or indirectly, require reports from institutional investment managers of information substantially similar to that called for by this subsection, national securities exchanges, and registered securities associations,

(A) to achieve uniform, centralized reporting of information concerning the securities holdings of and transactions by or for accounts with respect to which institutional investment managers exercise investment discretion, and

(B) consistently with the objective set forth in the preceding subparagraph, to avoid unnecessarily duplicative reporting by, and minimize the compliance burden on, institutional investment managers. Federal authorities which, directly or indirectly, require reports from institutional investment managers of information substantially similar to that called for by this subsection shall cooperate with the Commission in the performance of its responsibilities under the preceding sentence. An institutional investment manager which is a bank, the deposits of which are insured in accordance with the Federal Deposit Insurance Act [12 U.S.C.A. § 1811 et seq.], shall file with the appropriate regulatory agency a copy of every report filed with the Commission pursuant to this subsection.

(6)

(A) For purposes of this subsection the term "institutional investment manager" includes any person, other than a natural person, investing in or buying and selling securities for its own account, and any person exercising investment discretion with respect to the account of any other person.

(B) The Commission shall adopt such rules as it deems necessary or appropriate to prevent duplicative reporting pursuant to this subsection by two or more institutional investment managers exercising investment discretion with respect to the same amount.

(g) Statement of equity security ownership

(1) Any person who is directly or indirectly the beneficial owner of more than 5 per centum of any security of a class described in subsection (d)(1) of this section or otherwise becomes or is deemed to become a beneficial owner of any security of a class described in subsection (d)(1) upon the purchase or sale of a security-based swap that the Commission may define by rule shall file with the Commission a statement setting forth, in such form and at such time as the Commission may, by rule, prescribe—

(A) such person's identity, residence, and citizenship; and

(B) the number and description of the shares in which such person has an interest and the nature of such interest.

(2) If any material change occurs in the facts set forth in the statement filed with the Commission, an amendment shall be filed with the Commission, in accordance with such rules and regulations as the Commission may prescribe as necessary or appropriate in the public interest or for the protection of investors.

(3) When two or more persons act as a partnership, limited partnership, syndicate, or other group for the purpose of acquiring, holding, or disposing of securities of an issuer, such syndicate or group shall be deemed a "person" for the purposes of this subsection.

(4) In determining, for purposes of this subsection, any percentage of a class of any security, such class shall be deemed to consist of the amount of the outstanding securities of such class, exclusive of any securities of such class held by or for the account of the issuer or a subsidiary of the issuer.

(5) In exercising its authority under this subsection, the Commission shall take such steps as it deems necessary or appropriate in the public interest or for the protection of investors

(A) to achieve centralized reporting of information regarding ownership,

(B) to avoid unnecessarily duplicative reporting by and minimize the compliance burden on persons required to report, and

(C) to tabulate and promptly make available the information contained in any report filed pursuant to this subsection in a manner which will, in the view of the Commission, maximize the usefulness of the information to other Federal and State agencies and the public.

(6) The Commission may, by rule or order, exempt, in whole or in part, any person or class of persons from any or all of the reporting requirements of this subsection as it deems necessary or appropriate in the public interest or for the protection of investors.

(h) Large trader reporting

(1) Identification requirements for large traders

For the purpose of monitoring the impact on the securities markets of securities transactions involving a substantial volume or a large fair market value or exercise value and for the purpose of otherwise assisting the Commission in the enforcement of this chapter, each large trader shall—

(A) provide such information to the Commission as the Commission may by rule or regulation prescribe as necessary or appropriate, identifying such large trader and all accounts in or through which such large trader effects such transactions; and

(B) identify, in accordance with such rules or regulations as the Commission may prescribe as necessary or appropriate, to any registered broker or dealer by or through whom such large trader directly or indirectly effects securities transactions, such large trader and all accounts directly or indirectly maintained with such broker or dealer by such large trader in or through which such transactions are effected.

(2) Recordkeeping and reporting requirements for brokers and dealers

Every registered broker or dealer shall make and keep for prescribed periods such records as the Commission by rule or regulation prescribes as necessary or appropriate in the public interest, for the protection of investors, or otherwise in furtherance of the purposes of this chapter, with respect to securities transactions that equal or exceed the reporting activity level effected directly or indirectly by or through such registered broker or dealer of or for any person that such broker or dealer knows is a large trader, or any person that such broker or dealer has reason to know is a large trader on the basis of transactions in securities effected by or through such broker or dealer. Such records shall be available for reporting to the Commission, or any self-regulatory organization that the Commission shall designate to receive such reports, on the morning of the day following the day the transactions were effected, and shall be reported to the Commission or a self-regulatory organization designated by the Commission immediately upon request by the Commission or such a self-regulatory organization. Such records and reports shall be in a format and transmitted in a manner prescribed by the Commission (including, but not limited to, machine readable form).

(3) Aggregation rules

The Commission may prescribe rules or regulations governing the manner in which transactions and accounts shall be aggregated for the purpose of this subsection, including aggregation on the basis of common ownership or control.

(4) Examination of broker and dealer records

All records required to be made and kept by registered brokers and dealers pursuant to this subsection with respect to transactions effected by large traders are subject at any time, or from time to time, to such reasonable periodic, special, or other examinations by representatives of the Commission as the Commission deems necessary or appropriate in the public interest, for the protection of investors, or otherwise in furtherance of the purposes of this chapter.

(5) Factors to be considered in Commission actions

In exercising its authority under this subsection, the Commission shall take into account—

(A) existing reporting systems;

(B) the costs associated with maintaining information with respect to transactions effected by large traders and reporting such information to the Commission or self-regulatory organizations; and

(C) the relationship between the United States and international securities markets.

(6) Exemptions

The Commission, by rule, regulation, or order, consistent with the purposes of this chapter, may exempt any person or class of persons or any transaction or class of transactions, either conditionally or upon specified terms and conditions or for stated periods, from the operation of this subsection, and the rules and regulations thereunder.

(7) Authority of Commission to limit disclosure of information

Notwithstanding any other provision of law, the Commission shall not be compelled to disclose any information required to be kept or reported under this subsection. Nothing in this subsection shall authorize the Commission to withhold information from Congress, or prevent the Commission from complying with a request for information from any other Federal department or agency requesting information for purposes within the scope of its jurisdiction, or complying with an order of a court of the United States in an action brought by the United States or the Commission. For purposes of section 552 of Title 5, this subsection shall be considered a statute described in subsection (b)(3)(B) of such section 552.

(8) Definitions

For purposes of this subsection—

(A) the term "large trader" means every person who, for his own account or an account for which he exercises investment discretion, effects transactions for the purchase or sale of any publicly traded security or securities by use of any means or instrumentality of interstate commerce or of the mails, or of any facility of a national securities exchange, directly or indirectly by or through a registered broker or dealer in an aggregate amount equal to or in excess of the identifying activity level;

(B) the term "publicly traded security" means any equity security (including an option on individual equity securities, and an option on a group or index of such securities) listed, or admitted to unlisted trading privileges, on a national securities exchange, or quoted in an automated interdealer quotation system;

(C) the term "identifying activity level" means transactions in publicly traded securities at or above a level of volume, fair market value, or exercise value as shall be fixed from time to time by the Commission by rule or regulation, specifying the time interval during which such transactions shall be aggregated;

(D) the term "reporting activity level" means transactions in publicly traded securities at or above a level of volume, fair market value, or exercise value as shall be fixed from time to time by the Commission by rule, regulation, or order, specifying the time interval during which such transactions shall be aggregated; and

(E) the term "person" has the meaning given in section 78c(a)(9) of this title and also includes two or more persons acting as a partnership, limited partnership, syndicate, or other group, but does not include a foreign central bank.

(i) Accuracy of financial reports

Each financial report that contains financial statements, and that is required to be prepared in accordance with (or reconciled to) generally accepted accounting principles under this chapter and filed with the Commission shall reflect all material correcting adjustments that have been identified by a registered public accounting firm in accordance with generally accepted accounting principles and the rules and regulations of the Commission.

(j) Off-balance sheet transactions

Not later than 180 days after July 30, 2002, the Commission shall issue final rules providing that each annual and quarterly financial report required to be filed with the Commission shall disclose all material off-balance sheet transactions, arrangements, obligations (including contingent obligations), and other relationships of the issuer with unconsolidated entities or other persons, that may have a material current or future effect on financial condition, changes in financial condition, results of operations, liquidity, capital expenditures, capital resources, or significant components of revenues or expenses.

(k) Prohibition on personal loans to executives

(1) In general

It shall be unlawful for any issuer (as defined in section 7201 of this title), directly or indirectly, including through any subsidiary, to extend or maintain credit, to arrange for the extension of credit, or to renew an extension of credit, in the form of a personal loan to or for any director or executive officer (or equivalent thereof) of that issuer. An extension of credit maintained by the issuer on July 30, 2002, shall not be subject to the provisions of this subsection, provided that there is no material modification to any term of any such extension of credit or any renewal of any such extension of credit on or after July 30, 2002.

(2) Limitation

Paragraph (1) does not preclude any home improvement and manufactured home loans (as that term is defined insection 1464 of Title 12), consumer credit (as defined in section 1602 of this title), or any extension of credit under an open end credit plan (as defined in section 1602 of this title), or a charge card (as defined in section 1637(c)(4)(e) of this title), or any extension of credit by a broker or dealer registered under section 78o of this title to an employee of that broker or dealer to buy, trade, or carry securities, that is permitted under rules or regulations of the Board of Governors of the Federal Reserve System pursuant to section 78g of this title (other than an extension of credit that would be used to purchase the stock of that issuer), that is—

(A) made or provided in the ordinary course of the consumer credit business of such issuer;

(B) of a type that is generally made available by such issuer to the public; and

(C) made by such issuer on market terms, or terms that are no more favorable than those offered by the issuer to the general public for such extensions of credit.

(3) Rule of construction for certain loans

Paragraph (1) does not apply to any loan made or maintained by an insured depository institution (as defined insection 1813 of Title 12), if the loan is subject to the insider lending restrictions of section 375b of Title 12.

(l) Real time issuer disclosures

Each issuer reporting under subsection (a) of this section or section 78o(d) of this title shall disclose to the public on a rapid and current basis such additional information concerning material changes in the financial condition or operations of the issuer, in plain English, which may include trend and qualitative information and graphic presentations, as the Commission determines, by rule, is necessary or useful for the protection of investors and in the public interest.

(m) Public availability of security-based swap transaction data

(1) In general

(A) Definition of real-time public reporting

In this paragraph, the term "real-time public reporting" means to report data relating to a security-based swap transaction, including price and volume, as soon as technologically practicable after the time at which the security-based swap transaction has been executed.

(B) Purpose

The purpose of this subsection is to authorize the Commission to make security-based swap transaction and pricing data available to the public in such form and at such times as the Commission determines appropriate to enhance price discovery.

(C) General rule

The Commission is authorized to provide by rule for the public availability of security-based swap transaction, volume, and pricing data as follows:

(i) With respect to those security-based swaps that are subject to the mandatory clearing requirement described in section 78c-3(a)(1) of this title (including those security-based swaps that are excepted from the requirement pursuant to section 78c-3(g) of this title), the Commission shall require real-time public reporting for such transactions.

(ii) With respect to those security-based swaps that are not subject to the mandatory clearing requirement described in section 78c-3(a)(1) of this title, but are cleared at a registered clearing agency, the Commission shall require real-time public reporting for such transactions.

(iii) With respect to security-based swaps that are not cleared at a registered clearing agency and which are reported to a security-based swap data repository or the Commission under section 78c-3(a)(6) of this title,2the Commission shall require real-time public reporting for such transactions, in a manner that does not disclose the business transactions and market positions of any person.

(iv) With respect to security-based swaps that are determined to be required to be cleared under section 78c-3(b) of this title but are not cleared, the Commission shall require real-time public reporting for such transactions.

(D) Registered entities and public reporting

The Commission may require registered entities to publicly disseminate the security-based swap transaction and pricing data required to be reported under this paragraph.

(E) Rulemaking required

With respect to the rule providing for the public availability of transaction and pricing data for security-based swaps described in clauses (i) and (ii) of subparagraph (C), the rule promulgated by the Commission shall contain provisions—

(i) to ensure such information does not identify the participants;

(ii) to specify the criteria for determining what constitutes a large notional security-based swap transaction (block trade) for particular markets and contracts;

(iii) to specify the appropriate time delay for reporting large notional security-based swap transactions (block trades) to the public; and

(iv) that take into account whether the public disclosure will materially reduce market liquidity.

(F) Timeliness of reporting

Parties to a security-based swap (including agents of the parties to a security-based swap) shall be responsible for reporting security-based swap transaction information to the appropriate registered entity in a timely manner as may be prescribed by the Commission.

(G) Reporting of swaps to registered security-based swap data repositories

Each security-based swap (whether cleared or uncleared) shall be reported to a registered security-based swap data repository.

(H) Registration of clearing agencies

A clearing agency may register as a security-based swap data repository.

(2) Semiannual and annual public reporting of aggregate security-based swap data

(A) In general

In accordance with subparagraph (B), the Commission shall issue a written report on a semiannual and annual basis to make available to the public information relating to—

(i) the trading and clearing in the major security-based swap categories; and

(ii) the market participants and developments in new products.

(B) Use; consultation

In preparing a report under subparagraph (A), the Commission shall—

(i) use information from security-based swap data repositories and clearing agencies; and

(ii) consult with the Office of the Comptroller of the Currency, the Bank for International Settlements, and such other regulatory bodies as may be necessary.

(C) Authority of Commission

The Commission may, by rule, regulation, or order, delegate the public reporting responsibilities of the Commission under this paragraph in accordance with such terms and conditions as the Commission determines to be appropriate and in the public interest.

(n) Security-based swap data repositories

(1) Registration requirement

It shall be unlawful for any person, unless registered with the Commission, directly or indirectly, to make use of the mails or any means or instrumentality of interstate commerce to perform the functions of a security-based swap data repository.

(2) Inspection and examination

It shall be unlawful for any person, unless registered with the Commission, directly or indirectly, to make use of the mails or any means or instrumentality of interstate commerce to perform the functions of a security-based swap data repository.

Each registered security-based swap data repository shall be subject to inspection and examination by any representative of the Commission.

(3) Compliance with core principles

(A) In general

To be registered, and maintain registration, as a security-based swap data repository, the security-based swap data repository shall comply with—

(i) the requirements and core principles described in this subsection; and

(ii) any requirement that the Commission may impose by rule or regulation.

(B) Reasonable discretion of security-based swap data repository

Unless otherwise determined by the Commission, by rule or regulation, a security-based swap data repository described in subparagraph (A) shall have reasonable discretion in establishing the manner in which the security-based swap data repository complies with the core principles described in this subsection.

(4) Standard setting

(A) Data identification

(i) In general

In accordance with clause (ii), the Commission shall prescribe standards that specify the data elements for each security-based swap that shall be collected and maintained by each registered security-based swap data repository.

(ii) Requirement

In carrying out clause (i), the Commission shall prescribe consistent data element standards applicable to registered entities and reporting counterparties.

(B) Data collection and maintenance

The Commission shall prescribe data collection and data maintenance standards for security-based swap data repositories.

(C) Comparability

The standards prescribed by the Commission under this subsection shall be comparable to the data standards imposed by the Commission on clearing agencies in connection with their clearing of security-based swaps.

(5) Duties

A security-based swap data repository shall—

(A) accept data prescribed by the Commission for each security-based swap under subsection (b);

(B) confirm with both counterparties to the security-based swap the accuracy of the data that was submitted;

(C) maintain the data described in subparagraph (A) in such form, in such manner, and for such period as may be required by the Commission;

(D)

(i) provide direct electronic access to the Commission (or any designee of the Commission, including another registered entity); and

(ii) provide the information described in subparagraph (A) in such form and at such frequency as the Commission may require to comply with the public reporting requirements set forth in subsection (m);

(E) at the direction of the Commission, establish automated systems for monitoring, screening, and analyzing security-based swap data;

(F) maintain the privacy of any and all security-based swap transaction information that the security-based swap data repository receives from a security-based swap dealer, counterparty, or any other registered entity; and

(G) on a confidential basis pursuant to section 78x of this title, upon request, and after notifying the Commission of the request, make available all data obtained by the security-based swap data repository, including individual counterparty trade and position data, to—

(i) each appropriate prudential regulator;

(ii) the Financial Stability Oversight Council;

(iii) the Commodity Futures Trading Commission;

(iv) the Department of Justice; and

(v) any other person that the Commission determines to be appropriate, including—

(I) foreign financial supervisors (including foreign futures authorities);

(II) foreign central banks; and

(III) foreign ministries.

(H) Confidentiality and indemnification agreement

Before the security-based swap data repository may share information with any entity described in subparagraph (G)—

(i) the security-based swap data repository shall receive a written agreement from each entity stating that the entity shall abide by the confidentiality requirements described in section 78x of this title relating to the information on security-based swap transactions that is provided; and

(ii) each entity shall agree to indemnify the security-based swap data repository and the Commission for any expenses arising from litigation relating to the information provided under section 78x of this title.

(6) Designation of chief compliance officer

(A) In general

Each security-based swap data repository shall designate an individual to serve as a chief compliance officer.

(B) Duties

The chief compliance officer shall—

(i) report directly to the board or to the senior officer of the security-based swap data repository;

(ii) review the compliance of the security-based swap data repository with respect to the requirements and core principles described in this subsection;

(iii) in consultation with the board of the security-based swap data repository, a body performing a function similar to the board of the security-based swap data repository, or the senior officer of the security-based swap data repository, resolve any conflicts of interest that may arise;

(iv) be responsible for administering each policy and procedure that is required to be established pursuant to this section;

(v) ensure compliance with this chapter (including regulations) relating to agreements, contracts, or transactions, including each rule prescribed by the Commission under this section;

(vi) establish procedures for the remediation of noncompliance issues identified by the chief compliance officer through any—

(I) compliance office review;

(II) look-back;

(III) internal or external audit finding;

(IV) self-reported error; or

(V) validated complaint; and

(vii) establish and follow appropriate procedures for the handling, management response, remediation, retesting, and closing of noncompliance issues.

(C) Annual reports

(i) In general

In accordance with rules prescribed by the Commission, the chief compliance officer shall annually prepare and sign a report that contains a description of—

(I) the compliance of the security-based swap data repository of the chief compliance officer with respect to this chapter (including regulations); and

(II) each policy and procedure of the security-based swap data repository of the chief compliance officer (including the code of ethics and conflict of interest policies of the security-based swap data repository).

(ii) Requirements

A compliance report under clause (i) shall—

(I) accompany each appropriate financial report of the security-based swap data repository that is required to be furnished to the Commission pursuant to this section; and

(II) include a certification that, under penalty of law, the compliance report is accurate and complete.

(7) Core principles applicable to security-based swap data repositories

(A) Antitrust considerations

Unless necessary or appropriate to achieve the purposes of this chapter, the swap data repository shall not—

(i) adopt any rule or take any action that results in any unreasonable restraint of trade; or

(ii) impose any material anticompetitive burden on the trading, clearing, or reporting of transactions.

(B) Governance arrangements

Each security-based swap data repository shall establish governance arrangements that are transparent—

(i) to fulfill public interest requirements; and

(ii) to support the objectives of the Federal Government, owners, and participants.

(C) Conflicts of interest

Each security-based swap data repository shall—

(i) establish and enforce rules to minimize conflicts of interest in the decision-making process of the security-based swap data repository; and

(ii) establish a process for resolving any conflicts of interest described in clause (i).

(D) Additional duties developed by Commission

(i) In general

The Commission may develop 1 or more additional duties applicable to security-based swap data repositories.

(ii) Consideration of evolving standards

In developing additional duties under subparagraph (A), the Commission may take into consideration any evolving standard of the United States or the international community.

(iii) Additional duties for Commission designees

The Commission shall establish additional duties for any registrant described in subsection (m)(2)(C) in order to minimize conflicts of interest, protect data, ensure compliance, and guarantee the safety and security of the security-based swap data repository.

(8) Required registration for security-based swap data repositories

Any person that is required to be registered as a security-based swap data repository under this subsection shall register with the Commission, regardless of whether that person is also licensed under the Commodity Exchange Act as a swap data repository.

(9) Rules

The Commission shall adopt rules governing persons that are registered under this subsection.

(o) Beneficial ownership

For purposes of this section and section 78p of this title, a person shall be deemed to acquire beneficial ownership of an equity security based on the purchase or sale of a security-based swap, only to the extent that the Commission, by rule, determines after consultation with the prudential regulators and the Secretary of the Treasury, that the purchase or sale of the security-based swap, or class of security-based swap, provides incidents of ownership comparable to direct ownership of the equity security, and that it is necessary to achieve the purposes of this section that the purchase or sale of the security-based swaps, or class of security-based swap, be deemed the acquisition of beneficial ownership of the equity security.

(p) Disclosures relating to conflict minerals originating in the Democratic Republic of the Congo

(1) Regulations

(A) In general

Not later than 270 days after July 21, 2010, the Commission shall promulgate regulations requiring any person described in paragraph (2) to disclose annually, beginning with the person's first full fiscal year that begins after the date of promulgation of such regulations, whether conflict minerals that are necessary as described in paragraph (2)(B), in the year for which such reporting is required, did originate in the Democratic Republic of the Congo or an adjoining country and, in cases in which such conflict minerals did originate in any such country, submit to the Commission a report that includes, with respect to the period covered by the report—

(i) a description of the measures taken by the person to exercise due diligence on the source and chain of custody of such minerals, which measures shall include an independent private sector audit of such report submitted through the Commission that is conducted in accordance with standards established by the Comptroller General of the United States, in accordance with rules promulgated by the Commission, in consultation with the Secretary of State; and

(ii) a description of the products manufactured or contracted to be manufactured that are not DRC conflict free ("DRC conflict free" is defined to mean the products that do not contain minerals that directly or indirectly finance or benefit armed groups in the Democratic Republic of the Congo or an adjoining country), the entity that conducted the independent private sector audit in accordance with clause (i), the facilities used to process the conflict minerals, the country of origin of the conflict minerals, and the efforts to determine the mine or location of origin with the greatest possible specificity.

(B) Certification

The person submitting a report under subparagraph (A) shall certify the audit described in clause (i) of such subparagraph that is included in such report. Such a certified audit shall constitute a critical component of due diligence in establishing the source and chain of custody of such minerals.

(C) Unreliable determination

If a report required to be submitted by a person under subparagraph (A) relies on a determination of an independent private sector audit, as described under subparagraph (A)(i), or other due diligence processes previously determined by the Commission to be unreliable, the report shall not satisfy the requirements of the regulations promulgated under subparagraph (A)(i).

(D) DRC conflict free

For purposes of this paragraph, a product may be labeled as "DRC conflict free" if the product does not contain conflict minerals that directly or indirectly finance or benefit armed groups in the Democratic Republic of the Congo or an adjoining country.

(E) Information available to the public

Each person described under paragraph (2) shall make available to the public on the Internet website of such person the information disclosed by such person under subparagraph (A).

(2) Person described

A person is described in this paragraph if—

(A) the person is required to file reports with the Commission pursuant to paragraph (1)(A); and

(B) conflict minerals are necessary to the functionality or production of a product manufactured by such person.

(3) Revisions and waivers

The Commission shall revise or temporarily waive the requirements described in paragraph (1) if the President transmits to the Commission a determination that—

(A) such revision or waiver is in the national security interest of the United States and the President includes the reasons therefor; and

(B) establishes a date, not later than 2 years after the initial publication of such exemption, on which such exemption shall expire.

(4) Termination of disclosure requirements

The requirements of paragraph (1) shall terminate on the date on which the President determines and certifies to the appropriate congressional committees, but in no case earlier than the date that is one day after the end of the 5-year period beginning on July 21, 2010, that no armed groups continue to be directly involved and benefitting from commercial activity involving conflict minerals.

(5) Definitions

For purposes of this subsection, the terms "adjoining country", "appropriate congressional committees", "armed group", and "conflict mineral" have the meaning given those terms under section 1502 of the Dodd-Frank Wall Street Reform and Consumer Protection Act.

(q) Disclosure of payments by resource extraction issuers

(1) Definitions

In this subsection—

(A) the term "commercial development of oil, natural gas, or minerals" includes exploration, extraction, processing, export, and other significant actions relating to oil, natural gas, or minerals, or the acquisition of a license for any such activity, as determined by the Commission;

(B) the term "foreign government" means a foreign government, a department, agency, or instrumentality of a foreign government, or a company owned by a foreign government, as determined by the Commission;

(C) the term "payment"—

(i) means a payment that is—

(I) made to further the commercial development of oil, natural gas, or minerals; and

(II) not de minimis; and

(ii) includes taxes, royalties, fees (including license fees), production entitlements, bonuses, and other material benefits, that the Commission, consistent with the guidelines of the Extractive Industries Transparency Initiative (to the extent practicable), determines are part of the commonly recognized revenue stream for the commercial development of oil, natural gas, or minerals;

(D) the term "resource extraction issuer" means an issuer that—

(i) is required to file an annual report with the Commission; and

(ii) engages in the commercial development of oil, natural gas, or minerals;

(E) the term "interactive data format" means an electronic data format in which pieces of information are identified using an interactive data standard; and

(F) the term "interactive data standard" means standardized list of electronic tags that mark information included in the annual report of a resource extraction issuer.

(2) Disclosure

(A) Information required

Not later than 270 days after July 21, 2010, the Commission shall issue final rules that require each resource extraction issuer to include in an annual report of the resource extraction issuer information relating to any payment made by the resource extraction issuer, a subsidiary of the resource extraction issuer, or an entity under the control of the resource extraction issuer to a foreign government or the Federal Government for the purpose of the commercial development of oil, natural gas, or minerals, including—

(i) the type and total amount of such payments made for each project of the resource extraction issuer relating to the commercial development of oil, natural gas, or minerals; and

(ii) the type and total amount of such payments made to each government.

(B) Consultation in rulemaking

In issuing rules under subparagraph (A), the Commission may consult with any agency or entity that the Commission determines is relevant.

(C) Interactive data format

The rules issued under subparagraph (A) shall require that the information included in the annual report of a resource extraction issuer be submitted in an interactive data format.

(D) Interactive data standard

(i) In general

The rules issued under subparagraph (A) shall establish an interactive data standard for the information included in the annual report of a resource extraction issuer.

(ii) Electronic tags

The interactive data standard shall include electronic tags that identify, for any payments made by a resource extraction issuer to a foreign government or the Federal Government—

(I) the total amounts of the payments, by category;

(II) the currency used to make the payments;

(III) the financial period in which the payments were made;

(IV) the business segment of the resource extraction issuer that made the payments;

(V) the government that received the payments, and the country in which the government is located;

(VI) the project of the resource extraction issuer to which the payments relate; and

(VII) such other information as the Commission may determine is necessary or appropriate in the public interest or for the protection of investors.

(E) Interactive data format

To the extent practicable, the rules issued under subparagraph (A) shall support the commitment of the Federal Government to international transparency promotion efforts relating to the commercial development of oil, natural gas, or minerals.

(F) Effective date

With respect to each resource extraction issuer, the final rules issued under subparagraph (A) shall take effect on the date on which the resource extraction issuer is required to submit an annual report relating to the fiscal year of the resource extraction issuer that ends not earlier than 1 year after the date on which the Commission issues final rules under subparagraph (A).

(3) Public availability of information

(A) In general

To the extent practicable, the Commission shall make available online, to the public, a compilation of the information required to be submitted under the rules issued under paragraph (2)(A).

(B) Other information

Nothing in this paragraph shall require the Commission to make available online information other than the information required to be submitted under the rules issued under paragraph (2)(A).

(4) Authorization of appropriations

There are authorized to be appropriated to the Commission such sums as may be necessary to carry out this subsection.

(r) Disclosure of certain activities relating to Iran

(1) In general

Each issuer required to file an annual or quarterly report under subsection (a) shall disclose in that report the information required by paragraph (2) if, during the period covered by the report, the issuer or any affiliate of the issuer—

(A) knowingly engaged in an activity described in subsection (a) or (b) of section 5 of the Iran Sanctions Act of 1996 (Public Law 104-172; 50 U.S.C. 1701 note);

(B) knowingly engaged in an activity described in subsection (c)(2) of section 104 of the Comprehensive Iran Sanctions, Accountability, and Divestment Act of 2010 (22 U.S.C. 8513) or a transaction described in subsection (d)(1) of that section;

(C) knowingly engaged in an activity described in section 105A(b)(2) of that Act; or

(D) knowingly conducted any transaction or dealing with—

(i) any person the property and interests in property of which are blocked pursuant to Executive Order No. 13224 (66 Fed. Reg. 49079; relating to blocking property and prohibiting transactions with persons who commit, threaten to commit, or support terrorism);

(ii) any person the property and interests in property of which are blocked pursuant to Executive Order No. 13382 (70 Fed. Reg. 38567; relating to blocking of property of weapons of mass destruction proliferators and their supporters); or

(iii) any person or entity identified under section 560.304 of title 31, Code of Federal Regulations (relating to the definition of the Government of Iran) without the specific authorization of a Federal department or agency.

(2) Information required

If an issuer or an affiliate of the issuer has engaged in any activity described in paragraph (1), the issuer shall disclose a detailed description of each such activity, including—

(A) the nature and extent of the activity;

(B) the gross revenues and net profits, if any, attributable to the activity; and

(C) whether the issuer or the affiliate of the issuer (as the case may be) intends to continue the activity.

(3) Notice of disclosures

If an issuer reports under paragraph (1) that the issuer or an affiliate of the issuer has knowingly engaged in any activity described in that paragraph, the issuer shall separately file with the Commission, concurrently with the annual or quarterly report under subsection (a), a notice that the disclosure of that activity has been included in that annual or quarterly report that identifies the issuer and contains the information required by paragraph (2).

(4) Public disclosure of information

Upon receiving a notice under paragraph (3) that an annual or quarterly report includes a disclosure of an activity described in paragraph (1), the Commission shall promptly—

(A) transmit the report to—

(i) the President;

(ii) the Committee on Foreign Affairs and the Committee on Financial Services of the House of Representatives; and

(iii) the Committee on Foreign Relations and the Committee on Banking, Housing, and Urban Affairs of the Senate; and

(B) make the information provided in the disclosure and the notice available to the public by posting the information on the Internet website of the Commission.

(5) Investigations

Upon receiving a report under paragraph (4) that includes a disclosure of an activity described in paragraph (1) (other than an activity described in subparagraph (D)(iii) of that paragraph), the President shall—

(A) initiate an investigation into the possible imposition of sanctions under the Iran Sanctions Act of 1996 (Public Law 104-172; 50 U.S.C. 1701 note), section 8513 or 8514a of Title 22, an Executive order specified in clause (i) or (ii) of paragraph (1)(D), or any other provision of law relating to the imposition of sanctions with respect to Iran, as applicable; and

(B) not later than 180 days after initiating such an investigation, make a determination with respect to whether sanctions should be imposed with respect to the issuer or the affiliate of the issuer (as the case may be).

(6) Sunset

The provisions of this subsection shall terminate on the date that is 30 days after the date on which the President makes the certification described in section 8551(a) of Title 22.

§ 78n.   Proxies

(a)

(1) Solicitation of proxies in violation of rules and regulations

It shall be unlawful for any person, by the use of the mails or by any means or instrumentality of interstate commerce or of any facility of a national securities exchange or otherwise, in contravention of such rules and regulations as the Commission may prescribe as necessary or appropriate in the public interest or for the protection of investors, to solicit or to permit the use of his name to solicit any proxy or consent or authorization in respect of any security (other than an exempted security) registered pursuant to section 78*l* of this title.

(2) The rules and regulations prescribed by the Commission under paragraph (1) may include

(A) a requirement that a solicitation of proxy, consent, or authorization by (or on behalf of) an issuer include a nominee submitted by a shareholder to serve on the board of directors of the issuer; and

(B) a requirement that an issuer follow a certain procedure in relation to a solicitation described in subparagraph (A).

(b) Giving or refraining from giving proxy in respect of any security carried for account of customer

(1) It shall be unlawful for any member of a national securities exchange, or any broker or dealer registered under this chapter, or any bank, association, or other entity that exercises fiduciary powers, in contravention of such rules and regulations as the Commission may prescribe as necessary or appropriate in the

public interest or for the protection of investors, to give, or to refrain from giving a proxy, consent, authorization, or information statement in respect of any security registered pursuant to section 78l of this title, or any security issued by an investment company registered under the Investment Company Act of 1940 [15 U.S.C.A. § 80a-1 et seq.], and carried for the account of a customer.

(2) With respect to banks, the rules and regulations prescribed by the Commission under paragraph (1) shall not require the disclosure of the names of beneficial owners of securities in an account held by the bank on December 28, 1985, unless the beneficial owner consents to the disclosure. The provisions of this paragraph shall not apply in the case of a bank which the Commission finds has not made a good faith effort to obtain such consent from such beneficial owners.

(c) Information to holders of record prior to annual or other meetings

(1) Unless proxies, consents, or authorizations in respect of a security registered pursuant to section 78l of this title, or a security issued by an investment company registered under the Investment Company Act of 1940 [15 U.S.C.A. § 80a-1 et seq.], are solicited by or on behalf of the management of the issuer from the holders of record of such security in accordance with the rules and regulations prescribed under subsection (a) of this section, prior to any annual or other meeting of the holders of such security, such issuer shall, in accordance with rules and regulations prescribed by the Commission, file with the Commission and transmit to all holders of record of such security information substantially equivalent to the information which would be required to be transmitted if a solicitation were made, but no information shall be required to be filed or transmitted pursuant to this subsection before July 1, 1964.

(d) Tender offer by owner of more than five per centum of class of securities; exceptions

(1) It shall be unlawful for any person, directly or indirectly, by use of the mails or by any means or instrumentality of interstate commerce or of any facility of a national securities exchange or otherwise, to make a tender offer for, or a request or invitation for tenders of, any class of any equity security which is registered pursuant to section 78l of this title, or any equity security of an insurance company which would have been required to be so registered except for the exemption contained in section 78l(g)(2)(G) of this title, or any equity security issued by a closed-end investment company registered under the Investment Company Act of 1940 [15 U.S.C.A. § 80a-1 et seq.], if, after consummation thereof, such person would, directly or indirectly, be the beneficial owner of more than 5 per centum of such class, unless at the time copies of the offer or request or invitation are first published or sent or given to security holders such person has filed with the Commission a statement containing such of the information specified in section 78m(d) of this title, and such additional information as the Commission may by rules and regulations prescribe as necessary or appropriate in the public interest or for the protection of investors. All requests or invitations for tenders or advertisements making a tender offer or requesting or inviting tenders of such a security shall be filed as a part of such statement and shall contain such of the information contained in such statement as the Commission may by rules and regulations prescribe. Copies of any additional

material soliciting or requesting such tender offers subsequent to the initial solicitation or request shall contain such information as the Commission may by rules and regulations prescribe as necessary or appropriate in the public interest or for the protection of investors, and shall be filed with the Commission not later than the time copies of such material are first published or sent or given to security holders. Copies of all statements, in the form in which such material is furnished to security holders and the Commission, shall be sent to the issuer not later than the date such material is first published or sent or given to any security holders.

(2) When two or more persons act as a partnership, limited partnership, syndicate, or other group for the purpose of acquiring, holding, or disposing of securities of an issuer, such syndicate or group shall be deemed a "person" for purposes of this subsection.

(3) In determining, for purposes of this subsection, any percentage of a class of any security, such class shall be deemed to consist of the amount of the outstanding securities of such class, exclusive of any securities of such class held by or for the account of the issuer or a subsidiary of the issuer.

(4) Any solicitation or recommendation to the holders of such a security to accept or reject a tender offer or request or invitation for tenders shall be made in accordance with such rules and regulations as the Commission may prescribe as necessary or appropriate in the public interest or for the protection of investors.

(5) Securities deposited pursuant to a tender offer or request or invitation for tenders may be withdrawn by or on behalf of the depositor at any time until the expiration of seven days after the time definitive copies of the offer or request or invitation are first published or sent or given to security holders, and at any time after sixty days from the date of the original tender offer or request or invitation, except as the Commission may otherwise prescribe by rules, regulations, or order as necessary or appropriate in the public interest or for the protection of investors.

(6) Where any person makes a tender offer, or request or invitation for tenders, for less than all the outstanding equity securities of a class, and where a greater number of securities is deposited pursuant thereto within ten days after copies of the offer or request or invitation are first published or sent or given to security holders than such person is bound or willing to take up and pay for, the securities taken up shall be taken up as nearly as may be pro rata, disregarding fractions, according to the number of securities deposited by each depositor. The provisions of this subsection shall also apply to securities deposited within ten days after notice of an increase in the consideration offered to security holders, as described in paragraph (7), is first published or sent or given to security holders.

(7) Where any person varies the terms of a tender offer or request or invitation for tenders before the expiration thereof by increasing the consideration offered to holders of such securities, such person shall pay the increased consideration to each security holder whose securities are taken up and paid for pursuant to the tender offer or request or invitation for tenders whether or not such securities

have been taken up by such person before the variation of the tender offer or request or invitation.

(8) The provisions of this subsection shall not apply to any offer for, or request or invitation for tenders of, any security—

(A) if the acquisition of such security, together with all other acquisitions by the same person of securities of the same class during the preceding twelve months, would not exceed 2 per centum of that class;

(B) by the issuer of such security; or

(C) which the Commission, by rules or regulations or by order, shall exempt from the provisions of this subsection as not entered into for the purpose of, and not having the effect of, changing or influencing the control of the issuer or otherwise as not comprehended within the purposes of this subsection.

(e) Untrue statement of material fact or omission of fact with respect to tender offer

It shall be unlawful for any person to make any untrue statement of a material fact or omit to state any material fact necessary in order to make the statements made, in the light of the circumstances under which they are made, not misleading, or to engage in any fraudulent, deceptive, or manipulative acts or practices, in connection with any tender offer or request or invitation for tenders, or any solicitation of security holders in opposition to or in favor of any such offer, request, or invitation. The Commission shall, for the purposes of this subsection, by rules and regulations define, and prescribe means reasonably designed to prevent, such acts and practices as are fraudulent, deceptive, or manipulative.

(f) Election or designation of majority of directors of issuer by owner of more than five per centum of class of securities at other than meeting of security holders

If, pursuant to any arrangement or understanding with the person or persons acquiring securities in a transaction subject to subsection (d) of this section or subsection (d) of section 78m of this title, any persons are to be elected or designated as directors of the issuer, otherwise than at a meeting of security holders, and the persons so elected or designated will constitute a majority of the directors of the issuer, then, prior to the time any such person takes office as a director, and in accordance with rules and regulations prescribed by the Commission, the issuer shall file with the Commission, and transmit to all holders of record of securities of the issuer who would be entitled to vote at a meeting for election of directors, information substantially equivalent to the information which would be required by subsection (a) or (c) of this section to be transmitted if such person or persons were nominees for election as directors at a meeting of such security holders.

(g) Filing fees

(1)

(A) At the time of filing such preliminary proxy solicitation material as the Commission may require by rule pursuant to subsection (a) of this section that concerns an acquisition, merger, consolidation, or proposed sale or other disposition of substantially all the assets of a company, the person making such filing, other than a company registered under the Investment Company Act of 1940 [15 U.S.C.A. § 80a-1 et seq.], shall pay to the Commission the following fees:

(i) for preliminary proxy solicitation material involving an acquisition, merger, or consolidation, if there is a proposed payment of cash or transfer of securities or property to shareholders, a fee at a rate that, subject to paragraph (4), is equal to $92 per $1,000,000 of such proposed payment, or of the value of such securities or other property proposed to be transferred; and

(ii) for preliminary proxy solicitation material involving a proposed sale or other disposition of substantially all of the assets of a company, a fee at a rate that, subject to paragraph (4), is equal to $92 per $1,000,000 of the cash or of the value of any securities or other property proposed to be received upon such sale or disposition.

(B) The fee imposed under subparagraph (A) shall be reduced with respect to securities in an amount equal to any fee paid to the Commission with respect to such securities in connection with the proposed transaction under section 77f(b) of this title, or the fee paid under that section shall be reduced in an amount equal to the fee paid to the Commission in connection with such transaction under this subsection. Where two or more companies involved in an acquisition, merger, consolidation, sale, or other disposition of substantially all the assets of a company must file such proxy material with the Commission, each shall pay a proportionate share of such fee.

(2) At the time of filing such preliminary information statement as the Commission may require by rule pursuant to subsection (c) of this section, the issuer shall pay to the Commission the same fee as required for preliminary proxy solicitation material under paragraph (1) of this subsection.

(3) At the time of filing such statement as the Commission may require by rule pursuant to subsection (d)(1) of this section, the person making the filing shall pay to the Commission a fee at a rate that, subject to paragraph (4), is equal to $92 per $1,000,000 of the aggregate amount of cash or of the value of securities or other property proposed to be offered. The fee shall be reduced with respect to securities in an amount equal to any fee paid with respect to such securities in connection with the proposed transaction under section 77f(b) of this title, or the fee paid under that section shall be reduced in an amount equal to the fee paid to the Commission in connection with such transaction under this subsection.

(4) Annual adjustment

For each fiscal year, the Commission shall by order adjust the rate required by paragraphs (1) and (3) for such fiscal year to a rate that is equal to the rate (expressed in dollars per million) that is applicable under section 6(b) of the Securities Act of 1933 (15 U.S.C. 77f(b)) for such fiscal year.

(5) Fee collection

Fees collected pursuant to this subsection for fiscal year 2012 and each fiscal year thereafter shall be deposited and credited as general revenue of the Treasury and shall not be available for obligation.

(6) Review; effective date; publication

In exercising its authority under this subsection, the Commission shall not be required to comply with the provisions of section 553 of Title 5. An adjusted rate prescribed under paragraph (4) shall be published and take effect in accordance with section 6(b) of the Securities Act of 1933 (15 U.S.C. 77f(b)).

(7) Pro rata application

The rates per $1,000,000 required by this subsection shall be applied pro rata to amounts and balances of less than $1,000,000.

(8) Notwithstanding any other provision of law, the Commission may impose fees, charges, or prices for matters not involving any acquisition, merger, consolidation, sale, or other disposition of assets described in this subsection, as authorized by section 9701 of Title 31, or otherwise.

(9), (10) Repealed. Pub. L. 111-203, Title IX, § 991(b)(3), July 21, 2010, 124 Stat. 1953

(11) Redesignated (8)

(h) Proxy solicitations and tender offers in connection with limited partnership rollup transactions

(1) Proxy rules to contain special provisions

It shall be unlawful for any person to solicit any proxy, consent, or authorization concerning a limited partnership rollup transaction, or to make any tender offer in furtherance of a limited partnership rollup transaction, unless such transaction is conducted in accordance with rules prescribed by the Commission under subsections (a) and (d) of this section as required by this subsection. Such rules shall—

(A) permit any holder of a security that is the subject of the proposed limited partnership rollup transaction to engage in preliminary communications for the purpose of determining whether to solicit proxies, consents, or authorizations in opposition to the proposed limited partnership rollup transaction, without regard to whether any such communication would otherwise be considered a solicitation of proxies, and without being required to file soliciting material with the Commission prior to making that determination, except that—

(i) nothing in this subparagraph shall be construed to limit the application of any provision of this chapter prohibiting, or reasonably designed to prevent, fraudulent, deceptive, or manipulative acts or practices under this chapter; and

(ii) any holder of not less than 5 percent of the outstanding securities that are the subject of the proposed limited partnership rollup transaction who engages in the business of buying and selling limited partnership interests in the secondary market shall be required to disclose such ownership interests and any potential conflicts of interests in such preliminary communications;

(B) require the issuer to provide to holders of the securities that are the subject of the limited partnership rollup transaction such list of the holders of the issuer's securities as the Commission may determine in such form and subject to such terms and conditions as the Commission may specify;

(C) prohibit compensating any person soliciting proxies, consents, or authorizations directly from security holders concerning such a limited partnership rollup transaction—

(i) on the basis of whether the solicited proxy, consent, or authorization either approves or disapproves the proposed limited partnership rollup transaction; or

(ii) contingent on the approval, disapproval, or completion of the limited partnership rollup transaction;

(D) set forth disclosure requirements for soliciting material distributed in connection with a limited partnership rollup transaction, including requirements for clear, concise, and comprehensible disclosure with respect to

(i) any changes in the business plan, voting rights, form of ownership interest, or the compensation of the general partner in the proposed limited partnership rollup transaction from each of the original limited partnerships;

(ii) the conflicts of interest, if any, of the general partner;

(iii) whether it is expected that there will be a significant difference between the exchange values of the limited partnerships and the trading price of the securities to be issued in the limited partnership rollup transaction;

(iv) the valuation of the limited partnerships and the method used to determine the value of the interests of the limited partners to be exchanged for the securities in the limited partnership rollup transaction;

(v) the differing risks and effects of the limited partnership rollup transaction for investors in different limited partnerships proposed to be included, and the risks and effects of completing the limited partnership rollup transaction with less than all limited partnerships;

(vi) the statement by the general partner required under subparagraph (E);

(vii) such other matters deemed necessary or appropriate by the Commission;

(E) require a statement by the general partner as to whether the proposed limited partnership rollup transaction is fair or unfair to investors in each limited partnership, a discussion of the basis for that conclusion, and an evaluation and a description by the general partner of alternatives to the limited partnership rollup transaction, such as liquidation;

(F) provide that, if the general partner or sponsor has obtained any opinion (other than an opinion of counsel), appraisal, or report that is prepared by an outside party and that is materially related to the limited partnership rollup transaction, such soliciting materials shall contain or be accompanied by clear, concise, and comprehensible disclosure with respect to—

(i) the analysis of the transaction, scope of review, preparation of the opinion, and basis for and methods of arriving at conclusions, and any representations and undertakings with respect thereto;

(ii) the identity and qualifications of the person who prepared the opinion, the method of selection of such person, and any material past, existing, or contemplated relationships between the person or any of its affiliates and the general partner, sponsor, successor, or any other affiliate;

(iii) any compensation of the preparer of such opinion, appraisal, or report that is contingent on the transaction's approval or completion; and

(iv) any limitations imposed by the issuer on the access afforded to such preparer to the issuer's personnel, premises, and relevant books and records;

(G) provide that, if the general partner or sponsor has obtained any opinion, appraisal, or report as described in subparagraph (F) from any person whose compensation is contingent on the transaction's approval or completion or who has not been given access by the issuer to its personnel and premises and relevant books and records, the general partner or sponsor shall state the reasons therefor;

(H) provide that, if the general partner or sponsor has not obtained any opinion on the fairness of the proposed limited partnership rollup transaction to investors in each of the affected partnerships, such soliciting materials shall contain or be accompanied by a statement of such partner's or sponsor's reasons for concluding that such an opinion is not necessary in order to permit the limited partners to make an informed decision on the proposed transaction;

(I) require that the soliciting material include a clear, concise, and comprehensible summary of the limited partnership rollup transaction (including a summary of the matters referred to in clauses (i) through (vii) of subparagraph (D) and a summary of the matter referred to in subparagraphs (F), (G), and (H)), with the risks of the limited partnership rollup transaction set forth prominently in the fore part thereof;

(J) provide that any solicitation or offering period with respect to any proxy solicitation, tender offer, or information statement in a limited partnership rollup transaction shall be for not less than the lesser of 60 calendar days or the maximum number of days permitted under applicable State law; and

(K) contain such other provisions as the Commission determines to be necessary or appropriate for the protection of investors in limited partnership rollup transactions.

(2) Exemptions

The Commission may, consistent with the public interest, the protection of investors, and the purposes of this chapter, exempt by rule or order any security or class of securities, any transaction or class of transactions, or any person or class of persons, in whole or in part, conditionally or unconditionally, from the requirements imposed pursuant to paragraph (1) or from the definition contained in paragraph (4).

(3) Effect on Commission authority

Nothing in this subsection limits the authority of the Commission under subsection (a) or (d) of this section or any other provision of this chapter or precludes the Commission from imposing, under subsection (a) or (d) of this section or any other provision of this chapter, a remedy or procedure required to be imposed under this subsection.

(4) "Limited partnership rollup transaction" defined

Except as provided in paragraph (5), as used in this subsection, the term "limited partnership rollup transaction" means a transaction involving the combination or reorganization of one or more limited partnerships, directly or indirectly, in which—

(A) some or all of the investors in any of such limited partnerships will receive new securities, or securities in another entity, that will be reported under a transaction reporting plan declared effective before December 17, 1993, by the Commission under section 78k-1 of this title;

(B) any of the investors' limited partnership securities are not, as of the date of filing, reported under a transaction reporting plan declared effective before December 17, 1993, by the Commission under section 78k-1 of this title;

(C) investors in any of the limited partnerships involved in the transaction are subject to a significant adverse change with respect to voting rights, the term of existence of the entity, management compensation, or investment objectives; and

(D) any of such investors are not provided an option to receive or retain a security under substantially the same terms and conditions as the original issue.

(5) Exclusions from definition

Notwithstanding paragraph (4), the term "limited partnership rollup transaction" does not include—

(A) a transaction that involves only a limited partnership or partnerships having an operating policy or practice of retaining cash available for distribution and reinvesting proceeds from the sale, financing, or refinancing of assets in accordance with such criteria as the Commission determines appropriate;

(B) a transaction involving only limited partnerships wherein the interests of the limited partners are repurchased, recalled, or exchanged in accordance with the terms of the preexisting limited partnership agreements for securities in an operating company specifically identified at the time of the formation of the original limited partnership;

(C) a transaction in which the securities to be issued or exchanged are not required to be and are not registered under the Securities Act of 1933 [15 U.S.C.A. § 77a et seq.];

(D) a transaction that involves only issuers that are not required to register or report under section 78l of this title, both before and after the transaction;

(E) a transaction, except as the Commission may otherwise provide by rule for the protection of investors, involving the combination or reorganization of one or more limited partnerships in which a non-affiliated party succeeds to the interests of a general partner or sponsor, if—

(i) such action is approved by not less than 66 ⅔ percent of the outstanding units of each of the participating limited partnerships; and

(ii) as a result of the transaction, the existing general partners will receive only compensation to which they are entitled as expressly provided for in the preexisting limited partnership agreements; or

(F) a transaction, except as the Commission may otherwise provide by rule for the protection of investors, in which the securities offered to investors are securities of another entity that are reported under a transaction reporting plan declared effective before December 17, 1993, by the Commission under section 78k-1 of this title, if—

(i) such other entity was formed, and such class of securities was reported and regularly traded, not less than 12 months before the date on which soliciting material is mailed to investors; and

(ii) the securities of that entity issued to investors in the transaction do not exceed 20 percent of the total outstanding securities of the entity, exclusive of any securities of such class held by or for the account of the entity or a subsidiary of the entity.

(i) Disclosure of pay versus performance

The Commission shall, by rule, require each issuer to disclose in any proxy or consent solicitation material for an annual meeting of the shareholders of the issuer a clear description of any compensation required to be disclosed by the issuer under section 229.402 of title 17, Code of Federal Regulations (or any successor thereto), including, for any issuer other than an emerging growth company, information that shows the relationship between executive compensation actually paid and the financial performance of the issuer, taking into account any change in the value of the shares of stock and dividends of the issuer and any distributions. The disclosure under this subsection may include a graphic representation of the information required to be disclosed.

(j) Disclosure of hedging by employees and directors

The Commission shall, by rule, require each issuer to disclose in any proxy or consent solicitation material for an annual meeting of the shareholders of the issuer whether any employee or member of the board of directors of the issuer, or any designee of such employee or member, is permitted to purchase financial instruments (including prepaid variable forward contracts, equity swaps, collars, and exchange funds) that are designed to hedge or offset any decrease in the market value of equity securities—

(1) granted to the employee or member of the board of directors by the issuer as part of the compensation of the employee or member of the board of directors; or

(2) held, directly or indirectly, by the employee or member of the board of directors.

§ 78ff. Penalties

(a) Willful violations; false and misleading statements

Any person who willfully violates any provision of this chapter (other than section 78dd-1 of this title), or any rule or regulation thereunder the violation of which is made unlawful or the observance of which is required under the terms of this chapter, or any person who willfully and knowingly makes, or causes to be made, any statement in any application, report, or document required to be filed under this chapter or any rule or regulation thereunder or any undertaking contained in a registration statement as provided in subsection (d) of section 78o of this title, or by any self-regulatory organization in connection with an application for membership or participation therein or to become associated with a member thereof, which statement was false or misleading with respect to any material fact, shall upon conviction be fined not more than person other than a natural person, a fine not exceeding $25,000,000 may be imposed; but no person shall be subject to imprisonment under this section for the violation of any rule or regulation if he proves that he had no knowledge of such rule or regulation.

(b) Failure to file information, documents, or reports

Any issuer which fails to file information, documents, or reports required to be filed under subsection (d) of section 78o of this title or any rule or regulation thereunder shall forfeit to the United States the sum of $100 for each and every day such failure to file shall continue. Such forfeiture, which shall be in lieu of any criminal penalty for such failure to file which might be deemed to arise under subsection (a) of this section, shall be payable into the Treasury of the United States and shall be recoverable in a civil suit in the name of the United States.

(c) Violations by issuers, officers, directors, stockholders, employees, or agents of issuers

(1)

(A) Any issuer that violates subsection (a) or (g) of section 78dd-1 of this title shall be fined not more than $2,000,000.

(B) Any issuer that violates subsection (a) or (g) of section 78dd-1 of this title shall be subject to a civil penalty of not more than $10,000 imposed in an action brought by the Commission.

(2)

(A) Any officer, director, employee, or agent of an issuer, or stockholder acting on behalf of such issuer, who willfully violates subsection (a) or (g) of section 78dd-1 of this title shall be fined not more than $100,000, or imprisoned not more than 5 years, or both.

(B) Any officer, director, employee, or agent of an issuer, or stockholder acting on behalf of such issuer, who violates subsection (a) or (g) of section 78dd-1 of this title shall be subject to a civil penalty of not more than $10,000 imposed in an action brought by the Commission.

(3) Whenever a fine is imposed under paragraph (2) upon any officer, director, employee, agent, or stockholder of an issuer, such fine may not be paid, directly or indirectly, by such issuer.

§ 1125. False designations of origin, false descriptions, and dilution forbidden

(a) Civil action

(1) Any person who, on or in connection with any goods or services, or any container for goods, uses in commerce any word, term, name, symbol, or device, or any combination thereof, or any false designation of origin, false or misleading description of fact, or false or misleading representation of fact, which—

(A) is likely to cause confusion, or to cause mistake, or to deceive as to the affiliation, connection, or association of such person with another person, or as to the origin, sponsorship, or approval of his or her goods, services, or commercial activities by another person, or

(B) in commercial advertising or promotion, misrepresents the nature, characteristics, qualities, or geographic origin of his or her or another person's goods, services, or commercial activities, shall be liable in a civil action by any person who believes that he or she is or is likely to be damaged by such act.

(2) As used in this subsection, the term "any person" includes any State, instrumentality of a State or employee of a State or instrumentality of a State acting in his or her official capacity. Any State, and any such instrumentality, officer, or employee, shall be subject to the provisions of this chapter in the same manner and to the same extent as any nongovernmental entity.

(3) In a civil action for trade dress infringement under this chapter for trade dress not registered on the principal register, the person who asserts trade dress protection has the burden of proving that the matter sought to be protected is not functional.

(b) Importation

Any goods marked or labeled in contravention of the provisions of this section shall not be imported into the United States or admitted to entry at any customhouse of the United States. The owner, importer, or consignee of goods refused entry at any customhouse under this section may have any recourse by protest or appeal that is given under the customs revenue laws or may have the remedy given by this chapter in cases involving goods refused entry or seized.

(c) Dilution by blurring; dilution by tarnishment

(1) Injunctive relief

Subject to the principles of equity, the owner of a famous mark that is distinctive, inherently or through acquired distinctiveness, shall be entitled to an injunction against another person who, at any time after the owner's mark has become famous, commences use of a mark or trade name in commerce that is likely to cause dilution by blurring or dilution by tarnishment of the famous mark, regardless of the presence or absence of actual or likely confusion, of competition, or of actual economic injury.

(A) is likely to cause confusion, or to cause mistake, or to deceive as to the affiliation, connection, or association of such person with another person, or as to the origin, sponsorship, or approval of his or her goods, services, or commercial activities by another person, or

(2) Definitions

(A) For purposes of paragraph (1), a mark is famous if it is widely recognized by the general consuming public of the United States as a designation of source of the goods or services of the mark's owner. In determining whether a mark possesses the requisite degree of recognition, the court may consider all relevant factors, including the following:

(i) The duration, extent, and geographic reach of advertising and publicity of the mark, whether advertised or publicized by the owner or third parties.

(ii) The amount, volume, and geographic extent of sales of goods or services offered under the mark.

(iii) The extent of actual recognition of the mark.

(iv) Whether the mark was registered under the Act of March 3, 1881, or the Act of February 20, 1905, or on the principal register.

(B) For purposes of paragraph (1), "dilution by blurring" is association arising from the similarity between a mark or trade name and a famous mark that impairs the distinctiveness of the famous mark. In determining whether a mark or trade name is likely to cause dilution by blurring, the court may consider all relevant factors, including the following:

(i) The degree of similarity between the mark or trade name and the famous mark.

(ii) The degree of inherent or acquired distinctiveness of the famous mark.

(iii) The extent to which the owner of the famous mark is engaging in substantially exclusive use of the mark.

(iv) The degree of recognition of the famous mark.

(v) Whether the user of the mark or trade name intended to create an association with the famous mark.

(vi) Any actual association between the mark or trade name and the famous mark.

(C) For purposes of paragraph (1), "dilution by tarnishment" is association arising from the similarity between a mark or trade name and a famous mark that harms the reputation of the famous mark.

(3) Exclusions

The following shall not be actionable as dilution by blurring or dilution by tarnishment under this subsection:

(A) Any fair use, including a nominative or descriptive fair use, or facilitation of such fair use, of a famous mark by another person other than as a designation of source for the person's own goods or services, including use in connection with—

(i) advertising or promotion that permits consumers to compare goods or services; or

(ii) identifying and parodying, criticizing, or commenting upon the famous mark owner or the goods or services of the famous mark owner.

(B) All forms of news reporting and news commentary.

(C) Any noncommercial use of a mark.

(4) Burden of proof

In a civil action for trade dress dilution under this chapter for trade dress not registered on the principal register, the person who asserts trade dress protection has the burden of proving—

(A) the claimed trade dress, taken as a whole, is not functional and is famous; and

(B) if the claimed trade dress includes any mark or marks registered on the principal register, the unregistered matter, taken as a whole, is famous separate and apart from any fame of such registered marks.

(5) Additional remedies

In an action brought under this subsection, the owner of the famous mark shall be entitled to injunctive relief as set forth in section 1116 of this title. The owner of the famous mark shall also be entitled to the remedies set forth in sections 1117(a) and 1118 of this title, subject to the discretion of the court and the principles of equity if—

(A) the mark or trade name that is likely to cause dilution by blurring or dilution by tarnishment was first used in commerce by the person against whom the injunction is sought after October 6, 2006; and

(B) in a claim arising under this subsection—

(i) by reason of dilution by blurring, the person against whom the injunction is sought willfully intended to trade on the recognition of the famous mark; or

(ii) by reason of dilution by tarnishment, the person against whom the injunction is sought willfully intended to harm the reputation of the famous mark.

(6) Ownership of valid registration a complete bar to action

The ownership by a person of a valid registration under the Act of March 3, 1881, or the Act of February 20, 1905, or on the principal register under this chapter shall be a complete bar to an action against that person, with respect to that mark, that—

(A) is brought by another person under the common law or a statute of a State; and

(B)

(i) seeks to prevent dilution by blurring or dilution by tarnishment; or

(ii) asserts any claim of actual or likely damage or harm to the distinctiveness or reputation of a mark, label, or form of advertisement.

(7) Savings clause

Nothing in this subsection shall be construed to impair, modify, or supersede the applicability of the patent laws of the United States.

(d) Cyberpiracy prevention

(1)

(A) A person shall be liable in a civil action by the owner of a mark, including a personal name which is protected as a mark under this section, if, without regard to the goods or services of the parties, that person—

(i) has a bad faith intent to profit from that mark, including a personal name which is protected as a mark under this section; and

(ii) registers, traffics in, or uses a domain name that—

(I) in the case of a mark that is distinctive at the time of registration of the domain name, is identical or confusingly similar to that mark;

(II) in the case of a famous mark that is famous at the time of registration of the domain name, is identical or confusingly similar to or dilutive of that mark; or

(III) is a trademark, word, or name protected by reason of section 706 of Title 18 or section 220506 of Title 36.

(B)

(i) In determining whether a person has a bad faith intent described under subparagraph (A), a court may consider factors such as, but not limited to—

(I) the trademark or other intellectual property rights of the person, if any, in the domain name;

(II) the extent to which the domain name consists of the legal name of the person or a name that is otherwise commonly used to identify that person;

(III) the person's prior use, if any, of the domain name in connection with the bona fide offering of any goods or services;

(IV) the person's bona fide noncommercial or fair use of the mark in a site accessible under the domain name;

(V) the person's intent to divert consumers from the mark owner's online location to a site accessible under the domain name that could harm the goodwill represented by the mark, either for commercial gain or with the intent to tarnish or disparage the mark, by creating a likelihood of confusion as to the source, sponsorship, affiliation, or endorsement of the site;

(VI) the person's offer to transfer, sell, or otherwise assign the domain name to the mark owner or any third party for financial gain without having used, or having an intent to use, the domain name in the bona fide offering of any goods or services, or the person's prior conduct indicating a pattern of such conduct;

(VII) the person's provision of material and misleading false contact information when applying for the registration of the domain name, the person's intentional failure to maintain accurate contact information, or the person's prior conduct indicating a pattern of such conduct;

(VIII) the person's registration or acquisition of multiple domain names which the person knows are identical or confusingly similar to marks of others that are distinctive at the time of registration of such domain names, or dilutive of famous marks of others that are famous at the time of registration of such domain names, without regard to the goods or services of the parties; and

(IX) the extent to which the mark incorporated in the person's domain name registration is or is not distinctive and famous within the meaning of subsection (c) of this section.

(ii) Bad faith intent described under subparagraph (A) shall not be found in any case in which the court determines that the person believed and had reasonable grounds to believe that the use of the domain name was a fair use or otherwise lawful.

(C) In any civil action involving the registration, trafficking, or use of a domain name under this paragraph, a court may order the forfeiture or cancellation of the domain name or the transfer of the domain name to the owner of the mark.

(D) A person shall be liable for using a domain name under subparagraph (A) only if that person is the domain name registrant or that registrant's authorized licensee.

(E) As used in this paragraph, the term "traffics in" refers to transactions that include, but are not limited to, sales, purchases, loans, pledges, licenses, exchanges of currency, and any other transfer for consideration or receipt in exchange for consideration.

(2)

(A) The owner of a mark may file an in rem civil action against a domain name in the judicial district in which the domain name registrar, domain name registry, or other domain name authority that registered or assigned the domain name is located if—

(i) the domain name violates any right of the owner of a mark registered in the Patent and Trademark Office, or protected under subsection (a) or (c) of this section; and

(ii) the court finds that the owner—

(I) is not able to obtain in personam jurisdiction over a person who would have been a defendant in a civil action under paragraph (1); or

(II) through due diligence was not able to find a person who would have been a defendant in a civil action under paragraph (1) by—

(aa) sending a notice of the alleged violation and intent to proceed under this paragraph to the registrant of the domain name at the postal and e-mail address provided by the registrant to the registrar; and

(bb) publishing notice of the action as the court may direct promptly after filing the action.

(B) The actions under subparagraph (A)(ii) shall constitute service of process.

(C) In an in rem action under this paragraph, a domain name shall be deemed to have its situs in the judicial district in which—

(i) the domain name registrar, registry, or other domain name authority that registered or assigned the domain name is located; or

(ii) documents sufficient to establish control and authority regarding the disposition of the registration and use of the domain name are deposited with the court.

(D)

(i) The remedies in an in rem action under this paragraph shall be limited to a court order for the forfeiture or cancellation of the domain name or the transfer of the domain name to the owner of the mark. Upon receipt of written notification of a filed, stamped copy of a complaint filed by the owner of a mark in a United States district court under this paragraph, the domain name registrar, domain name registry, or other domain name authority shall—

(I) expeditiously deposit with the court documents sufficient to establish the court's control and authority regarding the disposition of the registration and use of the domain name to the court; and

(II) not transfer, suspend, or otherwise modify the domain name during the pendency of the action, except upon order of the court.

(ii) The domain name registrar or registry or other domain name authority shall not be liable for injunctive or monetary relief under this paragraph except in the case of bad faith or reckless disregard, which includes a willful failure to comply with any such court order.

(3) The civil action established under paragraph (1) and the in rem action established under paragraph (2), and any remedy available under either such action, shall be in addition to any other civil action or remedy otherwise applicable.

(4) The in rem jurisdiction established under paragraph (2) shall be in addition to any other jurisdiction that otherwise exists, whether in rem or in personem.

TITLE 17.   COPYRIGHTS

§ 506.   Criminal Offenses

(a) Criminal infringement.—

(1) In general.— Any person who willfully infringes a copyright shall be punished as provided under section 2319 of title 18, if the infringement was committed—

(A) for purposes of commercial advantage or private financial gain;

(B) by the reproduction or distribution, including by electronic means, during any 180-day period, of 1 or more copies or phonorecords of 1 or more copyrighted works, which have a total retail value of more than $1,000; or

(C) by the distribution of a work being prepared for commercial distribution, by making it available on a computer network accessible to members of the public, if such person knew or should have known that the work was intended for commercial distribution.

(2) Evidence.— For purposes of this subsection, evidence of reproduction or distribution of a copyrighted work, by itself, shall not be sufficient to establish willful infringement of a copyright.

(3) Definition.— In this subsection, the term "work being prepared for commercial distribution" means—

(A) a computer program, a musical work, a motion picture or other audiovisual work, or a sound recording, if, at the time of unauthorized distribution—

(i) the copyright owner has a reasonable expectation of commercial distribution; and

(ii) the copies or phonorecords of the work have not been commercially distributed; or

(B) a motion picture, if, at the time of unauthorized distribution, the motion picture—

(i) has been made available for viewing in a motion picture exhibition facility; and

(ii) has not been made available in copies for sale to the general public in the United States in a format intended to permit viewing outside a motion picture exhibition facility.

(b) Forfeiture, destruction, and restitution.— Forfeiture, destruction, and restitution relating to this section shall be subject to section 2323 of title 18, to the extent provided in that section, in addition to any other similar remedies provided by law.

(c) Fraudulent Copyright Notice.— Any person who, with fraudulent intent, places on any article a notice of copyright or words of the same purport that such person knows to be false, or who, with fraudulent intent, publicly distributes or imports for public distribution any article bearing such notice or words that such person knows to be false, shall be fined not more than $2,500.

(d) Fraudulent Removal of Copyright Notice.— Any person who, with fraudulent intent, removes or alters any notice of copyright appearing on a copy of a copyrighted work shall be fined not more than $2,500.

(e) False Representation.— Any person who knowingly makes a false representation of a material fact in the application for copyright registration provided for by section 409, or in any written statement filed in connection with the application, shall be fined not more than $2,500.

(f) Rights of Attribution and Integrity.— Nothing in this section applies to infringement of the rights conferred by section 106A(a).

TITLE 18. CRIMES AND CRIMINAL PROCEDURE

§ 2. Principals

(a) Whoever commits an offense against the United States or aids, abets, counsels, commands, induces or procures its commission, is punishable as a principal.

(b) Whoever willfully causes an act to be done which if directly performed by him or another would be an offense against the United States, is punishable as a principal.

§ 20. Financial Institution Defined

As used in this title, the term "financial institution" means—

(1) an insured depository institution (as defined in section 3(c)(2) of the Federal Deposit Insurance Act);

(2) a credit union with accounts insured by the National Credit Union Share Insurance Fund;

(3) a Federal home loan bank or a member, as defined in section 2 of the Federal Home Loan Bank Act (12 U.S.C. 1422), of the Federal home loan bank system;

(4) a System institution of the Farm Credit System, as defined in section

5.35(3) of the Farm Credit Act of 1971;

(5) a small business investment company, as defined in section 103 of the Small Business Investment Act of 1958 (15 U.S.C. 662);

(6) a depository institution holding company (as defined in section 3(w)(1) of the Federal Deposit Insurance Act);

(7) a Federal Reserve bank or a member bank of the Federal Reserve System;

(8) an organization operating under section 25 or section 25(a) of the Federal Reserve Act;

(9) a branch or agency of a foreign bank (as such terms are defined in paragraphs (1) and (3) of section 1(b) of the International Banking Act of 1978); or

(10) a mortgage lending business (as defined in section 27 of this title) or any person or entity that makes in whole or in part a federally related mortgage loan as defined in section 3 of the Real Estate Settlement Procedures Act of 1974.

§ 201. Bribery of public officials and witnesses

(a) For the purpose of this section—

(1) the term "public official" means Member of Congress, Delegate, or Resident Commissioner, either before or after such official has qualified, or an officer or employee or person acting for or on behalf of the United States, or any department, agency or branch of Government thereof, including the District of Columbia, in any official function, under or by authority of any such department, agency, or branch of Government, or a juror;

(2) the term "person who has been selected to be a public official" means any person who has been nominated or appointed to be a public official, or has been officially informed that such person will be so nominated or appointed; and

(3) the term "official act" means any decision or action on any question, matter, cause, suit, proceeding or controversy, which may at any time be pending, or which may by law be brought before any public official, in such official's official capacity, or in such official's place of trust or profit.

(b) Whoever—

(1) directly or indirectly, corruptly gives, offers or promises anything of value to any public official or person who has been selected to be a public official, or offers or promises any public official or any person who has been selected to be a public official to give anything of value to any other person or entity, with intent—

(A) to influence any official act; or

(B) to influence such public official or person who has been selected to be a public official to commit or aid in committing, or collude in, or allow, any fraud, or make opportunity for the commission of any fraud, on the United States; or

(C) to induce such public official or such person who has been selected to be a public official to do or omit to do any act in violation of the lawful duty of such official or person;

(2) being a public official or person selected to be a public official, directly or indirectly, corruptly demands, seeks, receives, accepts, or agrees to receive or accept anything of value personally or for any other person or entity, in return for:

(A) being influenced in the performance of any official act;

(B) being influenced to commit or aid in committing, or to collude in, or allow, any fraud, or make opportunity for the commission of any fraud, on the United States; or

(C) being induced to do or omit to do any act in violation of the official duty of such official or person;

(3) directly or indirectly, corruptly gives, offers, or promises anything of value to any person, or offers or promises such person to give anything of value to any other person or entity, with intent to influence the testimony under oath or affirmation of such first-mentioned person as a witness upon a trial, hearing, or other proceeding, before any court, any committee of either House or both Houses of Congress, or any agency, commission, or officer authorized by the laws of the United States to hear evidence or take testimony, or with intent to influence such person to absent himself therefrom;

(4) directly or indirectly, corruptly demands, seeks, receives, accepts, or agrees to receive or accept anything of value personally or for any other person or entity in return for being influenced in testimony under oath or affirmation as a witness upon any such trial, hearing, or other proceeding, or in return for absenting himself therefrom; shall be fined under this title or not more than three times the monetary equivalent of the thing of value, whichever is greater, or imprisoned for not more than fifteen years, or both, and may be disqualified from holding any office of honor, trust, or profit under the United States.

(c) Whoever—

(1) otherwise than as provided by law for the proper discharge of official duty—

(A) directly or indirectly gives, offers, or promises anything of value to any public official, former public official, or person selected to be a public official, for or because of any official act performed or to be performed by such public official, former public official, or person selected to be a public official; or

(B) being a public official, former public official, or person selected to be a public official, otherwise than as provided by law for the proper discharge of official duty, directly or indirectly demands, seeks, receives, accepts, or agrees to receive or accept anything of value personally for or because of any official act performed or to be performed by such official or person;

(2) directly or indirectly, gives, offers, or promises anything of value to any person, for or because of the testimony under oath or affirmation given or to be given by such person as a witness upon a trial, hearing, or other proceeding, before any court, any committee of either House or both Houses of Congress, or

any agency, commission, or officer authorized by the laws of the United States to hear evidence or take testimony, or for or because of such person's absence therefrom;

(3) directly or indirectly, demands, seeks, receives, accepts, or agrees to receive or accept anything of value personally for or because of the testimony under oath or affirmation given or to be given by such person as a witness upon any such trial, hearing, or other proceeding, or for or because of such person's absence therefrom; shall be fined under this title or imprisoned for not more than two years, or both.

(d) Paragraphs (3) and (4) of subsection (b) and paragraphs (2) and (3) subsection (c) shall not be construed to prohibit the payment or receipt of witness fees provided by law, or the payment, by the party upon whose behalf a witness is called and receipt by a witness, of the reasonable cost of travel and subsistence incurred and the reasonable value of time lost in attendance at any such trial, hearing, or proceeding, or in the case of expert witnesses, a reasonable fee for time spent in the preparation of such opinion, and in appearing and testifying.

(e) The offenses and penalties prescribed in this section are separate from and in addition to those prescribed in sections 1503, 1504, and 1505 of this title.

§ 242. Deprivation of rights under color of law

Whoever, under color of any law, statute, ordinance, regulation, or custom, willfully subjects any person in any State, Territory, Commonwealth, Possession, or District to the deprivation of any rights, privileges, or immunities secured or protected by the Constitution or laws of the United States, or to different punishments, pains, or penalties, on account of such person being an alien, or by reason of his color, or race, than are prescribed for the punishment of citizens, shall be fined under this title or imprisoned not more than one year, or both; and if bodily injury results from the acts committed in violation of this section or if such acts include the use, attempted use, or threatened use of a dangerous weapon, explosives, or fire, shall be fined under this title or imprisoned not more than ten years, or both; and if death results from the acts committed in violation of this section or if such acts include kidnapping or an attempt to kidnap, aggravated sexual abuse, or an attempt to commit aggravated sexual abuse, or an attempt to kill, shall be fined under this title, or imprisoned for any term of years or for life, or both, or may be sentenced to death.

§ 287. False, fictitious or fraudulent claims

Whoever makes or presents to any person or officer in the civil, military, or naval service of the United States, or to any department or agency thereof, any claim upon or against the United States, or any department or agency thereof, knowing such claim to be false, fictitious, or fraudulent, shall be imprisoned not more than five years and shall be subject to a fine in the amount provided in this title.

§ 371. Conspiracy to commit offense or to defraud United States

If two or more persons conspire either to commit any offense against the United States, or to defraud the United States, or any agency thereof in any manner or for any purpose, and one or more of such persons do any act to effect the object of the conspiracy, each shall be fined under this title or imprisoned not more than five years, or both.

If, however, the offense, the commission of which is the object of the conspiracy, is a misdemeanor only, the punishment for such conspiracy shall not exceed the maximum punishment provided for such misdemeanor.

§ 542. Entry of goods by means of false statements

Whoever enters or introduces, or attempts to enter or introduce, into the commerce of the United States any imported merchandise by means of any fraudulent or false invoice, declaration, affidavit, letter, paper, or by means of any false statement, written or verbal, or by means of any false or fraudulent practice or appliance, or makes any false statement in any declaration without reasonable cause to believe the truth of such statement, or procures the making of any such false statement as to any matter material thereto without reasonable cause to believe the truth of such statement, whether or not the United States shall or may be deprived of any lawful duties; or

Whoever is guilty of any willful act or omission whereby the United States shall or may be deprived of any lawful duties accruing upon merchandise embraced or referred to in such invoice, declaration, affidavit, letter, paper, or statement, or affected by such act or omission—

Shall be fined for each offense under this title or imprisoned not more than two years, or both.

Nothing in this section shall be construed to relieve imported merchandise from forfeiture under other provisions of law.

The term "commerce of the United States", as used in this section, shall not include commerce with the Virgin Islands, American Samoa, Wake Island, Midway Islands, Kingman Reef, Johnston Island, or Guam.

§ 641. Public money, property or records

Whoever embezzles, steals, purloins, or knowingly converts to his use or the use of another, or without authority, sells, conveys or disposes of any record, voucher, money, or thing of value of the United States or of any department or agency thereof, or any property made or being made under contract for the United States or any department or agency thereof; or

Whoever receives, conceals, or retains the same with intent to convert it to his use or gain, knowing it to have been embezzled, stolen, purloined or converted—

Shall be fined under this title or imprisoned not more than ten years, or both; but if the value of such property in the aggregate, combining amounts from all the counts for which the defendant is convicted in a single case, does not exceed the sum of $1,000, he shall be fined under this title or imprisoned not more than one year, or both.

The word "value" means face, par, or market value, or cost price, either wholesale or retail, whichever is greater.

§ 656. Theft, embezzlement, or misapplication by bank officer or employee

Whoever, being an officer, director, agent or employee of, or connected in any capacity with any Federal Reserve bank, member bank, depository institution holding company, national bank, insured bank, branch or agency of a foreign bank, or organization operating under section 25 or section 25(a) of the Federal Reserve Act, or a receiver of a national bank, insured bank, branch, agency, or organization or any agent or employee of the receiver, or a Federal Reserve Agent, or an agent or employee of a Federal Reserve Agent or of the Board of Governors of the Federal Reserve System, embezzles, abstracts, purloins or willfully misapplies any of the moneys, funds or credits of such bank, branch, agency, or organization or holding company or any moneys, funds, assets or securities intrusted to the custody or care of such bank, branch, agency, or organization, or holding company or to the custody or care of any such agent, officer, director, employee or receiver, shall be fined not more than $1,000,000 or imprisoned not more than 30 years, or both; but if the amount embezzled, abstracted, purloined or misapplied does not exceed $1,000, he shall be fined under this title or imprisoned not more than one year, or both.

As used in this section, the term "national bank" is synonymous with "national banking association"; "member bank" means and includes any national bank, state bank, or bank and trust company which has become a member of one of the Federal Reserve banks; "insured bank" includes any bank, banking association, trust company, savings bank, or other banking institution, the deposits of which are insured by the Federal Deposit Insurance Corporation; and the term "branch or agency of a foreign bank" means a branch or agency described in section 20(9) of this title. For purposes of this section, the term "depository institution holding company" has the meaning given such term in section 3 of the Federal Deposit Insurance Act.

§ 666. Theft or bribery concerning programs receiving Federal funds

(a) Whoever, if the circumstance described in subsection (b) of this section exists—

(1) being an agent of an organization, or of a State, local, or Indian tribal government, or any agency thereof—

(A) embezzles, steals, obtains by fraud, or otherwise without authority knowingly converts to the use of any person other than the rightful owner or intentionally misapplies, property that—

(i) is valued at $5,000 or more, and

(ii) is owned by, or is under the care, custody, or control of such organization, government, or agency; or

(B)

(i) corruptly solicits or demands for the benefit of any person, or accepts or agrees to accept, anything of value from any person, intending to be influenced or rewarded in connection with any business, transaction, or series of transactions of such organization, government, or agency involving any thing of value of $5,000 or more; or

(ii) corruptly gives, offers, or agrees to give anything of value to any person, with intent to influence or reward an agent of an organization or of a State, local or Indian tribal government, or any agency thereof, in connection with any business, transaction, or series of transactions of such organization, government, or agency involving anything of value of $5,000 or more; shall be fined under this title, imprisoned not more than 10 years, or both.

(b) The circumstance referred to in subsection (a) of this section is that the organization, government, or agency receives, in any one year period, benefits in excess of $10,000 under a Federal program involving a grant, contract, subsidy, loan, guarantee, insurance, or other form of Federal assistance.

(c) This section does not apply to bona fide salary, wages, fees, or other compensation paid, or expenses paid or reimbursed, in the usual course of business.

(d) As used in this section—

(1) the term "agent" means a person authorized to act on behalf of another person or a government and, in the case of an organization or government, includes a servant or employee, and a partner, director, officer, manager, and representative;

(2) the term "government agency" means a subdivision of the executive, legislative, judicial, or other branch of government, including a department, independent establishment, commission, administration, authority, board, and bureau, and a corporation or other legal entity established, and subject to control, by a government or governments for the execution of a governmental or intergovernmental program;

(3) the term "local" means of or pertaining to a political subdivision within a State;

(4) the term "State" includes a State of the United States, the District of Columbia, and any commonwealth, territory, or possession of the United States; and

(5) the term "in any one-year period" means a continuous period that commences no earlier than twelve months before the commission of the offense or that ends no later than twelve months after the commission of the offense. Such period may include time both before and after the commission of the offense.

§ 981. Civil forfeiture

(a)

(1) The following property is subject to forfeiture to the United States:

(A) Any property, real or personal, involved in a transaction or attempted transaction in violation of section 1956, 1957 or 1960 of this title, or any property traceable to such property.

(B) Any property, real or personal, within the jurisdiction of the United States, constituting, derived from, or traceable to, any proceeds obtained directly or indirectly from an offense against a foreign nation, or any property used to facilitate such an offense, if the offense—

(i) involves trafficking in nuclear, chemical, biological, or radiological weapons technology or material, or the manufacture, importation, sale, or distribution of a controlled substance (as that term is defined for purposes of the Controlled Substances Act), or any other conduct described in section 1956(c)(7)(B);

(ii) would be punishable within the jurisdiction of the foreign nation by death or for a term exceeding 1 year; and

(iii) would be punishable under the laws of the United States by imprisonment for a term exceeding 1 year, if the act or activity constituting the offense had occurred within the jurisdiction of the United States.

(C) Any property, real or personal, which constitutes or is derived from proceeds traceable to a violation of section 215, 471, 472, 473, 474, 476, 477, 478, 479, 480, 481, 485, 486, 487, 488, 501, 502, 510, 542, 545, 656, 657,670, 842, 844, 1005, 1006, 1007, 1014, 1028, 1029, 1030, 1032, or 1344 of this title or any offense constituting "specified unlawful activity" (as defined in section 1956(c)(7) of this title), or a conspiracy to commit such offense.

(D) Any property, real or personal, which represents or is traceable to the gross receipts obtained, directly or indirectly, from a violation of—

(i) section 666(a)(1) (relating to Federal program fraud);

(ii) section 1001 (relating to fraud and false statements);

(iii) section 1031 (relating to major fraud against the United States);

(iv) section 1032 (relating to concealment of assets from conservator or receiver of insured financial institution);

(v) section 1341 (relating to mail fraud); or

(vi) section 1343 (relating to wire fraud), if such violation relates to the sale of assets acquired or held by the Federal Deposit Insurance Corporation, as conservator or receiver for a financial institution, or any other conservator for a financial institution appointed by the Office of the Comptroller of the Currency or the National Credit Union Administration, as conservator or liquidating agent for a financial institution appointed by the Office of the Comptroller of the Currency or the National Credit Union Administration, as conservator or liquidating agent for a financial institution.

(E) With respect to an offense listed in subsection (a)(1)(D) committed for the purpose of executing or attempting to execute any scheme or artifice to defraud, or for obtaining money or property by means of false or fraudulent statements, pretenses, representations or promises, the gross receipts of such an offense shall include all property, real or personal, tangible or intangible, which thereby is obtained, directly or indirectly.

(F) Any property, real or personal, which represents or is traceable to the gross proceeds obtained, directly or indirectly, from a violation of—

(i) section 511 (altering or removing motor vehicle identification numbers);

(ii) section 553 (importing or exporting stolen motor vehicles);

(iii) section 2119 (armed robbery of automobiles);

(iv) section 2312 (transporting stolen motor vehicles in interstate commerce); or

(v) section 2313 (possessing or selling a stolen motor vehicle that has moved in interstate commerce).

(G) All assets, foreign or domestic—

(i) of any individual, entity, or organization engaged in planning or perpetrating any Federal crime of terrorism (as defined in section 2332b(g)(5)) against the United States, citizens or residents of the United States, or their property, and all assets, foreign or domestic, affording any person a source of influence over any such entity or organization;

(ii) acquired or maintained by any person with the intent and for the purpose of supporting, planning, conducting, or concealing any Federal crime of terrorism (as defined in section 2332b(g)(5) against the United States, citizens or residents of the United States, or their property;

(iii) derived from, involved in, or used or intended to be used to commit any Federal crime of terrorism (as defined in section 2332b(g)(5)) against the United States, citizens or residents of the United States, or their property; or

(iv) of any individual, entity, or organization engaged in planning or perpetrating any act of international terrorism (as defined in section 2331) against any international organization (as defined in section 209 of the State Department Basic Authorities Act of 1956 (22 U.S.C. 4309(b)) or against any foreign Government. Where the property sought for forfeiture is located beyond the territorial boundaries of the United States, an act in furtherance of such planning or perpetration must have occurred within the jurisdiction of the United States.

(H) Any property, real or personal, involved in a violation or attempted violation, or which constitutes or is derived from proceeds traceable to a violation, of section 2339C of this title.

(2) For purposes of paragraph (1), the term "proceeds" is defined as follows:

(A) In cases involving illegal goods, illegal services, unlawful activities, and telemarketing and health care fraud schemes, the term "proceeds" means property of any kind obtained directly or indirectly, as the result of the commission of the offense giving rise to forfeiture, and any property traceable thereto, and is not limited to the net gain or profit realized from the offense.

(B) In cases involving lawful goods or lawful services that are sold or provided in an illegal manner, the term "proceeds" means the amount of money acquired through the illegal transactions resulting in the forfeiture, less the direct costs incurred in providing the goods or services. The claimant shall have the burden of proof with respect to the issue of direct costs. The direct costs shall not include any part of the overhead expenses of the entity providing the goods or services, or any part of the income taxes paid by the entity.

(C) In cases involving fraud in the process of obtaining a loan or extension of credit, the court shall allow the claimant a deduction from the forfeiture to the extent that the loan was repaid, or the debt was satisfied, without any financial loss to the victim.

(b)

(1) Except as provided in section 985, any property subject to forfeiture to the United States under subsection (a) may be seized by the Attorney General and, in the case of property involved in a violation investigated by the Secretary of the Treasury or the United States Postal Service, the property may also be seized by the Secretary of the Treasury or the Postal Service, respectively.

(2) Seizures pursuant to this section shall be made pursuant to a warrant obtained in the same manner as provided for a search warrant under the Federal Rules of Criminal Procedure, except that a seizure may be made without a warrant if—

(A) a complaint for forfeiture has been filed in the United States district court and the court issued an arrest warrant in rem pursuant to the Supplemental Rules for Certain Admiralty and Maritime Claims;

(B) there is probable cause to believe that the property is subject to forfeiture and—

(i) the seizure is made pursuant to a lawful arrest or search; or

(ii) another exception to the Fourth Amendment warrant requirement would apply; or

(C) the property was lawfully seized by a State or local law enforcement agency and transferred to a Federal agency.

(3) Notwithstanding the provisions of rule 41(a) of the Federal Rules of Criminal Procedure, a seizure warrant may be issued pursuant to this subsection by a judicial officer in any district in which a forfeiture action against the property may be filed under section 1355(b) of title 28, and may be executed in any district in which the property is found, or transmitted to the central authority of any foreign state for service in accordance with any treaty or other international agreement. Any motion for the return of property seized under this section shall be filed in the district court in which the seizure warrant was issued or in the district court for the district in which the property was seized.

(4)

(A) If any person is arrested or charged in a foreign country in connection with an offense that would give rise to the forfeiture of property in the United States under this section or under the Controlled Substances Act, the Attorney General may apply to any Federal judge or magistrate judge in the district in which the property is located for an ex parte order restraining the property subject to forfeiture for not more than 30 days, except that the time may be extended for good cause shown at a hearing conducted in the manner provided in rule 43(e) of the Federal Rules of Civil Procedure.

(B) The application for the restraining order shall set forth the nature and circumstances of the foreign charges and the basis for belief that the person arrested or charged has property in the United States that would be subject to forfeiture, and shall contain a statement that the restraining order is needed to preserve the availability of property for such time as is necessary to receive evidence from the foreign country or elsewhere in support of probable cause for the seizure of the property under this subsection.

(c) Property taken or detained under this section shall not be repleviable, but shall be deemed to be in the custody of the Attorney General, the Secretary of the Treasury, or the Postal Service, as the case may be, subject only to the orders and decrees of the court or the official having jurisdiction thereof. Whenever property is seized under this subsection, the Attorney General, the Secretary of the Treasury, or the Postal Service, as the case may be, may—

(1) place the property under seal;

(2) remove the property to a place designated by him; or

(3) require that the General Services Administration take custody of the property and remove it, if practicable, to an appropriate location for disposition in accordance with law.

(d) For purposes of this section, the provisions of the customs laws relating to the seizure, summary and judicial forfeiture, condemnation of property for violation of the customs laws, the disposition of such property or the proceeds from the sale of such property under this section, the remission or mitigation of such forfeitures, and the compromise of claims (19 U.S.C. 1602 et seq.), insofar as they are applicable and not inconsistent with the provisions of this section, shall apply to seizures and forfeitures incurred, or alleged to have been incurred, under this section, except that such duties as are imposed upon the customs officer or any other person with respect to the seizure and forfeiture of property under the customs laws shall be performed with respect to seizures and forfeitures of property under this section by such officers, agents, or other persons as may be authorized or designated for that purpose by the Attorney General, the Secretary of the Treasury, or the Postal Service, as the case may be. The Attorney General shall have sole responsibility for disposing of petitions for remission or mitigation with respect to property involved in a judicial forfeiture proceeding.

(e) Notwithstanding any other provision of the law, except section 3 of the Anti Drug Abuse Act of 1986, the Attorney General, the Secretary of the Treasury, or the

Postal Service, as the case may be, is authorized to retain property forfeited pursuant to this section, or to transfer such property on such terms and conditions as he may determine—

(1) to any other Federal agency;

(2) to any State or local law enforcement agency which participated directly in any of the acts which led to the seizure or forfeiture of the property;

(3) in the case of property referred to in subsection (a)(1)(C), to any Federal financial institution regulatory agency—

(A) to reimburse the agency for payments to claimants or creditors of the institution; and

(B) to reimburse the insurance fund of the agency for losses suffered by the fund as a result of the receivership or liquidation;

(4) in the case of property referred to in subsection (a)(1)(C), upon the order of the appropriate Federal financial institution regulatory agency, to the financial institution as restitution, with the value of the property so transferred to be set off against any amount later recovered by the financial institution as compensatory damages in any State or Federal proceeding;

(5) in the case of property referred to in subsection (a)(1)(C), to any Federal financial institution regulatory agency, to the extent of the agency's contribution of resources to, or expenses involved in, the seizure and forfeiture, and the investigation leading directly to the seizure and forfeiture, of such property;

(6) as restoration to any victim of the offense giving rise to the forfeiture, including, in the case of a money laundering offense, any offense constituting the underlying specified unlawful activity; or

(7) In the case of property referred to in subsection (a)(1)(D), to the Resolution Trust Corporation, the Federal Deposit Insurance Corporation, or any other Federal financial institution regulatory agency (as defined in section 8(e)(7)(D) of the Federal Deposit Insurance Act).

The Attorney General, the Secretary of the Treasury, or the Postal Service, as the case may be, shall ensure the equitable transfer pursuant to paragraph (2) of any forfeited property to the appropriate State or local law enforcement agency so as to reflect generally the contribution of any such agency participating directly in any of the acts which led to the seizure or forfeiture of such property. A decision by the Attorney General, the Secretary of the Treasury, or the Postal Service pursuant to paragraph (2) shall not be subject to review. The United States shall not be liable in any action arising out of the use of any property the custody of which was transferred pursuant to this section to any non-Federal agency. The Attorney General, the Secretary of the Treasury, or the Postal Service may order the discontinuance of any forfeiture proceedings under this section in favor of the institution of forfeiture proceedings by State or local authorities under an appropriate State or local statute. After the filing of a complaint for forfeiture under this section, the Attorney General may seek dismissal of the complaint in favor of forfeiture proceedings under State or local law. Whenever forfeiture proceedings are discontinued by the United States in favor of State or local proceedings, the United States may transfer custody and possession of the seized property to the appropriate State or local official immediately upon the initiation of the proper actions by such officials. Whenever forfeiture proceedings are discontinued by the United States in favor of State or local proceedings, notice shall be sent to all known interested parties advising them of the discontinuance or dismissal. The United States shall not be liable in any action arising out of the seizure, detention, and transfer of seized property to State or local officials. The United States shall not be liable in any action arising out of a transfer under paragraph (3), (4), or (5) of this subsection.

(f) All right, title, and interest in property described in subsection (a) of this section shall vest in the United States upon commission of the act giving rise to forfeiture under this section.

(g)

(1) Upon the motion of the United States, the court shall stay the civil forfeiture proceeding if the court determines that civil discovery will adversely affect the ability of the Government to conduct a related criminal investigation or the prosecution of a related criminal case.

(2) Upon the motion of a claimant, the court shall stay the civil forfeiture proceeding with respect to that claimant if the court determines that—

(A) the claimant is the subject of a related criminal investigation or case;

(B) the claimant has standing to assert a claim in the civil forfeiture proceeding; and

(C) continuation of the forfeiture proceeding will burden the right of the claimant against self-incrimination in the related investigation or case.

(3) With respect to the impact of civil discovery described in paragraphs (1) and (2), the court may determine that a stay is unnecessary if a protective order limiting discovery would protect the interest of one party without unfairly limiting the ability of the opposing party to pursue the civil case. In no case, however, shall the court impose a protective order as an alternative to a stay if the effect of such protective order would be to allow one party to pursue discovery while the other party is substantially unable to do so.

(4) In this subsection, the terms "related criminal case" and "related criminal investigation" mean an actual prosecution or investigation in progress at the time at which the request for the stay, or any subsequent motion to lift the stay is made. In determining whether a criminal case or investigation is "related" to a civil forfeiture proceeding, the court shall consider the degree of similarity between the parties, witnesses, facts, and circumstances involved in the two proceedings, without requiring an identity with respect to any one or more factors.

(5) In requesting a stay under paragraph (1), the Government may, in appropriate cases, submit evidence ex parte in order to avoid disclosing any matter that may adversely affect an ongoing criminal investigation or pending

criminal trial

(6) Whenever a civil forfeiture proceeding is stayed pursuant to this subsection, the court shall enter any order necessary to preserve the value of the property or to protect the rights of lienholders or other persons with an interest in the property while the stay is in effect.

(7) A determination by the court that the claimant has standing to request a stay pursuant to paragraph (2) shall apply only to this subsection and shall not preclude the Government from objecting to the standing of the claimant by dispositive motion or at the time of trial.

(h) In addition to the venue provided for in section 1395 of title 28 or any other provision of law, in the case of property of a defendant charged with a violation that is the basis for forfeiture of the property under this section, a proceeding for forfeiture under this section may be brought in the judicial district in which the defendant owning such property is found or in the judicial district in which the criminal prosecution is brought.

(i)

(1) Whenever property is civilly or criminally forfeited under this chapter, the Attorney General or the Secretary of the Treasury, as the case may be, may transfer the forfeited personal property or the proceeds of the sale of any forfeited personal or real property to any foreign country which participated directly or indirectly in the seizure or forfeiture of the property, if such a transfer—

(A) has been agreed to by the Secretary of State;

(B) s authorized in an international agreement between the United States and the foreign country; and

(C) is made to a country which, if applicable, has been certified under section 481(h) of the Foreign Assistance Act of 1961.

A decision by the Attorney General or the Secretary of the Treasury pursuant to this paragraph shall not be subject to review. The foreign country shall, in the event of a transfer of property or proceeds of sale of property under this subsection, bear all expenses incurred by the United States in the seizure, maintenance, inventory, storage, forfeiture, and disposition of the property, and all transfer costs. The payment of all such expenses, and the transfer of assets pursuant to this paragraph, shall be upon such terms and conditions as the Attorney General or the Secretary of the Treasury may, in his discretion, set.

(2) The provisions of this section shall not be construed as limiting or superseding any other authority of the United States to provide assistance to a foreign country in obtaining property related to a crime committed in the foreign country, including property which is sought as evidence of a crime committed in the foreign country.

(3) A certified order or judgment of forfeiture by a court of competent jurisdiction of a foreign country concerning property which is the subject of

forfeiture under this section and was determined by such court to be the type of property described in subsection (a)(1)(B) of this section, and any certified recordings or transcripts of testimony taken in a foreign judicial proceeding concerning such order or judgment of forfeiture, shall be admissible in evidence in a proceeding brought pursuant to this section. Such certified order or judgment of forfeiture, when admitted into evidence, shall constitute probable cause that the property forfeited by such order or judgment of forfeiture is subject to forfeiture under this section and creates a rebuttable presumption of the forfeitability of such property under this section.

(4) A certified order or judgment of conviction by a court of competent jurisdiction of a foreign country concerning an unlawful drug activity which gives rise to forfeiture under this section and any certified recordings or transcripts of testimony taken in a foreign judicial proceeding concerning such order or judgment of conviction shall be admissible in evidence in a proceeding brought pursuant to this section. Such certified order or judgment of conviction, when admitted into evidence, creates a rebuttable presumption that the unlawful drug activity giving rise to forfeiture under this section has occurred.

(5) The provisions of paragraphs (3) and (4) of this subsection shall not be construed as limiting the admissibility of any evidence otherwise admissible, nor shall they limit the ability of the United States to establish probable cause that property is subject to forfeiture by any evidence otherwise admissible.

(j) For purposes of this section—

(1) the term "Attorney General" means the Attorney General or his delegate; and

(2) the term "Secretary of the Treasury" means the Secretary of the Treasury or his delegate.

(k) Interbank accounts.—

(1) In general.—

(A) In general.— For the purpose of a forfeiture under this section or under the Controlled Substances Act (21 U.S.C. 801 et seq.), if funds are deposited into an account at a foreign financial institution (as defined in section 984(c)(2)(A) of this title), and that foreign financial institution (as defined in section 984(c)(2)(A) of this title) has an interbank account in the United States with a covered financial institution (as defined in section 5318(j)(1) of title 31), the funds shall be deemed to have been deposited into the interbank account in the United States, and any restraining order, seizure warrant, or arrest warrant in rem regarding the funds may be served on the covered financial institution, and funds in the interbank account, up to the value of the funds deposited into the account at the foreign financial institution (as defined in section 984(c)(2)(A) of this title), may be restrained, seized, or arrested.

(B) Authority to suspend.— The Attorney General, in consultation with the Secretary of the Treasury, may suspend or terminate a forfeiture under this section if the Attorney General determines that a conflict of law exists between the laws of the jurisdiction in which the foreign financial institution (as defined in section 984(c)(2)(A) of this title) is located and the laws of the United States with respect to liabilities arising from the restraint, seizure, or arrest of such funds, and that such suspension or termination would be in the interest of justice and would not harm the national interests of the United States.

(2) No requirement for government to trace funds.— If a forfeiture action is brought against funds that are restrained, seized, or arrested under paragraph (1), it shall not be necessary for the Government to establish that the funds are directly traceable to the funds that were deposited into the foreign financial institution (as defined in section 984(c)(2)(A) of this title), nor shall it be necessary for the Government to rely on the application of section 984.

(3) Claims brought by owner of the funds.— If a forfeiture action is instituted against funds restrained, seized, or arrested under paragraph (1), the owner of the funds deposited into the account at the foreign financial institution (as defined in section 984(c)(2)(A) of this title) may contest the forfeiture by filing a claim under section 983.

(4) Definitions.— For purposes of this subsection, the following definitions shall apply:

(A) Interbank account.— The term "interbank account" has the same meaning as in section 984(c)(2)(B).

(B) Owner.—

(i) In general.— Except as provided in clause (ii), the term "owner"—

(I) means the person who was the owner, as that term is defined in section 983(d)(6), of the funds that were deposited into the foreign financial institution (as defined in section 984(c)(2)(A) of this title) at the time such funds were deposited; and

(II) does not include either the foreign financial institution (as defined in section 984(c)(2)(A) of this title) or any financial institution acting as an intermediary in the transfer of the funds into the interbank account.

(ii) Exception.— The foreign financial institution (as defined in section 984(c)(2)(A) of this title) may be considered the "owner" of the funds (and no other person shall qualify as the owner of such funds) only if—

(I) the basis for the forfeiture action is wrongdoing committed by the foreign financial institution (as defined in section 984(c)(2)(A) of this title); or

(II) the foreign financial institution (as defined in section 984(c)(2)(A) of this title) establishes, by a preponderance of the evidence, that prior to the restraint, seizure, or arrest of the funds, the foreign financial institution (as defined in section 984(c)(2)(A) of this title) had discharged all or part of its obligation to the prior owner of the funds, in which case the foreign financial institution (as defined in section 984(c)(2)(A) of this title) shall be deemed the owner of the funds to the extent of such discharged obligation.

§ 982. Criminal forfeiture

(a)

(1) The court, in imposing sentence on a person convicted of an offense in violation of section 1956, 1957, or 1960 of this title, shall order that the person forfeit to the United States any property, real or personal, involved in such offense, or any property traceable to such property.

(2) The court, in imposing sentence on a person convicted of a violation of, or a conspiracy to violate—

(A) section 215, 656, 657, 1005, 1006, 1007, 1014, 1341, 1343, or 1344 of this title, affecting a financial institution, or

(B) section 471, 472, 473, 474, 476, 477, 478, 479, 480, 481, 485, 486, 487, 488, 501, 502, 510, 542, 545, 555, 842, 844, 1028, 1029, or 1030 of this title, shall order that the person forfeit to the United States any property constituting, or derived from, proceeds the person obtained directly or indirectly, as the result of such violation.

(3) The court, in imposing a sentence on a person convicted of an offense under—

(A) section 666(a)(1) (relating to Federal program fraud);

(B) section 1001 (relating to fraud and false statements);

(C) section 1031 (relating to major fraud against the United States);

(D) section 1032 (relating to concealment of assets from conservator, receiver, or liquidating agent of insured financial institution);

(E) section 1341 (relating to mail fraud); or

(F) section 1343 (relating to wire fraud),

involving the sale of assets acquired or held by the Federal Deposit Insurance Corporation, as conservator or receiver for a financial institution or any other conservator for a financial institution appointed by the Office of the Comptroller of the Currency, or the National Credit Union Administration, as conservator or liquidating agent for a financial institution, shall order that the person forfeit to the United States any property, real or personal, which represents or is traceable to the gross receipts obtained, directly or indirectly, as a result of such violation.

(4) With respect to an offense listed in subsection (a)(3) committed for the purpose of executing or attempting to execute any scheme or artifice to defraud, or for obtaining money or property by means of false or fraudulent statements, pretenses, representations, or promises, the gross receipts of such an offense shall include any property, real or personal, tangible or intangible, which is obtained, directly or indirectly, as a result of such offense.

(5) The court, in imposing sentence on a person convicted of a violation or conspiracy to violate—

(A) section 511 (altering or removing motor vehicle identification numbers);

(B) section 553 (importing or exporting stolen motor vehicles);

(C) section 2119 (armed robbery of automobiles);

(D) section 2312 (transporting stolen motor vehicles in interstate commerce); or

(E) section 2313 (possessing or selling a stolen motor vehicle that has moved in interstate commerce); shall order that the person forfeit to the United States any property, real or personal, which represents or is traceable to the gross proceeds obtained, directly or indirectly, as a result of such violation.

(6)

(A) The court, in imposing sentence on a person convicted of a violation of, or conspiracy to violate, section 274(a), 274A(a)(1), or 274A(a)(2) of the Immigration and Nationality Act or section 555, 1425, 1426, 1427, 1541,1542, 1543, 1544, or 1546 of this title, or a violation of, or conspiracy to violate, section 1028 of this title if committed in connection with passport or visa issuance or use, shall order that the person forfeit to the United States, regardless of any provision of State law—

(i) any conveyance, including any vessel, vehicle, or aircraft used in the commission of the offense of which the person is convicted; and

(ii) any property real or personal—

(I) that constitutes, or is derived from or is traceable to the proceeds obtained directly or indirectly from the commission of the offense of which the person is convicted; or

(II) that is used to facilitate, or is intended to be used to facilitate, the commission of the offense of which the person is convicted.

(B) The court, in imposing sentence on a person described in subparagraph (A), shall order that the person forfeit to the United States all property described in that subparagraph.

(7) The court, in imposing sentence on a person convicted of a Federal health care offense, shall order the person to forfeit property, real or personal, that constitutes or is derived, directly or indirectly, from gross proceeds traceable to the commission of the offense.

(8) The court, in sentencing a defendant convicted of an offense under section 1028, 1029, 1341, 1342, 1343, or 1344, or of a conspiracy to commit such an offense, if the offense involves telemarketing (as that term is defined in section 2325), shall order that the defendant forfeit to the United States any real or personal property—

(A) used or intended to be used to commit, to facilitate, or to promote the commission of such offense; and

(B) constituting, derived from, or traceable to the gross proceeds that the defendant obtained directly or indirectly as a result of the offense.

(b)

(1) The forfeiture of property under this section, including any seizure and disposition of the property and any related judicial or administrative proceeding, shall be governed by the provisions of section 413 (other than subsection (d) of that section) of the Comprehensive Drug Abuse Prevention and Control Act of 1970 (21 U.S.C. 853).

(2) The substitution of assets provisions of subsection 413(p) shall not be used to order a defendant to forfeit assets in place of the actual property laundered where such defendant acted merely as an intermediary who handled but did not retain the property in the course of the money laundering offense unless the defendant, in committing the offense or offenses giving rise to the forfeiture, conducted three or more separate transactions involving a total of $100,000 or more in any twelve month period.

§ 983. General rules for civil forfeiture proceedings

(a) Notice; Claim; Complaint.—

(1)

(A)

(i) Except as provided in clauses (ii) through (v), in any nonjudicial civil forfeiture proceeding under a civil forfeiture statute, with respect to which the Government is required to send written notice to interested parties, such notice shall be sent in a manner to achieve proper notice as soon as practicable, and in no case more than 60 days after the date of the seizure.

(ii) No notice is required if, before the 60-day period expires, the Government files a civil judicial forfeiture action against the property and provides notice of that action as required by law.

(iii) If, before the 60-day period expires, the Government does not file a civil judicial forfeiture action, but does obtain a criminal indictment containing an allegation that the property is subject to forfeiture, the Government shall either—

(I) send notice within the 60 days and continue the nonjudicial civil forfeiture proceeding under this section; or

(II) terminate the nonjudicial civil forfeiture proceeding, and take the steps necessary to preserve its right to maintain custody of the property as provided in the applicable criminal forfeiture statute.

(iv) In a case in which the property is seized by a State or local law enforcement agency and turned over to a Federal law enforcement agency for the purpose of forfeiture under Federal law, notice shall be sent not more than 90 days after the date of seizure by the State or local law enforcement agency.

(v) If the identity or interest of a party is not determined until after the seizure or turnover but is determined before a declaration of forfeiture is entered, notice shall be sent to such interested party not later than 60 days after the determination by the Government of the identity of the party or the party's interest.

(B) A supervisory official in the headquarters office of the seizing agency may extend the period for sending notice under subparagraph (A) for a period not to exceed 30 days (which period may not be further extended except by a court), if the official determines that the conditions in subparagraph (D) are present.

(C) Upon motion by the Government, a court may extend the period for sending notice under subparagraph (A) for a period not to exceed 60 days, which period may be further extended by the court for 60-day periods, as necessary, if the court determines, based on a written certification of a supervisory official in the headquarters office of the seizing agency, that the conditions in subparagraph (D) are present.

(D) The period for sending notice under this paragraph may be extended only if there is reason to believe that notice may have an adverse result, including—

(i) endangering the life or physical safety of an individual;

(ii) flight from prosecution;

(iii) destruction of or tampering with evidence;

(iv) intimidation of potential witnesses; or

(v) otherwise seriously jeopardizing an investigation or unduly delaying a trial.

(E) Each of the Federal seizing agencies conducting nonjudicial forfeitures under this section shall report periodically to the Committees on the Judiciary of the House of Representatives and the Senate the number of occasions when an extension of time is granted under subparagraph (B).

(F) If the Government does not send notice of a seizure of property in accordance with subparagraph (A) to the person from whom the property was seized, and no extension of time is granted, the Government shall return the property to that person without prejudice to the right of the Government to commence a forfeiture proceeding at a later time. The Government shall not be required to return contraband or other property that the person from whom the property was seized may not legally possess.

(2)

(A) Any person claiming property seized in a nonjudicial civil forfeiture proceeding under a civil forfeiture statute may file a claim with the appropriate official after the seizure.

(B) A claim under subparagraph (A) may be filed not later than the deadline set forth in a personal notice letter (which deadline may be not earlier than 35 days after the date the letter is mailed), except that if that letter is not received, then a claim may be filed not later than 30 days after the date of final publication of notice of seizure.

(C) A claim shall—

(i) identify the specific property being claimed;

(ii) state the claimant's interest in such property; and

(iii) be made under oath, subject to penalty of perjury.

(D) A claim need not be made in any particular form. Each Federal agency conducting nonjudicial forfeitures under this section shall make claim forms generally available on request, which forms shall be written in easily understandable language.

(E) Any person may make a claim under subparagraph (A) without posting bond with respect to the property which is the subject of the claim.

(3)

(A) Not later than 90 days after a claim has been filed, the Government shall file a complaint for forfeiture in the manner set forth in the Supplemental Rules for Certain Admiralty and Maritime Claims or return the property pending the filing of a complaint, except that a court in the district in which the complaint will be filed may extend the period for filing a complaint for good cause shown or upon agreement of the parties.

(B) If the Government does not—

(i) file a complaint for forfeiture or return the property, in accordance with subparagraph (A); or

(ii) before the time for filing a complaint has expired—

(I) obtain a criminal indictment containing an allegation that the property is subject to forfeiture; and

(II) take the steps necessary to preserve its right to maintain custody of the property as provided in the applicable criminal forfeiture statute, the Government shall promptly release the property pursuant to regulations promulgated by the Attorney General, and may not take any further action to effect the civil forfeiture of such property in connection with the underlying offense.

(C) In lieu of, or in addition to, filing a civil forfeiture complaint, the Government may include a forfeiture allegation in a criminal indictment. If criminal forfeiture is the only forfeiture proceeding commenced by the Government, the Government's right to continued possession of the property shall be governed by the applicable criminal forfeiture statute.

(D) No complaint may be dismissed on the ground that the Government did not have adequate evidence at the time the complaint was filed to establish the forfeitability of the property.

(4)

(A) In any case in which the Government files in the appropriate United States district court a complaint for forfeiture of property, any person claiming an interest in the seized property may file a claim asserting such person's interest in the property in the manner set forth in the Supplemental Rules for Certain Admiralty and Maritime Claims, except that such claim may be filed not later than 30 days after the date of service of the Government's complaint or, as applicable, not later than 30 days after the date of final publication of notice of the filing of the complaint.

(B) A person asserting an interest in seized property, in accordance with subparagraph (A), shall file an answer to the Government's complaint for forfeiture not later than 20 days after the date of the filing of the claim.

(b) Representation.—

(1)

(A) If a person with standing to contest the forfeiture of property in a judicial civil forfeiture proceeding under a civil forfeiture statute is financially unable to obtain representation by counsel, and the person is represented by counsel appointed under section 3006A of this title in connection with a related criminal case, the court may authorize counsel to represent that person with respect to the claim.

(B) In determining whether to authorize counsel to represent a person under subparagraph (A), the court shall take into account such factors as—

(i) the person's standing to contest the forfeiture; and

(ii) whether the claim appears to be made in good faith.

(2)

(A) If a person with standing to contest the forfeiture of property in a judicial civil forfeiture proceeding under a civil forfeiture statute is financially unable to obtain representation by counsel, and the property subject to forfeiture is real property that is being used by the person as a primary residence, the court, at the request of the person, shall insure that the person is represented by an attorney for the Legal Services Corporation with respect to the claim.

(B)

(i) At appropriate times during a representation under subparagraph (A), the Legal Services Corporation shall submit a statement of reasonable attorney fees and costs to the court.

(ii) The court shall enter a judgment in favor of the Legal Services Corporation for reasonable attorney fees and costs submitted pursuant to clause (i) and treat such judgment as payable under section 2465 of title 28, United States Code, regardless of the outcome of the case.

(3) The court shall set the compensation for representation under this subsection, which shall be equivalent to that provided for court-appointed representation under section 3006A of this title.

(c) Burden of proof.— In a suit or action brought under any civil forfeiture statute for the civil forfeiture of any property—

(1) the burden of proof is on the Government to establish, by a preponderance of the evidence, that the property is subject to forfeiture;

(2) the Government may use evidence gathered after the filing of a complaint for forfeiture to establish, by a preponderance of the evidence, that property is subject to forfeiture; and

(3) if the Government's theory of forfeiture is that the property was used to commit or facilitate the commission of a criminal offense, or was involved in the commission of a criminal offense, the Government shall establish that there was a substantial connection between the property and the offense.

(d) Innocent Owner Defense.—

(1) An innocent owner's interest in property shall not be forfeited under any civil forfeiture statute. The claimant shall have the burden of proving that the claimant is an innocent owner by a preponderance of the evidence.

(2)

(A) With respect to a property interest in existence at the time the illegal conduct giving rise to forfeiture took place, the term "innocent owner" means an owner who—

(i) did not know of the conduct giving rise to forfeiture; or

(ii) upon learning of the conduct giving rise to the forfeiture, did all that reasonably could be expected under the circumstances to terminate such use of the property.

(B)

(i) For the purposes of this paragraph, ways in which a person may show that such person did all that reasonably could be expected may include demonstrating that such person, to the extent permitted by law—

(I) gave timely notice to an appropriate law enforcement agency of information that led the person to know the conduct giving rise to a forfeiture would occur or has occurred; and

(II) in a timely fashion revoked or made a good faith attempt to revoke permission for those engaging in such conduct to use the property or took reasonable actions in consultation with a law enforcement agency to discourage or prevent the illegal use of the property.

(ii) A person is not required by this subparagraph to take steps that the person reasonably believes would be likely to subject any person (other than the person whose conduct gave rise to the forfeiture) to physical danger.

(3)

(A) With respect to a property interest acquired after the conduct giving rise to the forfeiture has taken place, the term "innocent owner" means a person who, at the time that person acquired the interest in the property—

(i) was a bona fide purchaser or seller for value (including a purchaser or seller of goods or services for value); and

(ii) did not know and was reasonably without cause to believe that the property was subject to forfeiture.

(B) An otherwise valid claim under subparagraph (A) shall not be denied on the ground that the claimant gave nothing of value in exchange for the property if—

(i) the property is the primary residence of the claimant;

(ii) depriving the claimant of the property would deprive the claimant of the means to maintain reasonable shelter in the community for the claimant and all dependents residing with the claimant;

(iii) the property is not, and is not traceable to, the proceeds of any criminal offense; and

(iv) the claimant acquired his or her interest in the property through marriage, divorce, or legal separation, or the claimant was the spouse or legal dependent of a person whose death resulted in the transfer of the property to the claimant through inheritance or probate, except that the court shall limit the value of any real property interest for which innocent ownership is recognized under this subparagraph to the value necessary to maintain reasonable shelter in the community for such claimant and all dependents residing with the claimant.

(4) Notwithstanding any provision of this subsection, no person may assert an ownership interest under this subsection in contraband or other property that it is illegal to possess.

(5) If the court determines, in accordance with this section, that an innocent owner has a partial interest in property otherwise subject to forfeiture, or a joint tenancy or tenancy by the entirety in such property, the court may enter an appropriate order—

(A) severing the property;

(B) transferring the property to the Government with a provision that the Government compensate the innocent owner to the extent of his or her ownership interest once a final order of forfeiture has been entered and the property has been reduced to liquid assets; or

(C) permitting the innocent owner to retain the property subject to a lien in favor of the Government to the extent of the forfeitable interest in the property.

(6) In this subsection, the term "owner"—

(A) means a person with an ownership interest in the specific property sought to be forfeited, including a leasehold, lien, mortgage, recorded security interest, or valid assignment of an ownership interest; and

(B) does not include—

(i) a person with only a general unsecured interest in, or claim against, the property or estate of another;

(ii) a bailee unless the bailor is identified and the bailee shows a colorable legitimate interest in the property seized; or

(iii) a nominee who exercises no dominion or control over the property.

(e) Motion To Set Aside Forfeiture.—

(1) Any person entitled to written notice in any nonjudicial civil forfeiture proceeding under a civil forfeiture statute who does not receive such notice may file a motion to set aside a declaration of forfeiture with respect to that person's interest in the property, which motion shall be granted if—

(A) the Government knew, or reasonably should have known, of the moving party's interest and failed to take reasonable steps to provide such party with notice; and

(B) the moving party did not know or have reason to know of the seizure within sufficient time to file a timely claim.

(2)

(A) Notwithstanding the expiration of any applicable statute of limitations, if the court grants a motion under paragraph (1), the court shall set aside the declaration of forfeiture as to the interest of the moving party without prejudice to the right of the Government to commence a subsequent forfeiture proceeding as to the interest of the moving party.

(B) Any proceeding described in subparagraph (A) shall be commenced—

(i) if nonjudicial, within 60 days of the entry of the order granting the motion; or

(ii) if judicial, within 6 months of the entry of the order granting the motion.

(3) A motion under paragraph (1) may be filed not later than 5 years after the date of final publication of notice of seizure of the property.

(4) If, at the time a motion made under paragraph (1) is granted, the forfeited property has been disposed of by the Government in accordance with law, the Government may institute proceedings against a substitute sum of money equal to the value of the moving party's interest in the property at the time the property was disposed of.

(5) A motion filed under this subsection shall be the exclusive remedy for seeking to set aside a declaration of forfeiture under a civil forfeiture statute.

(f) Release Of Seized Property.—

(1) A claimant under subsection (a) is entitled to immediate release of seized property if—

(A) the claimant has a possessory interest in the property;

(B) the claimant has sufficient ties to the community to provide assurance that the property will be available at the time of the trial;

(C) the continued possession by the Government pending the final disposition of forfeiture proceedings will cause substantial hardship to the claimant, such as preventing the functioning of a business, preventing an individual from working, or leaving an individual homeless;

(D) the claimant's likely hardship from the continued possession by the Government of the seized property outweighs the risk that the property will be destroyed, damaged, lost, concealed, or transferred if it is returned to the claimant during the pendency of the proceeding; and

(E) none of the conditions set forth in paragraph (8) applies.

(2) A claimant seeking release of property under this subsection must request possession of the property from the appropriate official, and the request must set forth the basis on which the requirements of paragraph (1) are met.

(3)

(A) If not later than 15 days after the date of a request under paragraph (2) the property has not been released, the claimant may file a petition in the district court in which the complaint has been filed or, if no complaint has been filed, in the district court in which the seizure warrant was issued or in the district court for the district in which the property was seized.

(B) The petition described in subparagraph (A) shall set forth—

(i) the basis on which the requirements of paragraph (1) are met; and

(ii) the steps the claimant has taken to secure release of the property from the appropriate official.

(4) If the Government establishes that the claimant's claim is frivolous, the court shall deny the petition. In responding to a petition under this subsection on other grounds, the Government may in appropriate cases submit evidence ex parte in order to avoid disclosing any matter that may adversely affect an ongoing criminal investigation or pending criminal trial.

(5) The court shall render a decision on a petition filed under paragraph (3) not later than 30 days after the date of the filing, unless such 30-day limitation is extended by consent of the parties or by the court for good cause shown.

(6) If—

(A) a petition is filed under paragraph (3); and

(B) the claimant demonstrates that the requirements of paragraph (1) have been met, the district court shall order that the property be returned to the claimant, pending completion of proceedings by the Government to obtain forfeiture of the property.

(7) If the court grants a petition under paragraph (3)—

(A) the court may enter any order necessary to ensure that the value of the property is maintained while the forfeiture action is pending, including—

(i) permitting the inspection, photographing, and inventory of the property;

(ii) fixing a bond in accordance with rule E(5) of the Supplemental Rules for Certain Admiralty and Maritime Claims; and

(iii) requiring the claimant to obtain or maintain insurance on the subject property; and

(B) the Government may place a lien against the property or file a lis pendens to ensure that the property is not transferred to another person.

(8) This subsection shall not apply if the seized property—

(A) is contraband, currency, or other monetary instrument, or electronic funds unless such currency or other monetary instrument or electronic funds constitutes the assets of a legitimate business which has been seized;

(B) is to be used as evidence of a violation of the law;

(C) by reason of design or other characteristic, is particularly suited for use in illegal activities; or

(D) is likely to be used to commit additional criminal acts if returned to the claimant.

(g) Proportionality.—

(1) The claimant under subsection (a)(4) may petition the court to determine whether the forfeiture was constitutionally excessive.

(2) In making this determination, the court shall compare the forfeiture to the gravity of the offense giving rise to the forfeiture.

(3) The claimant shall have the burden of establishing that the forfeiture is grossly disproportional by a preponderance of the evidence at a hearing conducted by the court without a jury.

(4) If the court finds that the forfeiture is grossly disproportional to the offense it shall reduce or eliminate the forfeiture as necessary to avoid a violation of the Excessive Fines Clause of the Eighth Amendment of the Constitution.

(h) Civil fine.—

(1) In any civil forfeiture proceeding under a civil forfeiture statute in which the Government prevails, if the court finds that the claimant's assertion of an interest in the property was frivolous, the court may impose a civil fine on the claimant of an amount equal to 10 percent of the value of the forfeited property, but in no event shall the fine be less than $250 or greater than $5,000.

(2) Any civil fine imposed under this subsection shall not preclude the court from imposing sanctions under rule 11 of the Federal Rules of Civil Procedure.

(3) In addition to the limitations of section 1915 of title 28, United States Code, in no event shall a prisoner file a claim under a civil forfeiture statute or appeal

a judgment in a civil action or proceeding based on a civil forfeiture statute if the prisoner has, on three or more prior occasions, while incarcerated or detained in any facility, brought an action or appeal in a court of the United States that was dismissed on the grounds that it is frivolous or malicious, unless the prisoner shows extraordinary and exceptional circumstances.

(i) Civil Forfeiture Statute Defined.— In this section, the term "civil forfeiture statute"—

(1) means any provision of Federal law providing for the forfeiture of property other than as a sentence imposed upon conviction of a criminal offense; and

(2) does not include—

(A) the Tariff Act of 1930 or any other provision of law codified in title 19;

(B) the Internal Revenue Code of 1986;

(C) the Federal Food, Drug, and Cosmetic Act (21 U.S.C. 301 et seq.);

(D) the Trading with the Enemy Act (50 U.S.C. App. 1 et seq.) or the International Emergency Economic Powers Act (IEEPA) (50 U.S.C. 1701 et seq.); or

(E) section 1 of title VI of the Act of June 15, 1917 (40 Stat. 233; 22 U.S.C. 401).

(j) Restraining orders; protective orders.—

(1) Upon application of the United States, the court may enter a restraining order or injunction, require the execution of satisfactory performance bonds, create receiverships, appoint conservators, custodians, appraisers, accountants, or trustees, or take any other action to seize, secure, maintain, or preserve the availability of property subject to civil forfeiture—

(A) upon the filing of a civil forfeiture complaint alleging that the property with respect to which the order is sought is subject to civil forfeiture; or

(B) prior to the filing of such a complaint, if, after notice to persons appearing to have an interest in the property and opportunity for a hearing, the court determines that—

(i) there is a substantial probability that the United States will prevail on the issue of forfeiture and that failure to enter the order will result in the property being destroyed, removed from the jurisdiction of the court, or otherwise made unavailable for forfeiture; and

(ii) the need to preserve the availability of the property through the entry of the requested order outweighs the hardship on any party against whom the order is to be entered.

(2) An order entered pursuant to paragraph (1)(B) shall be effective for not more than 90 days, unless extended by the court for good cause shown, or unless a complaint described in paragraph (1)(A) has been filed.

(3) A temporary restraining order under this subsection may be entered upon

application of the United States without notice or opportunity for a hearing when a complaint has not yet been filed with respect to the property, if the United States demonstrates that there is probable cause to believe that the property with respect to which the order is sought is subject to civil forfeiture and that provision of notice will jeopardize the availability of the property for forfeiture. Such a temporary order shall expire not more than 14 days after the date on which it is entered, unless extended for good cause shown or unless the party against whom it is entered consents to an extension for a longer period. A hearing requested concerning an order entered under this paragraph shall be held at the earliest possible time and prior to the expiration of the temporary order.

(4) The court may receive and consider, at a hearing held pursuant to this subsection, evidence and information that would be inadmissible under the Federal Rules of Evidence.

§ 985.   Civil forfeiture of real property

(a) Notwithstanding any other provision of law, all civil forfeitures of real property and interests in real property shall proceed as judicial forfeitures.

(b)

(1) Except as provided in this section—

(A) real property that is the subject of a civil forfeiture action shall not be seized before entry of an order of forfeiture; and

(B) the owners or occupants of the real property shall not be evicted from, or otherwise deprived of the use and enjoyment of, real property that is the subject of a pending forfeiture action.

(2) The filing of a lis pendens and the execution of a writ of entry for the purpose of conducting an inspection and inventory of the property shall not be considered a seizure under this subsection.

(c)

(1) The Government shall initiate a civil forfeiture action against real property by—

(A) failing a complaint for forfeiture;

(B) posting a notice of the complaint on the property; and

(C) serving notice on the property owner, along with a copy of the complaint.

(2) If the property owner cannot be served with the notice under paragraph (1) because the owner—

(A) is a fugitive;

(B) resides outside the United States and efforts at service pursuant to rule 4 of the Federal Rules of Civil Procedure are unavailing; or

(C) cannot be located despite the exercise of due diligence, constructive service may be made in accordance with the laws of the State in which the property is located.

(3) If real property has been posted in accordance with this subsection, it shall not be necessary for the court to issue an arrest warrant in rem, or to take any other action to establish in rem jurisdiction over the property.

(d)

(1) Real property may be seized prior to the entry of an order of forfeiture if—

(A) the Government notifies the court that it intends to seize the property before trial; and

(B) the court—

(i) issues a notice of application for warrant, causes the notice to be served on the property owner and posted on the property, and conducts a hearing in which the property owner has a meaningful opportunity to be heard; or

(ii) makes an ex parte determination that there is probable cause for the forfeiture and that there are exigent circumstances that permit the Government to seize the property without prior notice and an opportunity for the property owner to be heard.

(2) For purposes of paragraph (1)(B)(ii), to establish exigent circumstances, the Government shall show that less restrictive measures such as a lis pendens, restraining order, or bond would not suffice to protect the Government's interests in preventing the sale, destruction, or continued unlawful use of the real property.

(e) If the court authorizes a seizure of real property under subsection (d)(1)(B)(ii), it shall conduct a prompt post-seizure hearing during which the property owner shall have an opportunity to contest the basis for the seizure.

(f) This section—

(1) applies only to civil forfeitures of real property and interests in real property;

(2) does not apply to forfeitures of the proceeds of the sale of such property or interests, or of money or other assets intended to be used to acquire such property or interests; and

(3) shall not affect the authority of the court to enter a restraining order relating to real property.

§ 1001.   Statements or entries generally

(a) Except as otherwise provided in this section, whoever, in any matter within the jurisdiction of the executive, legislative, or judicial branch of the Government of the United States, knowingly and willfully—

(1) falsifies, conceals, or covers up by any trick, scheme, or device a material fact;

(2) makes any materially false, fictitious, or fraudulent statement or representation; or

(3) makes or uses any false writing or document knowing the same to contain any materially false, fictitious, or fraudulent statement or entry;

shall be fined under this title, imprisoned not more than 5 years or, if the offense involves international or domestic terrorism (as defined in section 2331), imprisoned not more than 8 years, or both. If the matter relates to an offense under chapter 109A, 109B, 110, or 117, or section 1591, then the term of imprisonment imposed under this section shall be not more than 8 years.

(b) Subsection (a) does not apply to a party to a judicial proceeding, or that party's counsel, for statements, representations, writings or documents submitted by such party or counsel to a judge or magistrate in that proceeding.

(c) With respect to any matter within the jurisdiction of the legislative branch, subsection (a) shall apply only to—

(1) administrative matters, including a claim for payment, a matter related to the procurement of property or services, personnel or employment practices, or support services, or a document required by law, rule, or regulation to be submitted to the Congress or any office or officer within the legislative branch; or

(2) any investigation or review, conducted pursuant to the authority of any committee, subcommittee, commission or office of the Congress, consistent with applicable rules of the House or Senate.

§ 1005. Bank entries, reports and transactions

Whoever, being an officer, director, agent or employee of any Federal Reserve bank, member bank, depository institution holding company, national bank, insured bank, branch or agency of a foreign bank, or organization operating under section 25 or section 25(a) of the Federal Reserve Act, without authority from the directors of such bank, branch, agency, or organization or company, issues or puts in circulation any notes of such bank, branch, agency, or organization or company; or

Whoever, without such authority, makes, draws, issues, puts forth, or assigns any certificate of deposit, draft, order, bill of exchange, acceptance, note, debenture, bond, or other obligation, or mortgage, judgment or decree; or

Whoever makes any false entry in any book, report, or statement of such bank, company, branch, agency, or organization with intent to injure or defraud such bank, company, branch, agency, or organization, or any other company, body politic or corporate, or any individual person, or to deceive any officer of such bank, company, branch, agency, or organization, or the Comptroller of the Currency, or the Federal Deposit Insurance Corporation, or any agent or examiner appointed to examine the affairs of such bank, company, branch, agency, or organization, or the Board of Governors of the Federal Reserve System; or

Whoever with intent to defraud the United States or any agency thereof, or any financial institution referred to in this section, participates or shares in or receives (directly or indirectly) any money, profit, property, or benefits through any transaction, loan, commission, contract, or any other act of any such financial institution—

Shall be fined not more than $1,000,000 or imprisoned not more than 30 years, or both.

As used in this section, the term "national bank" is synonymous with "national banking association"; "member bank" means and includes any national bank, state bank, or bank or trust company, which has become a member of one of the Federal Reserve banks; "insured bank" includes any state bank, banking association, trust company, savings bank, or other banking institution, the deposits of which are insured by the Federal Deposit Insurance Corporation; and the term "branch or agency of a foreign bank" means a branch or agency described in section 20(9) of this title. For purposes of this section, the term "depository institution holding company" has the meaning given such term in section 3(w)(1) of the Federal Deposit Insurance Act.

§ 1014. Loan and credit applications generally; renewals and discounts; crop insurance

Whoever knowingly makes any false statement or report, or willfully overvalues any land, property or security, for the purpose of influencing in any way the action of the Federal Housing Administration, the Farm Credit Administration, Federal Crop Insurance Corporation or a company the Corporation reinsures, the Secretary of Agriculture acting through the Farmers Home Administration or successor agency, the Rural Development Administration or successor agency, any Farm Credit Bank, production credit association, agricultural credit association, bank for cooperatives, or any division, officer, or employee thereof, or of any regional agricultural credit corporation established pursuant to law, or a Federal land bank, a Federal land bank association, a Federal Reserve bank, a small business investment company, as defined in section 103 of the Small Business Investment Act of 1958 (15 U.S.C. 662), or the Small Business Administration in connection with any provision of that Act, a Federal credit union, an insured State-chartered credit union, any institution the accounts of which are insured by the Federal Deposit Insurance Corporation,,1 any Federal home loan bank, the Federal Housing Finance Agency, the Federal Deposit Insurance Corporation, the Farm Credit System Insurance Corporation, or the National Credit Union Administration Board, a branch or agency of a foreign bank (as such terms are defined in paragraphs (1) and (3) of section 1(b) of the International Banking Act of 1978), an organization operating under section 25 or section 25(a) of the Federal Reserve Act, or a mortgage lending business, or any person or entity that makes in whole or in part a federally related mortgage loan as defined in section 3 of the Real Estate Settlement Procedures Act of 1974, upon any application, advance, discount, purchase, purchase agreement, repurchase agreement, commitment, loan, or insurance agreement or application for insurance or a guarantee, or any change or extension of any of the same, by renewal, deferment of action or otherwise, or the acceptance, release, or substitution of security therefor, shall be fined not more than $1,000,000 or imprisoned not more than 30 years, or both. The term "State-chartered credit union" includes a credit union chartered under the laws of a State of the United States, the District of Columbia, or any commonwealth, territory, or possession of the United States.

§ 1029. Fraud and related activity in connection with access devices

(a) Whoever—

(1) knowingly and with intent to defraud produces, uses, or traffics in one or more counterfeit access devices;

(2) knowingly and with intent to defraud traffics in or uses one or more unauthorized access devices during any one-year period, and by such conduct obtains anything of value aggregating $1,000 or more during that period;

(3) knowingly and with intent to defraud possesses fifteen or more devices which are counterfeit or unauthorized access devices;

(4) knowingly, and with intent to defraud, produces, traffics in, has control or custody of, or possesses device-making equipment;

(5) knowingly and with intent to defraud effects transactions, with 1 or more access devices issued to another person or persons, to receive payment or any other thing of value during any 1-year period the aggregate value of which is equal to or greater than $1,000;

(6) without the authorization of the issuer of the access device, knowingly and with intent to defraud solicits a person for the purpose of—

(A) offering an access device; or

(B) selling information regarding or an application to obtain an access device;

(7) knowingly and with intent to defraud uses, produces, traffics in, has control or custody of, or possesses a telecommunications instrument that has been modified or altered to obtain unauthorized use of telecommunications services;

(8) knowingly and with intent to defraud uses, produces, traffics in, has control or custody of, or possesses a scanning receiver;

(9) knowingly uses, produces, traffics in, has control or custody of, or possesses hardware or software, knowing it has been configured to insert or modify telecommunication identifying information associated with or contained in a telecommunications instrument so that such instrument may be used to obtain telecommunications service without authorization; or

(10) without the authorization of the credit card system member or its agent, knowingly and with intent to defraud causes or arranges for another person to present to the member or its agent, for payment, 1 or more evidences or records of transactions made by an access device;

shall, if the offense affects interstate or foreign commerce, be punished as provided in subsection (c) of this section.

(b)

(1) Whoever attempts to commit an offense under subsection (a) of this section shall be subject to the same penalties as those prescribed for the offense attempted.

(2) Whoever is a party to a conspiracy of two or more persons to commit an offense under subsection (a) of this section, if any of the parties engages in any conduct in furtherance of such offense, shall be fined an amount not greater than the amount provided as the maximum fine for such offense under subsection (c) of this section or imprisoned not longer than one-half the period provided as the

maximum imprisonment for such offense under subsection (c) of this section, or both.

(c) Penalties.—

(1) Generally.— The punishment for an offense under subsection (a) of this section is—

(A) in the case of an offense that does not occur after a conviction for another offense under this section—

(i) if the offense is under paragraph (1), (2), (3), (6), (7), or (10) of subsection (a), a fine under this title or imprisonment for not more than 10 years, or both; and

(ii) if the offense is under paragraph (4), (5), (8), or (9) of subsection (a), a fine under this title or imprisonment for not more than 15 years, or both;

(B) in the case of an offense that occurs after a conviction for another offense under this section, a fine under this title or imprisonment for not more than 20 years, or both; and

(C) in either case, forfeiture to the United States of any personal property used or intended to be used to commit the offense.

(2) Forfeiture procedure.— The forfeiture of property under this section, including any seizure and disposition of the property and any related administrative and judicial proceeding, shall be governed by section 413 of the Controlled Substances Act, except for subsection (d) of that section.

(d) The United States Secret Service shall, in addition to any other agency having such authority, have the authority to investigate offenses under this section. Such authority of the United States Secret Service shall be exercised in accordance with an agreement which shall be entered into by the Secretary of the Treasury and the Attorney General.

(e) As used in this section—

(1) the term "access device" means any card, plate, code, account number, electronic serial number, mobile identification number, personal identification number, or other telecommunications service, equipment, or instrument identifier, or other means of account access that can be used, alone or in conjunction with another access device, to obtain money, goods, services, or any other thing of value, or that can be used to initiate a transfer of funds (other than a transfer originated solely by paper instrument);

(2) the term "counterfeit access device" means any access device that is counterfeit, fictitious, altered, or forged, or an identifiable component of an access device or a counterfeit access device;

(3) the term "unauthorized access device" means any access device that is lost, stolen, expired, revoked, canceled, or obtained with intent to defraud;

(4) the term "produce" includes design, alter, authenticate, duplicate, or assemble;

(5) the term "traffic" means transfer, or otherwise dispose of, to another, or obtain control of with intent to transfer or dispose of;

(6) the term "device-making equipment" means any equipment, mechanism, or impression designed or primarily used for making an access device or a counterfeit access device;

(7) the term "credit card system member" means a financial institution or other entity that is a member of a credit card system, including an entity, whether affiliated with or identical to the credit card issuer, that is the sole member of a credit card system;

(8) the term "scanning receiver" means a device or apparatus that can be used to intercept a wire or electronic communication in violation of chapter 119 or to intercept an electronic serial number, mobile identification number, or other identifier of any telecommunications service, equipment, or instrument

(9) the term "telecommunications service" has the meaning given such term in section 3 of title I of the Communications Act of 1934 (47 U.S.C. 153);

(10) the term "facilities-based carrier" means an entity that owns communications transmission facilities, is responsible for the operation and maintenance of those facilities, and holds an operating license issued by the Federal Communications Commission under the authority of title III of the Communications Act of 1934; and

(11) the term "telecommunication identifying information" means electronic serial number or any other number or signal that identifies a specific telecommunications instrument or account, or a specific communication transmitted from a telecommunications instrument.

(f) This section does not prohibit any lawfully authorized investigative, protective, or intelligence activity of a law enforcement agency of the United States, a State, or a political subdivision of a State, or of an Intelligence agency of the United States, or any activity authorized under chapter 224 of this title. For purposes of this subsection, the term "State" includes a State of the United States, the District of Columbia, and any commonwealth, territory, or possession of the United States.

(g)

(1) It is not a violation of subsection (a)(9) for an officer, employee, or agent of, or a person engaged in business with, a facilities-based carrier, to engage in conduct (other than trafficking) otherwise prohibited by that subsection for the purpose of protecting the property or legal rights of that carrier, unless such conduct is for the purpose of obtaining telecommunications service provided by another facilities-based carrier without the authorization of such carrier.

(2) In a prosecution for a violation of subsection (a)(9), (other than a violation consisting of producing or trafficking) it is an affirmative defense (which the defendant must establish by a preponderance of the evidence) that the conduct charged was engaged in for research or development in connection with a lawful purpose.

(h) Any person who, outside the jurisdiction of the United States, engages in any act that, if committed within the jurisdiction of the United States, would constitute an offense under subsection (a) or (b) of this section, shall be subject to the fines, penalties, imprisonment, and forfeiture provided in this title if—

(1) the offense involves an access device issued, owned, managed, or controlled by a financial institution, account issuer, credit card system member, or other entity within the jurisdiction of the United States; and

(2) the person transports, delivers, conveys, transfers to or through, or otherwise stores, secrets, or holds within the jurisdiction of the United States, any article used to assist in the commission of the offense or the proceeds of such offense or property derived therefrom.

§ 1030. Fraud and related activity in connection with computers

(a) Whoever—

(1) having knowingly accessed a computer without authorization or exceeding authorized access, and by means of such conduct having obtained information that has been determined by the United States Government pursuant to an Executive order or statute to require protection against unauthorized disclosure for reasons of national defense or foreign relations, or any restricted data, as defined in paragraph y. of section 11 of the Atomic Energy Act of 1954, with reason to believe that such information so obtained could be used to the injury of the United States, or to the advantage of any foreign nation willfully communicates, delivers, transmits, or causes to be communicated, delivered, or transmitted, or attempts to communicate, deliver, transmit or cause to be communicated, delivered, or transmitted the same to any person not entitled to receive it, or willfully retains the same and fails to deliver it to the officer or employee of the United States entitled to receive it;

(2) intentionally accesses a computer without authorization or exceeds authorized access, and thereby obtains—

(A) information contained in a financial record of a financial institution, or of a card issuer as defined in section 1602(n) of title 15, or contained in a file of a consumer reporting agency on a consumer, as such terms are defined in the Fair Credit Reporting Act (15 U.S.C. 1681 et seq.);

(B) information from any department or agency of the United States; or

(C) information from any protected computer;

(3) intentionally, without authorization to access any nonpublic computer of a department or agency of the United States, accesses such a computer of that department or agency that is exclusively for the use of the Government of the United States or, in the case of a computer not exclusively for such use, is used by or for the Government of the United States and such conduct affects that use by or for the Government of the United States;

(4) knowingly and with intent to defraud, accesses a protected computer without authorization, or exceeds authorized access, and by means of such conduct furthers the intended fraud and obtains anything of value, unless the object of the fraud and the thing obtained consists only of the use of the computer

and the value of such use is not more than $5,000 in any 1-year period;

(5)

(A) knowingly causes the transmission of a program, information, code, or command, and as a result of such conduct, intentionally causes damage without authorization, to a protected computer;

(B) intentionally accesses a protected computer without authorization, and as a result of such conduct, recklessly causes damage; or

(C) intentionally accesses a protected computer without authorization, and as a result of such conduct, causes damage and loss.

(6) knowingly and with intent to defraud traffics (as defined in section 1029) in any password or similar information through which a computer may be accessed without authorization, if—

(A) such trafficking affects interstate or foreign commerce; or

(B) such computer is used by or for the Government of the United States;

(7) with intent to extort from any person any money or other thing of value, transmits in interstate or foreign commerce any communication containing any—

(A) threat to cause damage to a protected computer;

(B) threat to obtain information from a protected computer without authorization or in excess of authorization or to impair the confidentiality of information obtained from a protected computer without authorization or by exceeding authorized access; or

(C) demand or request for money or other thing of value in relation to damage to a protected computer, where such damage was caused to facilitate the extortion;

shall be punished as provided in subsection (c) of this section.

(b) Whoever conspires to commit or attempts to commit an offense under subsection (a) of this section shall be punished as provided in subsection (c) of this section.

(c) The punishment for an offense under subsection (a) or (b) of this section is—

(1)

(A) a fine under this title or imprisonment for not more than ten years, or both, in the case of an offense under subsection (a)(1) of this section which does not occur after a conviction for another offense under this section, or an attempt to commit an offense punishable under this subparagraph; and

(B) a fine under this title or imprisonment for not more than twenty years, or both, in the case of an offense under subsection (a)(1) of this section which occurs after a conviction for another offense under this section, or an attempt to commit an offense punishable under this subparagraph;

(2)

(A) except as provided in subparagraph (B), a fine under this title or imprisonment for not more than one year, or both, in the case of an offense under subsection (a)(2), (a)(3), or (a)(6) of this section which does not occur after a conviction for another offense under this section, or an attempt to commit an offense punishable under this subparagraph;

(B) a fine under this title or imprisonment for not more than 5 years, or both, in the case of an offense under subsection (a)(2), or an attempt to commit an offense punishable under this subparagraph, if—

(i) the offense was committed for purposes of commercial advantage or private financial gain;

(ii) the offense was committed in furtherance of any criminal or tortious act in violation of the Constitution or laws of the United States or of any State; or

(iii) the value of the information obtained exceeds $5,000; and

(C) a fine under this title or imprisonment for not more than ten years, or both, in the case of an offense under subsection (a)(2), (a)(3) or (a)(6) of this section which occurs after a conviction for another offense under this section, or an attempt to commit an offense punishable under this subparagraph;

(3)

(A) a fine under this title or imprisonment for not more than five years, or both, in the case of an offense under subsection (a)(4) or (a)(7) of this section which does not occur after a conviction for another offense under this section, or an attempt to commit an offense punishable under this subparagraph; and

(B) a fine under this title or imprisonment for not more than ten years, or both, in the case of an offense under subsection (a)(4), or (a)(7) of this section which occurs after a conviction for another offense under this section, or an attempt to commit an offense punishable under this subparagraph;

(4)

(A) except as provided in subparagraphs (E) and (F), a fine under this title, imprisonment for not more than 5 years, or both, in the case of—

(i) an offense under subsection (a)(5)(B), which does not occur after a conviction for another offense under this section, if the offense caused (or, in the case of an attempted offense, would, if completed, have caused)—

(I) loss to 1 or more persons during any 1-year period (and, for purposes of an investigation, prosecution, or other proceeding brought by the United States only, loss resulting from a related course of conduct affecting 1 or more other protected computers) aggregating at least $5,000 in value;

(II) the modification or impairment, or potential modification or impairment, of the medical examination, diagnosis, treatment, or care of 1 or more individuals;

(III) physical injury to any person;

(IV) a threat to public health or safety;

(V) damage affecting a computer used by or for an entity of the United States Government in furtherance of the administration of justice, national defense, or national security; or

(VI) damage affecting 10 or more protected computers during any 1-year period; or

(ii) an attempt to commit an offense punishable under this subparagraph;

(B) except as provided in subparagraphs (E) and (F), a fine under this title, imprisonment for not more than 10 years, or both, in the case of—

(i) an offense under subsection (a)(5)(A), which does not occur after a conviction for another offense under this section, if the offense caused (or, in the case of an attempted offense, would, if completed, have caused) a harm provided in subclauses (I) through (VI) of subparagraph (A)(i); or

(ii) an attempt to commit an offense punishable under this subparagraph;

(C) except as provided in subparagraphs (E) and (F), a fine under this title, imprisonment for not more than 20 years, or both, in the case of—

(i) an offense or an attempt to commit an offense under subparagraphs (A) or (B) of subsection (a)(5) that occurs after a conviction for another offense under this section; or

(ii) an attempt to commit an offense punishable under this subparagraph;

(D) a fine under this title, imprisonment for not more than 10 years, or both, in the case of—

(i) an offense or an attempt to commit an offense under subsection (a) (5)(C) that occurs after a conviction for another offense under this section; or

(ii) an attempt to commit an offense punishable under this subparagraph;

(E) if the offender attempts to cause or knowingly or recklessly causes serious bodily injury from conduct in violation of subsection (a)(5)(A), a fine under this title, imprisonment for not more than 20 years, or both;

(F) if the offender attempts to cause or knowingly or recklessly causes death from conduct in violation of subsection (a)(5)(A), a fine under this title, imprisonment for any term of years or for life, or both; or

(G) a fine under this title, imprisonment for not more than 1 year, or both, for—

(i) any other offense under subsection (a)(5); or

(ii) an attempt to commit an offense punishable under this subparagraph.
[(5) Repealed. Pub.L. 110-326, Title II, § 204(a)(2)(D), Sept. 26, 2008, 122 Stat. 3562]

(d)

(1) The United States Secret Service shall, in addition to any other agency having such authority, have the authority to investigate offenses under this section.

(2) The Federal Bureau of Investigation shall have primary authority to investigate offenses under subsection (a)(1) for any cases involving espionage, foreign counterintelligence, information protected against unauthorized disclosure for reasons of national defense or foreign relations, or Restricted Data (as that term is defined in section 11y of the Atomic Energy Act of 1954 (42 U.S.C. 2014(y)), except for offenses affecting the duties of the United States Secret Service pursuant to section 3056(a) of this title.

(3) Such authority shall be exercised in accordance with an agreement which shall be entered into by the Secretary of the Treasury and the Attorney General.

(e) As used in this section—

(1) the term "computer" means an electronic, magnetic, optical, electrochemical, or other high speed data processing device performing logical, arithmetic, or storage functions, and includes any data storage facility or communications facility directly related to or operating in conjunction with such device, but such term does not include an automated typewriter or typesetter, a portable hand held calculator, or other similar device;

(2) the term "protected computer" means a computer—

(A) exclusively for the use of a financial institution or the United States Government, or, in the case of a computer not exclusively for such use, used by or for a financial institution or the United States Government and the conduct constituting the offense affects that use by or for the financial institution or the Government; or

(B) which is used in or affecting interstate or foreign commerce or communication, including a computer located outside the United States that is used in a manner that affects interstate or foreign commerce or communication of the United States;

(3) the term "State" includes the District of Columbia, the Commonwealth of Puerto Rico, and any other commonwealth, possession or territory of the United States;

(4) the term "financial institution" means—

(A) an institution, with deposits insured by the Federal Deposit Insurance Corporation;

(B) the Federal Reserve or a member of the Federal Reserve including any Federal Reserve Bank;

(C) a credit union with accounts insured by the National Credit Union Administration;

(D) a member of the Federal home loan bank system and any home loan bank;

(E) any institution of the Farm Credit System under the Farm Credit Act of 1971;

(F) a broker-dealer registered with the Securities and Exchange Commission pursuant to section 15 of the Securities Exchange Act of 1934;

(G) the Securities Investor Protection Corporation;

(H) a branch or agency of a foreign bank (as such terms are defined in paragraphs (1) and (3) of section 1(b) of the International Banking Act of 1978); and

(I) an organization operating under section 25 or section 25(a) of the Federal Reserve Act;

(5) the term "financial record" means information derived from any record held by a financial institution pertaining to a customer's relationship with the financial institution;

(6) the term "exceeds authorized access" means to access a computer with authorization and to use such access to obtain or alter information in the computer that the accesser is not entitled so to obtain or alter;

(7) the term "department of the United States" means the legislative or judicial branch of the Government or one of the executive departments enumerated in section 101 of title 5;

(8) the term "damage" means any impairment to the integrity or availability of data, a program, a system, or information;

(9) the term "government entity" includes the Government of the United States, any State or political subdivision of the United States, any foreign country, and any state, province, municipality, or other political subdivision of a foreign country;

(10) the term "conviction" shall include a conviction under the law of any State for a crime punishable by imprisonment for more than 1 year, an element of which is unauthorized access, or exceeding authorized access, to a computer;

(11) the term "loss" means any reasonable cost to any victim, including the cost of responding to an offense, conducting a damage assessment, and restoring the data, program, system, or information to its condition prior to the offense, and any revenue lost, cost incurred, or other consequential damages incurred because of interruption of service; and

(12) the term "person" means any individual, firm, corporation, educational institution, financial institution, governmental entity, or legal or other entity.

(f) This section does not prohibit any lawfully authorized investigative, protective, or intelligence activity of a law enforcement agency of the United States, a State, or a political subdivision of a State, or of an intelligence agency of the United States.

(g) Any person who suffers damage or loss by reason of a violation of this section may maintain a civil action against the violator to obtain compensatory damages and injunctive relief or other equitable relief. A civil action for a violation of this section may be brought only if the conduct involves 1 of the factors set forth in subclauses (I), (II), (III), (IV), or (V) of subsection (c)(4)(A)(i). Damages for a violation involving only conduct described in subsection (c)(4)(A)(i)(I) are limited to economic damages. No action may be brought under this subsection unless such action is begun within 2 years of the date of the act complained of or the date of the discovery of the damage. No action may be brought under this subsection for the negligent design or manufacture of computer hardware, computer software, or firmware.

(h) The Attorney General and the Secretary of the Treasury shall report to the Congress annually, during the first 3 years following the date of the enactment of this subsection, concerning investigations and prosecutions under subsection (a)(5).

(i)

(1) The court, in imposing sentence on any person convicted of a violation of this section, or convicted of conspiracy to violate this section, shall order, in addition to any other sentence imposed and irrespective of any provision of State law, that such person forfeit to the United States—

(A) such person's interest in any personal property that was used or intended to be used to commit or to facilitate the commission of such violation; and

(B) any property, real or personal, constituting or derived from, any proceeds that such person obtained, directly or indirectly, as a result of such violation.

(2) The criminal forfeiture of property under this subsection, any seizure and disposition thereof, and any judicial proceeding in relation thereto, shall be governed by the provisions of section 413 of the Comprehensive Drug Abuse Prevention and Control Act of 1970 (21 U.S.C. 853), except subsection (d) of that section.

(j) For purposes of subsection (i), the following shall be subject to forfeiture to the United States and no property right shall exist in them:

(1) Any personal property used or intended to be used to commit or to facilitate the commission of any violation of this section, or a conspiracy to violate this section.

(2) Any property, real or personal, which constitutes or is derived from proceeds traceable to any violation of this section, or a conspiracy to violate this section.

§ 1031. Major fraud against the United States

(a) Whoever knowingly executes, or attempts to execute, any scheme or artifice with the intent—

(1) to defraud the United States; or

(2) to obtain money or property by means of false or fraudulent pretenses, representations, or promises,

in any grant, contract, subcontract, subsidy, loan, guarantee, insurance, or other form of Federal assistance, including through the Troubled Asset Relief Program, an economic stimulus, recovery or rescue plan provided by the Government, or the Government's purchase of any troubled asset as defined in the Emergency Economic Stabilization Act of 2008, or in any procurement of property or services as a prime contractor with the United States or as a subcontractor or supplier on a contract in which there is a prime contract with the United States, if the value of such grant, contract, subcontract, subsidy, loan, guarantee, insurance, or other form of Federal assistance, or any constituent part thereof, is $1,000,000 or more shall, subject to the applicability of subsection (c) of this section, be fined not more than $1,000,000, or imprisoned not more than 10 years, or both.

(b) The fine imposed for an offense under this section may exceed the maximum otherwise provided by law, if such fine does not exceed $5,000,000 and—

(1) the gross loss to the Government or the gross gain to a defendant is $500,000 or greater; or

(2) the offense involves a conscious or reckless risk of serious personal injury.

(c) The maximum fine imposed upon a defendant for a prosecution including a prosecution with multiple counts under this section shall not exceed $10,000,000.

(d) Nothing in this section shall preclude a court from imposing any other sentences available under this title, including without limitation a fine up to twice the amount of the gross loss or gross gain involved in the offense pursuant to 18 U.S.C. section 3571(d).

(e) In determining the amount of the fine, the court shall consider the factors set forth in 18 U.S.C. sections 3553 and 3572, and the factors set forth in the guidelines and policy statements of the United States Sentencing Commission, including—

(1) the need to reflect the seriousness of the offense, including the harm or loss to the victim and the gain to the defendant;

(2) whether the defendant previously has been fined for a similar offense; and

(3) any other pertinent equitable considerations.

(f) A prosecution of an offense under this section may be commenced any time not later than 7 years after the offense is committed, plus any additional time otherwise allowed by law.

(g)

(1) In special circumstances and in his or her sole discretion, the Attorney General is authorized to make payments from funds appropriated to the Department of Justice to persons who furnish information relating to a possible prosecution under this section. The amount of such payment shall not exceed $250,000. Upon application by the Attorney General, the court may order that the Department shall be reimbursed for a payment from a criminal fine imposed under this section.

(2) An individual is not eligible for such a payment if—

(A) that individual is an officer or employee of a Government agency who furnishes information or renders service in the performance of official duties;

(B) that individual failed to furnish the information to the individual's employer prior to furnishing it to law enforcement authorities, unless the court determines the individual has justifiable reasons for that failure;

(C) the furnished information is based upon public disclosure of allegations or transactions in a criminal, civil, or administrative hearing, in a congressional, administrative, or GAO report, hearing, audit or investigation, or from the news media unless the person is the original source of the information. For the purposes of this subsection, "original source" means an individual who has direct and independent knowledge of the information on which the allegations are based and has voluntarily provided the information to the Government; or

(D) that individual participated in the violation of this section with respect to which such payment would be made.

(3) The failure of the Attorney General to authorize a payment shall not be subject to judicial review.

(h) Any individual who—

(1) is discharged, demoted, suspended, threatened, harassed, or in any other manner discriminated against in the terms and conditions of employment by an employer because of lawful acts done by the employee on behalf of the employee or others in furtherance of a prosecution under this section (including investigation for, initiation of, testimony for, or assistance in such prosecution), and

(2) was not a participant in the unlawful activity that is the subject of said prosecution, may, in a civil action, obtain all relief necessary to make such individual whole. Such relief shall include reinstatement with the same seniority status such individual would have had but for the discrimination, 2 times the amount of back pay, interest on the back pay, and compensation for any special damages sustained as a result of the discrimination, including litigation costs and reasonable attorney's fees.

§ 1035. False statements relating to health care matters

(a) Whoever, in any matter involving a health care benefit program, knowingly and willfully—

(1) falsifies, conceals, or covers up by any trick, scheme, or device a material fact; or

(2) makes any materially false, fictitious, or fraudulent statements or representations, or makes or uses any materially false writing or document knowing the same to contain any materially false, fictitious, or fraudulent statement or entry,

in connection with the delivery of or payment for health care benefits, items, or services, shall be fined under this title or imprisoned not more than 5 years, or both.

(b) As used in this section, the term "health care benefit program" has the meaning given such term in section 24(b) of this title.

§ 1341. Frauds and swindles

Whoever, having devised or intending to devise any scheme or artifice to defraud, or for obtaining money or property by means of false or fraudulent pretenses, representations, or promises, or to sell, dispose of, loan, exchange, alter, give away, distribute, supply, or furnish or procure for unlawful use any counterfeit or spurious coin, obligation, security, or other article, or anything represented to be or intimated or held out to be such counterfeit or spurious article, for the purpose of executing such scheme or artifice or attempting so to do, places in any post office or authorized depository for mail matter, any matter or thing whatever to be sent or delivered by the Postal Service, or deposits or causes to be deposited any matter or thing whatever to be sent or delivered by any private or commercial interstate carrier, or takes or receives therefrom, any such matter or thing, or knowingly causes to be delivered by mail or such carrier according to the direction thereon, or at the place at which it is directed to be delivered by the person to whom it is addressed, any such matter or thing, shall be fined under this title or imprisoned not more than 20 years, or both. If the violation occurs in relation to, or involving any benefit authorized, transported, transmitted, transferred, disbursed, or paid in connection with, a presidentially declared major disaster or emergency (as those terms are defined in section 102 of the Robert T. Stafford Disaster Relief and Emergency Assistance Act (42 U.S.C. 5122)), or affects a financial institution, such person shall be fined not more than $1,000,000 or imprisoned not more than 30 years, or both.

§ 1343. Fraud by wire, radio, or television

Whoever, having devised or intending to devise any scheme or artifice to defraud, or for obtaining money or property by means of false or fraudulent pretenses, representations, or promises, transmits or causes to be transmitted by means of wire, radio, or television communication in interstate or foreign commerce, any writings, signs, signals, pictures, or sounds for the purpose of executing such scheme or artifice, shall be fined under this title or imprisoned not more than 20 years, or both. If the violation occurs in relation to, or involving any benefit authorized, transported, transmitted, transferred, disbursed, or paid in connection with, a presidentially declared major disaster or emergency (as those terms are defined in section 102 of the Robert T. Stafford Disaster Relief and Emergency Assistance Act (42 U.S.C. 5122)), or affects a financial institution, such person shall be fined not more than $1,000,000 or imprisoned not more than 30 years, or both.

§ 1344. Bank fraud

Whoever knowingly executes, or attempts to execute, a scheme or artifice—

(1) to defraud a financial institution; or

(2) to obtain any of the moneys, funds, credits, assets, securities, or other property owned by, or under the custody or control of, a financial institution, by means of false or fraudulent pretenses, representations, or promises;

shall be fined not more than $1,000,000 or imprisoned not more than 30 years, or both.

§ 1346.   Definition of "scheme or artifice to defraud"

For the purposes of this chapter, the term "scheme or artifice to defraud" includes a scheme or artifice to deprive another of the intangible right of honest services.

§ 1347.   Health care fraud

(a) Whoever knowingly and willfully executes, or attempts to execute, a scheme or artifice—

(1) to defraud any health care benefit program; or

(2) to obtain, by means of false or fraudulent pretenses, representations, or promises, any of the money or property owned by, or under the custody or control of, any health care benefit program,

in connection with the delivery of or payment for health care benefits, items, or services, shall be fined under this title or imprisoned not more than 10 years, or both. If the violation results in serious bodily injury (as defined in section 1365 of this title), such person shall be fined under this title or imprisoned not more than 20 years, or both; and if the violation results in death, such person shall be fined under this title, or imprisoned for any term of years or for life, or both.

(b) With respect to violations of this section, a person need not have actual knowledge of this section or specific intent to commit a violation of this section.

§ 1348.   Securities and commodities fraud

Whoever knowingly executes, or attempts to execute, a scheme or artifice—

(1) to defraud any person in connection with any commodity for future delivery, or any option on a commodity for future delivery, or any security of an issuer with a class of securities registered under section 12 of the Securities Exchange Act of 1934 (15 U.S.C. 78l) or that is required to file reports under section 15(d) of the Securities Exchange Act of 1934 (15 U.S.C. 78o(d)); or

(2) to obtain, by means of false or fraudulent pretenses, representations, or promises, any money or property in connection with the purchase or sale of any commodity for future delivery, or any option on a commodity for future delivery, or any security of an issuer with a class of securities registered under section 12 of the Securities Exchange Act of 1934 (15 U.S.C. 78l) or that is required to file reports under section 15(d) of the Securities Exchange Act of 1934 (15 U.S.C. 78o(d));

shall be fined under this title, or imprisoned not more than 25 years, or both.

§ 1349.   Attempt and conspiracy

Any person who attempts or conspires to commit any offense under this chapter shall be subject to the same penalties as those prescribed for the offense, the commission of which was the object of the attempt or conspiracy.

§ 1350.   Failure of corporate officers to certify financial reports

(a) Certification of Periodic Financial Reports.— Each periodic report containing financial statements filed by an issuer with the Securities Exchange Commission pursuant to section 13(a) or 15(d) of the Securities Exchange Act of 1934 (15 U.S.C. 78m(a) or 78o(d)) shall be accompanied by a written statement by the chief executive officer and chief financial officer (or equivalent thereof) of the issuer.

(b) Content.— The statement required under subsection (a) shall certify that the periodic report containing the financial statements fully complies with the requirements of section 13(a) or 15(d) of the Securities Exchange Act of 1934 (15 U.S.C. 78m or 78o(d)) and that information contained in the periodic report fairly presents, in all material respects, the financial condition and results of operations of the issuer.

(c) Criminal Penalties.— Whoever—

(1) certifies any statement as set forth in subsections (a) and (b) of this section knowing that the periodic report accompanying the statement does not comport with all the requirements set forth in this section shall be fined not more than $1,000,000 or imprisoned not more than 10 years, or both; or

(2) willfully certifies any statement as set forth in subsections (a) and (b) of this section knowing that the periodic report accompanying the statement does not comport with all the requirements set forth in this section shall be fined not more than $5,000,000, or imprisoned not more than 20 years, or both.

§ 1503.   Influencing or injuring officer or juror generally

(a) Whoever corruptly, or by threats or force, or by any threatening letter or communication, endeavors to influence, intimidate, or impede any grand or petit juror, or officer in or of any court of the United States, or officer who may be serving at any examination or other proceeding before any United States magistrate judge or other committing magistrate, in the discharge of his duty, or injures any such grand or petit juror in his person or property on account of any verdict or indictment assented to by him, or on account of his being or having been such juror, or injures any such officer, magistrate judge, or other committing magistrate in his person or property on account of the performance of his official duties, or corruptly or by threats or force, or by any threatening letter or communication, influences, obstructs, or impedes, or endeavors to influence, obstruct, or impede, the due administration of justice, shall be punished as provided in subsection (b). If the offense under this section occurs in connection with a trial of a criminal case, and the act in violation of this section involves the threat of physical force or physical force, the maximum term of imprisonment which may be imposed for the offense shall be the higher of that otherwise provided by law or the maximum term that could have been imposed for any offense charged in such case.

(b) The punishment for an offense under this section is—

(1) in the case of a killing, the punishment provided in sections 1111 and 1112;

(2) in the case of an attempted killing, or a case in which the offense was committed against a petit juror and in which a class A or B felony was charged, imprisonment for not more than 20 years, a fine under this title, or both; and

(3) in any other case, imprisonment for not more than 10 years, a fine under

this title, or both.

§ 1505. Obstruction of proceedings before departments, agencies, and committees

Whoever, with intent to avoid, evade, prevent, or obstruct compliance, in whole or in part, with any civil investigative demand duly and properly made under the Antitrust Civil Process Act, willfully withholds, misrepresents, removes from any place, conceals, covers up, destroys, mutilates, alters, or by other means falsifies any documentary material, answers to written interrogatories, or oral testimony, which is the subject of such demand; or attempts to do so or solicits another to do so; or

Whoever corruptly, or by threats or force, or by any threatening letter or communication influences, obstructs, or impedes or endeavors to influence, obstruct, or impede the due and proper administration of the law under which any pending proceeding is being had before any department or agency of the United States, or the due and proper exercise of the power of inquiry under which any inquiry or investigation is being had by either House, or any committee of either House or any joint committee of the Congress—

Shall be fined under this title, imprisoned not more than 5 years or, if the offense involves international or domestic terrorism (as defined in section 2331), imprisoned not more than 8 years, or both.

§ 1510. Obstruction of criminal investigations

(a) Whoever willfully endeavors by means of bribery to obstruct, delay, or prevent the communication of information relating to a violation of any criminal statute of the United States by any person to a criminal investigator shall be fined under this title, or imprisoned not more than five years, or both.

(b)

(1) Whoever, being an officer of a financial institution, with the intent to obstruct a judicial proceeding, directly or indirectly notifies any other person about the existence or contents of a subpoena for records of that financial institution, or information that has been furnished in response to that subpoena, shall be fined under this title or imprisoned not more than 5 years, or both.

(2) Whoever, being an officer of a financial institution, directly or indirectly notifies—

(A) a customer of that financial institution whose records are sought by a subpoena for records; or

(B) any other person named in that subpoena;

about the existence or contents of that subpoena or information that has been furnished in response to that subpoena, shall be fined under this title or imprisoned not more than one year, or both.

(3) As used in this subsection—

(A) the term "an officer of a financial institution" means an officer, director, partner, employee, agent, or attorney of or for a financial institution; and

(B) the term "subpoena for records" means a Federal grand jury subpoena or a Department of Justice subpoena (issued under section 3486 of title 18), for customer records that has been served relating to a violation of, or a conspiracy to violate—

(i) section 215, 656, 657, 1005, 1006, 1007, 1014, 1344, 1956, 1957, or chapter 53 of title 31; or

(ii) section 1341 or 1343 affecting a financial institution.

(c) As used in this section, the term "criminal investigator" means any individual duly authorized by a department, agency, or armed force of the United States to conduct or engage in investigations of or prosecutions for violations of the criminal laws of the United States.

(d)

(1) Whoever—

(A) acting as, or being, an officer, director, agent or employee of a person engaged in the business of insurance whose activities affect interstate commerce, or

(B) is engaged in the business of insurance whose activities affect interstate commerce or is involved (other than as an insured or beneficiary under a policy of insurance) in a transaction relating to the conduct of affairs of such a business,

with intent to obstruct a judicial proceeding, directly or indirectly notifies any other person about the existence or contents of a subpoena for records of that person engaged in such business or information that has been furnished to a Federal grand jury in response to that subpoena, shall be fined as provided by this title or imprisoned not more than 5 years, or both.

(2) As used in paragraph (1), the term "subpoena for records" means a Federal grand jury subpoena for records that has been served relating to a violation of, or a conspiracy to violate, section 1033 of this title.

(e) Whoever, having been notified of the applicable disclosure prohibitions or confidentiality requirements of section 2709(c)(1) of this title, section 626(d)(1) or 627(c)(1) of the Fair Credit Reporting Act (15 U.S.C. 1681u(d)(1) or1681v(c)(1)), section 1114(a)(3)(A) or 1114(a)(5)(D)(i) of the Right to Financial Privacy Act (12 U.S.C. 3414(a)(3)(A) or 3414(a)(5)(D)(i)), or section 802(b)(1) of the National Security Act of 1947 (50 U.S.C. 436(b)(1)), knowingly and with the intent to obstruct an investigation or judicial proceeding violates such prohibitions or requirements applicable by law to such person shall be imprisoned for not more than five years, fined under this title, or both.

§ 1512. Tampering with a witness, victim, or an informant

(a)

(1) Whoever kills or attempts to kill another person, with intent to—

(A) prevent the attendance or testimony of any person in an official proceeding;

(B) prevent the production of a record, document, or other object, in an official proceeding; or

(C) prevent the communication by any person to a law enforcement officer or judge of the United States of information relating to the commission or possible commission of a Federal offense or a violation of conditions of probation, parole, or release pending judicial proceedings;

shall be punished as provided in paragraph (3).

(2) Whoever uses physical force or the threat of physical force against any person, or attempts to do so, with intent to—

(A) influence, delay, or prevent the testimony of any person in an official proceeding;

(B) cause or induce any person to—

(i) withhold testimony, or withhold a record, document, or other object, from an official proceeding;

(ii) alter, destroy, mutilate, or conceal an object with intent to impair the integrity or availability of the object for use in an official proceeding;

(iii) evade legal process summoning that person to appear as a witness, or to produce a record, document, or other object, in an official proceeding; or

(iv) be absent from an official proceeding to which that person has been summoned by legal process; or

(C) hinder, delay, or prevent the communication to a law enforcement officer or judge of the United States of information relating to the commission or possible commission of a Federal offense or a violation of conditions of probation, supervised release, parole, or release pending judicial proceedings;

shall be punished as provided in paragraph (3).

(3) The punishment for an offense under this subsection is—

(A) in the case of a killing, the punishment provided in sections 1111 and 1112;

(B) in the case of—

(i) an attempt to murder; or

(ii) the use or attempted use of physical force against any person; imprisonment for not more than 30 years; and

(C) in the case of the threat of use of physical force against any person, imprisonment for not more than 20 years.

(b) Whoever knowingly uses intimidation, threatens, or corruptly persuades another person, or attempts to do so, or engages in misleading conduct toward another person, with intent to—

(1) influence, delay, or prevent the testimony of any person in an official

proceeding;

(2) cause or induce any person to—

(A) withhold testimony, or withhold a record, document, or other object, from an official proceeding;

(B) alter, destroy, mutilate, or conceal an object with intent to impair the object's integrity or availability for use in an official proceeding;

(C) evade legal process summoning that person to appear as a witness, or to produce a record, document, or other object, in an official proceeding; or

(D) be absent from an official proceeding to which such person has been summoned by legal process; or

(3) hinder, delay, or prevent the communication to a law enforcement officer or judge of the United States of information relating to the commission or possible commission of a Federal offense or a violation of conditions of probation supervised release, parole, or release pending judicial proceedings;

shall be fined under this title or imprisoned not more than 20 years, or both.

(c) Whoever corruptly—

(1) alters, destroys, mutilates, or conceals a record, document, or other object, or attempts to do so, with the intent to impair the object's integrity or availability for use in an official proceeding; or

(2) otherwise obstructs, influences, or impedes any official proceeding, or attempts to do so,

shall be fined under this title or imprisoned not more than 20 years, or both.

(d) Whoever intentionally harasses another person and thereby hinders, delays, prevents, or dissuades any person from—

(1) attending or testifying in an official proceeding;

(2) reporting to a law enforcement officer or judge of the United States the commission or possible commission of a Federal offense or a violation of conditions of probation supervised release, parole, or release pending judicial proceedings;

(3) arresting or seeking the arrest of another person in connection with a Federal offense; or

(4) causing a criminal prosecution, or a parole or probation revocation proceeding, to be sought or instituted, or assisting in such prosecution or proceeding;

or attempts to do so, shall be fined under this title or imprisoned not more than 3 years, or both.

(e) In a prosecution for an offense under this section, it is an affirmative defense, as to which the defendant has the burden of proof by a preponderance of the evidence, that the conduct consisted solely of lawful conduct and that the defendant's sole intention was to encourage, induce, or cause the other person to testify truthfully.

(f) For the purposes of this section—

(1) an official proceeding need not be pending or about to be instituted at the time of the offense; and

(2) the testimony, or the record, document, or other object need not be admissible in evidence or free of a claim of privilege.

(g) In a prosecution for an offense under this section, no state of mind need be proved with respect to the circumstance—

(1) that the official proceeding before a judge, court, magistrate judge, grand jury, or government agency is before a judge or court of the United States, a United States magistrate judge, a bankruptcy judge, a Federal grand jury, or a Federal Government agency; or

(2) that the judge is a judge of the United States or that the law enforcement officer is an officer or employee of the Federal Government or a person authorized to act for or on behalf of the Federal Government or serving the Federal Government as an adviser or consultant.

(h) There is extraterritorial Federal jurisdiction over an offense under this section.

(i) A prosecution under this section or section 1503 may be brought in the district in which the official proceeding (whether or not pending or about to be instituted) was intended to be affected or in the district in which the conduct constituting the alleged offense occurred.

(j) If the offense under this section occurs in connection with a trial of a criminal case, the maximum term of imprisonment which may be imposed for the offense shall be the higher of that otherwise provided by law or the maximum term that could have been imposed for any offense charged in such case.

(k) Whoever conspires to commit any offense under this section shall be subject to the same penalties as those prescribed for the offense the commission of which was the object of the conspiracy.

§ 1513. Retaliating against a witness, victim, or an informant

(a)

(1) Whoever kills or attempts to kill another person with intent to retaliate against any person for—

(A) the attendance of a witness or party at an official proceeding, or any testimony given or any record, document, or other object produced by a witness in an official proceeding; or

(B) providing to a law enforcement officer any information relating to the commission or possible commission of a Federal offense or a violation of conditions of probation, supervised release, parole, or release pending judicial proceedings, shall be punished as provided in paragraph (2).

(2) The punishment for an offense under this subsection is—

(A) in the case of a killing, the punishment provided in sections 1111 and 1112; and

(B) in the case of an attempt, imprisonment for not more than 30 years.

(b) Whoever knowingly engages in any conduct and thereby causes bodily injury to another person or damages the tangible property of another person, or threatens to do so, with intent to retaliate against any person for—

(1) the attendance of a witness or party at an official proceeding, or any testimony given or any record, document, or other object produced by a witness in an official proceeding; or

(2) any information relating to the commission or possible commission of a Federal offense or a violation of conditions of probation, supervised release, parole, or release pending judicial proceedings given by a person to a law enforcement officer;

or attempts to do so, shall be fined under this title or imprisoned not more than 20 years, or both.

(c) If the retaliation occurred because of attendance at or testimony in a criminal case, the maximum term of imprisonment which may be imposed for the offense under this section shall be the higher of that otherwise provided by law or the maximum term that could have been imposed for any offense charged in such case.

(d) There is extraterritorial Federal jurisdiction over an offense under this section.

(e) Whoever knowingly, with the intent to retaliate, takes any action harmful to any person, including interference with the lawful employment or livelihood of any person, for providing to a law enforcement officer any truthful information relating to the commission or possible commission of any Federal offense, shall be fined under this title or imprisoned not more than 10 years, or both.

(f) Whoever conspires to commit any offense under this section shall be subject to the same penalties as those prescribed for the offense the commission of which was the object of the conspiracy.

(g) A prosecution under this section may be brought in the district in which the official proceeding (whether pending, about to be instituted, or completed) was intended to be affected, or in which the conduct constituting the alleged offense occurred.

§ 1515. Definitions for certain provisions; general provision

(a) As used in sections 1512 and 1513 of this title and in this section—

(1) the term "official proceeding" means—

(A) a proceeding before a judge or court of the United States, a United States magistrate judge, a bankruptcy judge, a judge of the United States Tax

Court, a special trial judge of the Tax Court, a judge of the United States
Court of Federal Claims, or a Federal grand jury;

(B) a proceeding before the Congress;

(C) a proceeding before a Federal Government agency which is authorized
by law; or

(D) a proceeding involving the business of insurance whose activities affect
interstate commerce before any insurance regulatory official or agency or any
agent or examiner appointed by such official or agency to examine the affairs
of any person engaged in the business of insurance whose activities affect
interstate commerce;

(2) the term "physical force" means physical action against another, and
includes confinement;

(3) the term "misleading conduct" means—

(A) knowingly making a false statement;

(B) intentionally omitting information from a statement and thereby causing
a portion of such statement to be misleading, or intentionally concealing a
material fact, and thereby creating a false impression by such statement;

(C) with intent to mislead, knowingly submitting or inviting reliance on a
writing or recording that is false, forged, altered, or otherwise lacking in
authenticity;

(D) with intent to mislead, knowingly submitting or inviting reliance on a
sample, specimen, map, photograph, boundary mark, or other object that is
misleading in a material respect; or

(E) knowingly using a trick, scheme, or device with intent to mislead;

(4) the term "law enforcement officer" means an officer or employee of the
Federal Government, or a person authorized to act for or on behalf of the Federal
Government or serving the Federal Government as an adviser or consultant—

(A) authorized under law to engage in or supervise the prevention, detection,
investigation, or prosecution of an offense; or

(B) serving as a probation or pretrial services officer under this title;

(5) the term "bodily injury" means—

(A) a cut, abrasion, bruise, burn, or disfigurement;

(B) physical pain;

(C) illness;

(D) impairment of the function of a bodily member, organ, or mental faculty;
or

(E) any other injury to the body, no matter how temporary; and

(6) the term "corruptly persuades" does not include conduct which would be

misleading conduct but for a lack of a state of mind.

(b) As used in section 1505, the term "corruptly" means acting with an improper purpose, personally or by influencing another, including making a false or misleading statement, or withholding, concealing, altering, or destroying a document or other information.

(c) This chapter does not prohibit or punish the providing of lawful, bona fide, legal representation services in connection with or anticipation of an official proceeding.

§ 1519. Destruction, alteration, or falsification of records in Federal investigations and bankruptcy

Whoever knowingly alters, destroys, mutilates, conceals, covers up, falsifies, or makes a false entry in any record, document, or tangible object with the intent to impede, obstruct, or influence the investigation or proper administration of any matter within the jurisdiction of any department or agency of the United States or any case filed under title 11, or in relation to or contemplation of any such matter or case, shall be fined under this title, imprisoned not more than 20 years, or both.

§ 1520. Destruction of corporate audit records

(a)

(1) Any accountant who conducts an audit of an issuer of securities to which section 10A(a) of the Securities Exchange Act of 1934 (15 U.S.C. 78j-1(a)) applies, shall maintain all audit or review workpapers for a period of 5 years from the end of the fiscal period in which the audit or review was concluded.

(2) The Securities and Exchange Commission shall promulgate, within 180 days, after adequate notice and an opportunity for comment, such rules and regulations, as are reasonably necessary, relating to the retention of relevant records such as workpapers, documents that form the basis of an audit or review, memoranda, correspondence, communications, other documents, and records (including electronic records) which are created, sent, or received in connection with an audit or review and contain conclusions, opinions, analyses, or financial data relating to such an audit or review, which is conducted by any accountant who conducts an audit of an issuer of securities to which section 10A(a) of the Securities Exchange Act of 1934 (15 U.S.C. 78j-1(a)) applies. The Commission may, from time to time, amend or supplement the rules and regulations that it is required to promulgate under this section, after adequate notice and an opportunity for comment, in order to ensure that such rules and regulations adequately comport with the purposes of this section.

(b) Whoever knowingly and willfully violates subsection (a)(1), or any rule or regulation promulgated by the Securities and Exchange Commission under subsection (a)(2), shall be fined under this title, imprisoned not more than 10 years, or both.

(c) Nothing in this section shall be deemed to diminish or relieve any person of any other duty or obligation imposed by Federal or State law or regulation to maintain, or refrain from destroying, any document.

§ 1621.   Perjury generally

Whoever—

(1) having taken an oath before a competent tribunal, officer, or person, in any case in which a law of the United States authorizes an oath to be administered, that he will testify, declare, depose, or certify truly, or that any written testimony, declaration, deposition, or certificate by him subscribed, is true, willfully and contrary to such oath states or subscribes any material matter which he does not believe to be true; or

(2) in any declaration, certificate, verification, or statement under penalty of perjury as permitted under section 1746 of title 28, United States Code, willfully subscribes as true any material matter which he does not believe to be true;

is guilty of perjury and shall, except as otherwise expressly provided by law, be fined under this title or imprisoned not more than five years, or both. This section is applicable whether the statement or subscription is made within or without the United States.

§ 1623.   False declarations before grand jury or court

(a) Whoever under oath (or in any declaration, certificate, verification, or statement under penalty of perjury as permitted under section 1746 of title 28, United States Code) in any proceeding before or ancillary to any court or grand jury of the United States knowingly makes any false material declaration or makes or uses any other information, including any book, paper, document, record, recording, or other material, knowing the same to contain any false material declaration, shall be fined under this title or imprisoned not more than five years, or both.

(b) This section is applicable whether the conduct occurred within or without the United States.

(c) An indictment or information for violation of this section alleging that, in any proceedings before or ancillary to any court or grand jury of the United States, the defendant under oath has knowingly made two or more declarations, which are inconsistent to the degree that one of them is necessarily false, need not specify which declaration is false if—

(1) each declaration was material to the point in question, and

(2) each declaration was made within the period of the statute of limitations for the offense charged under this section.

In any prosecution under this section, the falsity of a declaration set forth in the indictment or information shall be established sufficient for conviction by proof that the defendant while under oath made irreconcilably contradictory declarations material to the point in question in any proceeding before or ancillary to any court or grand jury. It shall be a defense to an indictment or information made pursuant to the first sentence of this subsection that the defendant at the time he made each declaration believed the declaration was true.

(d) Where, in the same continuous court or grand jury proceeding in which a declaration is made, the person making the declaration admits such declaration to be false, such admission shall bar prosecution under this section if, at the time the admission is made, the declaration has not substantially affected the proceeding, or it has not become manifest that such falsity has been or will be exposed.

(e) Proof beyond a reasonable doubt under this section is sufficient for conviction. It shall not be necessary that such proof be made by any particular number of witnesses or by documentary or other type of evidence.

§ 1951. Interference with commerce by threats or violence

(a) Whoever in any way or degree obstructs, delays, or affects commerce or the movement of any article or commodity in commerce, by robbery or extortion or attempts or conspires so to do, or commits or threatens physical violence to any person or property in furtherance of a plan or purpose to do anything in violation of this section shall be fined under this title or imprisoned not more than twenty years, or both.

(b) As used in this section—

(1) The term "robbery" means the unlawful taking or obtaining of personal property from the person or in the presence of another, against his will, by means of actual or threatened force, or violence, or fear of injury, immediate or future, to his person or property, or property in his custody or possession, or the person or property of a relative or member of his family or of anyone in his company at the time of the taking or obtaining.

(2) The term "extortion" means the obtaining of property from another, with his consent, induced by wrongful use of actual or threatened force, violence, or fear, or under color of official right.

(3) The term "commerce" means commerce within the District of Columbia, or any Territory or Possession of the United States; all commerce between any point in a State, Territory, Possession, or the District of Columbia and any point outside thereof; all commerce between points within the same State through any place outside such State; and all other commerce over which the United States has jurisdiction.

(c) This section shall not be construed to repeal, modify or affect section 17 of Title 15, sections 52, 101–115, 151–166 of Title 29 or sections 151–188 of Title 45.

§ 1952. Interstate and foreign travel or transportation in aid of racketeering enterprises

(a) Whoever travels in interstate or foreign commerce or uses the mail or any facility in interstate or foreign commerce, with intent to—

(1) distribute the proceeds of any unlawful activity; or

(2) commit any crime of violence to further any unlawful activity; or

(3) otherwise promote, manage, establish, carry on, or facilitate the promotion, management, establishment, or carrying on, of any unlawful activity,

and thereafter performs or attempts to perform—

(A) an act described in paragraph (1) or (3) shall be fined under this title, imprisoned not more than 5 years, or both; or

(B) an act described in paragraph (2) shall be fined under this title, imprisoned for not more than 20 years, or both, and if death results shall be imprisoned for any term of years or for life.

(b) As used in this section

(i) "unlawful activity" means

(1) any business enterprise involving gambling, liquor on which the Federal excise tax has not been paid, narcotics or controlled substances (as defined in section 102(6) of the Controlled Substances Act), or prostitution offenses in violation of the laws of the State in which they are committed or of the United States,

(2) extortion, bribery, or arson in violation of the laws of the State in which committed or of the United States, or

(3) any act which is indictable under subchapter II of chapter 53 of title 31, United States Code, or under section 1956 or 1957 of this title and (ii) the term "State" includes a State of the United States, the District of Columbia, and any commonwealth, territory, or possession of the United States.

(c) Investigations of violations under this section involving liquor shall be conducted under the supervision of the Attorney General.

(d) If the offense under this section involves an act described in paragraph (1) or (3) of subsection (a) and also involves a pre-retail medical product (as defined in section 670), the punishment for the offense shall be the same as the punishment for an offense under section 670 unless the punishment under subsection (a) is greater.

(e)

(1) This section shall not apply to a savings promotion raffle conducted by an insured depository institution or an insured credit union.

(2) In this subsection—

(A) the term "insured credit union" shall have the meaning given the term in section 101 of the Federal Credit Union Act (12 U.S.C. 1752);

(B) the term "insured depository institution" shall have the meaning given the term in section 3 of the Federal Deposit Insurance Act (12 U.S.C. 1813); and

(C) the term "savings promotion raffle" means a contest in which the sole consideration required for a chance of winning designated prizes is obtained by the deposit of a specified amount of money in a savings account or other savings program, where each ticket or entry has an equal chance of being drawn, such contest being subject to regulations that may from time to time be promulgated by the appropriate prudential regulator (as defined in section 1002 of the Consumer Financial Protection Act of 2010 (12 U.S.C. 5481)).

§ 1955. Prohibition of illegal gambling businesses

(a) Whoever conducts, finances, manages, supervises, directs, or owns all or part of an illegal gambling business shall be fined under this title or imprisoned not more than five years, or both.

(b) As used in this section—

(1) "illegal gambling business" means a gambling business which—

(i) is a violation of the law of a State or political subdivision in which it is conducted;

(ii) involves five or more persons who conduct, finance, manage, supervise, direct, or own all or part of such business; and

(iii) has been or remains in substantially continuous operation for a period in excess of thirty days or has a gross revenue of $2,000 in any single day.

(2) "insured credit union" shall have the meaning given the term in section 101 of the Federal Credit Union Act (12 U.S.C. 1752).

(3) "insured depository institution" shall have the meaning given the term in section 3 of the Federal Deposit Insurance Act (12 U.S.C. 1813).

(4) "gambling" includes but is not limited to pool-selling, bookmaking, maintaining slot machines, roulette wheels or dice tables, and conducting lotteries, policy, bolita or numbers games, or selling chances therein.

(5) "savings promotion raffle" means a contest in which the sole consideration required for a chance of winning designated prizes is obtained by the deposit of a specified amount of money in a savings account or other savings program, where each ticket or entry has an equal chance of being drawn, such contest being subject to regulations that may from time to time be promulgated by the appropriate prudential regulator (as defined in section 1002 of the Consumer Financial Protection Act of 2010 (12 U.S.C. 5481)).

(6) "State" means any State of the United States, the District of Columbia, the Commonwealth of Puerto Rico, and any territory or possession of the United States.

(c) If five or more persons conduct, finance, manage, supervise, direct, or own all or part of a gambling business and such business operates for two or more successive days, then, for the purpose of obtaining warrants for arrests, interceptions, and other searches and seizures, probable cause that the business receives gross revenue in excess of $2,000 in any single day shall be deemed to have been established.

(d) Any property, including money, used in violation of the provisions of this section may be seized and forfeited to the United States. All provisions of law relating to the seizures, summary, and judicial forfeiture procedures, and condemnation of vessels, vehicles, merchandise, and baggage for violation of the customs laws; the disposition of such vessels, vehicles, merchandise, and baggage or the proceeds from such sale; the remission or mitigation of such forfeitures; and the compromise of claims and the award of compensation to informers in respect of such forfeitures shall apply to seizures and forfeitures incurred or alleged to have been incurred under the provisions of this section, insofar as applicable and not inconsistent with such provisions. Such duties as are imposed upon the collector of customs or any other person in respect to the seizure and forfeiture of vessels, vehicles, merchandise, and baggage under the customs laws shall be performed with respect to seizures and forfeitures of property used or intended for use in violation of this section by such officers, agents, or other persons as may be designated for that purpose by the Attorney General.

(e) This section shall not apply to—

(1) any bingo game, lottery, or similar game of chance conducted by an organization exempt from tax under paragraph (3) of subsection (c) of section 501 of the Internal Revenue Code of 1986, as amended, if no part of the gross receipts derived from such activity inures to the benefit of any private shareholder, member, or employee of such organization except as compensation for actual expenses incurred by him in the conduct of such activity; or

(2) any savings promotion raffle.

§ 1956. Laundering of monetary instruments

(a)

(1) Whoever, knowing that the property involved in a financial transaction represents the proceeds of some form of unlawful activity, conducts or attempts to conduct such a financial transaction which in fact involves the proceeds of specified unlawful activity—

(A)

(i) with the intent to promote the carrying on of specified unlawful activity; or

(ii) with intent to engage in conduct constituting a violation of section 7201 or 7206 of the Internal Revenue Code of 1986; or

(B) knowing that the transaction is designed in whole or in part—

(i) to conceal or disguise the nature, the location, the source, the ownership, or the control of the proceeds of specified unlawful activity; or

(ii) to avoid a transaction reporting requirement under State or Federal law,

shall be sentenced to a fine of not more than $500,000 or twice the value of the property involved in the transaction, whichever is greater, or imprisonment for not more than twenty years, or both. For purposes of this paragraph, a financial transaction shall be considered to be one involving the proceeds of specified unlawful activity if it is part of a set of parallel or dependent transactions, any one of which involves the proceeds of specified unlawful activity, and all of which are part of a single plan or arrangement.

(2) Whoever transports, transmits, or transfers, or attempts to transport, transmit, or transfer a monetary instrument or funds from a place in the United

States to or through a place outside the United States or to a place in the United States from or through a place outside the United States—

(A) with the intent to promote the carrying on of specified unlawful activity; or

(B) knowing that the monetary instrument or funds involved in the transportation, transmission, or transfer represent the proceeds of some form of unlawful activity and knowing that such transportation, transmission, or transfer is designed in whole or in part—

(i) to conceal or disguise the nature, the location, the source, the ownership, or the control of the proceeds of specified unlawful activity; or

(ii) to avoid a transaction reporting requirement under State or Federal law,

shall be sentenced to a fine of not more than $500,000 or twice the value of the monetary instrument or funds involved in the transportation, transmission, or transfer, whichever is greater, or imprisonment for not more than twenty years, or both. For the purpose of the offense described in subparagraph (B), the defendant's knowledge may be established by proof that a law enforcement officer represented the matter specified in subparagraph (B) as true, and the defendant's subsequent statements or actions indicate that the defendant believed such representations to be true.

(3) Whoever, with the intent—

(A) to promote the carrying on of specified unlawful activity;

(B) to conceal or disguise the nature, location, source, ownership, or control of property believed to be the proceeds of specified unlawful activity; or

(C) to avoid a transaction reporting requirement under State or Federal law,

conducts or attempts to conduct a financial transaction involving property represented to be the proceeds of specified unlawful activity, or property used to conduct or facilitate specified unlawful activity, shall be fined under this title or imprisoned for not more than 20 years, or both. For purposes of this paragraph and paragraph (2), the term "represented" means any representation made by a law enforcement officer or by another person at the direction of, or with the approval of, a Federal official authorized to investigate or prosecute violations of this section.

(b) Penalties.—

(1) In general.— Whoever conducts or attempts to conduct a transaction described in subsection (a)(1) or (a)(3), or section 1957, or a transportation, transmission, or transfer described in subsection (a)(2), is liable to the United States for a civil penalty of not more than the greater of—

(A) the value of the property, funds, or monetary instruments involved in the transaction; or

(B) $10,000.

(2) Jurisdiction over foreign persons.— For purposes of adjudicating an action filed or enforcing a penalty ordered under this section, the district courts shall have jurisdiction over any foreign person, including any financial institution authorized under the laws of a foreign country, against whom the action is brought, if service of process upon the foreign person is made under the Federal Rules of Civil Procedure or the laws of the country in which the foreign person is found, and—

(A) the foreign person commits an offense under subsection (a) involving a financial transaction that occurs in whole or in part in the United States;

(B) the foreign person converts, to his or her own use, property in which the United States has an ownership interest by virtue of the entry of an order of forfeiture by a court of the United States; or

(C) the foreign person is a financial institution that maintains a bank account at a financial institution in the United States.

(3) Court authority over assets.— A court may issue a pretrial restraining order or take any other action necessary to ensure that any bank account or other property held by the defendant in the United States is available to satisfy a judgment under this section.

(4) Federal receiver.—

(A) In general.— A court may appoint a Federal Receiver, in accordance with subparagraph (B)of this paragraph, to collect, marshal, and take custody, control, and possession of all assets of the defendant, wherever located, to satisfy a civil judgment under this subsection, a forfeiture judgment under section 981 or 982, or a criminal sentence under section 1957 or subsection (a) of this section, including an order of restitution to any victim of a specified unlawful activity.

(B) Appointment and authority.— A Federal Receiver described in subparagraph (A)—

(i) may be appointed upon application of a Federal prosecutor or a Federal or State regulator, by the court having jurisdiction over the defendant in the case;

(ii) shall be an officer of the court, and the powers of the Federal Receiver shall include the powers set out in section 754 of title 28, United States Code; and

(iii) shall have standing equivalent to that of a Federal prosecutor for the purpose of submitting requests to obtain information regarding the assets of the defendant—

(I) from the Financial Crimes Enforcement Network of the Department of the Treasury; or

(II) from a foreign country pursuant to a mutual legal assistance treaty, multilateral agreement, or other arrangement for international law enforcement assistance, provided that such requests are in accordance with the policies and procedures of the Attorney General.

(c) As used in this section—

(1) the term "knowing that the property involved in a financial transaction represents the proceeds of some form of unlawful activity" means that the person knew the property involved in the transaction represented proceeds from some form, though not necessarily which form, of activity that constitutes a felony under State, Federal, or foreign law, regardless of whether or not such activity is specified in paragraph (7);

(2) the term "conducts" includes initiating, concluding, or participating in initiating, or concluding a transaction;

(3) the term "transaction" includes a purchase, sale, loan, pledge, gift, transfer, delivery, or other disposition, and with respect to a financial institution includes a deposit, withdrawal, transfer between accounts, exchange of currency, loan, extension of credit, purchase or sale of any stock, bond, certificate of deposit, or other monetary instrument, use of a safe deposit box, or any other payment, transfer, or delivery by, through, or to a financial institution, by whatever means effected;

(4) the term "financial transaction" means

(A) a transaction which in any way or degree affects interstate or foreign commerce

(i) involving the movement of funds by wire or other means or

(ii) involving one or more monetary instruments, or

(iii) involving the transfer of title to any real property, vehicle, vessel, or aircraft, or

(B) a transaction involving the use of a financial institution which is engaged in, or the activities of which affect, interstate or foreign commerce in any way or degree;

(5) the term "monetary instruments" means (i) coin or currency of the United States or of any other country, travelers' checks, personal checks, bank checks, and money orders, or (ii) investment securities or negotiable instruments, in bearer form or otherwise in such form that title thereto passes upon delivery;

(6) the term "financial institution" includes—

(A) any financial institution, as defined in section 5312(a)(2) of title 31, United States Code, or the regulations promulgated thereunder; and

(B) any foreign bank, as defined in section 1 of the International Banking Act of 1978 (12 U.S.C. 3101);

(7) the term "specified unlawful activity" means—

(A) any act or activity constituting an offense listed in section 1961(1) of this title except an act which is indictable under subchapter II of chapter 53 of title 31;

(B) with respect to a financial transaction occurring in whole or in part in the United States, an offense against a foreign nation involving—

(i) the manufacture, importation, sale, or distribution of a controlled substance (as such term is defined for the purposes of the Controlled Substances Act);

(ii) murder, kidnapping, robbery, extortion, destruction of property by means of explosive or fire, or a crime of violence (as defined in section 16);

(iii) fraud, or any scheme or attempt to defraud, by or against a foreign bank (as defined in paragraph 7 of section 1(b) of the International Banking Act of 1978));

(iv) bribery of a public official, or the misappropriation, theft, or embezzlement of public funds by or for the benefit of a public official;

(v) smuggling or export control violations involving—

(I) an item controlled on the United States Munitions List established under section 38 of the Arms Export Control Act (22 U.S.C. 2778); or

(II) an item controlled under regulations under the Export Administration Regulations (15 C.F.R. Parts 730–774);

(vi) an offense with respect to which the United States would be obligated by a multilateral treaty, either to extradite the alleged offender or to submit the case for prosecution, if the offender were found within the territory of the United States; or

(vii) trafficking in persons, selling or buying of children, sexual exploitation of children, or transporting, recruiting or harboring a person, including a child, for commercial sex acts;

(C) any act or acts constituting a continuing criminal enterprise, as that term is defined in section 408 of the Controlled Substances Act (21 U.S.C. 848);

(D) an offense under section 32 (relating to the destruction of aircraft), section 37 (relating to violence at international airports), section 115 (relating to influencing, impeding, or retaliating against a Federal official by threatening or injuring a family member), section 152 (relating to concealment of assets; false oaths and claims; bribery), section 175c (relating to the variola virus), section 215 (relating to commissions or gifts for procuring loans), section 351 (relating to congressional or Cabinet officer assassination), any of sections 500 through 503 (relating to certain counterfeiting offenses), section 513 (relating to securities of States and private entities), section 541 (relating to goods falsely classified), section 542 (relating to entry of goods by means of false statements), section 545 (relating to smuggling goods into the United States), section 549 (relating to removing goods from Customs custody), section 554 (relating to smuggling goods from the United States), section 555 (relating to border tunnels), section 641 (relating to public money, property, or records), section 656 (relating to theft, embezzlement, or misapplication by bank officer or employee), section 657 (relating to lending, credit, and insurance institutions), section 658 (relating to property mortgaged or pledged to farm credit agencies), section 666 (relating to theft or bribery concerning programs receiving Federal funds), section 793, 794, or 798 (relating to espionage), section 831 (relating to prohibited transactions involving nuclear materials), section 844(f) or (i) (relating to destruction by explosives or fire of Government property or property affecting interstate or foreign commerce), section 875 (relating to interstate communications), section 922(l) (relating to the unlawful importation of firearms), section 924(n) (relating to firearms trafficking), section 956 (relating to conspiracy to kill, kidnap, maim, or injure certain property in a foreign country), section 1005 (relating to fraudulent bank entries), 1006 (relating to fraudulent Federal credit institution entries), 1007 (relating to Federal Deposit Insurance transactions), 1014 (relating to fraudulent loan or credit applications), section 1030 (relating to computer fraud and abuse), 1032 (relating to concealment of assets from conservator, receiver, or liquidating agent of financial institution), section 1111 (relating to murder), section 1114 (relating to murder of United States law enforcement officials), section 1116 (relating to murder of foreign officials, official guests, or internationally protected persons), section 1201 (relating to kidnaping), section 1203 (relating to hostage taking), section 1361 (relating to willful injury of Government property), section 1363 (relating to destruction of property within the special maritime and territorial jurisdiction), section 1708 (theft from the mail), section 1751 (relating to Presidential assassination), section 2113 or 2114 (relating to bank and postal robbery and theft), section 2252A (relating to child pornography) where the child pornography contains a visual depiction of an actual minor engaging in sexually explicit conduct, section 2260 (production of certain child pornography for importation into the United States), section 2280 (relating to violence against maritime navigation), section 2281 (relating to violence against maritime fixed platforms), section 2319 (relating to copyright infringement), section 2320 (relating to trafficking in counterfeit goods and services), section 2332 (relating to terrorist acts abroad against United States nationals), section 2332a (relating to use of weapons of mass destruction), section 2332b (relating to international terrorist acts transcending national boundaries), section 2332g (relating to missile systems designed to destroy aircraft), section 2332h (relating to radiological dispersal devices), section 2339A or 2339B (relating to providing material support to terrorists), section 2339C (relating to financing of terrorism), or section 2339D (relating to receiving military-type training from a foreign terrorist organization) of this title, section 46502 of title 49, United States Code, a felony violation of the Chemical Diversion and Trafficking Act of 1988 (relating to precursor and essential chemicals), section 590 of the Tariff Act of 1930 (19 U.S.C. 1590) (relating to aviation smuggling), section 422 of the Controlled Substances Act (relating to transportation of drug paraphernalia), section 38(c) (relating to criminal violations) of the Arms Export Control Act, section 11 (relating to violations) of the Export Administration Act of 1979, section 206 (relating to penalties) of the International Emergency Economic Powers Act, section 16 (relating to offenses and punishment) of the Trading with the Enemy Act, any felony violation of section 15 of the Food and Nutrition Act of 2008 [7 U.S.C.A. § 2024] (relating to supplemental nutrition assistance program benefits fraud) involving a quantity of benefits having a value of not less than $5,000, any violation of section 543(a)(1) of the Housing Act of 1949 [42 U.S.C.A. § 1490s(a)(1)] (relating to equity skimming), any felony violation of the Foreign Agents Registration Act of 1938, any felony violation of the Foreign Corrupt Practices Act, or section 92 of the Atomic Energy Act of 1954 (42 U.S.C. 2122) (relating to prohibitions governing atomic weapons) ENVIRONMENTAL CRIMES

(E) a felony violation of the Federal Water Pollution Control Act (33 U.S.C. 1251 et seq.), the Ocean Dumping Act (33 U.S.C. 1401 et seq.), the Act to Prevent Pollution from Ships (33 U.S.C. 1901 et seq.), the Safe Drinking Water Act (42 U.S.C. 300f et seq.), or the Resources Conservation and Recovery Act (42 U.S.C. 6901 et seq.); or

(F) any act or activity constituting an offense involving a Federal health care offense;

(8) the term "State" includes a State of the United States, the District of Columbia, and any commonwealth, territory, or possession of the United States; and

(9) the term "proceeds" means any property derived from or obtained or retained, directly or indirectly, through some form of unlawful activity, including the gross receipts of such activity.

(d) Nothing in this section shall supersede any provision of Federal, State, or other law imposing criminal penalties or affording civil remedies in addition to those provided for in this section.

(e) Violations of this section may be investigated by such components of the Department of Justice as the Attorney General may direct, and by such components of the Department of the Treasury as the Secretary of the Treasury may direct, as appropriate, and, with respect to offenses over which the Department of Homeland Security has jurisdiction, by such components of the Department of Homeland Security as the Secretary of Homeland Security may direct, and, with respect to offenses over which the United States Postal Service has jurisdiction, by the Postal Service. Such authority of the Secretary of the Treasury, the Secretary of Homeland Security, and the Postal Service shall be exercised in accordance with an agreement which shall be entered into by the Secretary of the Treasury, the Secretary of Homeland Security, the Postal Service, and the Attorney General. Violations of this section involving offenses described in paragraph (c)(7)(E) may be investigated by such components of the Department of Justice as the Attorney General may direct, and the National Enforcement Investigations Center of the Environmental Protection Agency.

(f) There is extraterritorial jurisdiction over the conduct prohibited by this section if—

(1) the conduct is by a United States citizen or, in the case of a non-United States citizen, the conduct occurs in part in the United States; and

(2) the transaction or series of related transactions involves funds or monetary instruments of a value exceeding $10,000.

(g) Notice of conviction of financial institutions.— If any financial institution or any officer, director, or employee of any financial institution has been found guilty of an offense under this section, section 1957 or 1960 of this title, or section 5322 or 5324 of title 31, the Attorney General shall provide written notice of such fact to the appropriate regulatory agency for the financial institution.

(h) Any person who conspires to commit any offense defined in this section or section 1957 shall be subject to the same penalties as those prescribed for the offense the commission of which was the object of the conspiracy.

(i) Venue.—

(1) Except as provided in paragraph (2), a prosecution for an offense under this section or section 1957 may be brought in—

(A) any district in which the financial or monetary transaction is conducted; or

(B) any district where a prosecution for the underlying specified unlawful activity could be brought, if the defendant participated in the transfer of the proceeds of the specified unlawful activity from that district to the district where the financial or monetary transaction is conducted.

(2) A prosecution for an attempt or conspiracy offense under this section or section 1957 may be brought in the district where venue would lie for the completed offense under paragraph (1), or in any other district where an act in furtherance of the attempt or conspiracy took place.

(3) For purposes of this section, a transfer of funds from 1 place to another, by wire or any other means, shall constitute a single, continuing transaction. Any person who conducts (as that term is defined in subsection (c)(2)) any portion of the transaction may be charged in any district in which the transaction takes place.

§ 1957. Engaging in monetary transactions in property derived from specified unlawful activity

(a) Whoever, in any of the circumstances set forth in subsection (d), knowingly engages or attempts to engage in a monetary transaction in criminally derived property of a value greater than $10,000 and is derived from specified unlawful activity, shall be punished as provided in subsection (b).

(b)

(1) Except as provided in paragraph (2), the punishment for an offense under this section is a fine under title 18, United States Code, or imprisonment for not more than ten years or both. If the offense involves a pre-retail medical product (as defined in section 670) the punishment for the offense shall be the same as the punishment for an offense under section 670 unless the punishment under this subsection is greater.

(2) The court may impose an alternate fine to that imposable under paragraph (1) of not more than twice the amount of the criminally derived property involved in the transaction.

(c) In a prosecution for an offense under this section, the Government is not required to prove the defendant knew that the offense from which the criminally derived property was derived was specified unlawful activity.

(d) The circumstances referred to in subsection (a) are—

(1) that the offense under this section takes place in the United States or in the special maritime and territorial jurisdiction of the United States; or

(2) that the offense under this section takes place outside the United States and such special jurisdiction, but the defendant is a United States person (as defined in section 3077 of this title, but excluding the class described in paragraph (2)(D) of such section).

(e) Violations of this section may be investigated by such components of the Department of Justice as the Attorney General may direct, and by such components of the Department of the Treasury as the Secretary of the Treasury may direct, as appropriate, and, with respect to offenses over which the Department of Homeland Security has jurisdiction, by such components of the Department of Homeland Security as the Secretary of Homeland Security may direct, and, with respect to offenses over which the United States Postal Service has jurisdiction, by the Postal Service. Such authority of the Secretary of the Treasury, the Secretary of Homeland Security, and the Postal Service shall be exercised in accordance with an agreement which shall be entered into by the Secretary of the Treasury, the Secretary of Homeland Security, the Postal Service, and the Attorney General.

(f) As used in this section—

(1) the term "monetary transaction" means the deposit, withdrawal, transfer, or exchange, in or affecting interstate or foreign commerce, of funds or a monetary instrument (as defined in section 1956(c)(5) of this title) by, through, or to a financial institution (as defined in section 1956 of this title), including any transaction that would be a financial transaction under section 1956(c)(4)(B) of this title, but such term does not include any transaction necessary to preserve a person's right to representation as guaranteed by the sixth amendment to the Constitution;

(2) the term "criminally derived property" means any property constituting, or derived from, proceeds obtained from a criminal offense; and

(3) the terms "specified unlawful activity" and "proceeds" shall have the meaning given those terms in section 1956 of this title.

§ 1961. Definitions

As used in this chapter—

(1) "racketeering activity" means

(A) any act or threat involving murder, kidnapping, gambling, arson, robbery, bribery, extortion, dealing in obscene matter, or dealing in a controlled substance or listed chemical (as defined in section 102 of the Controlled Substances Act), which is chargeable under State law and punishable by imprisonment for more than one year;

(B) any act which is indictable under any of the following provisions of title 18, United States Code: Section 201 (relating to bribery), section 224 (relating to sports bribery), sections 471, 472, and 473 (relating to counterfeiting), section 659 (relating to theft from interstate shipment) if the act indictable under section 659 is felonious, section 664 (relating to embezzlement from pension and welfare funds), sections 891–894 (relating to extortionate credit transactions), section 1028 (relating to fraud and related activity in connection with identification documents), section 1029 (relating to fraud and related activity in connection with access devices), section 1084 (relating to the transmission of gambling information), section 1341 (relating to mail fraud), section 1343 (relating to wire fraud), section 1344 (relating to financial institution fraud), section 1351 (relating to fraud in foreign labor contracting), section 1425 (relating to the procurement of citizenship or nationalization unlawfully), section 1426 (relating to the reproduction of naturalization or citizenship papers), section 1427 (relating to the sale of naturalization or citizenship papers), sections 1461–1465 (relating to obscene matter), section 1503 (relating to obstruction of justice), section 1510 (relating to obstruction of criminal investigations), section 1511 (relating to the obstruction of State or local law enforcement), section 1512 (relating to tampering with a witness, victim, or an informant), section 1513 (relating to retaliating against a witness, victim, or an informant), section 1542 (relating to false statement in application and use of passport), section 1543 (relating to forgery or false use of passport), section 1544 (relating to misuse of passport), section 1546 (relating to fraud and misuse of visas, permits, and other documents), sections 1581–1592 (relating to peonage, slavery, and trafficking in persons), section 1951 (relating to interference with commerce, robbery, or extortion), section 1952 (relating to racketeering), section 1953 (relating to interstate transportation of wagering paraphernalia), section 1954 (relating to unlawful welfare fund payments), section 1955 (relating to the prohibition of illegal gambling businesses), section 1956 (relating to the laundering of monetary instruments), section 1957 (relating to engaging in monetary transactions in property derived from specified unlawful activity), section 1958 (relating to use of interstate commerce facilities in the commission of murder-for-hire), section 1960 (relating to illegal money transmitters), sections 2251, 2251A, 2252, and 2260 (relating to sexual exploitation of children), sections 2312 and 2313 (relating to interstate transportation of stolen motor vehicles), sections 2314 and 2315 (relating to interstate transportation of stolen property), section 2318 (relating to trafficking in counterfeit labels for phonorecords, computer programs or computer program documentation or packaging and copies of motion pictures or other audiovisual works), section 2319 (relating to criminal infringement of a copyright), section 2319A (relating to unauthorized fixation of and trafficking in sound recordings and music videos of live musical performances), section 2320 (relating to trafficking in goods or services bearing counterfeit marks), section 2321 (relating to trafficking in certain motor vehicles or motor vehicle parts), sections 2341–2346 (relating to trafficking in contraband cigarettes), sections 2421–24 (relating to white slave traffic), sections 175–178 (relating to biological weapons), sections 229–229F (relating to chemical weapons), section 831 (relating to nuclear materials),

(C) any act which is indictable under title 29, United States Code, section 186 (dealing with restrictions on payments and loans to labor organizations) or section 501(c) (relating to embezzlement from union funds),

(D) any offense involving fraud connected with a case under title 11 (except a case under section 157 of this title), fraud in the sale of securities, or the felonious manufacture, importation, receiving, concealment, buying, selling, or otherwise dealing in a controlled substance or listed chemical (as defined in section 102 of the Controlled Substances Act), punishable under any law of the United States,

(E) any act which is indictable under the Currency and Foreign Transactions Reporting Act,

(F) any act which is indictable under the Immigration and Nationality Act, section 274 (relating to bringing in and harboring certain aliens), section 277 (relating to aiding or assisting certain aliens to enter the United States), or section 278 (relating to importation of alien for immoral purpose) if the act indictable under such section of such Act was committed for the purpose of financial gain, or

(G) any act that is indictable under any provision listed in section 2332b(g)(5)(B);

(2) "State" means any State of the United States, the District of Columbia, the Commonwealth of Puerto Rico, any territory or possession of the United States, any political subdivision, or any department, agency, or instrumentality thereof;

(3) "person" includes any individual or entity capable of holding a legal or beneficial interest in property;

(4) "enterprise" includes any individual, partnership, corporation, association, or other legal entity, and any union or group of individuals associated in fact although not a legal entity;

(5) "pattern of racketeering activity" requires at least two acts of racketeering activity, one of which occurred after the effective date of this chapter and the last of which occurred within ten years (excluding any period of imprisonment) after the commission of a prior act of racketeering activity;

(6) "unlawful debt" means a debt (A) incurred or contracted in gambling activity which was in violation of the law of the United States, a State or political subdivision thereof, or which is unenforceable under State or Federal law in whole or in part as to principal or interest because of the laws relating to usury, and (B) which was incurred in connection with the business of gambling in violation of the law of the United States, a State or political subdivision thereof, or the business of lending money or a thing of value at a rate usurious under State or Federal law, where the usurious rate is at least twice the enforceable rate;

(7) "racketeering investigator" means any attorney or investigator so designated by the Attorney General and charged with the duty of enforcing or carrying into effect this chapter;

(8) "racketeering investigation" means any inquiry conducted by any rack-

eteering investigator for the purpose of ascertaining whether any person has been involved in any violation of this chapter or of any final order, judgment, or decree of any court of the United States, duly entered in any case or proceeding arising under this chapter;

(9) "documentary material" includes any book, paper, document, record, recording, or other material; and

(10) "Attorney General" includes the Attorney General of the United States, the Deputy Attorney General of the United States, the Associate Attorney General of the United States, any Assistant Attorney General of the United States, or any employee of the Department of Justice or any employee of any department or agency of the United States so designated by the Attorney General to carry out the powers conferred on the Attorney General by this chapter. Any department or agency so designated may use in investigations authorized by this chapter either the investigative provisions of this chapter or the investigative power of such department or agency otherwise conferred by law.

§ 1962. Prohibited activities

(a) It shall be unlawful for any person who has received any income derived, directly or indirectly, from a pattern of racketeering activity or through collection of an unlawful debt in which such person has participated as a principal within the meaning of section 2, title 18, United States Code, to use or invest, directly or indirectly, any part of such income, or the proceeds of such income, in acquisition of any interest in, or the establishment or operation of, any enterprise which is engaged in, or the activities of which affect, interstate or foreign commerce. A purchase of securities on the open market for purposes of investment, and without the intention of controlling or participating in the control of the issuer, or of assisting another to do so, shall not be unlawful under this subsection if the securities of the issuer held by the purchaser, the members of his immediate family, and his or their accomplices in any pattern or racketeering activity or the collection of an unlawful debt after such purchase do not amount in the aggregate to one percent of the outstanding securities of any one class, and do not confer, either in law or in fact, the power to elect one or more directors of the issuer.

(b) It shall be unlawful for any person through a pattern of racketeering activity or through collection of an unlawful debt to acquire or maintain, directly or indirectly, any interest in or control of any enterprise which is engaged in, or the activities of which affect, interstate or foreign commerce.

(c) It shall be unlawful for any person employed by or associated with any enterprise engaged in, or the activities of which affect, interstate or foreign commerce, to conduct or participate, directly or indirectly, in the conduct of such enterprise's affairs through a pattern of racketeering activity or collection of unlawful debt.

(d) It shall be unlawful for any person to conspire to violate any of the provisions of subsection (a), (b), or (c) of this section.

§ 1963. Criminal penalties

(a) Whoever violates any provision of section 1962 of this chapter shall be fined under this title or imprisoned not more than 20 years (or for life if the violation is based on a racketeering activity for which the maximum penalty includes life imprisonment), or both, and shall forfeit to the United States, irrespective of any provision of State law—

(1) any interest the person has acquired or maintained in violation of section 1962;

(2) any—

(A) interest in;

(B) security of;

(C) claim against; or

(D) property or contractual right of any kind affording a source of influence over;

any enterprise which the person has established, operated, controlled, conducted, or participated in the conduct of, in violation of section 1962; and

(3) any property constituting, or derived from, any proceeds which the person obtained, directly or indirectly, from racketeering activity or unlawful debt collection in violation of section 1962.

The court, in imposing sentence on such person shall order, in addition to any other sentence imposed pursuant to this section, that the person forfeit to the United States all property described in this subsection. In lieu of a fine otherwise authorized by this section, a defendant who derives profits or other proceeds from an offense may be fined not more than twice the gross profits or other proceeds.

(b) Property subject to criminal forfeiture under this section includes—

(1) real property, including things growing on, affixed to, and found in land; and

(2) tangible and intangible personal property, including rights, privileges, interests, claims, and securities.

(c) All right, title, and interest in property described in subsection (a) vests in the United States upon the commission of the act giving rise to forfeiture under this section. Any such property that is subsequently transferred to a person other than the defendant may be the subject of a special verdict of forfeiture and thereafter shall be ordered forfeited to the United States, unless the transferee establishes in a hearing pursuant to subsection (l) that he is a bona fide purchaser for value of such property who at the time of purchase was reasonably without cause to believe that the property was subject to forfeiture under this section.

(d)

(1) Upon application of the United States, the court may enter a restraining order or injunction, require the execution of a satisfactory performance bond, or take any other action to preserve the availability of property described in

subsection (a) for forfeiture under this section—

(A) upon the filing of an indictment or information charging a violation of section 1962 of this chapter and alleging that the property with respect to which the order is sought would, in the event of conviction, be subject to forfeiture under this section; or

(B) prior to the filing of such an indictment or information, if, after notice to persons appearing to have an interest in the property and opportunity for a hearing, the court determines that—

(i) there is a substantial probability that the United States will prevail on the issue of forfeiture and that failure to enter the order will result in the property being destroyed, removed from the jurisdiction of the court, or otherwise made unavailable for forfeiture; and

(ii) the need to preserve the availability of the property through the entry of the requested order outweighs the hardship on any party against whom the order is to be entered:

Provided, however, That an order entered pursuant to subparagraph (B) shall be effective for not more than ninety days, unless extended by the court for good cause shown or unless an indictment or information described in subparagraph (A) has been filed.

(2) A temporary restraining order under this subsection may be entered upon application of the United States without notice or opportunity for a hearing when an information or indictment has not yet been filed with respect to the property, if the United States demonstrates that there is probable cause to believe that the property with respect to which the order is sought would, in the event of conviction, be subject to forfeiture under this section and that provision of notice will jeopardize the availability of the property for forfeiture. Such a temporary order shall expire not more than fourteen days after the date on which it is entered, unless extended for good cause shown or unless the party against whom it is entered consents to an extension for a longer period. A hearing requested concerning an order entered under this paragraph shall be held at the earliest possible time, and prior to the expiration of the temporary order.

(3) The court may receive and consider, at a hearing held pursuant to this subsection, evidence and information that would be inadmissible under the Federal Rules of Evidence.

(e) Upon conviction of a person under this section, the court shall enter a judgment of forfeiture of the property to the United States and shall also authorize the Attorney General to seize all property ordered forfeited upon such terms and conditions as the court shall deem proper. Following the entry of an order declaring the property forfeited, the court may, upon application of the United States, enter such appropriate restraining orders or injunctions, require the execution of satisfactory performance bonds, appoint receivers, conservators, appraisers, accountants, or trustees, or take any other action to protect the interest of the United States in the property ordered forfeited. Any income accruing to, or derived from, an enterprise or an interest in an enterprise which has been ordered forfeited under this section may be used to offset ordinary and necessary expenses to the enterprise which are required by law, or which are necessary to protect the interests of the United States or third parties.

(f) Following the seizure of property ordered forfeited under this section, the Attorney General shall direct the disposition of the property by sale or any other commercially feasible means, making due provision for the rights of any innocent persons. Any property right or interest not exercisable by, or transferable for value to, the United States shall expire and shall not revert to the defendant, nor shall the defendant or any person acting in concert with or on behalf of the defendant be eligible to purchase forfeited property at any sale held by the United States. Upon application of a person, other than the defendant or a person acting in concert with or on behalf of the defendant, the court may restrain or stay the sale or disposition of the property pending the conclusion of any appeal of the criminal case giving rise to the forfeiture, if the applicant demonstrates that proceeding with the sale or disposition of the property will result in irreparable injury, harm or loss to him. Notwithstanding 31 U.S.C. 3302(b), the proceeds of any sale or other disposition of property forfeited under this section and any moneys forfeited shall be used to pay all proper expenses for the forfeiture and the sale, including expenses of seizure, maintenance and custody of the property pending its disposition, advertising and court costs. The Attorney General shall deposit in the Treasury any amounts of such proceeds or moneys remaining after the payment of such expenses.

(g) With respect to property ordered forfeited under this section, the Attorney General is authorized to—

(1) grant petitions for mitigation or remission of forfeiture, restore forfeited property to victims of a violation of this chapter, or take any other action to protect the rights of innocent persons which is in the interest of justice and which is not inconsistent with the provisions of this chapter;

(2) compromise claims arising under this section;

(3) award compensation to persons providing information resulting in a forfeiture under this section;

(4) direct the disposition by the United States of all property ordered forfeited under this section by public sale or any other commercially feasible means, making due provision for the rights of innocent persons; and

(5) take appropriate measures necessary to safeguard and maintain property ordered forfeited under this section pending its disposition.

(h) The Attorney General may promulgate regulations with respect to—

(1) making reasonable efforts to provide notice to persons who may have an interest in property ordered forfeited under this section;

(2) granting petitions for remission or mitigation of forfeiture;

(3) the restitution of property to victims of an offense petitioning for remission or mitigation of forfeiture under this chapter;

(4) the disposition by the United States of forfeited property by public sale or

other commercially feasible means;

(5) the maintenance and safekeeping of any property forfeited under this section pending its disposition; and

(6) the compromise of claims arising under this chapter.

Pending the promulgation of such regulations, all provisions of law relating to the disposition of property, or the proceeds from the sale thereof, or the remission or mitigation of forfeitures for violation of the customs laws, and the compromise of claims and the award of compensation to informers in respect of such forfeitures shall apply to forfeitures incurred, or alleged to have been incurred, under the provisions of this section, insofar as applicable and not inconsistent with the provisions hereof. Such duties as are imposed upon the Customs Service or any person with respect to the disposition of property under the customs law shall be performed under this chapter by the Attorney General.

(i) Except as provided in subsection (l), no party claiming an interest in property subject to forfeiture under this section may—

(1) intervene in a trial or appeal of a criminal case involving the forfeiture of such property under this section; or

(2) commence an action at law or equity against the United States concerning the validity of his alleged interest in the property subsequent to the filing of an indictment or information alleging that the property is subject to forfeiture under this section.

(j) The district courts of the United States shall have jurisdiction to enter orders as provided in this section without regard to the location of any property which may be subject to forfeiture under this section or which has been ordered forfeited under this section.

(k) In order to facilitate the identification or location of property declared forfeited and to facilitate the disposition of petitions for remission or mitigation of forfeiture, after the entry of an order declaring property forfeited to the United States the court may, upon application of the United States, order that the testimony of any witness relating to the property forfeited be taken by deposition and that any designated book, paper, document, record, recording, or other material not privileged be produced at the same time and place, in the same manner as provided for the taking of depositions under Rule 15 of the Federal Rules of Criminal Procedure.

(l)

(1) Following the entry of an order of forfeiture under this section, the United States shall publish notice of the order and of its intent to dispose of the property in such manner as the Attorney General may direct. The Government may also, to the extent practicable, provide direct written notice to any person known to have alleged an interest in the property that is the subject of the order of forfeiture as a substitute for published notice as to those persons so notified.

(2) Any person, other than the defendant, asserting a legal interest in property which has been ordered forfeited to the United States pursuant to this section

may, within thirty days of the final publication of notice or his receipt of notice under paragraph (1), whichever is earlier, petition the court for a hearing to adjudicate the validity of his alleged interest in the property. The hearing shall be held before the court alone, without a jury.

(3) The petition shall be signed by the petitioner under penalty of perjury and shall set forth the nature and extent of the petitioner's right, title, or interest in the property, the time and circumstances of the petitioner's acquisition of the right, title, or interest in the property, any additional facts supporting the petitioner's claim, and the relief sought.

(4) The hearing on the petition shall, to the extent practicable and consistent with the interests of justice, be held within thirty days of the filing of the petition. The court may consolidate the hearing on the petition with a hearing on any other petition filed by a person other than the defendant under this subsection.

(5) At the hearing, the petitioner may testify and present evidence and witnesses on his own behalf, and cross-examine witnesses who appear at the hearing. The United States may present evidence and witnesses in rebuttal and in defense of its claim to the property and cross-examine witnesses who appear at the hearing. In addition to testimony and evidence presented at the hearing, the court shall consider the relevant portions of the record of the criminal case which resulted in the order of forfeiture.

(6) If, after the hearing, the court determines that the petitioner has established by a preponderance of the evidence that—

(A) the petitioner has a legal right, title, or interest in the property, and such right, title, or interest renders the order of forfeiture invalid in whole or in part because the right, title, or interest was vested in the petitioner rather than the defendant or was superior to any right, title, or interest of the defendant at the time of the commission of the acts which gave rise to the forfeiture of the property under this section; or

(B) the petitioner is a bona fide purchaser for value of the right, title, or interest in the property and was at the time of purchase reasonably without cause to believe that the property was subject to forfeiture under this section;

the court shall amend the order of forfeiture in accordance with its determination.

(7) Following the court's disposition of all petitions filed under this subsection, or if no such petitions are filed following the expiration of the period provided in paragraph (2) for the filing of such petitions, the United States shall have clear title to property that is the subject of the order of forfeiture and may warrant good title to any subsequent purchaser or transferee.

(m) If any of the property described in subsection (a), as a result of any act or omission of the defendant—

(1) cannot be located upon the exercise of due diligence;

(2) has been transferred or sold to, or deposited with, a third party;

(3) has been placed beyond the jurisdiction of the court;

(4) has been substantially diminished in value; or

(5) has been commingled with other property which cannot be divided without difficulty;

the court shall order the forfeiture of any other property of the defendant up to the value of any property described in paragraphs (1) through (5).

§ 1964. Civil remedies

(a) The district courts of the United States shall have jurisdiction to prevent and restrain violations of section 1962 of this chapter by issuing appropriate orders, including, but not limited to: ordering any person to divest himself of any interest, direct or indirect, in any enterprise; imposing reasonable restrictions on the future activities or investments of any person, including, but not limited to, prohibiting any person from engaging in the same type of endeavor as the enterprise engaged in, the activities of which affect interstate or foreign commerce; or ordering dissolution or reorganization of any enterprise, making due provision for the rights of innocent persons.

(b) The Attorney General may institute proceedings under this section. Pending final determination thereof, the court may at any time enter such restraining orders or prohibitions, or take such other actions, including the acceptance of satisfactory performance bonds, as it shall deem proper.

(c) Any person injured in his business or property by reason of a violation of section 1962 of this chapter may sue therefor in any appropriate United States district court and shall recover threefold the damages he sustains and the cost of the suit, including a reasonable attorney's fee, except that no person may rely upon any conduct that would have been actionable as fraud in the purchase or sale of securities to establish a violation of section 1962. The exception contained in the preceding sentence does not apply to an action against any person that is criminally convicted in connection with the fraud, in which case the statute of limitations shall start to run on the date on which the conviction becomes final.

(d) A final judgment or decree rendered in favor of the United States in any criminal proceeding brought by the United States under this chapter shall estop the defendant from denying the essential allegations of the criminal offense in any subsequent civil proceeding brought by the United States.

§ 1965. Venue and Process

(a) Any civil action or proceeding under this chapter against any person may be instituted in the district court of the United States for any district in which such person resides, is found, has an agent, or transacts his affairs.

(b) In any action under section 1964 of this chapter in any district court of the United States in which it is shown that the ends of justice require that other parties residing in any other district be brought before the court, the court may cause such parties to be summoned, and process for that purpose may be served in any judicial district of the United States by the marshal thereof.

(c) In any civil or criminal action or proceeding instituted by the United States under this chapter in the district court of the United States for any judicial district, subpenas issued by such court to compel the attendance of witnesses may be served in any other judicial district, except that in any civil action or proceeding no such subpena shall be issued for service upon any individual who resides in another district at a place more than one hundred miles from the place at which such court is held without approval given by a judge of such court upon a showing of good cause.

(d) All other process in any action or proceeding under this chapter may be served on any person in any judicial district in which such person resides, is found, has an agent, or transacts his affairs.

§ 1966. Expedition of Actions

In any civil action instituted under this chapter by the United States in any district court of the United States, the Attorney General may file with the clerk of such court a certificate stating that in his opinion the case is of general public importance. A copy of that certificate shall be furnished immediately by such clerk to the chief judge or in his absence to the presiding district judge of the district in which such action is pending. Upon receipt of such copy, such judge shall designate immediately a judge of that district to hear and determine action.

§ 1967. Evidence

In any proceeding ancillary to or in any civil action instituted by the United States under this chapter the proceedings may be open or closed to the public at the discretion of the court after consideration of the rights of affected persons.

§ 1968. Civil Investigation demand

(a) Whenever the Attorney General has reason to believe that any person or enterprise may be in possession, custody, or control of any documentary materials relevant to a racketeering investigation, he may, prior to the institution of a civil or criminal proceeding thereon, issue in writing, and cause to be served upon such person, a civil investigative demand requiring such person to produce such material for examination.

(b) Each such demand shall—

(1) state the nature of the conduct constituting the alleged racketeering violation which is under investigation and the provision of law applicable thereto;

(2) describe the class or classes of documentary material produced thereunder with such definiteness and certainty as to permit such material to be fairly identified;

(3) state that the demand is returnable forthwith or prescribe a return date which will provide a reasonable period of time within which the material so demanded may be assembled and made available for inspection and copying or reproduction; and

(4) identify the custodian to whom such material shall be made available.

(c) No such demand shall—

(1) contain any requirement which would be held to be unreasonable if contained in a subpena duces tecum issued by a court of the United States in aid of a grand jury investigation of such alleged racketeering violation; or

(2) require the production of any documentary evidence which would be privileged from disclosure if demanded by a subpena duces tecum issued by a court of the United States in aid of a grand jury investigation of such alleged racketeering violation.

(d) Service of any such demand or any petition filed under this section may be made upon a person by—

(1) delivering a duly executed copy thereof to any partner, executive officer, managing agent, or general agent thereof, or to any agent thereof authorized by appointment or by law to receive service of process on behalf of such person, or upon any individual person;

(2) delivering a duly executed copy thereof to the principal office or place of business of the person to be served; or

(3) depositing such copy in the United States mail, by registered or certified mail duly addressed to such person at its principal office or place of business.

(e) A verified return by the individual serving any such demand or petition setting forth the manner of such service shall be prima facie proof of such service. In the case of service by registered or certified mail, such return shall be accompanied by the return post office receipt of delivery of such demand.

(f)

(1) The Attorney General shall designate a racketeering investigator to serve as racketeer document custodian, and such additional racketeering investigators as he shall determine from time to time to be necessary to serve as deputies to such officer.

(2) Any person upon whom any demand issued under this section has been duly served shall make such material available for inspection and copying or reproduction to the custodian designated therein at the principal place of business of such person, or at such other place as such custodian and such person thereafter may agree and prescribe in writing or as the court may direct, pursuant to this section on the return date specified in such demand, or on such later date as such custodian may prescribe in writing. Such person may upon written agreement between such person and the custodian substitute for copies of all or any part of such material originals thereof.

(3) The custodian to whom any documentary material is so delivered shall take physical possession thereof, and shall be responsible for the use made thereof and for the return thereof pursuant to this chapter. The custodian may cause the preparation of such copies of such documentary material as may be required for official use under regulations which shall be promulgated by the Attorney General. While in the possession of the custodian, no material so produced shall be available for examination, without the consent of the person who produced

such material, by any individual other than the Attorney General. Under such reasonable terms and conditions as the Attorney General shall prescribe, documentary material while in the possession of the custodian shall be available for examination by the person who produced such material or any duly authorized representatives of such person.

(4) Whenever any attorney has been designated to appear on behalf of the United States before any court or grand jury in any case or proceeding involving any alleged violation of this chapter, the custodian may deliver to such attorney such documentary material in the possession of the custodian as such attorney determines to be required for use in the presentation of such case or proceeding on behalf of the United States. Upon the conclusion of any such case or proceeding, such attorney shall return to the custodian any documentary material so withdrawn which has not passed into the control of such court or grand jury through the introduction thereof into the record of such case or proceeding.

(5) Upon the completion of—

(i) the racketeering investigation for which any documentary material was produced under this chapter, and

(ii) any case or proceeding arising from such investigation,

the custodian shall return to the person who produced such material all such material other than copies thereof made by the Attorney General pursuant to this subsection which has not passed into the control of any court or grand jury through the introduction thereof into the record of such case or proceeding.

(6) When any documentary material has been produced by any person under this section for use in any racketeering investigation, and no such case or proceeding arising therefrom has been instituted within a reasonable time after completion of the examination and analysis of all evidence assembled in the course of such investigation, such person shall be entitled, upon written demand made upon the Attorney General, to the return of all documentary material other than copies thereof made pursuant to this subsection so produced by such person.

(7) In the event of the death, disability, or separation from service of the custodian of any documentary material produced under any demand issued under this section or the official relief of such custodian from responsibility for the custody and control of such material, the Attorney General shall promptly—

(i) designate another racketeering investigator to serve as custodian thereof, and

(ii) transmit notice in writing to the person who produced such material as to the identity and address of the successor so designated.

Any successor so designated shall have with regard to such materials all duties and responsibilities imposed by this section upon his predecessor in office with regard thereto, except that he shall not be held responsible for any default or dereliction which occurred before his designation as custodian.

(g) Whenever any person fails to comply with any civil investigative demand duly served upon him under this section or whenever satisfactory copying or reproduction of any such material cannot be done and such person refuses to surrender such material, the Attorney General may file, in the district court of the United States for any judicial district in which such person resides, is found, or transacts business, and serve upon such person a petition for an order of such court for the enforcement of this section, except that if such person transacts business in more than one such district such petition shall be filed in the district in which such person maintains his principal place of business, or in such other district in which such person transacts business as may be agreed upon by the parties to such petition.

(h) Within twenty days after the service of any such demand upon any person, or at any time before the return date specified in the demand, whichever period is shorter, such person may file, in the district court of the United States for the judicial district within which such person resides, is found, or transacts business, and serve upon such custodian a petition for an order of such court modifying or setting aside such demand. The time allowed for compliance with the demand in whole or in part as deemed proper and ordered by the court shall not run during the pendency of such petition in the court. Such petition shall specify each ground upon which the petitioner relies in seeking such relief, and may be based upon any failure of such demand to comply with the provisions of this section or upon any constitutional or other legal right or privilege of such person.

(i) At any time during which any custodian is in custody or control of any documentary material delivered by any person in compliance with any such demand, such person may file, in the district court of the United States for the judicial district within which the office of such custodian is situated, and serve upon such custodian a petition for an order of such court requiring the performance by such custodian of any duty imposed upon him by this section.

(j) Whenever any petition is filed in any district court of the United States under this section, such court shall have jurisdiction to hear and determine the matter so presented, and to enter such order or orders as may be required to carry into effect the provisions of this section.

§ 3553. Imposition of a sentence

(a) Factors to be considered in imposing a sentence.— The court shall impose a sentence sufficient, but not greater than necessary, to comply with the purposes set forth in paragraph (2) of this subsection. The court, in determining the particular sentence to be imposed, shall consider—

(1) the nature and circumstances of the offense and the history and characteristics of the defendant;

(2) the need for the sentence imposed—

(A) to reflect the seriousness of the offense, to promote respect for the law, and to provide just punishment for the offense;

(B) to afford adequate deterrence to criminal conduct;

(C) to protect the public from further crimes of the defendant; and

(D) to provide the defendant with needed educational or vocational training, medical care, or other correctional treatment in the most effective manner;

(3) the kinds of sentences available;

(4) the kinds of sentence and the sentencing range established for—

(A) the applicable category of offense committed by the applicable category of defendant as set forth in the guidelines—

(i) issued by the Sentencing Commission pursuant to section 994(a)(1) of title 28, United States Code, subject to any amendments made to such guidelines by act of Congress (regardless of whether such amendments have yet to be incorporated by the Sentencing Commission into amendments issued under section 994(p) of title 28); and

(ii) that, except as provided in section 3742(g), are in effect on the date the defendant is sentenced; or

(B) in the case of a violation of probation or supervised release, the applicable guidelines or policy statements issued by the Sentencing Commission pursuant to section 994(a)(3) of title 28, United States Code, taking into account any amendments made to such guidelines or policy statements by act of Congress (regardless of whether such amendments have yet to be incorporated by the Sentencing Commission into amendments issued under section 994(p) of title 28);

(5) any pertinent policy statement—

(A) issued by the Sentencing Commission pursuant to section 994(a)(2) of title 28, United States Code, subject to any amendments made to such policy statement by act of Congress (regardless of whether such amendments have yet to be incorporated by the Sentencing Commission into amendments issued under section 994(p) of title 28); and

(B) that, except as provided in section 3742(g), is in effect on the date the defendant is sentenced.

(6) the need to avoid unwarranted sentence disparities among defendants with similar records who have been found guilty of similar conduct; and

(7) the need to provide restitution to any victims of the offense.

(b) Application of guidelines in imposing a sentence.—

(1) In general.— Except as provided in paragraph (2), the court shall impose a sentence of the kind, and within the range, referred to in subsection (a)(4) unless the court finds that there exists an aggravating or mitigating circumstance of a kind, or to a degree, not adequately taken into consideration by the Sentencing Commission in formulating the guidelines that should result in a sentence different from that described. In determining whether a circumstance was adequately taken into consideration, the court shall consider only the sentencing guidelines, policy statements, and official commentary of the Sentencing Commission. In the absence of an applicable sentencing guideline, the court shall impose an appropriate sentence, having due regard for the purposes set forth in subsection (a)(2). In the absence of an applicable sentencing guideline in

the case of an offense other than a petty offense, the court shall also have due regard for the relationship of the sentence imposed to sentences prescribed by guidelines applicable to similar offenses and offenders, and to the applicable policy statements of the Sentencing Commission.

(2) Child crimes and sexual offenses.—

(A) Sentencing.— In sentencing a defendant convicted of an offense under section 1201 involving a minor victim, an offense under section 1591, or an offense under chapter 71, 109A, 110, or 117, the court shall impose a sentence of the kind, and within the range, referred to in subsection (a)(4) unless—

(i) the court finds that there exists an aggravating circumstance of a kind, or to a degree, not adequately taken into consideration by the Sentencing Commission in formulating the guidelines that should result in a sentence greater than that described;

(ii) the court finds that there exists a mitigating circumstance of a kind or to a degree, that—

(I) has been affirmatively and specifically identified as a permissible ground of downward departure in the sentencing guidelines or policy statements issued under section 994(a) of title 28, taking account of any amendments to such sentencing guidelines or policy statements by Congress;

(II) has not been taken into consideration by the Sentencing Commission in formulating the guidelines; and

(III) should result in a sentence different from that described; or

(iii) the court finds, on motion of the Government, that the defendant has provided substantial assistance in the investigation or prosecution of another person who has committed an offense and that this assistance established a mitigating circumstance of a kind, or to a degree, not adequately taken into consideration by the Sentencing Commission in formulating the guidelines that should result in a sentence lower than that described.

In determining whether a circumstance was adequately taken into consideration, the court shall consider only the sentencing guidelines, policy statements, and official commentary of the Sentencing Commission, together with any amendments thereto by act of Congress. In the absence of an applicable sentencing guideline, the court shall impose an appropriate sentence, having due regard for the purposes set forth in subsection (a)(2). In the absence of an applicable sentencing guideline in the case of an offense other than a petty offense, the court shall also have due regard for the relationship of the sentence imposed to sentences prescribed by guidelines applicable to similar offenses and offenders, and to the applicable policy statements of the Sentencing Commission, together with any amendments to such guidelines or policy statements by act of Congress.

(c) Statement of reasons for imposing a sentence.— The court, at the time of sentencing, shall state in open court the reasons for its imposition of the particular sentence, and, if the sentence—

(1) is of the kind, and within the range, described in subsection (a)(4) and that range exceeds 24 months, the reason for imposing a sentence at a particular point within the range; or

(2) is not of the kind, or is outside the range, described in subsection (a)(4), the specific reason for the imposition of a sentence different from that described, which reasons must also be stated with specificity in a statement of reasons form issued under section 994(w)(1)(B) of title 28, except to the extent that the court relies upon statements received in camera in accordance with Federal Rule of Criminal Procedure 32. In the event that the court relies upon statements received in camera in accordance with Federal Rule of Criminal Procedure 32 the court shall state that such statements were so received and that it relied upon the content of such statements.

If the court does not order restitution, or orders only partial restitution, the court shall include in the statement the reason therefor. The court shall provide a transcription or other appropriate public record of the court's statement of reasons, together with the order of judgment and commitment, to the Probation System and to the Sentencing Commission, and, if the sentence includes a term of imprisonment, to the Bureau of Prisons.

(d) Presentence procedure for an order of notice.— Prior to imposing an order of notice pursuant to section 3555, the court shall give notice to the defendant and the Government that it is considering imposing such an order. Upon motion of the defendant or the Government, or on its own motion, the court shall—

(1) permit the defendant and the Government to submit affidavits and written memoranda addressing matters relevant to the imposition of such an order;

(2) afford counsel an opportunity in open court to address orally the appropriateness of the imposition of such an order; and

(3) include in its statement of reasons pursuant to subsection (c) specific reasons underlying its determinations regarding the nature of such an order.

Upon motion of the defendant or the Government, or on its own motion, the court may in its discretion employ any additional procedures that it concludes will not unduly complicate or prolong the sentencing process.

(e) Limited authority to impose a sentence below a statutory minimum.— Upon motion of the Government, the court shall have the authority to impose a sentence below a level established by statute as a minimum sentence so as to reflect a defendant's substantial assistance in the investigation or prosecution of another person who has committed an offense. Such sentence shall be imposed in accordance with the guidelines and policy statements issued by the Sentencing Commission pursuant to section 994 of title 28, United States Code.

(f) Limitation on applicability of statutory minimums in certain cases.— Notwithstanding any other provision of law, in the case of an offense under section 401, 404, or 406 of the Controlled Substances Act (21 U.S.C. 841, 844, 846) or section 1010 or 1013 of the Controlled Substances Import and Export Act (21 U.S.C. 960, 963), the court shall impose a sentence pursuant to guidelines promulgated by the United States Sentencing Commission under section 994 of title 28 without regard to any statutory minimum sentence, if the court finds at sentencing, after the Government has been afforded the opportunity to make a recommendation, that—

(1) the defendant does not have more than 1 criminal history point, as determined under the sentencing guidelines;

(2) the defendant did not use violence or credible threats of violence or possess a firearm or other dangerous weapon (or induce another participant to do so) in connection with the offense;

(3) the offense did not result in death or serious bodily injury to any person;

(4) the defendant was not an organizer, leader, manager, or supervisor of others in the offense, as determined under the sentencing guidelines and was not engaged in a continuing criminal enterprise, as defined in section 408 of the Controlled Substances Act; and

(5) not later than the time of the sentencing hearing, the defendant has truthfully provided to the Government all information and evidence the defendant has concerning the offense or offenses that were part of the same course of conduct or of a common scheme or plan, but the fact that the defendant has no relevant or useful other information to provide or that the Government is already aware of the information shall not preclude a determination by the court that the defendant has complied with this requirement.

§ 3742. Review of a sentence

(a) Limited authority to impose a sentence below a statutory minimum.— Upon motion of the Government, the court shall have the authority to impose a sentence below a level established by statute as a minimum sentence so as to reflect a defendant's substantial assistance in the investigation or prosecution of another person who has committed an offense. Such sentence shall be imposed in accordance with the guidelines and policy statements issued by the Sentencing Commission pursuant to section 994 of title 28, United States Code.

(1) was imposed in violation of law;

(2) was imposed as a result of an incorrect application of the sentencing guidelines; or

(3) is greater than the sentence specified in the applicable guideline range to the extent that the sentence includes a greater fine or term of imprisonment, probation, or supervised release than the maximum established in the guideline range, or includes a more limiting condition of probation or supervised release under section 3563(b)(6)or (b)(11) than the maximum established in the guideline range; or

(4) was imposed for an offense for which there is no sentencing guideline and is plainly unreasonable.

(b) Appeal by the Government.— The Government may file a notice of appeal in the district court for review of an otherwise final sentence if the sentence—

(1) was imposed in violation of law;

(2) was imposed as a result of an incorrect application of the sentencing guidelines;

(3) is less than the sentence specified in the applicable guideline range to the extent that the sentence includes a lesser fine or term of imprisonment, probation, or supervised release than the minimum established in the guideline range, or includes a less limiting condition of probation or supervised release under section 3563(b)(6) or (b)(11) than the minimum established in the guideline range; or

(4) was imposed for an offense for which there is no sentencing guideline and is plainly unreasonable.

The Government may not further prosecute such appeal without the personal approval of the Attorney General, the Solicitor General, or a deputy solicitor general designated by the Solicitor General.

(c) Plea agreements.— In the case of a plea agreement that includes a specific sentence under rule 11(e)(1)(C) of the Federal Rules of Criminal Procedure—

(1) a defendant may not file a notice of appeal under paragraph (3) or (4) of subsection (a) unless the sentence imposed is greater than the sentence set forth in such agreement; and

(2) the Government may not file a notice of appeal under paragraph (3) or (4) of subsection (b) unless the sentence imposed is less than the sentence set forth in such agreement.

(d) Record on review.— If a notice of appeal is filed in the district court pursuant to subsection (a) or (b), the clerk shall certify to the court of appeals—

(1) that portion of the record in the case that is designated as pertinent by either of the parties;

(2) the presentence report; and

(3) the information submitted during the sentencing proceeding.

(e) Consideration.— Upon review of the record, the court of appeals shall determine whether the sentence—

(1) was imposed in violation of law;

(2) was imposed as a result of an incorrect application of the sentencing guidelines;

(3) is outside the applicable guideline range, and

(A) the district court failed to provide the written statement of reasons required by section 3553(c);

(B) the sentence departs from the applicable guideline range based on a factor that—

(i) does not advance the objectives set forth in section 3553(a)(2); or

(ii) is not authorized under section 3553(b); or

(iii) is not justified by the facts of the case; or

(C) the sentence departs to an unreasonable degree from the applicable guidelines range, having regard for the factors to be considered in imposing a sentence, as set forth in section 3553(a) of this title and the reasons for the imposition of the particular sentence, as stated by the district court pursuant to the provisions of section 3553(c); or

(4) was imposed for an offense for which there is no applicable sentencing guideline and is plainly unreasonable.

The court of appeals shall give due regard to the opportunity of the district court to judge the credibility of the witnesses, and shall accept the findings of fact of the district court unless they are clearly erroneous and, except with respect to determinations under subsection (3)(A) or (3)(B), shall give due deference to the district court's application of the guidelines to the facts. With respect to determinations under subsection (3)(A) or (3)(B), the court of appeals shall review de novo the district court's application of the guidelines to the facts.

(f) Decision and disposition.— If the court of appeals determines that—

(1) the sentence was imposed in violation of law or imposed as a result of an incorrect application of the sentencing guidelines, the court shall remand the case for further sentencing proceedings with such instructions as the court considers appropriate;

(2) the sentence is outside the applicable guideline range and the district court failed to provide the required statement of reasons in the order of judgment and commitment, or the departure is based on an impermissible factor, or is to an unreasonable degree, or the sentence was imposed for an offense for which there is no applicable sentencing guideline and is plainly unreasonable, it shall state specific reasons for its conclusions and—

(A) if it determines that the sentence is too high and the appeal has been filed under subsection (a), it shall set aside the sentence and remand the case for further sentencing proceedings with such instructions as the court considers appropriate, subject to subsection (g);

(B) if it determines that the sentence is too low and the appeal has been filed under subsection (b), it shall set aside the sentence and remand the case for further sentencing proceedings with such instructions as the court considers appropriate, subject to subsection (g);

(3) the sentence is not described in paragraph (1) or (2), it shall affirm the sentence.

(g) Sentencing upon remand.— A district court to which a case is remanded pursuant to subsection (f)(1) or (f)(2) shall resentence a defendant in accordance with section 3553 and with such instructions as may have been given by the court of appeals, except that—

(1) In determining the range referred to in subsection 3553(a)(4), the court

shall apply the guidelines issued by the Sentencing Commission pursuant to section 994(a)(1) of title 28, United States Code, and that were in effect on the date of the previous sentencing of the defendant prior to the appeal, together with any amendments thereto by any act of Congress that was in effect on such date; and

(2) The court shall not impose a sentence outside the applicable guidelines range except upon a ground that—

(A) was specifically and affirmatively included in the written statement of reasons required by section 3553(c) in connection with the previous sentencing of the defendant prior to the appeal; and

(B) was held by the court of appeals, in remanding the case, to be a permissible ground of departure.

(h) Application to a sentence by a magistrate judge.— An appeal of an otherwise final sentence imposed by a United States magistrate judge may be taken to a judge of the district court, and this section shall apply (except for the requirement of approval by the Attorney General or the Solicitor General in the case of a Government appeal) as though the appeal were to a court of appeals from a sentence imposed by a district court.

(i) Guideline not expressed as a range.— For the purpose of this section, the term "guideline range" includes a guideline range having the same upper and lower limits.

(j) Definitions.— For purposes of this section—

(1) a factor is a "permissible" ground of departure if it—

(A) advances the objectives set forth in section 3553(a)(2); and

(B) is authorized under section 3553(b); and

(C) is justified by the facts of the case; and

(2) a factor is an "impermissible" ground of departure if it is not a permissible factor within the meaning of subsection (j)(1).

§ 6001. Definitions

As used in this chapter—

(1) "agency of the United States" means any executive department as defined in section 101 of title 5, United States Code, a military department as defined in section 102 of title 5, United States Code, the Nuclear Regulatory Commission, the Board of Governors of the Federal Reserve System, the China Trade Act registrar appointed under 53 Stat. 1432 (15 U.S.C. sec. 143), the Commodity Futures Trading Commission, the Federal Communications Commission, the Federal Deposit Insurance Corporation, the Federal Maritime Commission, the Federal Power Commission, the Federal Trade Commission, the Surface Transportation Board, the National Labor Relations Board, the National Transportation Safety Board, the Railroad Retirement Board, an arbitration board established under 48 Stat. 1193 (45 U.S.C. sec. 157), the Securities and Exchange

Commission, or a board established under 49 Stat. 31 (15 U.S.C. sec. 715d);

(2) "other information" includes any book, paper, document, record, recording, or other material;

(3) "proceeding before an agency of the United States" means any proceeding before such an agency with respect to which it is authorized to issue subpenas and to take testimony or receive other information from witnesses under oath; and

(4) "court of the United States" means any of the following courts: the Supreme Court of the United States, a United States court of appeals, a United States district court established under chapter 5, title 28, United States Code, a United States bankruptcy court established under chapter 6, title 28, United States Code, the District of Columbia Court of Appeals, the Superior Court of the District of Columbia, the District Court of Guam, the District Court of the Virgin Islands, the United States Court of Federal Claims, the Tax Court of the United States, the Court of International Trade, and the Court of Appeals for the Armed Forces.

§ 6002. Immunity generally

Whenever a witness refuses, on the basis of his privilege against self-incrimination, to testify or provide other information in a proceeding before or ancillary to—

(1) a court or grand jury of the United States,

(2) an agency of the United States, or

(3) either House of Congress, a joint committee of the two Houses, or a committee or a subcommittee of either House,

and the person presiding over the proceeding communicates to the witness an order issued under this title, the witness may not refuse to comply with the order on the basis of his privilege against self-incrimination; but no testimony or other information compelled under the order (or any information directly or indirectly derived from such testimony or other information) may be used against the witness in any criminal case, except a prosecution for perjury, giving a false statement, or otherwise failing to comply with the order.

§ 6003. Court and grand jury proceedings

(a) In the case of any individual who has been or may be called to testify or provide other information at any proceeding before or ancillary to a court of the United States or a grand jury of the United States, the United States district court for the judicial district in which the proceeding is or may be held shall issue, in accordance with subsection (b) of this section, upon the request of the United States attorney for such district, an order requiring such individual to give testimony or provide other information which he refuses to give or provide on the basis of his privilege against self-incrimination, such order to become effective as provided in section 6002 of this title.

(b) A United States attorney may, with the approval of the Attorney General, the

Deputy Attorney General, the Associate Attorney General, or any designated Assistant Attorney General or Deputy Assistant Attorney General, request an order under subsection (a) of this section when in his judgment—

(1) the testimony or other information from such individual may be necessary to the public interest; and

(2) such individual has refused or is likely to refuse to testify or provide other information on the basis of his privilege against self-incrimination.

TITLE 21.   FOOD AND DRUGS

§ 846.   Attempt and Conspiracy

Any person who attempts or conspires to commit any offense defined in this subchapter shall be subject to the same penalties as those prescribed for the offense, the commission of which was the object of the attempt or conspiracy.

§ 848.   Continuing criminal enterprise

(a) Penalties; forfeitures

Any person who engages in a continuing criminal enterprise shall be sentenced to a term of imprisonment which may not be less than 20 years and which may be up to life imprisonment, to a fine not to exceed the greater of that authorized in accordance with the provisions of Title 18 or $2,000,000 if the defendant is an individual or $5,000,000 if the defendant is other than an individual, and to the forfeiture prescribed in section 853 of this title; except that if any person engages in such activity after one or more prior convictions of him under this section have become final, he shall be sentenced to a term of imprisonment which may not be less than 30 years and which may be up to life imprisonment, to a fine not to exceed the greater of twice the amount authorized in accordance with the provisions of Title 18 or $4,000,000 if the defendant is an individual or $10,000,000 if the defendant is other than an individual, and to the forfeiture prescribed in section 853 of this title.

(b) Life imprisonment for engaging in continuing criminal enterprise

Any person who engages in a continuing criminal enterprise shall be imprisoned for life and fined in accordance with subsection (a) of this section, if—

(1) such person is the principal administrator, organizer, or leader of the enterprise or is one of several such principal administrators, organizers, or leaders; and

(2)

(A) the violation referred to in subsection (c)(1) of this section involved at least 300 times the quantity of a substance described in subsection 841(b)(1)(B) of this title, or

(B) the enterprise, or any other enterprise in which the defendant was the principal or one of several principal administrators, organizers, or leaders, received $10 million dollars in gross receipts during any twelve-month period of its existence for the manufacture, importation, or distribution of a substance described in section 841(b)(1)(B) of this title.

(c) "Continuing criminal enterprise" defined

For purposes of subsection (a) of this section, a person is engaged in a continuing criminal enterprise if—

(1) he violates any provision of this subchapter or subchapter II of this chapter the punishment for which is a felony, and

(2) such violation is a part of a continuing series of violations of this subchapter or subchapter II of this chapter—

(A) which are undertaken by such person in concert with five or more other persons with respect to whom such person occupies a position of organizer, a supervisory position, or any other position of management, and

(B) from which such person obtains substantial income or resources.

(d) Suspension of sentence and probation prohibited

In the case of any sentence imposed under this section, imposition or execution of such sentence shall not be suspended, probation shall not be granted, and the Act of July 15, 1932 (D.C.Code, secs. 24-203–24-207), shall not apply.

(e) Death penalty

(1) In addition to the other penalties set forth in this section—

(A) any person engaging in or working in furtherance of a continuing criminal enterprise, or any person engaging in an offense punishable under section 841(b)(1)(A) of this title or section 960(b)(1) of this title who intentionally kills or counsels, commands, induces, procures, or causes the intentional killing of an individual and such killing results, shall be sentenced to any term of imprisonment, which shall not be less than 20 years, and which may be up to life imprisonment, or may be sentenced to death; and

(B) any person, during the commission of, in furtherance of, or while attempting to avoid apprehension, prosecution or service of a prison sentence for, a felony violation of this subchapter or subchapter II of this chapter who intentionally kills or counsels, commands, induces, procures, or causes the intentional killing of any Federal, State, or local law enforcement officer engaged in, or on account of, the performance of such officer's official duties and such killing results, shall be sentenced to any term of imprisonment, which shall not be less than 20 years, and which may be up to life imprisonment, or may be sentenced to death.

(2) As used in paragraph (1)(B), the term "law enforcement officer" means a public servant authorized by law or by a Government agency or Congress to conduct or engage in the prevention, investigation, prosecution or adjudication of an offense, and includes those engaged in corrections, probation, or parole functions.

(g) to (p) Repealed. Pub.L. 109-177, Title II, § 221(2), Mar. 9, 2006, 120 Stat. 231

(q) Repealed. Pub.L. 109-177, Title II, §§ 221(4), 222(c), Mar. 9, 2006, 120 Stat. 231, 232

(r) Repealed. Pub.L. 109-177, Title II, § 221(3), Mar. 9, 2006, 120 Stat. 231

(s) Special provision for methamphetamine

For the purposes of subsection (b), in the case of continuing criminal enterprise involving methamphetamine or its salts, isomers, or salts of isomers, paragraph (2)(A) shall be applied by substituting "200" for "300", and paragraph (2)(B) shall be applied by substituting "$5,000,000" for "$10 million dollars".

§ 853. Criminal forfeitures

(a) Property subject to criminal forfeiture

Any person convicted of a violation of this subchapter or subchapter II of this chapter punishable by imprisonment for more than one year shall forfeit to the United States, irrespective of any provision of State law—

(1) any property constituting, or derived from, any proceeds the person obtained, directly or indirectly, as the result of such violation;

(2) any of the person's property used, or intended to be used, in any manner or part, to commit, or to facilitate the commission of, such violation; and

(3) in the case of a person convicted of engaging in a continuing criminal enterprise in violation of section 848 of this title, the person shall forfeit, in addition to any property described in paragraph (1) or (2), any of his interest in, claims against, and property or contractual rights affording a source of control over, the continuing criminal enterprise.

The court, in imposing sentence on such person, shall order, in addition to any other sentence imposed pursuant to this subchapter or subchapter II of this chapter, that the person forfeit to the United States all property described in this subsection. In lieu of a fine otherwise authorized by this part, a defendant who derives profits or other proceeds from an offense may be fined not more than twice the gross profits or other proceeds.

(b) Meaning of term "property"

Property subject to criminal forfeiture under this section includes—

(1) real property, including things growing on, affixed to, and found in land; and

(2) tangible and intangible personal property, including rights, privileges, interests, claims, and securities.

(c) Third party transfers

All right, title, and interest in property described in subsection (a) of this section vests in the United States upon the commission of the act giving rise to forfeiture under this section. Any such property that is subsequently transferred to a person other than the defendant may be the subject of a special verdict of forfeiture and thereafter shall be ordered forfeited to the United States, unless the transferee establishes in a hearing pursuant to subsection (n) of this section that he is a bona fide purchaser for value of such property who at the time of purchase was reasonably without cause to believe that the property was subject to forfeiture under this section.

(d) Rebuttable presumption

There is a rebuttable presumption at trial that any property of a person convicted of a felony under this subchapter or subchapter II of this chapter is subject to forfeiture under this section if the United States establishes by a preponderance of the evidence that—

(1) such property was acquired by such person during the period of the violation of this subchapter or subchapter II of this chapter or within a reasonable time after such period; and

(2) there was no likely source for such property other than the violation of this subchapter or subchapter II of this chapter.

(e) Protective orders

(1) Upon application of the United States, the court may enter a restraining order or injunction, require the execution of a satisfactory performance bond, or take any other action to preserve the availability of property described in subsection (a) of this section for forfeiture under this section—

(A) upon the filing of an indictment or information charging a violation of this subchapter or subchapter II of this chapter for which criminal forfeiture may be ordered under this section and alleging that the property with respect to which the order is sought would, in the event of conviction, be subject to forfeiture under this section; or

(B) prior to the filing of such an indictment or information, if, after notice to persons appearing to have an interest in the property and opportunity for a hearing, the court determines that—

(i) there is a substantial probability that the United States will prevail on the issue of forfeiture and that failure to enter the order will result in the property being destroyed, removed from the jurisdiction of the court, or otherwise made unavailable for forfeiture; and

(ii) the need to preserve the availability of the property through the entry of the requested order outweighs the hardship on any party against whom the order is to be entered:

Provided, however, That an order entered pursuant to subparagraph (B) shall be effective for not more than ninety days, unless extended by the court for good cause shown or unless an indictment or information described in subparagraph (A) has been filed.

(2) A temporary restraining order under this subsection may be entered upon application of the United States without notice or opportunity for a hearing when an information or indictment has not yet been filed with respect to the property, if the United States demonstrates that there is probable cause to believe that the property with respect to which the order is sought would, in the event of conviction, be subject to forfeiture under this section and that provision of notice will jeopardize the availability of the property for forfeiture. Such a temporary order shall expire not more than fourteen days after the date on which it is entered, unless extended for good cause shown or unless the party against whom

it is entered consents to an extension for a longer period. A hearing requested concerning an order entered under this paragraph shall be held at the earliest possible time and prior to the expiration of the temporary order.

(3) The court may receive and consider, at a hearing held pursuant to this subsection, evidence and information that would be inadmissible under the Federal Rules of Evidence.

(4) Order to repatriate and deposit

(A) In general

Pursuant to its authority to enter a pretrial restraining order under this section, the court may order a defendant to repatriate any property that may be seized and forfeited, and to deposit that property pending trial in the registry of the court, or with the United States Marshals Service or the Secretary of the Treasury, in an interest-bearing account, if appropriate.

(B) Failure to comply

Failure to comply with an order under this subsection, or an order to repatriate property under subsection (p) of this section, shall be punishable as a civil or criminal contempt of court, and may also result in an enhancement of the sentence of the defendant under the obstruction of justice provision of the Federal Sentencing Guidelines.

(f) Warrant of seizure

The Government may request the issuance of a warrant authorizing the seizure of property subject to forfeiture under this section in the same manner as provided for a search warrant. If the court determines that there is probable cause to believe that the property to be seized would, in the event of conviction, be subject to forfeiture and that an order under subsection (e) of this section may not be sufficient to assure the availability of the property for forfeiture, the court shall issue a warrant authorizing the seizure of such property.

(g) Execution

Upon entry of an order of forfeiture under this section, the court shall authorize the Attorney General to seize all property ordered forfeited upon such terms and conditions as the court shall deem proper. Following entry of an order declaring the property forfeited, the court may, upon application of the United States, enter such appropriate restraining orders or injunctions, require the execution of satisfactory performance bonds, appoint receivers, conservators, appraisers, accountants, or trustees, or take any other action to protect the interest of the United States in the property ordered forfeited. Any income accruing to or derived from property ordered forfeited under this section may be used to offset ordinary and necessary expenses to the property which are required by law, or which are necessary to protect the interests of the United States or third parties.

(h) Disposition of property

Following the seizure of property ordered forfeited under this section, the Attorney General shall direct the disposition of the property by sale or any other commercially feasible means, making due provision for the rights of any innocent persons. Any property right or interest not exercisable by, or transferable for value to, the United States shall expire and shall not revert to the defendant, nor shall the defendant or any person acting in concert with him or on his behalf be eligible to purchase forfeited property at any sale held by the United States. Upon application of a person, other than the defendant or a person acting in concert with him or on his behalf, the court may restrain or stay the sale or disposition of the property pending the conclusion of any appeal of the criminal case giving rise to the forfeiture, if the applicant demonstrates that proceeding with the sale or disposition of the property will result in irreparable injury, harm, or loss to him.

(i) Authority of the Attorney General

With respect to property ordered forfeited under this section, the Attorney General is authorized to—

(1) grant petitions for mitigation or remission of forfeiture, restore forfeited property to victims of a violation of this subchapter, or take any other action to protect the rights of innocent persons which is in the interest of justice and which is not inconsistent with the provisions of this section;

(2) compromise claims arising under this section;

(3) award compensation to persons providing information resulting in a forfeiture under this section;

(4) direct the disposition by the United States, in accordance with the provisions of section 881(e) of this title, of all property ordered forfeited under this section by public sale or any other commercially feasible means, making due provision for the rights of innocent persons; and

(5) take appropriate measures necessary to safeguard and maintain property ordered forfeited under this section pending its disposition.

(j) Applicability of civil forfeiture provisions

Except to the extent that they are inconsistent with the provisions of this section, the provisions of section 881(d) of this title shall apply to a criminal forfeiture under this section.

(k) Bar on intervention

Except as provided in subsection (n) of this section, no party claiming an interest in property subject to forfeiture under this section may—

(1) intervene in a trial or appeal of a criminal case involving the forfeiture of such property under this section; or

(2) commence an action at law or equity against the United States concerning the validity of his alleged interest in the property subsequent to the filing of an indictment or information alleging that the property is subject to forfeiture under this section.

(l) Jurisdiction to enter orders

The district courts of the United States shall have jurisdiction to enter orders as provided in this section without regard to the location of any property which may be subject to forfeiture under this section or which has been ordered forfeited under this section.

(m) Depositions

In order to facilitate the identification and location of property declared forfeited and to facilitate the disposition of petitions for remission or mitigation of forfeiture, after the entry of an order declaring property forfeited to the United States, the court may, upon application of the United States, order that the testimony of any witness relating to the property forfeited be taken by deposition and that any designated book, paper, document, record, recording, or other material not privileged be produced at the same time and place, in the same manner as provided for the taking of depositions under Rule 15 of the Federal Rules of Criminal Procedure.

(n) Third party interests

(1) Following the entry of an order of forfeiture under this section, the United States shall publish notice of the order and of its intent to dispose of the property in such manner as the Attorney General may direct. The Government may also, to the extent practicable, provide direct written notice to any person known to have alleged an interest in the property that is the subject of the order of forfeiture as a substitute for published notice as to those persons so notified.

(2) Any person, other than the defendant, asserting a legal interest in property which has been ordered forfeited to the United States pursuant to this section may, within thirty days of the final publication of notice or his receipt of notice under paragraph (1), whichever is earlier, petition the court for a hearing to adjudicate the validity of his alleged interest in the property. The hearing shall be held before the court alone, without a jury.

(3) The petition shall be signed by the petitioner under penalty of perjury and shall set forth the nature and extent of the petitioner's right, title, or interest in the property, the time and circumstances of the petitioner's acquisition of the right, title, or interest in the property, any additional facts supporting the petitioner's claim, and the relief sought.

(4) The hearing on the petition shall, to the extent practicable and consistent with the interests of justice, be held within thirty days of the filing of the petition. The court may consolidate the hearing on the petition with a hearing on any other petition filed by a person other than the defendant under this subsection.

(5) At the hearing, the petitioner may testify and present evidence and witnesses on his own behalf, and cross-examine witnesses who appear at the hearing. The United States may present evidence and witnesses in rebuttal and in defense of its claim to the property and cross-examine witnesses who appear at the hearing. In addition to testimony and evidence presented at the hearing, the court shall consider the relevant portions of the record of the criminal case which resulted in the order of forfeiture.

(6) If, after the hearing, the court determines that the petitioner has established by a preponderance of the evidence that—

(A) the petitioner has a legal right, title, or interest in the property, and such right, title, or interest renders the order of forfeiture invalid in whole or in part because the right, title, or interest was vested in the petitioner rather than the defendant or was superior to any right, title, or interest of the defendant at the time of the commission of the acts which gave rise to the forfeiture of the property under this section; or

(B) the petitioner is a bona fide purchaser for value of the right, title, or interest in the property and was at the time of purchase reasonably without cause to believe that the property was subject to forfeiture under this section;

the court shall amend the order of forfeiture in accordance with its determination.

(7) Following the court's disposition of all petitions filed under this subsection, or if no such petitions are filed following the expiration of the period provided in paragraph (2) for the filing of such petitions, the United States shall have clear title to property that is the subject of the order of forfeiture and may warrant good title to any subsequent purchaser or transferee.

(o) Construction

The provisions of this section shall be liberally construed to effectuate its remedial purposes.

(p) Forfeiture of substitute property

(1) In general

Paragraph (2) of this subsection shall apply, if any property described in subsection (a), as a result of any act or omission of the defendant—

(A) cannot be located upon the exercise of due diligence;

(B) has been transferred or sold to, or deposited with, a third party;

(C) has been placed beyond the jurisdiction of the court;

(D) has been substantially diminished in value; or

(E) has been commingled with other property which cannot be divided without difficulty.

(2) Substitute property

In any case described in any of subparagraphs (A) through (E) of paragraph (1), the court shall order the forfeiture of any other property of the defendant, up to the value of any property described in subparagraphs (A) through (E) of paragraph (1), as applicable.

(3) Return of property to jurisdiction

In the case of property described in paragraph (1)(C), the court may, in addition to any other action authorized by this subsection, order the defendant to return the property to the jurisdiction of the court so that the property may be seized and forfeited.

(q) Restitution for cleanup of clandestine laboratory sites

The court, when sentencing a defendant convicted of an offense under this subchapter or subchapter II of this chapter involving the manufacture, the possession, or the possession with intent to distribute, of amphetamine or methamphetamine, shall—

(1) order restitution as provided in sections 3612 and 3664 of Title 18;

(2) order the defendant to reimburse the United States, the State or local government concerned, or both the United States and the State or local government concerned for the costs incurred by the United States or the State or local government concerned, as the case may be, for the cleanup associated with the manufacture of amphetamine or methamphetamine by the defendant, or on premises or in property that the defendant owns, resides, or does business in; and

(3) order restitution to any person injured as a result of the offense as provided in section 3663A of Title 18.

§ 881.   Forfeitures

(a) Subject property

The following shall be subject to forfeiture to the United States and no property right shall exist in them:

(1) All controlled substances which have been manufactured, distributed, dispensed, or acquired in violation of this subchapter.

(2) All raw materials, products, and equipment of any kind which are used, or intended for use, in manufacturing, compounding, processing, delivering, importing, or exporting any controlled substance or listed chemical in violation of this subchapter.

(3) All property which is used, or intended for use, as a container for property described in paragraph (1), (2), or (9).

(4) All conveyances, including aircraft, vehicles, or vessels, which are used, or are intended for use, to transport, or in any manner to facilitate the transportation, sale, receipt, possession, or concealment of property described in paragraph (1), (2), or (9).

(5) All books, records, and research, including formulas, microfilm, tapes, and data which are used, or intended for use, in violation of this subchapter.

(6) All moneys, negotiable instruments, securities, or other things of value furnished or intended to be furnished by any person in exchange for a controlled substance or listed chemical in violation of this subchapter, all proceeds traceable to such an exchange, and all moneys, negotiable instruments, and securities used or intended to be used to facilitate any violation of this subchapter.

(7) All real property, including any right, title, and interest (including any leasehold interest) in the whole of any lot or tract of land and any appurtenances or improvements, which is used, or intended to be used, in any manner or part, to commit, or to facilitate the commission of, a violation of this subchapter punishable by more than one year's imprisonment.

(8) All controlled substances which have been possessed in violation of this subchapter.

(9) All listed chemicals, all drug manufacturing equipment, all tableting machines, all encapsulating machines, and all gelatin capsules, which have been imported, exported, manufactured, possessed, distributed, dispensed, acquired, or intended to be distributed, dispensed, acquired, imported, or exported, in violation of this subchapter or subchapter II of this chapter.

(10) Any drug paraphernalia (as defined in section 863 of this title).

(11) Any firearm (as defined in section 921 of Title 18) used or intended to be used to facilitate the transportation, sale, receipt, possession, or concealment of property described in paragraph (1) or (2) and any proceeds traceable to such property.

(b) Seizure procedures

Any property subject to forfeiture to the United States under this section may be seized by the Attorney General in the manner set forth in section 981(b) of Title 18.

(c) Custody of Attorney General

Property taken or detained under this section shall not be repleviable, but shall be deemed to be in the custody of the Attorney General, subject only to the orders and decrees of the court or the official having jurisdiction thereof. Whenever property is seized under any of the provisions of this subchapter, the Attorney General may—

(1) place the property under seal;

(2) remove the property to a place designated by him; or

(3) require that the General Services Administration take custody of the property and remove it, if practicable, to an appropriate location for disposition in accordance with law.

(d) Other laws and proceedings applicable

The provisions of law relating to the seizure, summary and judicial forfeiture, and condemnation of property for violation of the customs laws; the disposition of such property or the proceeds from the sale thereof; the remission or mitigation of such forfeitures; and the compromise of claims shall apply to seizures and forfeitures incurred, or alleged to have been incurred, under any of the provisions of this subchapter, insofar as applicable and not inconsistent with the provisions hereof; except that such duties as are imposed upon the customs officer or any other person with respect to the seizure and forfeiture of property under the customs laws shall be performed with respect to seizures and forfeitures of property under this subchapter by such officers, agents, or other persons as may be authorized or designated for that purpose by the Attorney General, except to the extent that such duties arise from seizures and forfeitures effected by any customs officer.

(e) Disposition of forfeited property

(1) Whenever property is civilly or criminally forfeited under this subchapter the Attorney General may—

(A) retain the property for official use or, in the manner provided with respect to transfers under section 1616a of Title 19, transfer the property to any Federal agency or to any State or local law enforcement agency which participated directly in the seizure or forfeiture of the property;

(B) except as provided in paragraph (4), sell, by public sale or any other commercially feasible means, any forfeited property which is not required to be destroyed by law and which is not harmful to the public;

(C) require that the General Services Administration take custody of the property and dispose of it in accordance with law;

(D) forward it to the Bureau of Narcotics and Dangerous Drugs for disposition (including delivery for medical or scientific use to any Federal or State agency under regulations of the Attorney General); or

(E) transfer the forfeited personal property or the proceeds of the sale of any forfeited personal or real property to any foreign country which participated directly or indirectly in the seizure or forfeiture of the property, if such a transfer—

(i) has been agreed to by the Secretary of State;

(ii) is authorized in an international agreement between the United States and the foreign country; and

(iii) is made to a country which, if applicable, has been certified under section 2291j(b) of Title 22.

(2)

(A) The proceeds from any sale under subparagraph (B) of paragraph (1) and any moneys forfeited under this subchapter shall be used to pay—

(i) all property expenses of the proceedings for forfeiture and sale including expenses of seizure, maintenance of custody, advertising, and court costs; and

(ii) awards of up to $100,000 to any individual who provides original information which leads to the arrest and conviction of a person who kills or kidnaps a Federal drug law enforcement agent.

Any award paid for information concerning the killing or kidnapping of a Federal drug law enforcement agent, as provided in clause (ii), shall be paid at the discretion of the Attorney General.

(B) The Attorney General shall forward to the Treasurer of the United States for deposit in accordance with section 524(c) of Title 28, any amounts of such moneys and proceeds remaining after payment of the expenses provided in subparagraph (A), except that, with respect to forfeitures conducted by the Postal Service, the Postal Service shall deposit in the Postal Service Fund, under section 2003(b)(7) of Title 39, such moneys and proceeds.

(3) The Attorney General shall assure that any property transferred to a State or local law enforcement agency under paragraph (1)(A)—

(A) has a value that bears a reasonable relationship to the degree of direct participation of the State or local agency in the law enforcement effort resulting in the forfeiture, taking into account the total value of all property forfeited and the total law enforcement effort with respect to the violation of law on which the forfeiture is based; and

(B) will serve to encourage further cooperation between the recipient State or local agency and Federal law enforcement agencies.

(4)

(A) With respect to real property described in subparagraph (B), if the chief executive officer of the State involved submits to the Attorney General a request for purposes of such subparagraph, the authority established in such subparagraph is in lieu of the authority established in paragraph (1)(B).

(B) In the case of property described in paragraph (1)(B) that is civilly or criminally forfeited under this subchapter, if the property is real property that is appropriate for use as a public area reserved for recreational or historic purposes or for the preservation of natural conditions, the Attorney General, upon the request of the chief executive officer of the State in which the property is located, may transfer title to the property to the State, either without charge or for a nominal charge, through a legal instrument providing that—

(i) such use will be the principal use of the property; and

(ii) title to the property reverts to the United States in the event that the property is used otherwise.

(f) Forfeiture and destruction of schedule I and II substances

(1) All controlled substances in schedule I or II that are possessed, transferred, sold, or offered for sale in violation of the provisions of this subchapter; all dangerous, toxic, or hazardous raw materials or products subject to forfeiture under subsection (a)(2) of this section; and any equipment or container subject to forfeiture under subsection (a)(2) or (3) of this section which cannot be separated safely from such raw materials or products shall be deemed contraband and seized and summarily forfeited to the United States. Similarly, all substances in schedule I or II, which are seized or come into the possession of the United States, the owners of which are unknown, shall be deemed contraband and summarily forfeited to the United States.

(2) The Attorney General may direct the destruction of all controlled substances in schedule I or II seized for violation of this subchapter; all dangerous, toxic, or hazardous raw materials or products subject to forfeiture under subsection (a)(2) of this section; and any equipment or container subject to forfeiture under subsection (a)(2) or (3) of this section which cannot be separated safely from such raw materials or products under such circumstances as the Attorney General may deem necessary.

(g) Plants

(1) All species of plants from which controlled substances in schedules I and II

may be derived which have been planted or cultivated in violation of this subchapter, or of which the owners or cultivators are unknown, or which are wild growths, may be seized and summarily forfeited to the United States.

(2) The failure, upon demand by the Attorney General or his duly authorized agent, of the person in occupancy or in control of land or premises upon which such species of plants are growing or being stored, to produce an appropriate registration, or proof that he is the holder thereof, shall constitute authority for the seizure and forfeiture.

(3) The Attorney General, or his duly authorized agent, shall have authority to enter upon any lands, or into any dwelling pursuant to a search warrant, to cut, harvest, carry off, or destroy such plants.

(h) Vesting of title in United States

All right, title, and interest in property described in subsection (a) of this section shall vest in the United States upon commission of the act giving rise to forfeiture under this section.

(i) Stay of civil forfeiture proceedings

The provisions of section 981(g) of Title 18 regarding the stay of a civil forfeiture proceeding shall apply to forfeitures under this section.

(j) Venue

In addition to the venue provided for in section 1395 of Title 28 or any other provision of law, in the case of property of a defendant charged with a violation that is the basis for forfeiture of the property under this section, a proceeding for forfeiture under this section may be brought in the judicial district in which the defendant owning such property is found or in the judicial district in which the criminal prosecution is brought.

(l) Agreement between Attorney General and Postal Service for performance of functions

The functions of the Attorney General under this section shall be carried out by the Postal Service pursuant to such agreement as may be entered into between the Attorney General and the Postal Service.

TITLE 26.   INTERNAL REVENUE CODE

§ 1001.   Determination of amount of and recognition of gain or loss

(a) Computation of gain or loss.— The gain from the sale or other disposition of property shall be the excess of the amount realized therefrom over the adjusted basis provided in section 1011 for determining gain, and the loss shall be the excess of the adjusted basis provided in such section for determining loss over the amount realized.

(b) Amount realized.— The amount realized from the sale or other disposition of property shall be the sum of any money received plus the fair market value of the property (other than money) received. In determining the amount realized—

(1) there shall not be taken into account any amount received as reimburse-

ment for real property taxes which are treated under section 164(d) as imposed on the purchaser, and

(2) there shall be taken into account amounts representing real property taxes which are treated under section 164(d) as imposed on the taxpayer if such taxes are to be paid by the purchaser.

(c) Recognition of gain or loss.— Except as otherwise provided in this subtitle, the entire amount of the gain or loss, determined under this section, on the sale or exchange of property shall be recognized.

(d) Installment sales.— Nothing in this section shall be construed to prevent (in the case of property sold under contract providing for payment in installments) the taxation of that portion of any installment payment representing gain or profit in the year in which such payment is received.

(e) Certain term interests.—

(1) In general.— In determining gain or loss from the sale or other disposition of a term interest in property, that portion of the adjusted basis of such interest which is determined pursuant to section 1014, 1015, or 1041 (to the extent that such adjusted basis is a portion of the entire adjusted basis of the property) shall be disregarded.

(2) Term interest in property defined.— For purposes of paragraph (1), the term "term interest in property" means—

(A) a life interest in property,

(B) an interest in property for a term of years, or

(C) an income interest in a trust.

(3) Exception.— Paragraph (1) shall not apply to a sale or other disposition which is a part of a transaction in which the entire interest in property is transferred to any person or persons.

§ 6050I. Returns relating to cash received in trade or business, etc.

(a) Cash receipts of more than $10,000.— Any person—

(1) who is engaged in a trade or business, and

(2) who, in the course of such trade or business, receives more than $10,000 in cash in 1 transaction (or 2 or more related transactions),

shall make the return described in subsection (b) with respect to such transaction (or related transactions) at such time as the Secretary may by regulations prescribe.

(b) Form and manner of returns.— A return is described in this subsection if such return—

(1) is in such form as the Secretary may prescribe,

(2) contains—

(A) the name, address, and TIN of the person from whom the cash was received,

 (B) the amount of cash received,

 (C) the date and nature of the transaction, and

 (D) such other information as the Secretary may prescribe.

(c) Exceptions.—

 (1) Cash received by financial institutions.— Subsection (a) shall not apply to—

 (A) cash received in a transaction reported under title 31, United States Code, if the Secretary determines that reporting under this section would duplicate the reporting to the Treasury under title 31, United States Code, or

 (B) cash received by any financial institution (as defined in subparagraph (A), (B), (C), (D), (E), (F), (G), (J), (K), (R), and (S) of section 5312(a)(2) of title 31, United States Code).

 (2) Transactions occurring outside the United States.— Except to the extent provided in regulations prescribed by the Secretary, subsection (a) shall not apply to any transaction if the entire transaction occurs outside the United States.

(d) Cash includes foreign currency and certain monetary instruments.— For purposes of this section, the term "cash" includes—

 (1) foreign currency, and

 (2) to the extent provided in regulations prescribed by the Secretary, any monetary instrument (whether or not in bearer form) with a face amount of not more than $10,000.

Paragraph (2) shall not apply to any check drawn on the account of the writer in a financial institution referred to in subsection (c)(1)(B).

(e) Statements to be furnished to persons with respect to whom information is required.— Every person required to make a return under subsection (a) shall furnish to each person whose name is required to be set forth in such return a written statement showing—

 (1) the name, address, and phone number of the information contact of the person required to make such return, and

 (2) the aggregate amount of cash described in subsection (a) received by the person required to make such return.

The written statement required under the preceding sentence shall be furnished to the person on or before January 31 of the year following the calendar year for which the return under subsection (a) was required to be made.

(f) Structuring transactions to evade reporting requirements prohibited.—

 (1) In general.— No person shall for the purpose of evading the return requirements of this section—

 (A) cause or attempt to cause a trade or business to fail to file a return required under this section,

(B) cause or attempt to cause a trade or business to file a return required under this section that contains a material omission or misstatement of fact, or

(C) structure or assist in structuring, or attempt to structure or assist in structuring, any transaction with one or more trades or businesses.

(2) Penalties.— A person violating paragraph (1) of this subsection shall be subject to the same civil and criminal sanctions applicable to a person which fails to file or completes a false or incorrect return under this section.

(g) Cash received by criminal court clerks.—

(1) In general.— Every clerk of a Federal or State criminal court who receives more than $10,000 in cash as bail for any individual charged with a specified criminal offense shall make a return described in paragraph (2) (at such time as the Secretary may by regulations prescribe) with respect to the receipt of such bail.

(2) Return.— A return is described in this paragraph if such return—

(A) is in such form as the Secretary may prescribe, and

(B) contains—

(i) the name, address, and TIN of—

(I) the individual charged with the specified criminal offense, and

(II) each person posting the bail (other than a person licensed as a bail bondsman),

(ii) the amount of cash received,

(iii) the date the cash was received, and

(iv) such other information as the Secretary may prescribe.

(3) Specified criminal offense.— For purposes of this subsection, the term "specified criminal offense" means—

(A) any Federal criminal offense involving a controlled substance,

(B) racketeering (as defined in section 1951, 1952, or 1955 of title 18, United States Code),

(C) money laundering (as defined in section 1956 or 1957 of such title), and

(D) any State criminal offense substantially similar to an offense described in subparagraph (A), (B), or (C).

(4) Information to Federal prosecutors.— Each clerk required to include on a return under paragraph (1) the information described in paragraph (2)(B) with respect to an individual described in paragraph (2)(B)(i)(I) shall furnish (at such time as the Secretary may by regulations prescribe) a written statement showing such information to the United States Attorney for the jurisdiction in which such individual resides and the jurisdiction in which the specified criminal offense

occurred.

(5) Information to payors of bail.— Each clerk required to make a return under paragraph (1) shall furnish (at such time as the Secretary may by regulations prescribe) to each person whose name is required to be set forth in such return by reason of paragraph (2)(B)(i)(II) a written statement showing—

(A) the name and address of the clerk's office required to make the return, and

(B) the aggregate amount of cash described in paragraph (1) received by such clerk.

§ 7201. Attempt to evade or defeat tax

Any person who willfully attempts in any manner to evade or defeat any tax imposed by this title or the payment thereof shall, in addition to other penalties provided by law, be guilty of a felony and, upon conviction thereof, shall be fined not more than $100,000 ($500,000 in the case of a corporation), or imprisoned not more than 5 years, or both, together with the costs of prosecution.

§ 7203. Willful failure to file return, supply information, or pay tax

Any person required under this title to pay any estimated tax or tax, or required by this title or by regulations made under authority thereof to make a return, keep any records, or supply any information, who willfully fails to pay such estimated tax or tax, make such return, keep such records, or supply such information, at the time or times required by law or regulations, shall, in addition to other penalties provided by law, be guilty of a misdemeanor and, upon conviction thereof, shall be fined not more than $25,000 ($100,000 in the case of a corporation), or imprisoned not more than 1 year, or both, together with the costs of prosecution. In the case of any person with respect to whom there is a failure to pay any estimated tax, this section shall not apply to such person with respect to such failure if there is no addition to tax under section 6654 or 6655 with respect to such failure. In the case of a willful violation of any provision of section 6050I, the first sentence of this section shall be applied by substituting "felony" for "misdemeanor" and "5 years" for "1 year".

§ 7206. Fraud and false statements

Any person who—

(1) Declaration under penalties of perjury.— Willfully makes and subscribes any return, statement, or other document, which contains or is verified by a written declaration that it is made under the penalties of perjury, and which he does not believe to be true and correct as to every material matter; or

(2) Aid or assistance.— Willfully aids or assists in, or procures, counsels, or advises the preparation or presentation under, or in connection with any matter arising under, the internal revenue laws, of a return, affidavit, claim, or other document, which is fraudulent or is false as to any material matter, whether or not such falsity or fraud is with the knowledge or consent of the person authorized or required to present such return, affidavit, claim, or document; or

(3) Fraudulent bonds, permits, and entries.— Simulates or falsely or fraudu-

lently executes or signs any bond, permit, entry, or other document required by the provisions of the internal revenue laws, or by any regulation made in pursuance thereof, or procures the same to be falsely or fraudulently executed, or advises, aids in, or connives at such execution thereof; or

(4) Removal or concealment with intent to defraud.— Removes, deposits, or conceals, or is concerned in removing, depositing, or concealing, any goods or commodities for or in respect whereof any tax is or shall be imposed, or any property upon which levy is authorized by section 6331, with intent to evade or defeat the assessment or collection of any tax imposed by this title; or

(5) Compromises and closing agreements.— In connection with any compromise under section 7122, or offer of such compromise, or in connection with any closing agreement under section 7121, or offer to enter into any such agreement, willfully—

(A) Concealment of property.— Conceals from any officer or employee of the United States any property belonging to the estate of a taxpayer or other person liable in respect of the tax, or

(B) Withholding, falsifying, and destroying records.— Receives, withholds, destroys, mutilates, or falsifies any book, document, or record, or makes any false statement, relating to the estate or financial condition of the taxpayer or other person liable in respect of the tax;

shall be guilty of a felony and, upon conviction thereof, shall be fined not more than $100,000 ($500,000 in the case of a corporation), or imprisoned not more than 3 years, or both, together with the costs of prosecution.

§ 7213. Unauthorized disclosure of information

(a) Returns and return information.—

(1) Federal employees and other persons.— It shall be unlawful for any officer or employee of the United States or any person described in section 6103(n) (or an officer or employee of any such person), or any former officer or employee, willfully to disclose to any person, except as authorized in this title, any return or return information (as defined in section 6103(b)). Any violation of this paragraph shall be a felony punishable upon conviction by a fine in any amount not exceeding $5,000, or imprisonment of not more than 5 years, or both, together with the costs of prosecution, and if such offense is committed by any officer or employee of the United States, he shall, in addition to any other punishment, be dismissed from office or discharged from employment upon conviction for such offense.

(2) State and other employees.— It shall be unlawful for any person (not described in paragraph (1)) willfully to disclose to any person, except as authorized in this title, any return or return information (as defined in section 6103(b)) acquired by him or another person under subsection (d), (i)(3)(B)(i) or (7)(A)(ii), (k)(10), (l)(6), (7), (8), (9), (10), (12), (15), (16), (19), (20), or (21) or (m)(2), (4), (5), (6), or (7) of section 6103 or under section 6104(c). Any violation of this paragraph shall be a felony punishable by a fine in any amount not exceeding $5,000, or imprisonment of not more than 5 years, or both, together with the costs of prosecution.

(3) Other persons.— It shall be unlawful for any person to whom any return or return information (as defined insection 6103(b)) is disclosed in a manner unauthorized by this title thereafter willfully to print or publish in any manner not provided by law any such return or return information. Any violation of this paragraph shall be a felony punishable by a fine in any amount not exceeding $5,000, or imprisonment of not more than 5 years, or both, together with the costs of prosecution.

(4) Solicitation.— It shall be unlawful for any person willfully to offer any item of material value in exchange for any return or return information (as defined in section 6103(b)) and to receive as a result of such solicitation any such return or return information. Any violation of this paragraph shall be a felony punishable by a fine in any amount not exceeding $5,000, or imprisonment of not more than 5 years, or both, together with the costs of prosecution.

(5) Shareholders.— It shall be unlawful for any person to whom a return or return information (as defined in section 6103(b)) is disclosed pursuant to the provisions of section 6103(e)(1)(D)(iii) willfully to disclose such return or return information in any manner not provided by law. Any violation of this paragraph shall be a felony punishable by a fine in any amount not to exceed $5,000, or imprisonment of not more than 5 years, or both, together with the costs of prosecution.

(b) Disclosure of operations of manufacturer or producer.— Any officer or employee of the United States who divulges or makes known in any manner whatever not provided by law to any person the operations, style of work, or apparatus of any manufacturer or producer visited by him in the discharge of his official duties shall be guilty of a misdemeanor and, upon conviction thereof, shall be fined not more than $1,000, or imprisoned not more than 1 year, or both, together with the costs of prosecution; and the offender shall be dismissed from office or discharged from employment.

(c) Disclosures by certain delegates of Secretary.— All provisions of law relating to the disclosure of information, and all provisions of law relating to penalties for unauthorized disclosure of information, which are applicable in respect of any function under this title when performed by an officer or employee of the Treasury Department are likewise applicable in respect of such function when performed by any person who is a "delegate" within the meaning of section 7701(a)(12)(B).

(d) Disclosure of software.— Any person who willfully divulges or makes known software (as defined in section 7612(d)(1)) to any person in violation of section 7612 shall be guilty of a felony and, upon conviction thereof, shall be fined not more than $5,000, or imprisoned not more than 5 years, or both, together with the costs of prosecution.

(e) Cross references.—

(1) Penalties for disclosure of information by preparers of returns.—

For penalty for disclosure or use of information by preparers of returns, see section 7216.

(2) Penalties for disclosure of confidential information.—

For penalties for disclosure of confidential information by any officer or employee of the United States or any department or agency thereof, see 18 U.S.C. 1905.

§ 7609. Special procedures for third-party summonses

(a) Notice.—

(1) In general.— If any summons to which this section applies requires the giving of testimony on or relating to, the production of any portion of records made or kept on or relating to, or the production of any computer software source code (as defined in 7612(d)(2)) with respect to, any person (other than the person summoned) who is identified in the summons, then notice of the summons shall be given to any person so identified within 3 days of the day on which such service is made, but no later than the 23rd day before the day fixed in the summons as the day upon which such records are to be examined. Such notice shall be accompanied by a copy of the summons which has been served and shall contain an explanation of the right under subsection (b)(2) to bring a proceeding to quash the summons.

(2) Sufficiency of notice.— Such notice shall be sufficient if, on or before such third day, such notice is served in the manner provided in section 7603 (relating to service of summons) upon the person entitled to notice, or is mailed by certified or registered mail to the last known address of such person, or, in the absence of a last known address, is left with the person summoned. If such notice is mailed, it shall be sufficient if mailed to the last known address of the person entitled to notice or, in the case of notice to the Secretary under section 6903 of the existence of a fiduciary relationship, to the last known address of the fiduciary of such person, even if such person or fiduciary is then deceased, under a legal disability, or no longer in existence.

(3) Nature of summons.— Any summons to which this subsection applies (and any summons in aid of collection described in subsection (c)(2)(D)) shall identify the taxpayer to whom the summons relates or the other person to whom the records pertain and shall provide such other information as will enable the person summoned to locate the records required under the summons.

(b) Right to intervene; right to proceeding to quash.—

(1) Intervention.— Notwithstanding any other law or rule of law, any person who is entitled to notice of a summons under subsection (a) shall have the right to intervene in any proceeding with respect to the enforcement of such summons under section 7604.

(2) Proceeding to quash.—

(A) In general.— Notwithstanding any other law or rule of law, any person who is entitled to notice of a summons under subsection (a) shall have the right to begin a proceeding to quash such summons not later than the 20th day after the day such notice is given in the manner provided in subsection (a)(2). In any such proceeding, the Secretary may seek to compel compliance with the summons.

(B) Requirement of notice to person summoned and to Secretary.— If any person begins a proceeding under subparagraph (A) with respect to any summons, not later than the close of the 20-day period referred to in subparagraph (A) such person shall mail by registered or certified mail a copy of the petition to the person summoned and to such office as the Secretary may direct in the notice referred to in subsection (a)(1).

(C) Intervention; etc.— Notwithstanding any other law or rule of law, the person summoned shall have the right to intervene in any proceeding under subparagraph (A). Such person shall be bound by the decision in such proceeding (whether or not the person intervenes in such proceeding).

(c) Summons to which section applies.—

(1) In general.— Except as provided in paragraph (2), this section shall apply to any summons issued under paragraph (2) of section 7602(a) or under section 6420(e)(2), 6421(g)(2), 6427(j)(2), or 7612.

(2) Exceptions.— This section shall not apply to any summons—

(A) served on the person with respect to whose liability the summons is issued, or any officer or employee of such person;

(B) issued to determine whether or not records of the business transactions or affairs of an identified person have been made or kept;

(C) issued solely to determine the identity of any person having a numbered account (or similar arrangement) with a bank or other institution described in section 7603(b)(2)(A);

(D) issued in aid of the collection of—

(i) an assessment made or judgment rendered against the person with respect to whose liability the summons is issued; or

(ii) the liability at law or in equity of any transferee or fiduciary of any person referred to in clause (i); or

(E)

(i) issued by a criminal investigator of the Internal Revenue Service in connection with the investigation of an offense connected with the administration or enforcement of the internal revenue laws; and

(ii) served on any person who is not a third-party record keeper (as defined in section 7603(b)).

(3) John Doe and certain other summonses.— Subsection (a) shall not apply to any summons described in subsection (f) or (g).

(4) Records.— For purposes of this section, the term "records" includes books, papers, and other data.

(d) Restriction on examination of records.— No examination of any records required to be produced under a summons as to which notice is required under subsection (a) may be made—

(1) before the close of the 23rd day after the day notice with respect to the summons is given in the manner provided in subsection (a)(2), or

(2) where a proceeding under subsection (b)(2)(A) was begun within the 20-day period referred to in such subsection and the requirements of subsection (b)(2)(B) have been met, except in accordance with an order of the court having jurisdiction of such proceeding or with the consent of the person beginning the proceeding to quash.

(e) Suspension of statute of limitations.—

(1) Subsection (b) action.— If any person takes any action as provided in subsection (b) and such person is the person with respect to whose liability the summons is issued (or is the agent, nominee, or other person acting under the direction or control of such person), then the running of any period of limitations under section 6501(relating to the assessment and collection of tax) or under section 6531 (relating to criminal prosecutions) with respect to such person shall be suspended for the period during which a proceeding, and appeals therein, with respect to the enforcement of such summons is pending.

(2) Suspension after 6 months of service of summons.— In the absence of the resolution of the summoned party's response to the summons, the running of any period of limitations under section 6501 or under section 6531 with respect to any person with respect to whose liability the summons is issued (other than a person taking action as provided in subsection (b)) shall be suspended for the period—

(A) beginning on the date which is 6 months after the service of such summons, and

(B) ending with the final resolution of such response.

(f) Additional requirement in the case of a John Doe summons.— Any summons described in subsection (c)(1) which does not identify the person with respect to whose liability the summons is issued may be served only after a court proceeding in which the Secretary establishes that—

(1) the summons relates to the investigation of a particular person or ascertainable group or class of persons,

(2) there is a reasonable basis for believing that such person or group or class of persons may fail or may have failed to comply with any provision of any internal revenue law, and

(3) the information sought to be obtained from the examination of the records or testimony (and the identity of the person or persons with respect to whose liability the summons is issued) is not readily available from other sources.

(g) Special exception for certain summonses.— A summons is described in this subsection if, upon petition by the Secretary, the court determines, on the basis of the facts and circumstances alleged, that there is reasonable cause to believe the giving of notice may lead to attempts to conceal, destroy, or alter records relevant to the examination, to prevent the communication of information from other persons through intimidation, bribery, or collusion, or to flee to avoid prosecution, testifying, or production of records.

(h) Jurisdiction of district court; etc.—

(1) Jurisdiction.— The United States district court for the district within which the person to be summoned resides or is found shall have jurisdiction to hear and determine any proceeding brought under subsection (b)(2), (f), or (g). An order denying the petition shall be deemed a final order which may be appealed.

(2) Special rule for proceedings under subsections (f) and (g).— The determinations required to be made under subsections (f) and (g) shall be made ex parte and shall be made solely on the petition and supporting affidavits.

(i) Duty of summoned party.—

(1) Recordkeeper must assemble records and be prepared to produce records.— On receipt of a summons to which this section applies for the production of records, the summoned party shall proceed to assemble the records requested, or such portion thereof as the Secretary may prescribe, and shall be prepared to produce the records pursuant to the summons on the day on which the records are to be examined.

(2) Secretary may give summoned party certificate.— The Secretary may issue a certificate to the summoned party that the period prescribed for beginning a proceeding to quash a summons has expired and that no such proceeding began within such period, or that the taxpayer consents to the examination.

(3) Protection for summoned party who discloses.— Any summoned party, or agent or employee thereof, making a disclosure of records or testimony pursuant to this section in good faith reliance on the certificate of the Secretary or an order of a court requiring production of records or the giving of such testimony shall not be liable to any customer or other person for such disclosure.

(4) Notice of suspension of statute of limitations in the case of a John Doe summons.— In the case of a summons described in subsection (f) with respect to which any period of limitations has been suspended under subsection (e)(2), the summoned party shall provide notice of such suspension to any person described in subsection (f).

(j) Use of summons not required.— Nothing in this section shall be construed to limit the Secretary's ability to obtain information, other than by summons, through formal or informal procedures authorized by sections 7601 and 7602.

TITLE 28. JUDICIARY AND JUDICIAL PROCEDURE

§ 991. United States Sentencing Commission; establishment and purposes

(a) There is established as an independent commission in the judicial branch of the United States a United States Sentencing Commission which shall consist of seven voting members and one nonvoting member. The President, after consultation with representatives of judges, prosecuting attorneys, defense attorneys, law enforcement officials, senior citizens, victims of crime, and others interested in the criminal justice process, shall appoint the voting members of the Commission, by and with the advice and consent of the Senate, one of whom shall be appointed, by and with the advice and consent of the Senate, as the Chair and three of whom shall be designated by the President as Vice Chairs. At least 3 of the members shall be Federal judges selected after considering a list of six judges recommended to the President by the Judicial Conference of the United States. Not more than four of the members of the Commission shall be members of the same political party, and of the three Vice Chairs, no more than two shall be members of the same political party. The Attorney General, or the Attorney General's designee, shall be an ex officio, nonvoting member of the Commission. The Chair, Vice Chairs, and members of the Commission shall be subject to removal from the Commission by the President only for neglect of duty or malfeasance in office or for other good cause shown.

(b) The purposes of the United States Sentencing Commission are to—

(1) establish sentencing policies and practices for the Federal criminal justice system that—

(A) assure the meeting of the purposes of sentencing as set forth in section 3553(a)(2) of title 18, United States Code;

(B) provide certainty and fairness in meeting the purposes of sentencing, avoiding unwarranted sentencing disparities among defendants with similar records who have been found guilty of similar criminal conduct while maintaining sufficient flexibility to permit individualized sentences when warranted by mitigating or aggravating factors not taken into account in the establishment of general sentencing practices; and

(C) reflect, to the extent practicable, advancement in knowledge of human behavior as it relates to the criminal justice process; and

(2) develop means of measuring the degree to which the sentencing, penal, and correctional practices are effective in meeting the purposes of sentencing as set forth in section 3553(a)(2) of title 18, United States Code.

§ 994. Duties of the Commission

(a) The Commission, by affirmative vote of at least four members of the Commission, and pursuant to its rules and regulations and consistent with all pertinent provisions of any Federal statute shall promulgate and distribute to all courts of the United States and to the United States Probation System—

(1) guidelines, as described in this section, for use of a sentencing court in determining the sentence to be imposed in a criminal case, including—

(A) a determination whether to impose a sentence to probation, a fine, or a term of imprisonment;

(B) a determination as to the appropriate amount of a fine or the appropriate length of a term of probation or a term of imprisonment;

(C) a determination whether a sentence to a term of imprisonment should include a requirement that the defendant be placed on a term of supervised release after imprisonment, and, if so, the appropriate length of such a term;

(D) a determination whether multiple sentences to terms of imprisonment should be ordered to run concurrently or consecutively; and

(E) a determination under paragraphs (6) and (11) of section 3563(b) of title 18;

(2) general policy statements regarding application of the guidelines or any other aspect of sentencing or sentence implementation that in the view of the Commission would further the purposes set forth in section 3553(a)(2) of title 18, United States Code, including the appropriate use of—

(A) the sanctions set forth in sections 3554, 3555, and 3556 of title 18;

(B) the conditions of probation and supervised release set forth in sections 3563(b) and 3583(d) of title 18;

(C) the sentence modification provisions set forth in sections 3563(c), 3564, 3573, and 3582(c) of title 18;

(D) the fine imposition provisions set forth in section 3572 of title 18;

(E) the authority granted under rule 11(e)(2) of the Federal Rules of Criminal Procedure to accept or reject a plea agreement entered into pursuant to rule 11(e)(1); and

(F) the temporary release provisions set forth in section 3622 of title 18, and the prerelease custody provisions set forth in section 3624(c) of title 18; and

(2) guidelines or general policy statements regarding the appropriate use of the provisions for revocation of probation set forth in section 3565 of title 18, and the provisions for modification of the term or conditions of supervised release and revocation of supervised release set forth in section 3583(e) of title 18.

(b)

(1) The Commission, in the guidelines promulgated pursuant to subsection (a)(1), shall, for each category of offense involving each category of defendant, establish a sentencing range that is consistent with all pertinent provisions of title 18, United States Code.

(2) If a sentence specified by the guidelines includes a term of imprisonment, the maximum of the range established for such a term shall not exceed the minimum of that range by more than the greater of 25 percent or 6 months, except that, if the minimum term of the range is 30 years or more, the maximum may be life imprisonment.

(c) The Commission, in establishing categories of offenses for use in the guidelines and policy statements governing the imposition of sentences of probation, a fine, or imprisonment, governing the imposition of other authorized sanctions, governing the size of a fine or the length of a term of probation, imprisonment, or supervised release, and governing the conditions of probation, supervised release, or imprisonment, shall consider whether the following matters, among others, have any relevance to the nature, extent, place of service, or other incidents of an appropriate sentence, and shall take them into account only to the extent that they do have relevance—

(1) the grade of the offense;

(2) the circumstances under which the offense was committed which mitigate or aggravate the seriousness of the offense;

(3) the nature and degree of the harm caused by the offense, including whether it involved property, irreplaceable property, a person, a number of persons, or a breach of public trust;

(4) the community view of the gravity of the offense;

(5) the public concern generated by the offense;

(6) the deterrent effect a particular sentence may have on the commission of the offense by others; and

(7) the current incidence of the offense in the community and in the Nation as a whole.

(d) The Commission in establishing categories of defendants for use in the guidelines and policy statements governing the imposition of sentences of probation, a fine, or imprisonment, governing the imposition of other authorized sanctions, governing the size of a fine or the length of a term of probation, imprisonment, or supervised release, and governing the conditions of probation, supervised release, or imprisonment, shall consider whether the following matters, among others, with respect to a defendant, have any relevance to the nature, extent, place of service, or other incidents of an appropriate sentence, and shall take them into account only to the extent that they do have relevance—

(1) age;

(2) education;

(3) vocational skills;

(4) mental and emotional condition to the extent that such condition mitigates the defendant's culpability or to the extent that such condition is otherwise plainly relevant;

(5) physical condition, including drug dependence;

(6) previous employment record;

(7) family ties and responsibilities;

(8) community ties;

(9) role in the offense;

(10) criminal history; and

(11) degree of dependence upon criminal activity for a livelihood.

The Commission shall assure that the guidelines and policy statements are entirely neutral as to the race, sex, national origin, creed, and socioeconomic status of offenders.

(e) The Commission shall assure that the guidelines and policy statements, in recommending a term of imprisonment or length of a term of imprisonment, reflect the general inappropriateness of considering the education, vocational skills, employment record, family ties and responsibilities, and community ties of the defendant.

(f) The Commission, in promulgating guidelines pursuant to subsection (a)(1), shall promote the purposes set forth in section 991(b)(1), with particular attention to the requirements of subsection 991(b)(1)(B) for providing certainty and fairness in sentencing and reducing unwarranted sentence disparities.

(g) The Commission, in promulgating guidelines pursuant to subsection (a)(1) to meet the purposes of sentencing as set forth in section 3553(a)(2) of title 18, United States Code, shall take into account the nature and capacity of the penal, correctional, and other facilities and services available, and shall make recommendations concerning any change or expansion in the nature or capacity of such facilities and services that might become necessary as a result of the guidelines promulgated pursuant to the provisions of this chapter. The sentencing guidelines prescribed under this chapter shall be formulated to minimize the likelihood that the Federal prison population will exceed the capacity of the Federal prisons, as determined by the Commission.

(h) The Commission shall assure that the guidelines specify a sentence to a term of imprisonment at or near the maximum term authorized for categories of defendants in which the defendant is eighteen years old or older and—

(1) has been convicted of a felony that is—

(A) a crime of violence; or

(B) an offense described in section 401 of the Controlled Substances Act (21 U.S.C. 841), sections 1002(a), 1005, and 1009 of the Controlled Substances Import and Export Act (21 U.S.C. 952(a), 955, and 959), and chapter 705 of title 46; and

(2) has previously been convicted of two or more prior felonies, each of which is—

(A) a crime of violence; or

(B) an offense described in section 401 of the Controlled Substances Act (21 U.S.C. 841), sections 1002(a), 1005, and 1009 of the Controlled Substances Import and Export Act (21 U.S.C. 952(a), 955, and 959), and chapter 705 of title 46.

(i) The Commission shall assure that the guidelines specify a sentence to a substantial term of imprisonment for categories of defendants in which the defendant—

(1) has a history of two or more prior Federal, State, or local felony convictions for offenses committed on different occasions;

(2) committed the offense as part of a pattern of criminal conduct from which the defendant derived a substantial portion of the defendant's income;

(3) committed the offense in furtherance of a conspiracy with three or more persons engaging in a pattern of racketeering activity in which the defendant participated in a managerial or supervisory capacity;

(4) committed a crime of violence that constitutes a felony while on release pending trial, sentence, or appeal from a Federal, State, or local felony for which he was ultimately convicted; or

(5) committed a felony that is set forth in section 401 or 1010 of the Comprehensive Drug Abuse Prevention and Control Act of 1970 (21 U.S.C. 841 and 960), and that involved trafficking in a substantial quantity of a controlled substance.

(j) The Commission shall insure that the guidelines reflect the general appropriateness of imposing a sentence other than imprisonment in cases in which the defendant is a first offender who has not been convicted of a crime of violence or an otherwise serious offense, and the general appropriateness of imposing a term of imprisonment on a person convicted of a crime of violence that results in serious bodily injury.

(k) The Commission shall insure that the guidelines reflect the inappropriateness of imposing a sentence to a term of imprisonment for the purpose of rehabilitating the defendant or providing the defendant with needed educational or vocational training, medical care, or other correctional treatment.

(l) The Commission shall insure that the guidelines promulgated pursuant to subsection (a)(1) reflect—

(1) the appropriateness of imposing an incremental penalty for each offense in a case in which a defendant is convicted of—

(A) multiple offenses committed in the same course of conduct that result in the exercise of ancillary jurisdiction over one or more of the offenses; and

(B) multiple offenses committed at different times, including those cases in which the subsequent offense is a violation of section 3146 (penalty for failure to appear) or is committed while the person is released pursuant to the provisions of section 3147 (penalty for an offense committed while on release) of title 18; and

(2) the general inappropriateness of imposing consecutive terms of imprisonment for an offense of conspiring to commit an offense or soliciting commission of an offense and for an offense that was the sole object of the conspiracy or solicitation.

(m) The Commission shall insure that the guidelines reflect the fact that, in many cases, current sentences do not accurately reflect the seriousness of the offense. This will require that, as a starting point in its development of the initial sets of guidelines for particular categories of cases, the Commission ascertain the average sentences imposed in such categories of cases prior to the creation of the Commission, and in cases involving sentences to terms of imprisonment, the length of such terms actually served. The Commission shall not be bound by such average sentences, and shall independently develop a sentencing range that is consistent with the purposes of sentencing described in section 3553(a)(2) of title 18, United States Code.

(n) The Commission shall assure that the guidelines reflect the general appropriateness of imposing a lower sentence than would otherwise be imposed, including a sentence that is lower than that established by statute as a minimum sentence, to take into account a defendant's substantial assistance in the investigation or prosecution of another person who has committed an offense.

(o) The Commission periodically shall review and revise, in consideration of comments and data coming to its attention, the guidelines promulgated pursuant to the provisions of this section. In fulfilling its duties and in exercising its powers, the Commission shall consult with authorities on, and individual and institutional representatives of, various aspects of the Federal criminal justice system. The United States Probation System, the Bureau of Prisons, the Judicial Conference of the United States, the Criminal Division of the United States Department of Justice, and a representative of the Federal Public Defenders shall submit to the Commission any observations, comments, or questions pertinent to the work of the Commission whenever they believe such communication would be useful, and shall, at least annually, submit to the Commission a written report commenting on the operation of the Commission's guidelines, suggesting changes in the guidelines that appear to be warranted, and otherwise assessing the Commission's work.

(p) The Commission, at or after the beginning of a regular session of Congress, but not later than the first day of May, may promulgate under subsection (a) of this section and submit to Congress amendments to the guidelines and modifications to previously submitted amendments that have not taken effect, including modifications to the effective dates of such amendments. Such an amendment or modification shall be accompanied by a statement of the reasons therefor and shall take effect on a date specified by the Commission, which shall be no earlier than 180 days after being so submitted and no later than the first day of November of the calendar year in which the amendment or modification is submitted, except to the extent that the effective date is revised or the amendment is otherwise modified or disapproved by Act of Congress.

(q) The Commission and the Bureau of Prisons shall submit to Congress an analysis and recommendations concerning maximum utilization of resources to deal effectively with the Federal prison population. Such report shall be based upon consideration of a variety of alternatives, including—

(1) modernization of existing facilities;

(2) inmate classification and periodic review of such classification for use in placing inmates in the least restrictive facility necessary to ensure adequate security; and

(3) use of existing Federal facilities, such as those currently within military jurisdiction.

(r) The Commission, not later than two years after the initial set of sentencing guidelines promulgated under subsection (a) goes into effect, and thereafter whenever it finds it advisable, shall recommend to the Congress that it raise or lower the grades, or otherwise modify the maximum penalties, of those offenses for which such an adjustment appears appropriate.

(s) The Commission shall give due consideration to any petition filed by a defendant requesting modification of the guidelines utilized in the sentencing of such defendant, on the basis of changed circumstances unrelated to the defendant, including changes in—

(1) the community view of the gravity of the offense;

(2) the public concern generated by the offense; and

(3) the deterrent effect particular sentences may have on the commission of the offense by others.

(t) The Commission, in promulgating general policy statements regarding the sentencing modification provisions insection 3582(c)(1)(A) of title 18, shall describe what should be considered extraordinary and compelling reasons for sentence reduction, including the criteria to be applied and a list of specific examples. Rehabilitation of the defendant alone shall not be considered an extraordinary and compelling reason.

(u) If the Commission reduces the term of imprisonment recommended in the guidelines applicable to a particular offense or category of offenses, it shall specify in what circumstances and by what amount the sentences of prisoners serving terms of imprisonment for the offense may be reduced.

(v) The Commission shall ensure that the general policy statements promulgated pursuant to subsection (a)(2) include a policy limiting consecutive terms of imprisonment for an offense involving a violation of a general prohibition and for an offense involving a violation of a specific prohibition encompassed within the general prohibition.

(w)

(1) The Chief Judge of each district court shall ensure that, within 30 days following entry of judgment in every criminal case, the sentencing court submits to the Commission, in a format approved and required by the Commission, a written report of the sentence, the offense for which it is imposed, the age, race, sex of the offender, and information regarding factors made relevant by the guidelines. The report shall also include—

(A) the judgment and commitment order;

(B) the written statement of reasons for the sentence imposed (which shall include the reason for any departure from the otherwise applicable guideline range and which shall be stated on the written statement of reasons form issued by the Judicial Conference and approved by the United States Sentencing Commission);

(C) any plea agreement;

(D) the indictment or other charging document;

(E) the presentence report; and

(F) any other information as the Commission finds appropriate.

The information referred to in subparagraphs (A) through (F) shall be submitted by the sentencing court in a format approved and required by the Commission.

(2) The Commission shall, upon request, make available to the House and Senate Committees on the Judiciary, the written reports and all underlying records accompanying those reports described in this section, as well as other records received from courts.

(3) The Commission shall submit to Congress at least annually an analysis of these documents, any recommendations for legislation that the Commission concludes is warranted by that analysis, and an accounting of those districts that the Commission believes have not submitted the appropriate information and documents required by this section.

(4) The Commission shall make available to the Attorney General, upon request, such data files as the Commission itself may assemble or maintain in electronic form as a result of the information submitted under paragraph (1). Such data files shall be made available in electronic form and shall include all data fields requested, including the identity of the sentencing judge.

(x) The provisions of section 553 of title 5, relating to publication in the Federal Register and public hearing procedure, shall apply to the promulgation of guidelines pursuant to this section.

(y) The Commission, in promulgating guidelines pursuant to subsection (a)(1), may include, as a component of a fine, the expected costs to the Government of any imprisonment, supervised release, or probation sentence that is ordered.

§ 2461.   Mode of recovery

(a) Whenever a civil fine, penalty or pecuniary forfeiture is prescribed for the violation of an Act of Congress without specifying the mode of recovery or enforcement thereof, it may be recovered in a civil action.

(b) Unless otherwise provided by Act of Congress, whenever a forfeiture of property is prescribed as a penalty for violation of an Act of Congress and the seizure takes place on the high seas or on navigable waters within the admiralty and maritime jurisdiction of the United States, such forfeiture may be enforced by libel in admiralty but in cases of seizures on land the forfeiture may be enforced by a proceeding by libel which shall conform as near as may be to proceedings in admiralty.

(c) If a person is charged in a criminal case with a violation of an Act of Congress for which the civil or criminal forfeiture of property is authorized, the Government may include notice of the forfeiture in the indictment or information pursuant to the Federal Rules of Criminal Procedure. If the defendant is convicted of the offense giving rise to the forfeiture, the court shall order the forfeiture of the property as part of the sentence in the criminal case pursuant to to the Federal Rules of Criminal Procedure and section 3554 of title 18, United States Code. The procedures in section 413 of the Controlled Substances Act (21 U.S.C. 853) apply to all stages of a criminal forfeiture proceeding, except that subsection (d) of such section applies only in cases in which the defendant is convicted of a violation of such Act.

TITLE 31. MONEY AND FINANCE

§ 3729. False claims

(a) Liability for certain acts.—

(1) In general.— Subject to paragraph (2), any person who—

(A) knowingly presents, or causes to be presented, a false or fraudulent claim for payment or approval;

(B) knowingly makes, uses, or causes to be made or used, a false record or statement material to a false or fraudulent claim;

(C) conspires to commit a violation of subparagraph (A), (B), (D), (E), (F), or (G);

(D) has possession, custody, or control of property or money used, or to be used, by the Government and knowingly delivers, or causes to be delivered, less than all of that money or property;

(E) is authorized to make or deliver a document certifying receipt of property used, or to be used, by the Government and, intending to defraud the Government, makes or delivers the receipt without completely knowing that the information on the receipt is true;

(F) knowingly buys, or receives as a pledge of an obligation or debt, public property from an officer or employee of the Government, or a member of the Armed Forces, who lawfully may not sell or pledge property; or

(G) knowingly makes, uses, or causes to be made or used, a false record or statement material to an obligation to pay or transmit money or property to the Government, or knowingly conceals or knowingly and improperly avoids or decreases an obligation to pay or transmit money or property to the Government,

is liable to the United States Government for a civil penalty of not less than $5,000 and not more than $10,000, as adjusted by the Federal Civil Penalties Inflation Adjustment Act of 1990 (28 U.S.C. 2461 note; Public Law 104-410), plus 3 times the amount of damages which the Government sustains because of the act of that person.

(2) Reduced damages.— If the court finds that—

(A) the person committing the violation of this subsection furnished officials of the United States responsible for investigating false claims violations with all information known to such person about the violation within 30 days after the date on which the defendant first obtained the information;

(B) such person fully cooperated with any Government investigation of such violation; and

(C) at the time such person furnished the United States with the information about the violation, no criminal prosecution, civil action, or administrative action had commenced under this title with respect to such violation, and the person did not have actual knowledge of the existence of an investigation into such violation,

the court may assess not less than 2 times the amount of damages which the Government sustains because of the act of that person.

(3) Costs of civil actions.— A person violating this subsection shall also be liable to the United States Government for the costs of a civil action brought to recover any such penalty or damages.

(b) Definitions.— For purposes of this section—

(1) the terms "knowing" and "knowingly"—

(A) mean that a person, with respect to information—

(i) has actual knowledge of the information;

(ii) acts in deliberate ignorance of the truth or falsity of the information; or

(iii) acts in reckless disregard of the truth or falsity of the information; and

(B) require no proof of specific intent to defraud;

(2) the term "claim"—

(A) means any request or demand, whether under a contract or otherwise, for money or property and whether or not the United States has title to the money or property, that—

(i) is presented to an officer, employee, or agent of the United States; or

(ii) is made to a contractor, grantee, or other recipient, if the money or property is to be spent or used on the Government's behalf or to advance a Government program or interest, and if the United States Government—

(I) provides or has provided any portion of the money or property requested or demanded; or

(II) will reimburse such contractor, grantee, or other recipient for any portion of the money or property which is requested or demanded; and

(B) does not include requests or demands for money or property that the Government has paid to an individual as compensation for Federal employment or as an income subsidy with no restrictions on that individual's use of the money or property;

(3) the term "obligation" means an established duty, whether or not fixed, arising from an express or implied contractual, grantor-grantee, or licensor-licensee relationship, from a fee-based or similar relationship, from statute or regulation, or from the retention of any overpayment; and

(4) the term "material" means having a natural tendency to influence, or be capable of influencing, the payment or receipt of money or property.

(c) Exemption from disclosure.— Any information furnished pursuant to subsection (a)(2) shall be exempt from disclosure under section 552 of title 5.

(d) Exclusion.— This section does not apply to claims, records, or statements made under the Internal Revenue Code of 1986.

(e) Redesignated (d)

§ 3730. Civil actions for false claims

(a) Responsibilities of the Attorney General.— The Attorney General diligently shall investigate a violation under section 3729. If the Attorney General finds that a person has violated or is violating section 3729, the Attorney General may bring a civil action under this section against the person.

(b) Actions by private persons.—

(1) A person may bring a civil action for a violation of section 3729 for the person and for the United States Government. The action shall be brought in the name of the Government. The action may be dismissed only if the court and the Attorney General give written consent to the dismissal and their reasons for consenting.

(2) A copy of the complaint and written disclosure of substantially all material evidence and information the person possesses shall be served on the Government pursuant to Rule 4(d)(4) of the Federal Rules of Civil Procedure.[1] The complaint shall be filed in camera, shall remain under seal for at least 60 days, and shall not be served on the defendant until the court so orders. The Government may elect to intervene and proceed with the action within 60 days after it receives both the complaint and the material evidence and information.

(3) The Government may, for good cause shown, move the court for extensions of the time during which the complaint remains under seal under paragraph (2). Any such motions may be supported by affidavits or other submissions in camera. The defendant shall not be required to respond to any complaint filed under this section until 20 days after the complaint is unsealed and served upon the defendant pursuant to Rule 4 of the Federal Rules of Civil Procedure.

(4) Before the expiration of the 60-day period or any extensions obtained under paragraph (3), the Government shall—

(A) proceed with the action, in which case the action shall be conducted by the Government; or

(B) notify the court that it declines to take over the action, in which case the person bringing the action shall have the right to conduct the action.

(5) When a person brings an action under this subsection, no person other than the Government may intervene or bring a related action based on the facts underlying the pending action.

(c) Rights of the parties to qui tam actions.—

(1) If the Government proceeds with the action, it shall have the primary responsibility for prosecuting the action, and shall not be bound by an act of the

---

[1] So in original. Probably should be a reference to Rule 4(i).

person bringing the action. Such person shall have the right to continue as a party to the action, subject to the limitations set forth in paragraph (2).

(2)

(A) The Government may dismiss the action notwithstanding the objections of the person initiating the action if the person has been notified by the Government of the filing of the motion and the court has provided the person with an opportunity for a hearing on the motion.

(B) The Government may settle the action with the defendant notwithstanding the objections of the person initiating the action if the court determines, after a hearing, that the proposed settlement is fair, adequate, and reasonable under all the circumstances. Upon a showing of good cause, such hearing may be held in camera.

(C) Upon a showing by the Government that unrestricted participation during the course of the litigation by the person initiating the action would interfere with or unduly delay the Government's prosecution of the case, or would be repetitious, irrelevant, or for purposes of harassment, the court may, in its discretion, impose limitations on the person's participation, such as—

(i) limiting the number of witnesses the person may call;

(ii) limiting the length of the testimony of such witnesses;

(iii) limiting the person's cross-examination of witnesses; or

(iv) otherwise limiting the participation by the person in the litigation.

(D) Upon a showing by the defendant that unrestricted participation during the course of the litigation by the person initiating the action would be for purposes of harassment or would cause the defendant undue burden or unnecessary expense, the court may limit the participation by the person in the litigation.

(3) If the Government elects not to proceed with the action, the person who initiated the action shall have the right to conduct the action. If the Government so requests, it shall be served with copies of all pleadings filed in the action and shall be supplied with copies of all deposition transcripts (at the Government's expense). When a person proceeds with the action, the court, without limiting the status and rights of the person initiating the action, may nevertheless permit the Government to intervene at a later date upon a showing of good cause.

(4) Whether or not the Government proceeds with the action, upon a showing by the Government that certain actions of discovery by the person initiating the action would interfere with the Government's investigation or prosecution of a criminal or civil matter arising out of the same facts, the court may stay such discovery for a period of not more than 60 days. Such a showing shall be conducted in camera. The court may extend the 60-day period upon a further showing in camera that the Government has pursued the criminal or civil investigation or proceedings with reasonable diligence and any proposed discovery in the civil action will interfere with the ongoing criminal or civil investigation or proceedings.

(5) Notwithstanding subsection (b), the Government may elect to pursue its claim through any alternate remedy available to the Government, including any administrative proceeding to determine a civil money penalty. If any such alternate remedy is pursued in another proceeding, the person initiating the action shall have the same rights in such proceeding as such person would have had if the action had continued under this section. Any finding of fact or conclusion of law made in such other proceeding that has become final shall be conclusive on all parties to an action under this section. For purposes of the preceding sentence, a finding or conclusion is final if it has been finally determined on appeal to the appropriate court of the United States, if all time for filing such an appeal with respect to the finding or conclusion has expired, or if the finding or conclusion is not subject to judicial review.

(d) Award to qui tam plaintiff.—

(1) If the Government proceeds with an action brought by a person under subsection (b), such person shall, subject to the second sentence of this paragraph, receive at least 15 percent but not more than 25 percent of the proceeds of the action or settlement of the claim, depending upon the extent to which the person substantially contributed to the prosecution of the action. Where the action is one which the court finds to be based primarily on disclosures of specific information (other than information provided by the person bringing the action) relating to allegations or transactions in a criminal, civil, or administrative hearing, in a congressional, administrative, or Government Accounting Office report, hearing, audit, or investigation, or from the news media, the court may award such sums as it considers appropriate, but in no case more than 10 percent of the proceeds, taking into account the significance of the information and the role of the person bringing the action in advancing the case to litigation. Any payment to a person under the first or second sentence of this paragraph shall be made from the proceeds. Any such person shall also receive an amount for reasonable expenses which the court finds to have been necessarily incurred, plus reasonable attorneys fees and costs. All such expenses, fees, and costs shall be awarded against the defendant.

(2) If the Government proceeds with an action brought by a person under subsection (b), such person shall, subject to the second sentence of this paragraph, receive at least 15 percent but not more than 25 percent of the proceeds of the action or settlement of the claim, depending upon the extent to which the person substantially contributed to the prosecution of the action. Where the action is one which the court finds to be based primarily on disclosures of specific information (other than information provided by the person bringing the action) relating to allegations or transactions in a criminal, civil, or administrative hearing, in a congressional, administrative, or Government Accounting Office report, hearing, audit, or investigation, or from the news media, the court may award such sums as it considers appropriate, but in no case more than 10 percent of the proceeds, taking into account the significance of the information and the role of the person bringing the action in advancing the case to litigation. Any payment to a person under the first or second sentence of this paragraph shall be made from the proceeds. Any such person shall also receive an amount for reasonable expenses which the court finds to have been necessarily incurred,

plus reasonable attorneys fees and costs. All such expenses, fees, and costs shall be awarded against the defendant.

(3) Whether or not the Government proceeds with the action, if the court finds that the action was brought by a person who planned and initiated the violation of section 3729 upon which the action was brought, then the court may, to the extent the court considers appropriate, reduce the share of the proceeds of the action which the person would otherwise receive under paragraph (1) or (2) of this subsection, taking into account the role of that person in advancing the case to litigation and any relevant circumstances pertaining to the violation. If the person bringing the action is convicted of criminal conduct arising from his or her role in the violation of section 3729, that person shall be dismissed from the civil action and shall not receive any share of the proceeds of the action. Such dismissal shall not prejudice the right of the United States to continue the action, represented by the Department of Justice.

(4) If the Government does not proceed with the action and the person bringing the action conducts the action, the court may award to the defendant its reasonable attorneys' fees and expenses if the defendant prevails in the action and the court finds that the claim of the person bringing the action was clearly frivolous, clearly vexatious, or brought primarily for purposes of harassment.

(e) Certain actions barred.—

(1) No court shall have jurisdiction over an action brought by a former or present member of the armed forces under subsection (b) of this section against a member of the armed forces arising out of such person's service in the armed forces.

(2)

(A) No court shall have jurisdiction over an action brought under subsection (b) against a Member of Congress, a member of the judiciary, or a senior executive branch official if the action is based on evidence or information known to the Government when the action was brought.

(B) For purposes of this paragraph, "senior executive branch official" means any officer or employee listed in paragraphs (1) through (8) of section 101(f) of the Ethics in Government Act of 1978 (5 U.S.C. App.).

(3) In no event may a person bring an action under subsection (b) which is based upon allegations or transactions which are the subject of a civil suit or an administrative civil money penalty proceeding in which the Government is already a party.

(4)

(A) The court shall dismiss an action or claim under this section, unless opposed by the Government, if substantially the same allegations or transactions as alleged in the action or claim were publicly disclosed—

(i) in a Federal criminal, civil, or administrative hearing in which the Government or its agent is a party;

(ii) in a congressional, Government Accountability Office, or other Federal report, hearing, audit, or investigation; or

(iii) from the news media,

unless the action is brought by the Attorney General or the person bringing the action is an original source of the information.

(B) For purposes of this paragraph, "original source" means an individual who either (i) prior to a public disclosure under subsection (e)(4)(a), has voluntarily disclosed to the Government the information on which allegations or transactions in a claim are based, or (2) who has knowledge that is independent of and materially adds to the publicly disclosed allegations or transactions, and who has voluntarily provided the information to the Government before filing an action under this section.

(f) Government not liable for certain expenses.— The Government is not liable for expenses which a person incurs in bringing an action under this section.

(g) Fees and expenses to prevailing defendant.— In civil actions brought under this section by the United States, the provisions of section 2412(d) of title 28 shall apply.

(h) Relief from retaliatory actions.—

(1) In general.— Any employee, contractor, or agent shall be entitled to all relief necessary to make that employee, contractor, or agent whole, if that employee, contractor, or agent is discharged, demoted, suspended, threatened, harassed, or in any other manner discriminated against in the terms and conditions of employment because of lawful acts done by the employee, contractor, agent or associated others in furtherance of an action under this section or other efforts to stop 1 or more violations of this subchapter.

(2) Relief.— Relief under paragraph (1) shall include reinstatement with the same seniority status that employee, contractor, or agent would have had but for the discrimination, 2 times the amount of back pay, interest on the back pay, and compensation for any special damages sustained as a result of the discrimination, including litigation costs and reasonable attorneys' fees. An action under this subsection may be brought in the appropriate district court of the United States for the relief provided in this subsection.

(3) Limitation on bringing civil action.— A civil action under this subsection may not be brought more than 3 years after the date when the retaliation occurred.

§ 3731.   False claims procedure

(a) A subpena requiring the attendance of a witness at a trial or hearing conducted under section 3730 of this title may be served at any place in the United States.

(b) A civil action under section 3730 may not be brought—

(1) more than 6 years after the date on which the violation of section 3729 is committed, or

(2) more than 3 years after the date when facts material to the right of action are known or reasonably should have been known by the official of the United States charged with responsibility to act in the circumstances, but in no event more than 10 years after the date on which the violation is committed,

whichever occurs last.

(c) If the Government elects to intervene and proceed with an action brought under 3730(b), the Government may file its own complaint or amend the complaint of a person who has brought an action under section 3730(b) to clarify or add detail to the claims in which the Government is intervening and to add any additional claims with respect to which the Government contends it is entitled to relief. For statute of limitations purposes, any such Government pleading shall relate back to the filing date of the complaint of the person who originally brought the action, to the extent that the claim of the Government arises out of the conduct, transactions, or occurrences set forth, or attempted to be set forth, in the prior complaint of that person.

(d) In any action brought under section 3730, the United States shall be required to prove all essential elements of the cause of action, including damages, by a preponderance of the evidence.

(e) Notwithstanding any other provision of law, the Federal Rules of Criminal Procedure, or the Federal Rules of Evidence, a final judgment rendered in favor of the United States in any criminal proceeding charging fraud or false statements, whether upon a verdict after trial or upon a plea of guilty or nolo contendere, shall estop the defendant from denying the essential elements of the offense in any action which involves the same transaction as in the criminal proceeding and which is brought under subsection (a) or (b) of section 3730.

§ 5311. Declaration of purpose

It is the purpose of this subchapter (except section 5315) to require certain reports or records where they have a high degree of usefulness in criminal, tax, or regulatory investigations or proceedings, or in the conduct of intelligence or counterintelligence activities, including analysis, to protect against international terrorism.

§ 5312. Definitions and application

(a) In this subchapter—

(1) "financial agency" means a person acting for a person (except for a country, a monetary or financial authority acting as a monetary or financial authority, or an international financial institution of which the United States Government is a member) as a financial institution, bailee, depository trustee, or agent, or acting in a similar way related to money, credit, securities, gold, or a transaction in money, credit, securities, or gold.

(2) "financial institution" means—

(A) an insured bank (as defined in section 3(h) of the Federal Deposit Insurance Act (12 U.S.C. 1813(h)));

(B) a commercial bank or trust company;

(C) a private banker;

(D) an agency or branch of a foreign bank in the United States;

(E) any credit union;

(F) a thrift institution;

(G) a broker or dealer registered with the Securities and Exchange Commission under the Securities Exchange Act of 1934 (15 U.S.C. 78a et seq.);

(H) a broker or dealer in securities or commodities;

(I) an investment banker or investment company;

(J) a currency exchange;

(K) an issuer, redeemer, or cashier of travelers' checks, checks, money orders, or similar instruments;

(L) an operator of a credit card system;

(M) an insurance company;

(N) a dealer in precious metals, stones, or jewels;

(O) a pawnbroker;

(P) a loan or finance company;

(Q) a travel agency;

(R) a licensed sender of money or any other person who engages as a business in the transmission of funds, including any person who engages as a business in an informal money transfer system or any network of people who engage as a business in facilitating the transfer of money domestically or internationally outside of the conventional financial institutions system;

(S) a telegraph company;

(T) a business engaged in vehicle sales, including automobile, airplane, and boat sales;

(U) persons involved in real estate closings and settlements;

(V) the United States Postal Service;

(W) an agency of the United States Government or of a State or local government carrying out a duty or power of a business described in this paragraph;

(X) a casino, gambling casino, or gaming establishment with an annual gaming revenue of more than $1,000,000 which—

    (i) is licensed as a casino, gambling casino, or gaming establishment under the laws of any State or any political subdivision of any State; or

    (ii) is an Indian gaming operation conducted under or pursuant to the

Indian Gaming Regulatory Act other than an operation which is limited to class I gaming (as defined in section 4(6) of such Act);

(Y) any business or agency which engages in any activity which the Secretary of the Treasury determines, by regulation, to be an activity which is similar to, related to, or a substitute for any activity in which any business described in this paragraph is authorized to engage; or

(Z) any other business designated by the Secretary whose cash transactions have a high degree of usefulness in criminal, tax, or regulatory matters.

(3) "monetary instruments" means—

(A) United States coins and currency;

(B) as the Secretary may prescribe by regulation, coins and currency of a foreign country, travelers' checks, bearer negotiable instruments, bearer investment securities, bearer securities, stock on which title is passed on delivery, and similar material; and

(C) as the Secretary of the Treasury shall provide by regulation for purposes of sections 5316 and 5331, checks, drafts, notes, money orders, and other similar instruments which are drawn on or by a foreign financial institution and are not in bearer form.

(4) Nonfinancial trade or business.— The term "nonfinancial trade or business" means any trade or business other than a financial institution that is subject to the reporting requirements of section 5313 and regulations prescribed under such section.

(5) "person", in addition to its meaning under section 1 of title 1, includes a trustee, a representative of an estate and, when the Secretary prescribes, a governmental entity.

(6) "United States" means the States of the United States, the District of Columbia, and, when the Secretary prescribes by regulation, the Commonwealth of Puerto Rico, the Virgin Islands, Guam, the Northern Mariana Islands, American Samoa, the Trust Territory of the Pacific Islands, a territory or possession of the United States, or a military or diplomatic establishment.

(b) In this subchapter—

(1) "domestic financial agency" and "domestic financial institution" apply to an action in the United States of a financial agency or institution.

(2) "foreign financial agency" and "foreign financial institution" apply to an action outside the United States of a financial agency or institution.

(c) Additional definitions.— For purposes of this subchapter, the following definitions shall apply:

(1) Certain institutions included in definition.— The term "financial institution" (as defined in subsection (a)) includes the following:

(A) Any futures commission merchant, commodity trading advisor, or commodity pool operator registered, or required to register, under the

Commodity Exchange Act [7 U.S.C.A. § 1 et seq.].

§ 5313. Reports on domestic coins and currency transactions

(a) When a domestic financial institution is involved in a transaction for the payment, receipt, or transfer of United States coins or currency (or other monetary instruments the Secretary of the Treasury prescribes), in an amount, denomination, or amount and denomination, or under circumstances the Secretary prescribes by regulation, the institution and any other participant in the transaction the Secretary may prescribe shall file a report on the transaction at the time and in the way the Secretary prescribes. A participant acting for another person shall make the report as the agent or bailee of the person and identify the person for whom the transaction is being made.

(b) The Secretary may designate a domestic financial institution as an agent of the United States Government to receive a report under this section. However, the Secretary may designate a domestic financial institution that is not insured, chartered, examined, or registered as a domestic financial institution only if the institution consents. The Secretary may suspend or revoke a designation for a violation of this subchapter or a regulation under this subchapter (except a violation of section 5315 of this title or a regulation prescribed under section 5315), section 411 of the National Housing Act (12 U.S.C. 1730d), or section 21 of the Federal Deposit Insurance Act (12 U.S.C. 1829b).

(c)

(1) A person (except a domestic financial institution designated under subsection (b) of this section) required to file a report under this section shall file the report—

(A) with the institution involved in the transaction if the institution was designated;

(B) in the way the Secretary prescribes when the institution was not designated; or

(C) with the Secretary.

(2) The Secretary shall prescribe—

(A) the filing procedure for a domestic financial institution designated under subsection (b) of this section; and

(B) the way the institution shall submit reports filed with it.

(d) Mandatory exemptions from reporting requirements.—

(1) In general.— The Secretary of the Treasury shall exempt, pursuant to section 5318(a)(6), a depository institution from the reporting requirements of subsection (a) with respect to transactions between the depository institution and the following categories of entities:

(A) Another depository institution.

(B) A department or agency of the United States, any State, or any political subdivision of any State.

(C) Any entity established under the laws of the United States, any State, or any political subdivision of any State, or under an interstate compact between 2 or more States, which exercises governmental authority on behalf of the United States or any such State or political subdivision.

(D) Any business or category of business the reports on which have little or no value for law enforcement purposes.

(2) Notice of exemption.— The Secretary of the Treasury shall publish in the Federal Register at such times as the Secretary determines to be appropriate (but not less frequently than once each year) a list of all the entities whose transactions with a depository institution are exempt under this subsection from the reporting requirements of subsection (a).

(e) Discretionary exemptions from reporting requirements.—

(1) In general.— The Secretary of the Treasury may exempt, pursuant to section 5318(a)(6), a depository institution from the reporting requirements of subsection (a) with respect to transactions between the depository institution and a qualified business customer of the institution on the basis of information submitted to the Secretary by the institution in accordance with procedures which the Secretary shall establish.

(2) Qualified business customer defined.— For purposes of this subsection, the term "qualified business customer" means a business which—

(A) maintains a transaction account (as defined in section 19(b)(1)(C) of the Federal Reserve Act) at the depository institution;

(B) frequently engages in transactions with the depository institution which are subject to the reporting requirements of subsection (a); and

(C) meets criteria which the Secretary determines are sufficient to ensure that the purposes of this subchapter are carried out without requiring a report with respect to such transactions.

(3) Criteria for exemption.— The Secretary of the Treasury shall establish, by regulation, the criteria for granting and maintaining an exemption under paragraph (1).

(4) Guidelines.—

(A) In general.— The Secretary of the Treasury shall establish guidelines for depository institutions to follow in selecting customers for an exemption under this subsection.

(B) Contents.— The guidelines may include a description of the types of businesses or an itemization of specific businesses for which no exemption will be granted under this subsection to any depository institution.

(5) Annual review.— The Secretary of the Treasury shall prescribe regulations requiring each depository institution to—

(A) review, at least once each year, the qualified business customers of such institution with respect to whom an exemption has been granted under this subsection; and

(B) upon the completion of such review, resubmit information about such customers, with such modifications as the institution determines to be appropriate, to the Secretary for the Secretary's approval.

(6) 2-Year phase-in provision.— During the 2-year period beginning on the date of enactment of the Money Laundering Suppression Act of 1994, this subsection shall be applied by the Secretary on the basis of such criteria as the Secretary determines to be appropriate to achieve an orderly implementation of the requirements of this subsection.

(f) Provisions applicable to mandatory and discretionary exemptions.—

(1) Limitation on liability of depository institutions.— No depository institution shall be subject to any penalty which may be imposed under this subchapter for the failure of the institution to file a report with respect to a transaction with a customer for whom an exemption has been granted under subsection (d) or (e) unless the institution—

(A) knowingly files false or incomplete information to the Secretary with respect to the transaction or the customer engaging in the transaction; or

(B) has reason to believe at the time the exemption is granted or the transaction is entered into that the customer or the transaction does not meet the criteria established for granting such exemption.

(2) Coordination with other provisions.— Any exemption granted by the Secretary of the Treasury under section 5318(a) in accordance with this section, and any transaction which is subject to such exemption, shall be subject to any other provision of law applicable to such exemption, including—

(A) the authority of the Secretary, under section 5318(a)(6), to revoke such exemption at any time; and

(B) any requirement to report, or any authority to require a report on, any possible violation of any law or regulation or any suspected criminal activity.

(g) Depository institution defined.— For purposes of this section, the term "depository institution"—

(1) has the meaning given to such term in section 19(b)(1)(A) of the Federal Reserve Act; and

(2) includes—

(A) any branch, agency, or commercial lending company (as such terms are defined in section 1(b) of the International Banking Act of 1978);

(B) any corporation chartered under section 25A of the Federal Reserve Act; and

(C) any corporation having an agreement or undertaking with the Board of Governors of the Federal Reserve System under section 25 of the Federal Reserve Act.

§ 5314.   Records and reports on foreign financial agency transactions

(a) Considering the need to avoid impeding or controlling the export or import of monetary instruments and the need to avoid burdening unreasonably a person making a transaction with a foreign financial agency, the Secretary of the Treasury shall require a resident or citizen of the United States or a person in, and doing business in, the United States, to keep records, file reports, or keep records and file reports, when the resident, citizen, or person makes a transaction or maintains a relation for any person with a foreign financial agency. The records and reports shall contain the following information in the way and to the extent the Secretary prescribes:

(1) the identity and address of participants in a transaction or relationship.

(2) the legal capacity in which a participant is acting.

(3) the identity of real parties in interest.

(4) a description of the transaction.

(b) The Secretary may prescribe—

(1) a reasonable classification of persons subject to or exempt from a requirement under this section or a regulation under this section;

(2) a foreign country to which a requirement or a regulation under this section applies if the Secretary decides applying the requirement or regulation to all foreign countries is unnecessary or undesirable;

(3) the magnitude of transactions subject to a requirement or a regulation under this section;

(4) the kind of transaction subject to or exempt from a requirement or a regulation under this section; and

(5) other matters the Secretary considers necessary to carry out this section or a regulation under this section.

(c) A person shall be required to disclose a record required to be kept under this section or under a regulation under this section only as required by law.

§ 5315.   Reports on foreign currency transactions

(a) Congress finds that—

(1) moving mobile capital can have a significant impact on the proper functioning of the international monetary system;

(2) it is important to have the most feasible current and complete information on the kind and source of capital flows, including transactions by large United States businesses and their foreign affiliates; and

(3) additional authority should be provided to collect information on capital flows under section 5(b) of the Trading With the Enemy Act (50 App. U.S.C. 5(b)) and section 8 of the Bretton Woods Agreement Act (22 U.S.C. 286f).

(b) In this section, "United States person" and "foreign person controlled by a

United States person" have the same meanings given those terms in section 7(f)(2)(A) and (C), respectively, of the Securities and Exchange Act of 1934 (15 U.S.C. 78g(f)(2)(A), (C)).

(c) The Secretary of the Treasury shall prescribe regulations consistent with subsection (a) of this section requiring reports on foreign currency transactions conducted by a United States person or a foreign person controlled by a United States person. The regulations shall require that a report contain information and be submitted at the time and in the way, with reasonable exceptions and classifications, necessary to carry out this section.

§ 5316. Reports on exporting and importing monetary instruments

(a) Except as provided in subsection (c) of this section, a person or an agent or bailee of the person shall file a report under subsection (b) of this section when the person, agent, or bailee knowingly—

(1) transports, is about to transport, or has transported, monetary instruments of more than $10,000 at one time—

(A) from a place in the United States to or through a place outside the United States; or

(B) to a place in the United States from or through a place outside the United States; or

(2) receives monetary instruments of more than $10,000 at one time transported into the United States from or through a place outside the United States.

(b) A report under this section shall be filed at the time and place the Secretary of the Treasury prescribes. The report shall contain the following information to the extent the Secretary prescribes:

(1) the legal capacity in which the person filing the report is acting.

(2) the origin, destination, and route of the monetary instruments.

(3) when the monetary instruments are not legally and beneficially owned by the person transporting the instruments, or if the person transporting the instruments personally is not going to use them, the identity of the person that gave the instruments to the person transporting them, the identity of the person who is to receive them, or both.

(4) the amount and kind of monetary instruments transported.

(5) additional information.

(c) This section or a regulation under this section does not apply to a common carrier of passengers when a passenger possesses a monetary instrument, or to a common carrier of goods if the shipper does not declare the instrument.

(d) Cumulation of closely related events.— The Secretary of the Treasury may prescribe regulations under this section defining the term "at one time" for purposes of subsection (a). Such regulations may permit the cumulation of closely related events in order that such events may collectively be considered to occur at one time for the purposes of subsection (a).

§ 5318. Compliance, exemptions, and summons authority

(a) General powers of Secretary.— The Secretary of the Treasury may (except under section 5315 of this title and regulations prescribed under section 5315)—

(1) except as provided in subsection (b)(2), delegate duties and powers under this subchapter to an appropriate supervising agency and the United States Postal Service;

(2) require a class of domestic financial institutions or nonfinancial trades or businesses to maintain appropriate procedures to ensure compliance with this subchapter and regulations prescribed under this subchapter or to guard against money laundering;

(3) examine any books, papers, records, or other data of domestic financial institutions or nonfinancial trades or businesses relevant to the recordkeeping or reporting requirements of this subchapter;

(4) summon a financial institution or nonfinancial trade or business, an officer or employee of a financial institution or nonfinancial trade or business (including a former officer or employee), or any person having possession, custody, or care of the reports and records required under this subchapter, to appear before the Secretary of the Treasury or his delegate at a time and place named in the summons and to produce such books, papers, records, or other data, and to give testimony, under oath, as may be relevant or material to an investigation described in subsection (b);

(5) exempt from the requirements of this subchapter any class of transactions within any State if the Secretary determines that—

(A) under the laws of such State, that class of transactions is subject to requirements substantially similar to those imposed under this subchapter; and

(B) there is adequate provision for the enforcement of such requirements;

(6) rely on examinations conducted by a State supervisory agency of a category of financial institution, if the Secretary determines that—

(A) the category of financial institution is required to comply with this subchapter and regulations prescribed under this subchapter; or

(B) the State supervisory agency examines the category of financial institution for compliance with this subchapter and regulations prescribed under this subchapter; and

(7) prescribe an appropriate exemption from a requirement under this subchapter and regulations prescribed under this subchapter. The Secretary may revoke an exemption under this paragraph or paragraph (5) by actually or constructively notifying the parties affected. A revocation is effective during judicial review.

(b) Limitations on summons power.—

(1) Scope of power.— The Secretary of the Treasury may take any action

described in paragraph (3) or (4) of subsection (a) only in connection with investigations for the purpose of civil enforcement of violations of this subchapter, section 21 of the Federal Deposit Insurance Act, section 411 of the National Housing Act, or chapter 2 of Public Law 91-508 (12 U.S.C. 1951 et seq.) or any regulation under any such provision.

(2) Authority to issue.— A summons may be issued under subsection (a)(4) only by, or with the approval of, the Secretary of the Treasury or a supervisory level delegate of the Secretary of the Treasury.

(c) Administrative aspects of summons.—

(1) Production at designated site.— A summons issued pursuant to this section may require that books, papers, records, or other data stored or maintained at any place be produced at any designated location in any State or in any territory or other place subject to the jurisdiction of the United States not more than 500 miles distant from any place where the financial institution or nonfinancial trade or business operates or conducts business in the United States.

(2) Fees and travel expenses.— Persons summoned under this section shall be paid the same fees and mileage for travel in the United States that are paid witnesses in the courts of the United States.

(3) No liability for expenses.— The United States shall not be liable for any expense, other than an expense described in paragraph (2), incurred in connection with the production of books, papers, records, or other data under this section.

(d) Service of summons.— Service of a summons issued under this section may be by registered mail or in such other manner calculated to give actual notice as the Secretary may prescribe by regulation.

(e) Contumacy or refusal.—

(1) Referral to Attorney General.— In case of contumacy by a person issued a summons under paragraph (3) or (4) of subsection (a) or a refusal by such person to obey such summons, the Secretary of the Treasury shall refer the matter to the Attorney General.

(2) Jurisdiction of court.— The Attorney General may invoke the aid of any court of the United States within the jurisdiction of which—

(A) the investigation which gave rise to the summons is being or has been carried on;

(B) the person summoned is an inhabitant; or

(C) the person summoned carries on business or may be found, to compel compliance with the summons.

(3) Court order.— The court may issue an order requiring the person summoned to appear before the Secretary or his delegate to produce books, papers, records, and other data, to give testimony as may be necessary to explain how such material was compiled and maintained, and to pay the costs of the proceeding.

(4) Failure to comply with order.— Any failure to obey the order of the court may be punished by the court as a contempt thereof.

(5) Service of process.— All process in any case under this subsection may be served in any judicial district in which such person may be found.

(f) Written and signed statement required.— No person shall qualify for an exemption under subsection (a)(5) unless the relevant financial institution or nonfinancial trade or business prepares and maintains a statement which—

(1) describes in detail the reasons why such person is qualified for such exemption; and

(2) contains the signature of such person.

(g) Reporting of suspicious transactions.—

(1) In general.— The Secretary may require any financial institution, and any director, officer, employee, or agent of any financial institution, to report any suspicious transaction relevant to a possible violation of law or regulation.

(2) Notification prohibited.—

(A) In general.— If a financial institution or any director, officer, employee, or agent of any financial institution, voluntarily or pursuant to this section or any other authority, reports a suspicious transaction to a government agency—

(i) neither the financial institution, director, officer, employee, or agent of such institution (whether or not any such person is still employed by the institution), nor any other current or former director, officer, or employee of, or contractor for, the financial institution or other reporting person, may notify any person involved in the transaction that the transaction has been reported; and

(ii) no current or former officer or employee of or contractor for the Federal Government or of or for any State, local, tribal, or territorial government within the United States, who has any knowledge that such report was made may disclose to any person involved in the transaction that the transaction has been reported, other than as necessary to fulfill the official duties of such officer or employee.

(B) Disclosures in certain employment references.—

(i) Rule of construction.— Notwithstanding the application of subparagraph (A) in any other context, subparagraph (A) shall not be construed as prohibiting any financial institution, or any director, officer, employee, or agent of such institution, from including information that was included in a report to which subparagraph (A) applies—

(I) in a written employment reference that is provided in accordance with section 18(w) of the Federal Deposit Insurance Act in response to a request from another financial institution; or

(II) in a written termination notice or employment reference that is provided in accordance with the rules of a self-regulatory organization registered with the Securities and Exchange Commission or the Commodity Futures Trading Commission,

except that such written reference or notice may not disclose that such information was also included in any such report, or that such report was made.

(ii) Information not required.— Clause (i) shall not be construed, by itself, to create any affirmative duty to include any information described in clause (i) in any employment reference or termination notice referred to in clause (i).

(3) Liability for disclosures.—

(A) In general.— Any financial institution that makes a voluntary disclosure of any possible violation of law or regulation to a government agency or makes a disclosure pursuant to this subsection or any other authority, and any director, officer, employee, or agent of such institution who makes, or requires another to make any such disclosure, shall not be liable to any person under any law or regulation of the United States, any constitution, law, or regulation of any State or political subdivision of any State, or under any contract or other legally enforceable agreement (including any arbitration agreement), for such disclosure or for any failure to provide notice of such disclosure to the person who is the subject of such disclosure or any other person identified in the disclosure.

(B) Rule of construction.— Subparagraph (A) shall not be construed as creating—

(i) any inference that the term "person", as used in such subparagraph, may be construed more broadly than its ordinary usage so as to include any government or agency of government; or

(ii) any immunity against, or otherwise affecting, any civil or criminal action brought by any government or agency of government to enforce any constitution, law, or regulation of such government or agency.

(4) Single designee for reporting suspicious transactions.—

(A) In general.— In requiring reports under paragraph (1) of suspicious transactions, the Secretary of the Treasury shall designate, to the extent practicable and appropriate, a single officer or agency of the United States to whom such reports shall be made.

(B) Duty of designee.— The officer or agency of the United States designated by the Secretary of the Treasury pursuant to subparagraph (A) shall refer any report of a suspicious transaction to any appropriate law enforcement, supervisory agency, or United States intelligence agency for use in the conduct of intelligence or counterintelligence activities, including analysis, to protect against international terrorism.

(C) Coordination with other reporting requirements.— Subparagraph (A) shall not be construed as precluding any supervisory agency for any financial institution from requiring the financial institution to submit any information or report to the agency or another agency pursuant to any other applicable provision of law.

(h) Anti-money laundering programs.—

(1) In general.— In order to guard against money laundering through financial institutions, each financial institution shall establish anti-money laundering programs, including, at a minimum—

(A) the development of internal policies, procedures, and controls;

(B) the designation of a compliance officer;

(C) an ongoing employee training program; and

(D) an independent audit function to test programs.

(2) Regulations.— The Secretary of the Treasury, after consultation with the appropriate Federal functional regulator (as defined in section 509 of the Gramm-Leach-Bliley Act), may prescribe minimum standards for programs established under paragraph (1), and may exempt from the application of those standards any financial institution that is not subject to the provisions of the rules contained in part 103 of title 31, of the Code of Federal Regulations, or any successor rule thereto, for so long as such financial institution is not subject to the provisions of such rules.

(3) Concentration accounts.— The Secretary may prescribe regulations under this subsection that govern maintenance of concentration accounts by financial institutions, in order to ensure that such accounts are not used to prevent association of the identity of an individual customer with the movement of funds of which the customer is the direct or beneficial owner, which regulations shall, at a minimum—

(A) prohibit financial institutions from allowing clients to direct transactions that move their funds into, out of, or through the concentration accounts of the financial institution;

(B) prohibit financial institutions and their employees from informing customers of the existence of, or the means of identifying, the concentration accounts of the institution; and

(C) require each financial institution to establish written procedures governing the documentation of all transactions involving a concentration account, which procedures shall ensure that, any time a transaction involving a concentration account commingles funds belonging to 1 or more customers, the identity of, and specific amount belonging to, each customer is documented.

(i) Due diligence for United States private banking and correspondent bank accounts involving foreign persons.—

(1) In general.— Each financial institution that establishes, maintains, administers, or manages a private banking account or a correspondent account in the United States for a non-United States person, including a foreign individual

visiting the United States, or a representative of a non-United States person shall establish appropriate, specific, and, where necessary, enhanced, due diligence policies, procedures, and controls that are reasonably designed to detect and report instances of money laundering through those accounts.

(2) Additional standards for certain correspondent accounts.—

(A) In general.— Subparagraph (B) shall apply if a correspondent account is requested or maintained by, or on behalf of, a foreign bank operating—

(i) under an offshore banking license; or

(ii) under a banking license issued by a foreign country that has been designated—

(I) as noncooperative with international anti-money laundering principles or procedures by an intergovernmental group or organization of which the United States is a member, with which designation the United States representative to the group or organization concurs; or

(II) by the Secretary of the Treasury as warranting special measures due to money laundering concerns.

(B) Policies, procedures, and controls.— The enhanced due diligence policies, procedures, and controls required under paragraph (1) shall, at a minimum, ensure that the financial institution in the United States takes reasonable steps—

(i) to ascertain for any such foreign bank, the shares of which are not publicly traded, the identity of each of the owners of the foreign bank, and the nature and extent of the ownership interest of each such owner;

(ii) to conduct enhanced scrutiny of such account to guard against money laundering and report any suspicious transactions under subsection (g); and

(iii) to ascertain whether such foreign bank provides correspondent accounts to other foreign banks and, if so, the identity of those foreign banks and related due diligence information, as appropriate under paragraph (1).

(3) Minimum standards for private banking accounts.— If a private banking account is requested or maintained by, or on behalf of, a non-United States person, then the due diligence policies, procedures, and controls required under paragraph (1) shall, at a minimum, ensure that the financial institution takes reasonable steps—

(A) to ascertain the identity of the nominal and beneficial owners of, and the source of funds deposited into, such account as needed to guard against money laundering and report any suspicious transactions under subsection (g); and

(B) to conduct enhanced scrutiny of any such account that is requested or maintained by, or on behalf of, a senior foreign political figure, or any immediate family member or close associate of a senior foreign political figure, that is reasonably designed to detect and report transactions that may involve the proceeds of foreign corruption.

(4) Definitions.— For purposes of this subsection, the following definitions shall apply:

(A) Offshore banking license.— The term "offshore banking license" means a license to conduct banking activities which, as a condition of the license, prohibits the licensed entity from conducting banking activities with the citizens of, or with the local currency of, the country which issued the license.

(B) Private banking account.— The term "private banking account" means an account (or any combination of accounts) that—

(i) requires a minimum aggregate deposits of funds or other assets of not less than $1,000,000;

(ii) is established on behalf of 1 or more individuals who have a direct or beneficial ownership interest in the account; and

(iii) is assigned to, or is administered or managed by, in whole or in part, an officer, employee, or agent of a financial institution acting as a liaison between the financial institution and the direct or beneficial owner of the account.

(j) Prohibition on United States correspondent accounts with foreign shell banks.—

(1) In general.— A financial institution described in subparagraphs (A) through (G) of section 5312(a)(2) (in this subsection referred to as a "covered financial institution") shall not establish, maintain, administer, or manage a correspondent account in the United States for, or on behalf of, a foreign bank that does not have a physical presence in any country.

(2) Prevention of indirect service to foreign shell banks.— A covered financial institution shall take reasonable steps to ensure that any correspondent account established, maintained, administered, or managed by that covered financial institution in the United States for a foreign bank is not being used by that foreign bank to indirectly provide banking services to another foreign bank that does not have a physical presence in any country. The Secretary of the Treasury shall, by regulation, delineate the reasonable steps necessary to comply with this paragraph.

(3) Exception.— Paragraphs (1) and (2) do not prohibit a covered financial institution from providing a correspondent account to a foreign bank, if the foreign bank—

(A) is an affiliate of a depository institution, credit union, or foreign bank that maintains a physical presence in the United States or a foreign country, as applicable; and

(B) is subject to supervision by a banking authority in the country regulating the affiliated depository institution, credit union, or foreign bank described in subparagraph (A), as applicable.

(4) Definitions.— For purposes of this subsection—

(A) the term "affiliate" means a foreign bank that is controlled by or is under common control with a depository institution, credit union, or foreign bank; and

(B) the term "physical presence" means a place of business that—

(i) is maintained by a foreign bank;

(ii) is located at a fixed address (other than solely an electronic address) in a country in which the foreign bank is authorized to conduct banking activities, at which location the foreign bank—

(I) employs 1 or more individuals on a full-time basis; and

(II) maintains operating records related to its banking activities; and

(iii) is subject to inspection by the banking authority which licensed the foreign bank to conduct banking activities.

(k) Bank records related to anti-money laundering programs.—

(1) Definitions.— For purposes of this subsection, the following definitions shall apply:

(A) Appropriate Federal banking agency.— The term "appropriate Federal banking agency" has the same meaning as in section 3 of the Federal Deposit Insurance Act (12 U.S.C. 1813).

(B) Incorporated term.— The term "correspondent account" has the same meaning as in section 5318A(e)(1)(B).

(2) 120-hour rule.— Not later than 120 hours after receiving a request by an appropriate Federal banking agency for information related to anti-money laundering compliance by a covered financial institution or a customer of such institution, a covered financial institution shall provide to the appropriate Federal banking agency, or make available at a location specified by the representative of the appropriate Federal banking agency, information and account documentation for any account opened, maintained, administered or managed in the United States by the covered financial institution.

(3) Foreign bank records.—

(A) Summons or subpoena of records.—

(i) In general.— The Secretary of the Treasury or the Attorney General may issue a summons or subpoena to any foreign bank that maintains a correspondent account in the United States and request records related to such correspondent account, including records maintained outside of the United States relating to the deposit of funds into the foreign bank.

(ii) Service of summons or subpoena.— A summons or subpoena referred to in clause (i) may be served on the foreign bank in the United States if the foreign bank has a representative in the United States, or in a foreign country pursuant to any mutual legal assistance treaty, multilateral agreement, or other request for international law enforcement assistance.

(B) Acceptance of service.—

(i) Maintaining records in the United States.— Any covered financial institution which maintains a correspondent account in the United States for a foreign bank shall maintain records in the United States identifying the owners of such foreign bank and the name and address of a person who resides in the United States and is authorized to accept service of legal process for records regarding the correspondent account.

(ii) Law enforcement request.— Upon receipt of a written request from a Federal law enforcement officer for information required to be maintained under this paragraph, the covered financial institution shall provide the information to the requesting officer not later than 7 days after receipt of the request.

(C) Termination of correspondent relationship.—

(i) Termination upon receipt of notice.— A covered financial institution shall terminate any correspondent relationship with a foreign bank not later than 10 business days after receipt of written notice from the Secretary or the Attorney General (in each case, after consultation with the other) that the foreign bank has failed—

(I) to comply with a summons or subpoena issued under subparagraph (A); or

(II) to initiate proceedings in a United States court contesting such summons or subpoena.

(ii) Limitation on liability.— A covered financial institution shall not be liable to any person in any court or arbitration proceeding for terminating a correspondtent relationship in accordance with this subsection.

(iii) Failure to terminate relationship.— Failure to terminate a correspondent relationship in accordance with this subsection shall render the covered financial institution liable for a civil penalty of up to $10,000 per day until the correspondent relationship is so terminated.

(l) Identification and verification of accountholders.—

(1) In general.— Subject to the requirements of this subsection, the Secretary of the Treasury shall prescribe regulations setting forth the minimum standards for financial institutions and their customers regarding the identity of the customer that shall apply in connection with the opening of an account at a financial institution.

(2) Minimum requirements.— The regulations shall, at a minimum, require financial institutions to implement, and customers (after being given adequate notice) to comply with, reasonable procedures for—

(A) verifying the identity of any person seeking to open an account to the extent reasonable and practicable;

(B) maintaining records of the information used to verify a person's identity, including name, address, and other identifying information; and

(C) consulting lists of known or suspected terrorists or terrorist organizations provided to the financial institution by any government agency to determine whether a person seeking to open an account appears on any such list.

(3) Factors to be considered.— In prescribing regulations under this subsection, the Secretary shall take into consideration the various types of accounts maintained by various types of financial institutions, the various methods of opening accounts, and the various types of identifying information available.

(4) Certain financial institutions.— In the case of any financial institution the business of which is engaging in financial activities described in section 4(k) of the Bank Holding Company Act of 1956 (including financial activities subject to the jurisdiction of the Commodity Futures Trading Commission), the regulations prescribed by the Secretary under paragraph (1) shall be prescribed jointly with each Federal functional regulator (as defined in section 509 of the Gramm-Leach-Bliley Act, including the Commodity Futures Trading Commission) appropriate for such financial institution.

(5) Exemptions.— The Secretary (and, in the case of any financial institution described in paragraph (4), any Federal agency described in such paragraph) may, by regulation or order, exempt any financial institution or type of account from the requirements of any regulation prescribed under this subsection in accordance with such standards and procedures as the Secretary may prescribe.

(6) Effective date.— Final regulations prescribed under this subsection shall take effect before the end of the 1-year period beginning on the date of enactment of the International Money Laundering Abatement and Financial Anti-Terrorism Act of 2001.

(m) Applicability of rules.— Any rules promulgated pursuant to the authority contained in section 21 of the Federal Deposit Insurance Act (12 U.S.C. 1829b) shall apply, in addition to any other financial institution to which such rules apply, to any person that engages as a business in the transmission of funds, including any person who engages as a business in an informal money transfer system or any network of people who engage as a business in facilitating the transfer of money domestically or internationally outside of the conventional financial institutions system.

(n) Reporting of certain cross-border transmittals of funds.—

(1) In general.— Subject to paragraphs (3) and (4), the Secretary shall prescribe regulations requiring such financial institutions as the Secretary determines to be appropriate to report to the Financial Crimes Enforcement Network certain cross-border electronic transmittals of funds, if the Secretary determines that reporting of such transmittals is reasonably necessary to conduct the efforts of the Secretary against money laundering and terrorist financing.

(2) Limitation on reporting requirements.— Information required to be reported by the regulations prescribed under paragraph (1) shall not exceed the information required to be retained by the reporting financial institution pursuant to section 21 of the Federal Deposit Insurance Act and the regulations promulgated thereunder, unless—

(A) the Board of Governors of the Federal Reserve System and the Secretary jointly determine that a particular item or items of information are not currently required to be retained under such section or such regulations; and

(B) the Secretary determines, after consultation with the Board of Governors of the Federal Reserve System, that the reporting of such information is reasonably necessary to conduct the efforts of the Secretary to identify cross-border money laundering and terrorist financing.

(3) Form and manner of reports.— In prescribing the regulations required under paragraph (1), the Secretary shall, subject to paragraph (2), determine the appropriate form, manner, content, and frequency of filing of the required reports.

(4) Feasibility report.—

(A) In general.— Before prescribing the regulations required under paragraph (1), and as soon as is practicable after the date of enactment of the Intelligence Reform and Terrorism Prevention Act of 2004, the Secretary shall submit a report to the Committee on Banking, Housing, and Urban Affairs of the Senate and the Committee on Financial Services of the House of Representatives that—

(i) identifies the information in cross-border electronic transmittals of funds that may be found in particular cases to be reasonably necessary to conduct the efforts of the Secretary to identify money laundering and terrorist financing, and outlines the criteria to be used by the Secretary to select the situations in which reporting under this subsection may be required;

(ii) outlines the appropriate form, manner, content, and frequency of filing of the reports that may be required under such regulations;

(iii) identifies the technology necessary for the Financial Crimes Enforcement Network to receive, keep, exploit, protect the security of, and disseminate information from reports of cross-border electronic transmittals of funds to law enforcement and other entities engaged in efforts against money laundering and terrorist financing; and

(iv) discusses the information security protections required by the exercise of the Secretary's authority under this subsection.

(B) Consultation.— In reporting the feasibility report under subparagraph (A), the Secretary may consult with the Bank Secrecy Act Advisory Group established by the Secretary, and any other group considered by the Secretary to be relevant.

(5) Regulations.—

(A) In general.— Subject to subparagraph (B), the regulations required by paragraph (1) shall be prescribed in final form by the Secretary, in consultation with the Board of Governors of the Federal Reserve System, before the end of the 3-year period beginning on the date of enactment of the National

Intelligence Reform Act of 2004.

(B) Technological feasibility.— No regulations shall be prescribed under this subsection before the Secretary certifies to the Congress that the Financial Crimes Enforcement Network has the technological systems in place to effectively and efficiently receive, keep, exploit, protect the security of, and disseminate information from reports of cross-border electronic transmittals of funds to law enforcement and other entities engaged in efforts against money laundering and terrorist financing.

§ 5322.   Criminal penalties

(a) A person willfully violating this subchapter or a regulation prescribed or order issued under this subchapter (except section 5315 or 5324 of this title or a regulation prescribed under section 5315 or 5324), or willfully violating a regulation prescribed under section 21 of the Federal Deposit Insurance Act or section 123 of Public Law 91-508, shall be fined not more than $250,000, or imprisoned for not more than five years, or both.

(b) A person willfully violating this subchapter or a regulation prescribed or order issued under this subchapter (except section 5315 or 5324 of this title or a regulation prescribed under section 5315 or 5324), or willfully violating a regulation prescribed under section 21 of the Federal Deposit Insurance Act or section 123 of Public Law 91-508, while violating another law of the United States or as part of a pattern of any illegal activity involving more than $100,000 in a 12-month period, shall be fined not more than $500,000, imprisoned for not more than 10 years, or both.

(c) For a violation of section 5318(a)(2) of this title or a regulation prescribed under section 5318(a)(2), a separate violation occurs for each day the violation continues and at each office, branch, or place of business at which a violation occurs or continues.

(d) A financial institution or agency that violates any provision of subsection (i) or (j) of section 5318, or any 5318 or section 5318A, shall be fined in an amount equal to not less than 2 times the amount of the transaction, but not more than $1, 000,000.

§ 5324.   Structuring transactions to evade reporting requirement prohibited

(a) Domestic coin and currency transactions involving financial institutions.— No person shall, for the purpose of evading the reporting requirements of section 5313(a) or 5325 or any regulation prescribed under any such section, the reporting or recordkeeping requirements imposed by any order issued under section 5326, or the recordkeeping requirements imposed by any regulation prescribed under section 21 of the Federal Deposit Insurance Act or section 123 of Public Law 91-508—

    (1) cause or attempt to cause a domestic financial institution to fail to file a report required under section 5313(a) or5325 or any regulation prescribed under any such section, to file a report or to maintain a record required by an order issued under section 5326, or to maintain a record required pursuant to any regulation prescribed under section 21 of the Federal Deposit Insurance Act or section 123 of Public Law 91-508;

(2) cause or attempt to cause a domestic financial institution to file a report required under section 5313(a) or 5325or any regulation prescribed under any such section, to file a report or to maintain a record required by any order issued under section 5326, or to maintain a record required pursuant to any regulation prescribed under section 5326, or to maintain a record required pursuant to any regulation prescribed under section 21 of the Federal Deposit Insurance Act or section 123 of Public Law 91-508, that contains a material omission or misstatement of fact; or

(3) structure or assist in structuring, or attempt to structure or assist in structuring, any transaction with one or more domestic financial institutions.

(b) Domestic coin and currency transactions involving nonfinancial trades or businesses.— No person shall, for the purpose of evading the report requirements of section 5331 or any regulation prescribed under such section—

(1) cause or attempt to cause a nonfinancial trade or business to fail to file a report required under section 5331 or any regulation prescribed under such section;

(2) cause or attempt to cause a nonfinancial trade or business to file a report required under section 5331 or any regulation prescribed under such section that contains a material omission or misstatement of fact; or

(3) structure or assist in structuring, or attempt to structure or assist in structuring, any transaction with 1 or more nonfinancial trades or businesses.

(c) International monetary instrument transactions.— No person shall, for the purpose of evading the reporting requirements of section 5316—

(1) fail to file a report required by section 5316, or cause or attempt to cause a person to fail to file such a report;

(2) file or cause or attempt to cause a person to file a report required under section 5316 that contains a material omission or misstatement of fact; or

(3) structure or assist in structuring, or attempt to structure or assist in structuring, any importation or exportation of monetary instruments.

(d) Criminal penalty.—

(1) In general.— Whoever violates this section shall be fined in accordance with title 18, United States Code, imprisoned for not more than 5 years, or both.

(2) Enhanced penalty for aggravated cases.— Whoever violates this section while violating another law of the United States or as part of a pattern of any illegal activity involving more than $100,000 in a 12-month period shall be fined twice the amount provided in subsection (b)(3) or (c)(3) (as the case may be) of section 3571 of title 18, United States Code, imprisoned for not more than 10 years, or both.

§ 5325. Identification required to purchase certain monetary instruments

(a) In general.— No financial institution may issue or sell a bank check, cashier's check, traveler's check, or money order to any individual in connection with a transaction or group of such contemporaneous transactions which involves United States coins or currency (or such other monetary instruments as the Secretary may prescribe) in amounts or denominations of $3,000 or more unless—

(1) the individual has a transaction account with such financial institution and the financial institution—

(A) verifies that fact through a signature card or other information maintained by such institution in connection with the account of such individual; and

(B) records the method of verification in accordance with regulations which the Secretary of the Treasury shall prescribe; or

(2) the individual furnishes the financial institution with such forms of identification as the Secretary of the Treasury may require in regulations which the Secretary shall prescribe and the financial institution verifies and records such information in accordance with regulations which such Secretary shall prescribe.

(b) Report to Secretary upon request.— Any information required to be recorded by any financial institution under paragraph (1) or (2) of subsection (a) shall be reported by such institution to the Secretary of the Treasury at the request of such Secretary.

(c) Transaction account defined.— For purposes of this section, the term "transaction account" has the meaning given to such term in section 19(b)(1)(C) of the Federal Reserve Act.

§ 5332. Bulk cash smuggling into or out of the United States

(a) Criminal offense.—

(1) In general.— Whoever, with the intent to evade a currency reporting requirement under section 5316, knowingly conceals more than $10,000 in currency or other monetary instruments on the person of such individual or in any conveyance, article of luggage, merchandise, or other container, and transports or transfers or attempts to transport or transfer such currency or monetary instruments from a place within the United States to a place outside of the United States, or from a place outside the United States to a place within the United States, shall be guilty of a currency smuggling offense and subject to punishment pursuant to subsection (b).

(2) Concealment on person.— For purposes of this section, the concealment of currency on the person of any individual includes concealment in any article of clothing worn by the individual or in any luggage, backpack, or other container worn or carried by such individual.

(b) Penalty.—

(1) Term of imprisonment.— A person convicted of a currency smuggling offense under subsection (a), or a conspiracy to commit such offense, shall be imprisoned for not more than 5 years.

(2) Forfeiture.— In addition, the court, in imposing sentence under paragraph

(1), shall order that the defendant forfeit to the United States, any property, real or personal, involved in the offense, and any property traceable to such property.

(3) Procedure.— The seizure, restraint, and forfeiture of property under this section shall be governed by section 413 of the Controlled Substances Act.

(4) Personal money judgment.— If the property subject to forfeiture under paragraph (2) is unavailable, and the defendant has insufficient substitute property that may be forfeited pursuant to section 413(p) of the Controlled Substances Act, the court shall enter a personal money judgment against the defendant for the amount that would be subject to forfeiture.

(c) Civil forfeiture.—

(1) In general.— Any property involved in a violation of subsection (a), or a conspiracy to commit such violation, and any property traceable to such violation or conspiracy, may be seized and forfeited to the United States.

(2) Procedure.— The seizure and forfeiture shall be governed by the procedures governing civil forfeitures in money laundering cases pursuant to section 981(a)(1)(A) of title 18, United States Code.

(3) Treatment of certain property as involved in the offense.— For purposes of this subsection and subsection (b), any currency or other monetary instrument that is concealed or intended to be concealed in violation of subsection (a) or a conspiracy to commit such violation, any article, container, or conveyance used, or intended to be used, to conceal or transport the currency or other monetary instrument, and any other property used, or intended to be used, to facilitate the offense, shall be considered property involved in the offense.

TITLE 50.   WAR AND NATIONAL DEFENSE

§ 1702.   Unusual and extraordinary threat; declaration of national emergency; exercise of Presidential authorities

(a) Any authority granted to the President by section 1702 of this title may be exercised to deal with any unusual and extraordinary threat, which has its source in whole or substantial part outside the United States, to the national security, foreign policy, or economy of the United States, if the President declares a national emergency with respect to such threat.

(b) The authorities granted to the President by section 1702 of this title may only be exercised to deal with an unusual and extraordinary threat with respect to which a national emergency has been declared for purposes of this chapter and may not be exercised for any other purpose. Any exercise of such authorities to deal with any new threat shall be based on a new declaration of national emergency which must be with respect to such threat.

§ 1705.   Penalties

(a) Unlawful acts

It shall be unlawful for a person to violate, attempt to violate, conspire to violate, or cause a violation of any license, order, regulation, or prohibition issued under this chapter.

(b) Civil penalty

A civil penalty may be imposed on any person who commits an unlawful act described in subsection (a) of this section in an amount not to exceed the greater of—

(1) $250,000; or

(2) an amount that is twice the amount of the transaction that is the basis of the violation with respect to which the penalty is imposed.

(c) Criminal penalty

A person who willfully commits, willfully attempts to commit, or willfully conspires to commit, or aids or abets in the commission of, an unlawful act described in subsection (a) of this section shall, upon conviction, be fined not more than $1,000,000, or if a natural person, may be imprisoned for not more than 20 years, or both.

Chapter 2
CODE OF FEDERAL REGULATIONS

TITLE 17. COMMODITY AND SECURITIES EXCHANGES

§ 240.10b-5   Employment of manipulative and deceptive devices.

It shall be unlawful for any person, directly or indirectly, by the use of any means or instrumentality of interstate commerce, or of the mails or of any facility of any national securities exchange,

(a) To employ any device, scheme, or artifice to defraud,

(b) To make any untrue statement of a material fact or to omit to state a material fact necessary in order to make the statements made, in the light of the circumstances under which they were made, not misleading, or

(c) To engage in any act, practice, or course of business which operates or would operate as a fraud or deceit upon any person, in connection with the purchase or sale of any security.

§ 240.10b5-1   Trading "on the basis of" material nonpublic information in insider trading cases.

Preliminary Note to § 240.10b5-1: This provision defines when a purchase or sale constitutes trading "on the basis of" material nonpublic information in insider trading cases brought under Section 10(b) of the Act and Rule 10b-5 thereunder. The law of insider trading is otherwise defined by judicial opinions construing Rule 10b-5, and Rule 10b5-1 does not modify the scope of insider trading law in any other respect.

(a) General. The "manipulative and deceptive devices" prohibited by Section 10(b) of the Act (15 U.S.C. 78j) and § 240.10b-5 thereunder include, among other things, the purchase or sale of a security of any issuer, on the basis of material nonpublic information about that security or issuer, in breach of a duty of trust or confidence that is owed directly, indirectly, or derivatively, to the issuer of that security or the shareholders of that issuer, or to any other person who is the source of the material nonpublic information.

(b) Definition of "on the basis of." Subject to the affirmative defenses in paragraph (c) of this section, a purchase or sale of a security of an issuer is "on the basis of" material nonpublic information about that security or issuer if the person making the purchase or sale was aware of the material nonpublic information when the person made the purchase or sale.

(c) Affirmative defenses.

(1)

(i) Subject to paragraph (c)(1)(ii) of this section, a person's purchase or sale is not "on the basis of" material nonpublic information if the person making the purchase or sale demonstrates that:

(A) Before becoming aware of the information, the person had:

(1) Entered into a binding contract to purchase or sell the security,

(2) Instructed another person to purchase or sell the security for the instructing person's account, or

(3) Adopted a written plan for trading securities;

(B) The contract, instruction, or plan described in paragraph (c)(1)(i)(A) of this Section:

(1) Specified the amount of securities to be purchased or sold and the price at which and the date on which the securities were to be purchased or sold;

(2) Included a written formula or algorithm, or computer program, for determining the amount of securities to be purchased or sold and the price at which and the date on which the securities were to be purchased or sold; or

(3) Did not permit the person to exercise any subsequent influence over how, when, or whether to effect purchases or sales; provided, in addition, that any other person who, pursuant to the contract, instruction, or plan, did exercise such influence must not have been aware of the material nonpublic information when doing so; and

(C) The purchase or sale that occurred was pursuant to the contract, instruction, or plan. A purchase or sale is not "pursuant to a contract, instruction, or plan" if, among other things, the person who entered into the contract, instruction, or plan altered or deviated from the contract, instruction, or plan to purchase or sell securities (whether by changing the amount, price, or timing of the purchase or sale), or entered into or altered a corresponding or hedging transaction or position with respect to those securities.

(ii) Paragraph (c)(1)(i) of this section is applicable only when the contract, instruction, or plan to purchase or sell securities was given or entered into in good faith and not as part of a plan or scheme to evade the prohibitions of this section.

(iii) This paragraph (c)(1)(iii) defines certain terms as used in paragraph (c) of this Section.

(A) Amount. "Amount" means either a specified number of shares or other securities or a specified dollar value of securities.

(B) Price. "Price" means the market price on a particular date or a limit price, or a particular dollar price.

(C) Date. "Date" means, in the case of a market order, the specific day of the year on which the order is to be executed (or as soon thereafter as is practicable under ordinary principles of best execution). "Date" means, in the case of a limit order, a day of the year on which the limit order is in force.

(2) A person other than a natural person also may demonstrate that a purchase or sale of securities is not "on the basis of" material nonpublic information if the person demonstrates that:

(i) The individual making the investment decision on behalf of the person to purchase or sell the securities was not aware of the information; and

(ii) The person had implemented reasonable policies and procedures, taking into consideration the nature of the person's business, to ensure that individuals making investment decisions would not violate the laws prohibiting trading on the basis of material nonpublic information. These policies and procedures may include those that restrict any purchase, sale, and causing any purchase or sale of any security as to which the person has material nonpublic information, or those that prevent such individuals from becoming aware of such information.

§ 240.10b5-2   Duties of trust or confidence in misappropriation insider trading cases.

Preliminary Note to § 240.10b5-2: This section provides a non-exclusive definition of circumstances in which a person has a duty of trust or confidence for purposes of the "misappropriation" theory of insider trading under Section 10(b) of the Act and Rule 10b-5. The law of insider trading is otherwise defined by judicial opinions construing Rule 10b-5, and Rule 10b5-2 does not modify the scope of insider trading law in any other respect.

(a) Scope of Rule. This section shall apply to any violation of Section 10(b) of the Act (15 U.S.C. 78j(b)) and § 240.10b-5 thereunder that is based on the purchase or sale of securities on the basis of, or the communication of, material nonpublic information misappropriated in breach of a duty of trust or confidence.

(b) Enumerated "duties of trust or confidence." For purposes of this section, a "duty of trust or confidence" exists in the following circumstances, among others:

(1) Whenever a person agrees to maintain information in confidence;

(2) Whenever the person communicating the material nonpublic information and the person to whom it is communicated have a history, pattern, or practice of sharing confidences, such that the recipient of the information knows or reasonably should know that the person communicating the material nonpublic information expects that the recipient will maintain its confidentiality; or

(3) Whenever a person receives or obtains material nonpublic information from his or her spouse, parent, child, or sibling; provided, however, that the person receiving or obtaining the information may demonstrate that no duty of trust or confidence existed with respect to the information, by establishing that he or she neither knew nor reasonably should have known that the person who was the source of the information expected that the person would keep the information confidential, because of the parties' history, pattern, or practice of sharing and maintaining confidences, and because there was no agreement or understanding to maintain the confidentiality of the information.

§ 240.14a-9   False or misleading statements.

(a) No solicitation subject to this regulation shall be made by means of any proxy statement, form of proxy, notice of meeting or other communication, written or oral, containing any statement which, at the time and in the light of the circumstances under which it is made, is false or misleading with respect to any material fact, or which omits to state any material fact necessary in order to make the statements therein not false or misleading or necessary to correct any statement in any earlier communication with respect to the solicitation of a proxy for the same meeting or subject matter which has become false or misleading.

(b) The fact that a proxy statement, form of proxy or other soliciting material has been filed with or examined by the Commission shall not be deemed a finding by the Commission that such material is accurate or complete or not false or misleading, or that the Commission has passed upon the merits of or approved any statement contained therein or any matter to be acted upon by security holders. No representation contrary to the foregoing shall be made.

(c) No nominee, nominating shareholder or nominating shareholder group, or any member thereof, shall cause to be included in a registrant's proxy materials, either pursuant to the Federal proxy rules, an applicable state or foreign law provision, or a registrant's governing documents as they relate to including shareholder nominees for director in a registrant's proxy materials, include in a notice on Schedule 14N (§ 240.14n-101), or include in any other related communication, any statement which, at the time and in the light of the circumstances under which it is made, is false or misleading with respect to any material fact, or which omits to state any material fact necessary in order to make the statements therein not false or misleading or necessary to correct any statement in any earlier communication with respect to a solicitation for the same meeting or subject matter which has become false or misleading.

Note: The following are some examples of what, depending upon particular facts and circumstances, may be misleading within the meaning of this section.

(a) Predictions as to specific future market values.

(b) Material which directly or indirectly impugns character, integrity or personal reputation, or directly or indirectly makes charges concerning improper, illegal or immoral conduct or associations, without factual foundation.

(c) Failure to so identify a proxy statement, form of proxy and other soliciting material as to clearly distinguish it from the soliciting material of any other person or persons soliciting for the same meeting or subject matter.

(d) Claims made prior to a meeting regarding the results of a solicitation.

§ 240.14e-3   Transactions in securities on the basis of material, nonpublic information in the context of tender offers.

(a) If any person has taken a substantial step or steps to commence, or has commenced, a tender offer (the "offering person"), it shall constitute a fraudulent, deceptive or manipulative act or practice within the meaning of section 14(e) of the Act for any other person who is in possession of material information relating to such tender offer which information he knows or has reason to know is nonpublic and which he knows or has reason to know has been acquired directly or indirectly from:

(1) The offering person,

(2) The issuer of the securities sought or to be sought by such tender offer, or

(3) Any officer, director, partner or employee or any other person acting on behalf of the offering person or such issuer, to purchase or sell or cause to be purchased or sold any of such securities or any securities convertible into or exchangeable for any such securities or any option or right to obtain or to dispose of any of the foregoing securities, unless within a reasonable time prior to any purchase or sale such information and its source are publicly disclosed by press release or otherwise.

(b) A person other than a natural person shall not violate paragraph (a) of this section if such person shows that:

(1) The individual(s) making the investment decision on behalf of such person to purchase or sell any security described in paragraph (a) of this section or to cause any such security to be purchased or sold by or on behalf of others did not know the material, nonpublic information; and

(2) Such person had implemented one or a combination of policies and procedures, reasonable under the circumstances, taking into consideration the nature of the person's business, to ensure that individual(s) making investment decision(s) would not violate paragraph (a) of this section, which policies and procedures may include, but are not limited to,

(i) those which restrict any purchase, sale and causing any purchase and sale of any such security or

(ii) those which prevent such individual(s) from knowing such information.

(c) Notwithstanding anything in paragraph (a) of this section to contrary, the following transactions shall not be violations of paragraph (a) of this section:

(1) Purchase(s) of any security described in paragraph (a) of this section by a broker or by another agent on behalf of an offering person; or

(2) Sale(s) by any person of any security described in paragraph (a) of this section to the offering person.

(d)

(1) As a means reasonably designed to prevent fraudulent, deceptive or manipulative acts or practices within the meaning of section 14(e) of the Act, it shall be unlawful for any person described in paragraph (d)(2) of this section to communicate material, nonpublic information relating to a tender offer to any other person under circumstances in which it is reasonably foreseeable that such communication is likely to result in a violation of this section except that this paragraph shall not apply to a communication made in good faith,

(i) To the officers, directors, partners or employees of the offering person, to its advisors or to other persons, involved in the planning, financing, preparation or execution of such tender offer;

(ii) To the issuer whose securities are sought or to be sought by such tender offer, to its officers, directors, partners, employees or advisors or to other persons, involved in the planning, financing, preparation or execution of the activities of the issuer with respect to such tender offer; or

(iii) To any person pursuant to a requirement of any statute or rule or regulation promulgated thereunder.

(2) The persons referred to in paragraph (d)(1) of this section are:

(i) The offering person or its officers, directors, partners, employees or advisors;

(ii) The issuer of the securities sought or to be sought by such tender offer or its officers, directors, partners, employees or advisors;

(iii) Anyone acting on behalf of the persons in paragraph (d)(2)(i) of this section or the issuer or persons in paragraph (d)(2)(ii) of this section; and

(iv) Any person in possession of material information relating to a tender offer which information he knows or has reason to know is nonpublic and which he knows or has reason to know has been acquired directly or indirectly from any of the above.

TITLE 31.   MONEY AND FINANCE: TREASURY

§ 103.11   Meaning of terms.

(gg) Structure (structuring). For purposes of section 103.53, a person structures a transaction if that person, acting alone, or in conjunction with, or on behalf of, other persons, conducts or attempts to conduct one or more transactions in currency, in any amount, at one or more financial institutions, on one or more days, in any manner, for the purpose of evading the reporting requirements under section 103.22 of this part. "In any manner" includes, but is not limited to, the breaking down of a single sum of currency exceeding $10,000 into smaller sums, including sums at or below $10,000, or the conduct of a transaction, or series of currency transactions, including transactions at or below $10,000. The transaction or transactions need not exceed the $10,000 reporting threshold at any single financial institution on any single day in order to constitute structuring within the meaning of this definition.

TITLE 42.   MONEY AND FINANCE: TREASURY

§ 1320.   Approval of certain projects.

No payment shall be made under this chapter with respect to any experimental, pilot, demonstration, or other project all or any part of which is wholly financed with Federal funds made available under this chapter (without any State, local, or other non-Federal financial participation) unless such project shall have been personally approved by the Secretary or Deputy Secretary of Health and Human Services.

Chapter 3
FEDERAL RULES OF CRIMINAL PROCEDURE

Rule 6. The Grand Jury

(a) Summoning a Grand Jury.

(1) In General. When the public interest so requires, the court must order that one or more grand juries be summoned. A grand jury must have 16 to 23 members, and the court must order that enough legally qualified persons be summoned to meet this requirement.

(2) Alternate Jurors. When a grand jury is selected, the court may also select alternate jurors. Alternate jurors must have the same qualifications and be selected in the same manner as any other juror. Alternate jurors replace jurors in the same sequence in which the alternates were selected. An alternate juror who replaces a juror is subject to the same challenges, takes the same oath, and has the same authority as the other jurors.

(b) Objection to the Grand Jury or to a Grand Juror.

(1) Challenges. Either the government or a defendant may challenge the grand jury on the ground that it was not lawfully drawn, summoned, or selected, and may challenge an individual juror on the ground that the juror is not legally qualified.

(2) Motion to Dismiss an Indictment. A party may move to dismiss the indictment based on an objection to the grand jury or on an individual juror's lack of legal qualification, unless the court has previously ruled on the same objection under Rule 6(b)(1). The motion to dismiss is governed by 28 U.S.C. § 1867(e). The court must not dismiss the indictment on the ground that a grand juror was not legally qualified if the record shows that at least 12 qualified jurors concurred in the indictment.

(c) Foreperson and Deputy Foreperson. The court will appoint one juror as the foreperson and another as the deputy foreperson. In the foreperson's absence, the deputy foreperson will act as the foreperson. The foreperson may administer oaths and affirmations and will sign all indictments. The foreperson — or another juror designated by the foreperson — will record the number of jurors concurring in every indictment and will file the record with the clerk, but the record may not be made public unless the court so orders.

(d) Who May Be Present.

(1) While the Grand Jury Is in Session. The following persons may be present while the grand jury is in session: attorneys for the government, the witness being questioned, interpreters when needed, and a court reporter or an operator of a recording device.

(2) During Deliberations and Voting. No person other than the jurors, and any interpreter needed to assist a hearing-impaired or speech-impaired juror, may be

present while the grand jury is deliberating or voting.

(e) Recording and Disclosing the Proceedings.

(1) Recording the Proceedings. Except while the grand jury is deliberating or voting, all proceedings must be recorded by a court reporter or by a suitable recording device. But the validity of a prosecution is not affected by the unintentional failure to make a recording. Unless the court orders otherwise, an attorney for the government will retain control of the recording, the reporter's notes, and any transcript prepared from those notes.

(2) Secrecy.

(A) No obligation of secrecy may be imposed on any person except in accordance with Rule 6(e)(2)(B).

(B) Unless these rules provide otherwise, the following persons must not disclose a matter occurring before the grand jury:

(i) a grand juror;

(ii) an interpreter;

(iii) a court reporter;

(iv) an operator of a recording device;

(v) a person who transcribes recorded testimony;

(vi) an attorney for the government; or

(vii) a person to whom disclosure is made under Rule 6(e)(3)(A)(ii) or (iii).

(3) Exceptions.

(A) Disclosure of a grand-jury matter — other than the grand jury's deliberations or any grand juror's vote — may be made to:

(i) an attorney for the government for use in performing that attorney's duty;

(ii) any government personnel — including those of a state, state subdivision, Indian tribe, or foreign government — that an attorney for the government considers necessary to assist in performing that attorney's duty to enforce federal criminal law; or

(iii) a person authorized by 18 U.S.C. § 3322.

(B) A person to whom information is disclosed under Rule 6(e)(3)(A)(ii) may use that information only to assist an attorney for the government in performing that attorney's duty to enforce federal criminal law. An attorney for the government must promptly provide the court that impaneled the grand jury with the names of all persons to whom a disclosure has been made, and must certify that the attorney has advised those persons of their obligation of secrecy under this rule.

(C) An attorney for the government may disclose any grand-jury matter to another federal grand jury.

(D) An attorney for the government may disclose any grand-jury matter involving foreign intelligence, counterintelligence (as defined in 50 U.S.C. § 3003), or foreign intelligence information (as defined in Rule 6(e)(3)(D)(iii)) to any federal law enforcement, intelligence, protective, immigration, national defense, or national security official to assist the official receiving the information in the performance of that official's duties. An attorney for the government may also disclose any grand-jury matter involving, within the United States or elsewhere, a threat of attack or other grave hostile acts of a foreign power or its agent, a threat of domestic or international sabotage or terrorism, or clandestine intelligence gathering activities by an intelligence service or network of a foreign power or by its agent, to any appropriate federal, state, state subdivision, Indian tribal, or foreign government official, for the purpose of preventing or responding to such threat or activities.

(i) Any official who receives information under Rule 6(e)(3)(D) may use the information only as necessary in the conduct of that person's official duties subject to any limitations on the unauthorized disclosure of such information. Any state, state subdivision, Indian tribal, or foreign government official who receives information under Rule 6(e)(3)(D) may use the information only in a manner consistent with any guidelines issued by the Attorney General and the Director of National Intelligence.

(ii) Within a reasonable time after disclosure is made under Rule 6(e)(3)(D), an attorney for the government must file, under seal, a notice with the court in the district where the grand jury convened stating that such information was disclosed and the departments, agencies, or entities to which the disclosure was made.

(iii) As used in Rule 6(e)(3)(D), the term "foreign intelligence information" means:

(a) information, whether or not it concerns a United States person, that relates to the ability of the United States to protect against—

• actual or potential attack or other grave hostile acts of a foreign power or its agent;

• sabotage or international terrorism by a foreign power or its agent; or

• clandestine intelligence activities by an intelligence service or network of a foreign power or by its agent; or

(b) information, whether or not it concerns a United States person, with respect to a foreign power or foreign territory that relates to—

• the national defense or the security of the United States; or

• the conduct of the foreign affairs of the United States.

(E) The court may authorize disclosure — at a time, in a manner, and subject to any other conditions that it directs — of a grand-jury matter:

(i) preliminarily to or in connection with a judicial proceeding;

(ii) at the request of a defendant who shows that a ground may exist to dismiss the indictment because of a matter that occurred before the grand jury;

(iii) at the request of the government, when sought by a foreign court or prosecutor for use in an official criminal investigation;

(iv) at the request of the government if it shows that the matter may disclose a violation of State, Indian tribal, or foreign criminal law, as long as the disclosure is to an appropriate state, state-subdivision, Indian tribal, or foreign government official for the purpose of enforcing that law; or

(v) at the request of the government if it shows that the matter may disclose a violation of military criminal law under the Uniform Code of Military Justice, as long as the disclosure is to an appropriate military official for the purpose of enforcing that law.

(F) A petition to disclose a grand-jury matter under Rule 6(e)(3)(E)(i) must be filed in the district where the grand jury convened. Unless the hearing is ex parte — as it may be when the government is the petitioner — the petitioner must serve the petition on, and the court must afford a reasonable opportunity to appear and be heard to:

(i) an attorney for the government;

(ii) the parties to the judicial proceeding; and

(iii) any other person whom the court may designate.

(G) If the petition to disclose arises out of a judicial proceeding in another district, the petitioned court must transfer the petition to the other court unless the petitioned court can reasonably determine whether disclosure is proper. If the petitioned court decides to transfer, it must send to the transferee court the material sought to be disclosed, if feasible, and a written evaluation of the need for continued grand-jury secrecy. The transferee court must afford those persons identified in Rule 6(e)(3)(F) a reasonable opportunity to appear and be heard.

(4) Sealed Indictment. The magistrate judge to whom an indictment is returned may direct that the indictment be kept secret until the defendant is in custody or has been released pending trial. The clerk must then seal the indictment, and no person may disclose the indictment's existence except as necessary to issue or execute a warrant or summons.

(5) Closed Hearing. Subject to any right to an open hearing in a contempt proceeding, the court must close any hearing to the extent necessary to prevent disclosure of a matter occurring before a grand jury.

(6) Sealed Records. Records, orders, and subpoenas relating to grand-jury proceedings must be kept under seal to the extent and as long as necessary to prevent the unauthorized disclosure of a matter occurring before a grand jury.

(7) Contempt. A knowing violation of Rule 6, or of any guidelines jointly issued by the Attorney General and the Director of National Intelligence under Rule 6, may be punished as a contempt of court.

(f) **Indictment and Return.** A grand jury may indict only if at least 12 jurors concur. The grand jury — or its foreperson or deputy foreperson — must return the indictment to a magistrate judge in open court. To avoid unnecessary cost or delay, the magistrate judge may take the return by video teleconference from the court where the grand jury sits. If a complaint or information is pending against the defendant and 12 jurors do not concur in the indictment, the foreperson must promptly and in writing report the lack of concurrence to the magistrate judge.

(g) **Discharging the Grand Jury.** A grand jury must serve until the court discharges it, but it may serve more than 18 months only if the court, having determined that an extension is in the public interest, extends the grand jury's service. An extension may be granted for no more than 6 months, except as otherwise provided by statute.

(h) **Excusing a Juror.** At any time, for good cause, the court may excuse a juror either temporarily or permanently, and if permanently, the court may impanel an alternate juror in place of the excused juror.

(i) **"Indian Tribe" Defined.** "Indian tribe" means an Indian tribe recognized by the Secretary of the Interior on a list published in the Federal Register under 25 U.S.C. § 479a-1.

Rule 7.   The Indictment and the Information

(a) **When Used.**

(1) *Felony.* An offense (other than criminal contempt) must be prosecuted by an indictment if it is punishable:

(A) by death; or

(B) by imprisonment for more than one year.

(2) *Misdemeanor.* An offense punishable by imprisonment for one year or less may be prosecuted in accordance with Rule 58(b)(1).

(b) **Waiving Indictment.** An offense punishable by imprisonment for more than one year may be prosecuted by information if the defendant — in open court and after being advised of the nature of the charge and of the defendant's rights — waives prosecution by indictment.

(c) **Nature and Contents.**

(1) *In General.* The indictment or information must be a plain, concise, and definite written statement of the essential facts constituting the offense charged and must be signed by an attorney for the government. It need not contain a formal introduction or conclusion. A count may incorporate by reference an allegation made in another count. A count may allege that the means by which the defendant committed the offense are unknown or that the defendant committed it by one or more specified means. For each count, the indictment or information must give the official or customary citation of the statute, rule, regulation, or other provision of law that the defendant is alleged to have violated. For purposes of an indictment referred to in section 3282 of title 18, United States Code, for which the identity of the defendant is unknown, it shall be sufficient for the

indictment to describe the defendant as an individual whose name is unknown, but who has a particular DNA profile, as that term is defined in that section 3282.

(2) Citation Error. Unless the defendant was misled and thereby prejudiced, neither an error in a citation nor a citation's omission is a ground to dismiss the indictment or information or to reverse a conviction.

(3) Redesignated (2)

(d) Surplusage. Upon the defendant's motion, the court may strike surplusage from the indictment or information.

(e) Amending an Information. Unless an additional or different offense is charged or a substantial right of the defendant is prejudiced, the court may permit an information to be amended at any time before the verdict or finding.

(f) Bill of Particulars. The court may direct the government to file a bill of particulars. The defendant may move for a bill of particulars before or within 14 days after arraignment or at a later time if the court permits. The government may amend a bill of particulars subject to such conditions as justice requires.

Rule 8. Joinder of Offenses or Defendants

(a) Joinder of Offenses. The indictment or information may charge a defendant in separate counts with 2 or more offenses if the offenses charged — whether felonies or misdemeanors or both — are of the same or similar character, or are based on the same act or transaction, or are connected with or constitute parts of a common scheme or plan.

(b) Joinder of Defendants. The indictment or information may charge 2 or more defendants if they are alleged to have participated in the same act or transaction, or in the same series of acts or transactions, constituting an offense or offenses. The defendants may be charged in one or more counts together or separately. All defendants need not be charged in each count.

Rule 11. Pleas

(a) Entering a Plea.

(1) In General. A defendant may plead not guilty, guilty, or (with the court's consent) nolo contendere.

(2) Conditional Plea. With the consent of the court and the government, a defendant may enter a conditional plea of guilty or nolo contendere, reserving in writing the right to have an appellate court review an adverse determination of a specified pretrial motion. A defendant who prevails on appeal may then withdraw the plea.

(3) Nolo Contendere Plea. Before accepting a plea of nolo contendere, the court must consider the parties' views and the public interest in the effective administration of justice.

(4) Failure to Enter a Plea. If a defendant refuses to enter a plea or if a defendant organization fails to appear, the court must enter a plea of not guilty.

(b) Considering and Accepting a Guilty or Nolo Contendere Plea.

(1) Advising and Questioning the Defendant. Before the court accepts a plea of guilty or nolo contendere, the defendant may be placed under oath, and the court must address the defendant personally in open court. During this address, the court must inform the defendant of, and determine that the defendant understands, the following:

(A) the government's right, in a prosecution for perjury or false statement, to use against the defendant any statement that the defendant gives under oath;

(B) the right to plead not guilty, or having already so pleaded, to persist in that plea;

(C) the right to a jury trial;

(D) the right to be represented by counsel — and if necessary have the court appoint counsel — at trial and at every other stage of the proceeding;

(E) the right at trial to confront and cross-examine adverse witnesses, to be protected from compelled self-incrimination, to testify and present evidence, and to compel the attendance of witnesses;

(F) the defendant's waiver of these trial rights if the court accepts a plea of guilty or nolo contendere;

(G) the nature of each charge to which the defendant is pleading;

(H) any maximum possible penalty, including imprisonment, fine, and term of supervised release;

(I) any mandatory minimum penalty;

(J) any applicable forfeiture;

(K) the court's authority to order restitution;

(L) the court's obligation to impose a special assessment;

(M) in determining a sentence, the court's obligation to calculate the applicable sentencing-guideline range and to consider that range, possible departures under the Sentencing Guidelines, and other sentencing factors under 18 U.S.C. § 3553(a);

(N) the terms of any plea-agreement provision waiving the right to appeal or to collaterally attack the sentence; and

(O) that, if convicted, a defendant who is not a United States citizen may be removed from the United States, denied citizenship, and denied admission to the United States in the future.

(2) Ensuring That a Plea Is Voluntary. Before accepting a plea of guilty or nolo contendere, the court must address the defendant personally in open court and determine that the plea is voluntary and did not result from force, threats, or promises (other than promises in a plea agreement).

(3) Determining the Factual Basis for a Plea. Before entering judgment on a guilty plea, the court must determine that there is a factual basis for the plea.

(c) Plea Agreement Procedure.

(1) In General. An attorney for the government and the defendant's attorney, or the defendant when proceeding pro se, may discuss and reach a plea agreement. The court must not participate in these discussions. If the defendant pleads guilty or nolo contendere to either a charged offense or a lesser or related offense, the plea agreement may specify that an attorney for the government will:

(A) not bring, or will move to dismiss, other charges;

(B) recommend, or agree not to oppose the defendant's request, that a particular sentence or sentencing range is appropriate or that a particular provision of the Sentencing Guidelines, or policy statement, or sentencing factor does or does not apply (such a recommendation or request does not bind the court); or

(C) agree that a specific sentence or sentencing range is the appropriate disposition of the case, or that a particular provision of the Sentencing Guidelines, or policy statement, or sentencing factor does or does not apply (such a recommendation or request binds the court once the court accepts the plea agreement).

(2) Disclosing a Plea Agreement. The parties must disclose the plea agreement in open court when the plea is offered, unless the court for good cause allows the parties to disclose the plea agreement in camera.

(3) Judicial Consideration of a Plea Agreement.

(A) To the extent the plea agreement is of the type specified in Rule 11(c)(1)(A) or (C), the court may accept the agreement, reject it, or defer a decision until the court has reviewed the presentence report.

(B) To the extent the plea agreement is of the type specified in Rule 11(c)(1)(B), the court must advise the defendant that the defendant has no right to withdraw the plea if the court does not follow the recommendation or request.

(4) Accepting a Plea Agreement. If the court accepts the plea agreement, it must inform the defendant that to the extent the plea agreement is of the type specified in Rule 11(c)(1)(A) or (C), the agreed disposition will be included in the judgment.

(5) Rejecting a Plea Agreement. If the court rejects a plea agreement containing provisions of the type specified in Rule 11(c)(1)(A) or (C), the court must do the following on the record and in open court (or, for good cause, in camera):

(A) inform the parties that the court rejects the plea agreement;

(B) advise the defendant personally that the court is not required to follow the plea agreement and give the defendant an opportunity to withdraw the plea; and

(C) advise the defendant personally that if the plea is not withdrawn, the court may dispose of the case less favorably toward the defendant than the plea agreement contemplated.

(d) Withdrawing a Guilty or Nolo Contendere Plea. A defendant may withdraw a plea of guilty or nolo contendere:

(1) before the court accepts the plea, for any reason or no reason; or

(2) after the court accepts the plea, but before it imposes sentence if:

(A) the court rejects a plea agreement under Rule 11(c)(5); or

(B) the defendant can show a fair and just reason for requesting the withdrawal.

(e) Finality of a Guilty or Nolo Contendere Plea. After the court imposes sentence, the defendant may not withdraw a plea of guilty or nolo contendere, and the plea may be set aside only on direct appeal or collateral attack.

(f) Admissibility or Inadmissibility of a Plea, Plea Discussions, and Related Statements. The admissibility or inadmissibility of a plea, a plea discussion, and any related statement is governed by Federal Rule of Evidence 410.

(g) Recording the Proceedings. The proceedings during which the defendant enters a plea must be recorded by a court reporter or by a suitable recording device. If there is a guilty plea or a nolo contendere plea, the record must include the inquiries and advice to the defendant required under Rule 11(b) and (c).

(h) Harmless Error. A variance from the requirements of this rule is harmless error if it does not affect substantial rights.

Rule 12. Pleadings and Pretrial Motions

(a) Pleadings. The pleadings in a criminal proceeding are the indictment, the information, and the pleas of not guilty, guilty, and nolo contendere.

(b) Pretrial Motions.

(1) In General. A party may raise by pretrial motion any defense, objection, or request that the court can determine without a trial on the merits. Rule 47 applies to a pretrial motion.

(2) Motions That May Be Made at Any Time. A motion that the court lacks jurisdiction may be made at any time while the case is pending.

(3) Motions That Must Be Made Before Trial. The following defenses, objections, and requests must be raised by pretrial motion if the basis for the motion is then reasonably available and the motion can be determined without a trial on the merits:

(A) a defect in instituting the prosecution, including:

(i) improper venue;

(ii) preindictment delay;

(iii) a violation of the constitutional right to a speedy trial;

(iv) selective or vindictive prosecution; and

(v) an error in the grand-jury proceeding or preliminary hearing;

(B) a defect in the indictment or information, including:

(i) joining two or more offenses in the same count (duplicity);

(ii) charging the same offense in more than one count (multiplicity);

(iii) lack of specificity;

(iv) improper joinder; and

(v) failure to state an offense;

(C) suppression of evidence;

(D) severance of charges or defendants under Rule 14; and

(E) discovery under Rule 16.

(4) *Notice of the Government's Intent to Use Evidence.*

(A) At the Government's Discretion. At the arraignment or as soon afterward as practicable, the government may notify the defendant of its intent to use specified evidence at trial in order to afford the defendant an opportunity to object before trial under Rule 12(b)(3)(C).

(B) At the Defendant's Request. At the arraignment or as soon afterward as practicable, the defendant may, in order to have an opportunity to move to suppress evidence under Rule 12(b)(3)(C), request notice of the government's intent to use (in its evidence-in-chief at trial) any evidence that the defendant may be entitled to discover under Rule 16.

(c) Deadline for a Pretrial Motion; Consequences of Not Making a Timely Motion.

(1) Setting the Deadline. The court may, at the arraignment or as soon afterward as practicable, set a deadline for the parties to make pretrial motions and may also schedule a motion hearing. If the court does not set one, the deadline is the start of trial.

(2) Extending or Resetting the Deadline. At any time before trial, the court may extend or reset the deadline for pretrial motions.

(3) Consequences of Not Making a Timely Motion Under Rule 12(b)(3). If a party does not meet the deadline for making a Rule 12(b)(3) motion, the motion is untimely. But a court may consider the defense, objection, or request if the party shows good cause.

(d) Ruling on a Motion. The court must decide every pretrial motion before trial unless it finds good cause to defer a ruling. The court must not defer ruling on a pretrial motion if the deferral will adversely affect a party's right to appeal. When factual issues are involved in deciding a motion, the court must state its essential findings on the record.

(e) [Reserved]

(f) Recording the Proceedings. All proceedings at a motion hearing, including any findings of fact and conclusions of law made orally by the court, must be recorded by a court reporter or a suitable recording device.

(g) Defendant's Continued Custody or Release Status. If the court grants a motion to dismiss based on a defect in instituting the prosecution, in the indictment, or in the information, it may order the defendant to be released or detained under 18 U.S.C. § 3142 for a specified time until a new indictment or information is filed. This rule does not affect any federal statutory period of limitations.

(h) Producing Statements at a Suppression Hearing. Rule 26.2 applies at a suppression hearing under Rule 12(b)(3)(C). At a suppression hearing, a law enforcement officer is considered a government witness.

Rule 14. Relief from Prejudicial Joinder

(a) Relief. If the joinder of offenses or defendants in an indictment, an information, or a consolidation for trial appears to prejudice a defendant or the government, the court may order separate trials of counts, sever the defendants' trials, or provide any other relief that justice requires.

(b) Defendant's Statements. Before ruling on a defendant's motion to sever, the court may order an attorney for the government to deliver to the court for in camera inspection any defendant's statement that the government intends to use as evidence.

Rule 15. Depositions

(a) When Taken.

(1) In General. A party may move that a prospective witness be deposed in order to preserve testimony for trial. The court may grant the motion because of exceptional circumstances and in the interest of justice. If the court orders the deposition to be taken, it may also require the deponent to produce at the deposition any designated material that is not privileged, including any book, paper, document, record, recording, or data.

(2) Detained Material Witness. A witness who is detained under 18 U.S.C. § 3144 may request to be deposed by filing a written motion and giving notice to the parties. The court may then order that the deposition be taken and may discharge the witness after the witness has signed under oath the deposition transcript.

(b) Notice.

(1) In General. A party seeking to take a deposition must give every other party reasonable written notice of the deposition's date and location. The notice must state the name and address of each deponent. If requested by a party receiving the notice, the court may, for good cause, change the deposition's date or location.

(2) To the Custodial Officer. A party seeking to take the deposition must also notify the officer who has custody of the defendant of the scheduled date and location.

(c) Defendant's Presence.

(1) Defendant in Custody. Except as authorized by Rule 15(c)(3), the officer who has custody of the defendant must produce the defendant at the deposition and keep the defendant in the witness's presence during the examination, unless the defendant:

(A) waives in writing the right to be present; or

(B) persists in disruptive conduct justifying exclusion after being warned by the court that disruptive conduct will result in the defendant's exclusion.

(2) Defendant Not in Custody. Except as authorized by Rule 15(c)(3), a defendant who is not in custody has the right upon request to be present at the deposition, subject to any conditions imposed by the court. If the government tenders the defendant's expenses as provided in Rule 15(d) but the defendant still fails to appear, the defendant — absent good cause — waives both the right to appear and any objection to the taking and use of the deposition based on that right.

(3) Taking Depositions Outside the United States Without the Defendant's Presence. The deposition of a witness who is outside the United States may be taken without the defendant's presence if the court makes case-specific findings of all the following:

(A) the witness's testimony could provide substantial proof of a material fact in a felony prosecution;

(B) there is a substantial likelihood that the witness's attendance at trial cannot be obtained;

(C) the witness's presence for a deposition in the United States cannot be obtained;

(D) the defendant cannot be present because:

(i) the country where the witness is located will not permit the defendant to attend the deposition;

(ii) for an in-custody defendant, secure transportation and continuing custody cannot be assured at the witness's location; or

(iii) for an out-of-custody defendant, no reasonable conditions will assure an appearance at the deposition or at trial or sentencing; and

(E) the defendant can meaningfully participate in the deposition through reasonable means.

(d) Expenses. If the deposition was requested by the government, the court may — or if the defendant is unable to bear the deposition expenses, the court must — order the government to pay:

(1) any reasonable travel and subsistence expenses of the defendant and the defendant's attorney to attend the deposition; and

(2) the costs of the deposition transcript.

(e) Manner of Taking. Unless these rules or a court order provides otherwise, a deposition must be taken and filed in the same manner as a deposition in a civil action, except that:

(1) A defendant may not be deposed without that defendant's consent.

(2) The scope and manner of the deposition examination and cross-examination must be the same as would be allowed during trial.

(3) The government must provide to the defendant or the defendant's attorney, for use at the deposition, any statement of the deponent in the government's possession to which the defendant would be entitled at trial.

(f) Admissibility and Use as Evidence. An order authorizing a deposition to be taken under this rule does not determine its admissibility. A party may use all or part of a deposition as provided by the Federal Rules of Evidence.

(g) Objections. A party objecting to deposition testimony or evidence must state the grounds for the objection during the deposition.

(h) Depositions by Agreement Permitted. The parties may by agreement take and use a deposition with the court's consent.

Rule 16. Discovery and Inspection

(a) Government's Disclosure.

(1) Information Subject to Disclosure.

(A) Defendant's Oral Statement. Upon a defendant's request, the government must disclose to the defendant the substance of any relevant oral statement made by the defendant, before or after arrest, in response to interrogation by a person the defendant knew was a government agent if the government intends to use the statement at trial.

(B) Defendant's Written or Recorded Statement. Upon a defendant's request, the government must disclose to the defendant, and make available for inspection, copying, or photographing, all of the following:

(i) any relevant written or recorded statement by the defendant if:

• the statement is within the government's possession, custody, or control; and

• the attorney for the government knows — or through due diligence could know — that the statement exists;

(ii) the portion of any written record containing the substance of any relevant oral statement made before or after arrest if the defendant made the statement in response to interrogation by a person the defendant knew was a government agent; and

(iii) the defendant's recorded testimony before a grand jury relating to the charged offense.

(C) Organizational Defendant. Upon a defendant's request, if the defendant is an organization, the government must disclose to the defendant any statement described in Rule 16(a)(1)(A) and (B) if the government contends that the person making the statement:

(i) was legally able to bind the defendant regarding the subject of the statement because of that person's position as the defendant's director, officer, employee, or agent; or

(ii) was personally involved in the alleged conduct constituting the offense and was legally able to bind the defendant regarding that conduct because of that person's position as the defendant's director, officer, employee, or agent.

(D) Defendant's Prior Record. Upon a defendant's request, the government must furnish the defendant with a copy of the defendant's prior criminal record that is within the government's possession, custody, or control if the attorney for the government knows — or through due diligence could know — that the record exists.

(E) Documents and Objects. Upon a defendant's request, the government must permit the defendant to inspect and to copy or photograph books, papers, documents, data, photographs, tangible objects, buildings or places, or copies or portions of any of these items, if the item is within the government's possession, custody, or control and:

(i) the item is material to preparing the defense;

(ii) the government intends to use the item in its case-in-chief at trial; or

(iii) the item was obtained from or belongs to the defendant.

(F) Reports of Examinations and Tests. Upon a defendant's request, the government must permit a defendant to inspect and to copy or photograph the results or reports of any physical or mental examination and of any scientific test or experiment if:

(i) the item is within the government's possession, custody, or control;

(ii) the attorney for the government knows — or through due diligence could know — that the item exists; and

(iii) the item is material to preparing the defense or the government intends to use the item in its case-in-chief at trial.

(G) Expert witnesses.— At the defendant's request, the government must give to the defendant a written summary of any testimony that the government intends to use under Rules 702, 703, or 705 of the Federal Rules of Evidence during its case-in-chief at trial. If the government requests discovery under subdivision (b)(1)(C)(ii) and the defendant complies, the government must, at the defendant's request, give to the defendant a written summary of testimony that the government intends to use under Rules 702, 703, or 705 of the Federal Rules of Evidence as evidence at trial on the issue of the defendant's mental condition. The summary provided under this subparagraph must describe the witness's opinions, the bases and reasons for those opinions, and the witness's qualifications.

(2) Information Not Subject to Disclosure. Except as permitted by Rule 16(a)(1)(A)–(D), (F), and (G), this rule does not authorize the discovery or inspection of reports, memoranda, or other internal government documents made by an attorney for the government or other government agent in connection with investigating or prosecuting the case. Nor does this rule authorize the discovery or inspection of statements made by prospective government witnesses except as provided in 18 U.S.C. § 3500.

(3) Grand Jury Transcripts. This rule does not apply to the discovery or inspection of a grand jury's recorded proceedings, except as provided in Rules 6, 12(h), 16(a)(1), and 26.2.

(b) Defendant's Disclosure.

(1) Information Subject to Disclosure.

(A) Documents and Objects. If a defendant requests disclosure under Rule 16(a)(1)(E) and the government complies, then the defendant must permit the government, upon request, to inspect and to copy or photograph books, papers, documents, data, photographs, tangible objects, buildings or places, or copies or portions of any of these items if:

(i) the item is within the defendant's possession, custody, or control; and

(ii) the defendant intends to use the item in the defendant's case-in-chief at trial.

(B) Reports of Examinations and Tests. If a defendant requests disclosure under Rule 16(a)(1)(F) and the government complies, the defendant must permit the government, upon request, to inspect and to copy or photograph the results or reports of any physical or mental examination and of any scientific test or experiment if:

(i) the item is within the defendant's possession, custody, or control; and

(ii) the defendant intends to use the item in the defendant's case-in-chief at trial, or intends to call the witness who prepared the report and the report relates to the witness's testimony.

(C) Expert witnesses.— The defendant must, at the government's request, give to the government a written summary of any testimony that the defendant intends to use under Rules 702, 703, or 705 of the Federal Rules of Evidence as evidence at trial, if—

(i) the defendant requests disclosure under subdivision (a)(1)(G) and the government complies; or

(ii) the defendant has given notice under Rule 12.2(b) of an intent to present expert testimony on the defendant's mental condition.

This summary must describe the witness's opinions, the bases and reasons for those opinions, and the witness's qualifications.

(2) Information Not Subject to Disclosure. Except for scientific or medical reports, Rule 16(b)(1) does not authorize discovery or inspection of:

(A) reports, memoranda, or other documents made by the defendant, or the defendant's attorney or agent, during the case's investigation or defense; or

(B) a statement made to the defendant, or the defendant's attorney or agent, by:

(i) the defendant;

(ii) a government or defense witness; or

(iii) a prospective government or defense witness.

(c) Continuing Duty to Disclose. A party who discovers additional evidence or material before or during trial must promptly disclose its existence to the other party or the court if:

(1) the evidence or material is subject to discovery or inspection under this rule; and

(2) the other party previously requested, or the court ordered, its production.

(d) Regulating Discovery.

(1) Protective and Modifying Orders. At any time the court may, for good cause, deny, restrict, or defer discovery or inspection, or grant other appropriate relief. The court may permit a party to show good cause by a written statement that the court will inspect ex parte. If relief is granted, the court must preserve the entire text of the party's statement under seal.

(2) Failure to Comply. If a party fails to comply with this rule, the court may:

(A) order that party to permit the discovery or inspection; specify its time, place, and manner; and prescribe other just terms and conditions;

(B) grant a continuance;

(C) prohibit that party from introducing the undisclosed evidence; or

(D) enter any other order that is just under the circumstances.

Rule 17. Subpoena

(a) Content. A subpoena must state the court's name and the title of the proceeding, include the seal of the court, and command the witness to attend and testify at the time and place the subpoena specifies. The clerk must issue a blank subpoena — signed and sealed — to the party requesting it, and that party must fill in the blanks before the subpoena is served.

(b) Defendant Unable to Pay. Upon a defendant's ex parte application, the court must order that a subpoena be issued for a named witness if the defendant shows an inability to pay the witness's fees and the necessity of the witness's presence for an adequate defense. If the court orders a subpoena to be issued, the process costs and witness fees will be paid in the same manner as those paid for witnesses the government subpoenas.

(c) Producing Documents and Objects.

(1) In General. A subpoena may order the witness to produce any books,

papers, documents, data, or other objects the subpoena designates. The court may direct the witness to produce the designated items in court before trial or before they are to be offered in evidence. When the items arrive, the court may permit the parties and their attorneys to inspect all or part of them.

(2) Quashing or Modifying the Subpoena. On motion made promptly, the court may quash or modify the subpoena if compliance would be unreasonable or oppressive.

(3) Subpoena for Personal or Confidential Information About a Victim. After a complaint, indictment, or information is filed, a subpoena requiring the production of personal or confidential information about a victim may be served on a third party only by court order. Before entering the order and unless there are exceptional circumstances, the court must require giving notice to the victim so that the victim can move to quash or modify the subpoena or otherwise object.

(d) Service. A marshal, a deputy marshal, or any nonparty who is at least 18 years old may serve a subpoena. The server must deliver a copy of the subpoena to the witness and must tender to the witness one day's witness-attendance fee and the legal mileage allowance. The server need not tender the attendance fee or mileage allowance when the United States, a federal officer, or a federal agency has requested the subpoena.

(e) Place of Service.

(1) In the United States. A subpoena requiring a witness to attend a hearing or trial may be served at any place within the United States.

(2) In a Foreign Country. If the witness is in a foreign country, 28 U.S.C. § 1783 governs the subpoena's service.

(f) Issuing a Deposition Subpoena.

(1) Issuance. A court order to take a deposition authorizes the clerk in the district where the deposition is to be taken to issue a subpoena for any witness named or described in the order.

(2) Place. After considering the convenience of the witness and the parties, the court may order — and the subpoena may require — the witness to appear anywhere the court designates.

(g) Contempt. The court (other than a magistrate judge) may hold in contempt a witness who, without adequate excuse, disobeys a subpoena issued by a federal court in that district. A magistrate judge may hold in contempt a witness who, without adequate excuse, disobeys a subpoena issued by that magistrate judge as provided in 28 U.S.C. § 636(e).

(h) Information Not Subject to a Subpoena. No party may subpoena a statement of a witness or of a prospective witness under this rule. Rule 26.2 governs the production of the statement.

Rule 29. Motion for a Judgment of Acquittal

(a) Before Submission to the Jury. After the government closes its evidence or after the close of all the evidence, the court on the defendant's motion must enter a judgment of acquittal of any offense for which the evidence is insufficient to sustain a conviction. The court may on its own consider whether the evidence is insufficient to sustain a conviction. If the court denies a motion for a judgment of acquittal at the close of the government's evidence, the defendant may offer evidence without having reserved the right to do so.

(b) Reserving Decision. The court may reserve decision on the motion, proceed with the trial (where the motion is made before the close of all the evidence), submit the case to the jury, and decide the motion either before the jury returns a verdict or after it returns a verdict of guilty or is discharged without having returned a verdict. If the court reserves decision, it must decide the motion on the basis of the evidence at the time the ruling was reserved.

(c) After Jury Verdict or Discharge.

(1) Time for a Motion. A defendant may move for a judgment of acquittal, or renew such a motion, within 14 days after a guilty verdict or after the court discharges the jury, whichever is later.

(2) Ruling on the Motion. If the jury has returned a guilty verdict, the court may set aside the verdict and enter an acquittal. If the jury has failed to return a verdict, the court may enter a judgment of acquittal.

(3) No Prior Motion Required. A defendant is not required to move for a judgment of acquittal before the court submits the case to the jury as a prerequisite for making such a motion after jury discharge.

(d) Conditional Ruling on a Motion for a New Trial.

(1) Motion for a New Trial. If the court enters a judgment of acquittal after a guilty verdict, the court must also conditionally determine whether any motion for a new trial should be granted if the judgment of acquittal is later vacated or reversed. The court must specify the reasons for that determination.

(2) Finality. The court's order conditionally granting a motion for a new trial does not affect the finality of the judgment of acquittal.

(3) Appeal.

(A) Grant of a Motion for a New Trial. If the court conditionally grants a motion for a new trial and an appellate court later reverses the judgment of acquittal, the trial court must proceed with the new trial unless the appellate court orders otherwise.

(B) Denial of a Motion for a New Trial. If the court conditionally denies a motion for a new trial, an appellee may assert that the denial was erroneous. If the appellate court later reverses the judgment of acquittal, the trial court must proceed as the appellate court directs.

Rule 32.   Sentencing and Judgment

(a) [Reserved.]

(b) Time of Sentencing.

(1) In General. The court must impose sentence without unnecessary delay.

(2) Changing Time Limits. The court may, for good cause, change any time limits prescribed in this rule.

(c) Presentence Investigation.

(1) Required Investigation.

(A) In General. The probation officer must conduct a presentence investigation and submit a report to the court before it imposes sentence unless:

(i) 18 U.S.C. § 3593(c) or another statute requires otherwise; or

(ii) the court finds that the information in the record enables it to meaningfully exercise its sentencing authority under 18 U.S.C. § 3553, and the court explains its finding on the record.

(B) Restitution. If the law permits restitution, the probation officer must conduct an investigation and submit a report that contains sufficient information for the court to order restitution.

(2) Interviewing the Defendant. The probation officer who interviews a defendant as part of a presentence investigation must, on request, give the defendant's attorney notice and a reasonable opportunity to attend the interview.

(d) Presentence Report.

(1) Applying the Advisory Sentencing Guidelines. The presentence report must:

(A) identify all applicable guidelines and policy statements of the Sentencing Commission;

(B) calculate the defendant's offense level and criminal history category;

(C) state the resulting sentencing range and kinds of sentences available;

(D) identify any factor relevant to:

(i) the appropriate kind of sentence, or

(ii) the appropriate sentence within the applicable sentencing range; and

(E) identify any basis for departing from the applicable sentencing range.

(2) Additional Information. The presentence report must also contain the following:

(A) the defendant's history and characteristics, including:

(i) any prior criminal record;

(ii) the defendant's financial condition; and

(iii) any circumstances affecting the defendant's behavior that may be helpful in imposing sentence or in correctional treatment;

(B) information that assesses any financial, social, psychological, and medical impact on any victim;

(C) when appropriate, the nature and extent of nonprison programs and resources available to the defendant;

(D) when the law provides for restitution, information sufficient for a restitution order;

(E) if the court orders a study under 18 U.S.C. § 3552(b), any resulting report and recommendation;

(F) a statement of whether the government seeks forfeiture under Rule 32.2 and any other law; and

(G) any other information that the court requires, including information relevant to the factors under 18 U.S.C. § 3553(a).

(3) Exclusions. The presentence report must exclude the following:

(A) any diagnoses that, if disclosed, might seriously disrupt a rehabilitation program;

(B) any sources of information obtained upon a promise of confidentiality; and

(C) any other information that, if disclosed, might result in physical or other harm to the defendant or others.

(e) Disclosing the Report and Recommendation.

(1) Time to Disclose. Unless the defendant has consented in writing, the probation officer must not submit a presentence report to the court or disclose its contents to anyone until the defendant has pleaded guilty or nolo contendere, or has been found guilty.

(2) Minimum Required Notice. The probation officer must give the presentence report to the defendant, the defendant's attorney, and an attorney for the government at least 35 days before sentencing unless the defendant waives this minimum period.

(3) Sentence Recommendation. By local rule or by order in a case, the court may direct the probation officer not to disclose to anyone other than the court the officer's recommendation on the sentence.

(f) Objecting to the Report.

(1) Time to Object. Within 14 days after receiving the presentence report, the parties must state in writing any objections, including objections to material information, sentencing guideline ranges, and policy statements contained in or omitted from the report.

(2) Serving Objections. An objecting party must provide a copy of its objections to the opposing party and to the probation officer.

(3) Action on Objections. After receiving objections, the probation officer may meet with the parties to discuss the objections. The probation officer may then investigate further and revise the presentence report as appropriate.

(g) Submitting the Report. At least 7 days before sentencing, the probation officer must submit to the court and to the parties the presentence report and an addendum containing any unresolved objections, the grounds for those objections, and the probation officer's comments on them.

(h) Notice of Possible Departure from Sentencing Guidelines. Before the court may depart from the applicable sentencing range on a ground not identified for departure either in the presentence report or in a party's prehearing submission, the court must give the parties reasonable notice that it is contemplating such a departure. The notice must specify any ground on which the court is contemplating a departure.

(i) Sentencing.

(1) In General. At sentencing, the court:

(A) must verify that the defendant and the defendant's attorney have read and discussed the presentence report and any addendum to the report;

(B) must give to the defendant and an attorney for the government a written summary of — or summarize in camera — any information excluded from the presentence report under Rule 32(d)(3) on which the court will rely in sentencing, and give them a reasonable opportunity to comment on that information;

(C) must allow the parties' attorneys to comment on the probation officer's determinations and other matters relating to an appropriate sentence; and

(D) may, for good cause, allow a party to make a new objection at any time before sentence is imposed.

(2) Introducing Evidence; Producing a Statement. The court may permit the parties to introduce evidence on the objections. If a witness testifies at sentencing, Rule 26.2(a)–(d) and (f) applies. If a party fails to comply with a Rule 26.2 order to produce a witness's statement, the court must not consider that witness's testimony.

(3) Court Determinations. At sentencing, the court:

(A) may accept any undisputed portion of the presentence report as a finding of fact;

(B) must — for any disputed portion of the presentence report or other controverted matter — rule on the dispute or determine that a ruling is unnecessary either because the matter will not affect sentencing, or because the court will not consider the matter in sentencing; and

(C) must append a copy of the court's determinations under this rule to any copy of the presentence report made available to the Bureau of Prisons.

(4) Opportunity to Speak.

(A) By a Party. Before imposing sentence, the court must:

(i) provide the defendant's attorney an opportunity to speak on the defendant's behalf;

(ii) address the defendant personally in order to permit the defendant to speak or present any information to mitigate the sentence; and

(iii) provide an attorney for the government an opportunity to speak equivalent to that of the defendant's attorney.

(B) By a Victim. Before imposing sentence, the court must address any victim of the crime who is present at sentencing and must permit the victim to be reasonably heard.

(C) In Camera Proceedings. Upon a party's motion and for good cause, the court may hear in camera any statement made under Rule 32(i)(4).

(j) Defendant's Right to Appeal.

(1) Advice of a Right to Appeal.

(A) Appealing a Conviction. If the defendant pleaded not guilty and was convicted, after sentencing the court must advise the defendant of the right to appeal the conviction.

(B) Appealing a Sentence. After sentencing — regardless of the defendant's plea — the court must advise the defendant of any right to appeal the sentence.

(C) Appeal Costs. The court must advise a defendant who is unable to pay appeal costs of the right to ask for permission to appeal in forma pauperis.

(2) Clerk's Filing of Notice. If the defendant so requests, the clerk must immediately prepare and file a notice of appeal on the defendant's behalf.

(k) Judgment.

(1) In General. In the judgment of conviction, the court must set forth the plea, the jury verdict or the court's findings, the adjudication, and the sentence. If the defendant is found not guilty or is otherwise entitled to be discharged, the court must so order. The judge must sign the judgment, and the clerk must enter it.

(2) Criminal Forfeiture. Forfeiture procedures are governed by Rule 32.2.

Rule 32.2. Criminal Forfeiture

(a) Notice to the Defendant. A court must not enter a judgment of forfeiture in a criminal proceeding unless the indictment or information contains notice to the defendant that the government will seek the forfeiture of property as part of any sentence in accordance with the applicable statute. The notice should not be designated as a count of the indictment or information. The indictment or information need not identify the property subject to forfeiture or specify the amount of any forfeiture money judgment that the government seeks.

(b) Entering a Preliminary Order of Forfeiture.

(1) Forfeiture Phase of the Trial.

(A) Forfeiture Determinations. As soon as practical after a verdict or finding of guilty, or after a plea of guilty or nolo contendere is accepted, on any count in an indictment or information regarding which criminal forfeiture is sought, the court must determine what property is subject to forfeiture under the applicable statute. If the government seeks forfeiture of specific property, the court must determine whether the government has established the requisite nexus between the property and the offense. If the government seeks a personal money judgment, the court must determine the amount of money that the defendant will be ordered to pay.

(B) Evidence and Hearing. The court's determination may be based on evidence already in the record, including any written plea agreement, and on any additional evidence or information submitted by the parties and accepted by the court as relevant and reliable. If the forfeiture is contested, on either party's request the court must conduct a hearing after the verdict or finding of guilty.

(2) Preliminary Order.

(A) Contents of a Specific Order. If the court finds that property is subject to forfeiture, it must promptly enter a preliminary order of forfeiture setting forth the amount of any money judgment, directing the forfeiture of specific property, and directing the forfeiture of any substitute property if the government has met the statutory criteria. The court must enter the order without regard to any third party's interest in the property. Determining whether a third party has such an interest must be deferred until any third party files a claim in an ancillary proceeding under Rule 32.2(c).

(B) Timing. Unless doing so is impractical, the court must enter the preliminary order sufficiently in advance of sentencing to allow the parties to suggest revisions or modifications before the order becomes final as to the defendant under Rule 32.2(b)(4).

(C) General Order. If, before sentencing, the court cannot identify all the specific property subject to forfeiture or calculate the total amount of the money judgment, the court may enter a forfeiture order that:

(i) lists any identified property;

(ii) describes other property in general terms; and

(iii) states that the order will be amended under Rule 32.2(e)(1) when additional specific property is identified or the amount of the money judgment has been calculated.

(3) Seizing Property. The entry of a preliminary order of forfeiture authorizes the Attorney General (or a designee) to seize the specific property subject to forfeiture; to conduct any discovery the court considers proper in identifying, locating, or disposing of the property; and to commence proceedings that comply with any statutes governing third-party rights. The court may include in the order of forfeiture conditions reasonably necessary to preserve the property's value pending any appeal.

(4) Sentence and Judgment.

(A) When Final. At sentencing — or at any time before sentencing if the defendant consents — the preliminary forfeiture order becomes final as to the defendant. If the order directs the defendant to forfeit specific property, it remains preliminary as to third parties until the ancillary proceeding is concluded under Rule 32.2(c).

(B) Notice and Inclusion in the Judgment. The court must include the forfeiture when orally announcing the sentence or must otherwise ensure that the defendant knows of the forfeiture at sentencing. The court must also include the forfeiture order, directly or by reference, in the judgment, but the court's failure to do so may be corrected at any time under Rule 36.

(C) Time to Appeal. The time for the defendant or the government to file an appeal from the forfeiture order, or from the court's failure to enter an order, begins to run when judgment is entered. If the court later amends or declines to amend a forfeiture order to include additional property under Rule 32.2(e), the defendant or the government may file an appeal regarding that property under Federal Rule of Appellate Procedure 4(b). The time for that appeal runs from the date when the order granting or denying the amendment becomes final.

(5) Jury Determination.

(A) Retaining the Jury. In any case tried before a jury, if the indictment or information states that the government is seeking forfeiture, the court must determine before the jury begins deliberating whether either party requests that the jury be retained to determine the forfeitability of specific property if it returns a guilty verdict.

(B) Special Verdict Form. If a party timely requests to have the jury determine forfeiture, the government must submit a proposed Special Verdict Form listing each property subject to forfeiture and asking the jury to determine whether the government has established the requisite nexus between the property and the offense committed by the defendant.

(6) Notice of the Forfeiture Order.

(A) Publishing and Sending Notice. If the court orders the forfeiture of specific property, the government must publish notice of the order and send notice to any person who reasonably appears to be a potential claimant with standing to contest the forfeiture in the ancillary proceeding.

(B) Content of the Notice. The notice must describe the forfeited property, state the times under the applicable statute when a petition contesting the forfeiture must be filed, and state the name and contact information for the government attorney to be served with the petition.

(C) Means of Publication; Exceptions to Publication Requirement. Publication must take place as described in Supplemental Rule G(4)(a)(iii) of the Federal Rules of Civil Procedure, and may be by any means described in Supplemental Rule G(4)(a)(iv). Publication is unnecessary if any exception in Supplemental Rule G(4)(a)(i) applies.

(D) Means of Sending the Notice. The notice may be sent in accordance with Supplemental Rules G(4)(b)(iii)–(v) of the Federal Rules of Civil Procedure.

(7) Interlocutory Sale. At any time before entry of a final forfeiture order, the

court, in accordance with Supplemental Rule G(7) of the Federal Rules of Civil Procedure, may order the interlocutory sale of property alleged to be forfeitable.

(c) Ancillary Proceeding; Entering a Final Order of Forfeiture.

(1) In General. If, as prescribed by statute, a third party files a petition asserting an interest in the property to be forfeited, the court must conduct an ancillary proceeding, but no ancillary proceeding is required to the extent that the forfeiture consists of a money judgment.

(A) In the ancillary proceeding, the court may, on motion, dismiss the petition for lack of standing, for failure to state a claim, or for any other lawful reason. For purposes of the motion, the facts set forth in the petition are assumed to be true.

(B) After disposing of any motion filed under Rule 32.2(c)(1)(A) and before conducting a hearing on the petition, the court may permit the parties to conduct discovery in accordance with the Federal Rules of Civil Procedure if the court determines that discovery is necessary or desirable to resolve factual issues. When discovery ends, a party may move for summary judgment under Federal Rule of Civil Procedure 56.

(2) Entering a Final Order. When the ancillary proceeding ends, the court must enter a final order of forfeiture by amending the preliminary order as necessary to account for any third-party rights. If no third party files a timely petition, the preliminary order becomes the final order of forfeiture if the court finds that the defendant (or any combination of defendants convicted in the case) had an interest in the property that is forfeitable under the applicable statute. The defendant may not object to the entry of the final order on the ground that the property belongs, in whole or in part, to a codefendant or third party; nor may a third party object to the final order on the ground that the third party had an interest in the property.

(3) Multiple Petitions. If multiple third-party petitions are filed in the same case, an order dismissing or granting one petition is not appealable until rulings are made on all the petitions, unless the court determines that there is no just reason for delay.

(4) Ancillary Proceeding Not Part of Sentencing. An ancillary proceeding is not part of sentencing.

(d) Stay Pending Appeal. If a defendant appeals from a conviction or an order of forfeiture, the court may stay the order of forfeiture on terms appropriate to ensure that the property remains available pending appellate review. A stay does not delay the ancillary proceeding or the determination of a third party's rights or interests. If the court rules in favor of any third party while an appeal is pending, the court may amend the order of forfeiture but must not transfer any property interest to a third party until the decision on appeal becomes final, unless the defendant consents in writing or on the record.

(e) Subsequently Located Property; Substitute Property.

(1) In General. On the government's motion, the court may at any time enter

an order of forfeiture or amend an existing order of forfeiture to include property that:

(A) is subject to forfeiture under an existing order of forfeiture but was located and identified after that order was entered; or

(B) is substitute property that qualifies for forfeiture under an applicable statute.

(2) Procedure. If the government shows that the property is subject to forfeiture under Rule 32.2(e)(1), the court must:

(A) enter an order forfeiting that property, or amend an existing preliminary or final order to include it; and

(B) if a third party files a petition claiming an interest in the property, conduct an ancillary proceeding under Rule 32.2(c).

(3) Jury Trial Limited. There is no right to a jury trial under Rule 32.2(e).

Rule 33. New Trial

(a) Defendant's Motion. Upon the defendant's motion, the court may vacate any judgment and grant a new trial if the interest of justice so requires. If the case was tried without a jury, the court may take additional testimony and enter a new judgment.

(b) Time to File.

(1) Newly Discovered Evidence. Any motion for a new trial grounded on newly discovered evidence must be filed within 3 years after the verdict or finding of guilty. If an appeal is pending, the court may not grant a motion for a new trial until the appellate court remands the case.

(2) Other Grounds. Any motion for a new trial grounded on any reason other than newly discovered evidence must be filed within 14 days after the verdict or finding of guilty.

Chapter 4

FEDERAL RULES OF EVIDENCE

Rule 502. **Attorney-Client Privilege and Work Product; Limitations on Waiver**

The following provisions apply, in the circumstances set out, to disclosure of a communication or information covered by the attorney-client privilege or work-product protection.

(a) Disclosure Made in a Federal Proceeding or to a Federal Office or Agency; Scope of a Waiver. When the disclosure is made in a federal proceeding or to a federal office or agency and waives the attorney-client privilege or work-product protection, the waiver extends to an undisclosed communication or information in a federal or state proceeding only if:

(1) the waiver is intentional;

(2) the disclosed and undisclosed communications or information concern the same subject matter; and

(3) they ought in fairness to be considered together.

(b) Inadvertent Disclosure. When made in a federal proceeding or to a federal office or agency, the disclosure does not operate as a waiver in a federal or state proceeding if:

(1) the disclosure is inadvertent;

(2) the holder of the privilege or protection took reasonable steps to prevent disclosure; and

(3) the holder promptly took reasonable steps to rectify the error, including (if applicable) following Federal Rule of Civil Procedure 26(b)(5)(B).

(c) Disclosure Made in a State Proceeding. When the disclosure is made in a state proceeding and is not the subject of a state-court order concerning waiver, the disclosure does not operate as a waiver in a federal proceeding if the disclosure:

(1) would not be a waiver under this rule if it had been made in a federal proceeding; or

(2) is not a waiver under the law of the state where the disclosure occurred.

(d) Controlling Effect of a Court Order. A federal court may order that the privilege or protection is not waived by disclosure connected with the litigation pending before the court — in which event the disclosure is also not a waiver in any other federal or state proceeding.

(e) Controlling Effect of a Party Agreement. An agreement on the effect of disclosure in a federal proceeding is binding only on the parties to the agreement, unless it is incorporated into a court order.

(f) Controlling Effect of This Rule. Notwithstanding Rules 101 and 1101, this rule applies to state proceedings and to federal court-annexed and federal court-mandated arbitration proceedings, in the circumstances set out in the rule. And notwithstanding Rule 501, this rule applies even if state law provides the rule of decision.

(g) Definitions. In this rule:

(1) "attorney-client privilege" means the protection that applicable law provides for confidential attorney-client communications; and

(2) "work-product protection" means the protection that applicable law provides for tangible material (or its intangible equivalent) prepared in anticipation of litigation or for trial.

Chapter 5
MODEL PENAL CODE*

ARTICLE 2 — GENERAL PRINCIPLES OF LIABILITY

§ 2.02. General Requirements of Culpability

(1) Minimum Requirements of Culpability. Except as provided in Section 2.05, a person is not guilty of an offense unless he acted purposely, knowingly, recklessly or negligently, as the law may require, with respect to each material element of the offense.

(2) Kinds of Culpability Defined.

(a) Purposely.

A person acts purposely with respect to a material element of an offense when:

(i) if the element involves the nature of his conduct or a result thereof, it is his conscious object to engage in conduct of that nature or to cause such a result; and

(ii) if the element involves the attendant circumstances, he is aware of the existence of such circumstances or he believes or hopes that they exist.

(b) Knowingly.

A person acts knowingly with respect to a material element of an offense when:

(i) if the element involves the nature of his conduct or the attendant circumstances, he is aware that his conduct is of that nature or that such circumstances exist; and

(ii) if the element involves a result of his conduct, he is aware that it is practically certain that his conduct will cause such a result.

(c) Recklessly.

A person acts recklessly with respect to a material element of an offense when he consciously disregards a substantial and unjustifiable risk that the material element exists or will result from his conduct. The risk must be of such a nature and degree that, considering the nature and purpose of the actor's conduct and the circumstances known to him, its disregard involves a gross deviation from the standard of conduct that a law-abiding person would observe in the actor's situation.

(d) Negligently.

A person acts negligently with respect to a material element of an offense when he should be aware of a substantial and unjustifiable risk that the material element exists or will result from his conduct. The risk must be of such a nature and degree that the actor's failure to perceive it, considering the nature and purpose of his conduct and the circumstances known to him, involves a gross deviation from the standard of care that a reasonable person would observe in the actor's situation.

(3) Culpability Required Unless Otherwise Provided. When the culpability sufficient to establish a material element of an offense is not prescribed by law, such element is established if a person acts purposely, knowingly or recklessly with respect thereto.

(4) Prescribed Culpability Requirement Applies to All Material Elements. When the law defining an offense prescribes the kind of culpability that is sufficient for the commission of an offense, without distinguishing among the material elements thereof, such provision shall apply to all the material elements of the offense, unless a contrary purpose plainly appears.

(5) Substitutes for Negligence, Recklessness and Knowledge. When the law provides that negligence suffices to establish an element of an offense, such element also is established if a person acts purposely, knowingly or recklessly. When recklessness suffices to establish an element, such element also is established if a person acts purposely or knowingly. When acting knowingly suffices to establish an element, such element also is established if a person acts purposely.

(6) Requirement of Purpose Satisfied if Purpose Is Conditional. When a particular purpose is an element of an offense, the element is established although such purpose is conditional, unless the condition negatives the harm or evil sought to be prevented by the law defining the offense.

(7) Requirement of Knowledge Satisfied by Knowledge of High Probability. When knowledge of the existence of a particular fact is an element of an offense, such knowledge is established if a person is aware of a high probability of its existence, unless he actually believes that it does not exist.

(8) Requirement of Wilfulness Satisfied by Acting Knowingly. A requirement that an offense be committed wilfully is satisfied if a person acts knowingly with respect to the material elements of the offense, unless a purpose to impose further requirements appears.

(9) Culpability as to Illegality of Conduct. Neither knowledge nor recklessness or negligence as to whether conduct constitutes an offense or as to the existence, meaning or application of the law determining the elements of an offense is an element of such offense, unless the definition of the offense or the Code so provides.

(10) Culpability as Determinant of Grade of Offense. When the grade or degree of an offense depends on whether the offense is committed purposely, knowingly, recklessly or negligently, its grade or degree shall be the lowest for which the determinative kind of culpability is established with respect to any material element of the offense.

§ 2.07. Liability of Corporations, Unincorporated Associations and Persons Acting, or Under a Duty to Act, in Their Behalf

(1) A corporation may be convicted of the commission of an offense if:

(a) the offense is a violation or the offense is defined by a statute other than the Code in which a legislative purpose to impose liability on corporations plainly appears and the conduct is performed by an agent of the corporation acting in behalf of the corporation within the scope of his office or employment, except that if the law defining the offense designates the agents for whose conduct the corporation is accountable or the circumstances under which it is accountable, such provisions shall apply; or

(b) the offense consists of an omission to discharge a specific duty of affirmative performance imposed on corporations by law; or

(c) the commission of the offense was authorized, requested, commanded, performed or recklessly tolerated by the board of directors or by a high managerial agent acting in behalf of the corporation within the scope of his office or employment.

(2) When absolute liability is imposed for the commission of an offense, a legislative purpose to impose liability on a corporation shall be assumed, unless the contrary plainly appears.

(3) An unincorporated association may be convicted of the commission of an offense if:

(a) the offense is defined by a statute other than the Code that expressly provides for the liability of such an association and the conduct is performed by an agent of the association acting in behalf of the association within the scope of his office or employment, except that if the law defining the offense designates the agents for whose conduct the association is accountable or the circumstances under which it is accountable, such provisions shall apply; or

(b) the offense consists of an omission to discharge a specific duty of affirmative performance imposed on associations by law.

(4) As used in this Section:

(a) "corporation" does not include an entity organized as or by a governmental agency for the execution of a governmental program;

(b) "agent" means any director, officer, servant, employee or other person authorized to act in behalf of the corporation or association and, in the case of an unincorporated association, a member of such association;

(c) "high managerial agent" means an officer of a corporation or an unincorporated association, or, in the case of a partnership, a partner, or any other agent of a corporation or association having duties of such responsibility that his conduct may fairly be assumed to represent the policy of the corporation or association.

(5) In any prosecution of a corporation or an unincorporated association for the commission of an offense included within the terms of Subsection (1)(a) or Subsection (3)(a) of this Section, other than an offense for which absolute liability has been imposed, it shall be a defense if the defendant proves by a preponderance of evidence that the high managerial agent having supervisory responsibility over the subject matter of the offense employed due diligence to prevent its commission.

This paragraph shall not apply if it is plainly inconsistent with the legislative purpose in defining the particular offense.

(6)

(a) A person is legally accountable for any conduct he performs or causes to be performed in the name of the corporation or an unincorporated association or in its behalf to the same extent as if it were performed in his own name or behalf.

(b) Whenever a duty to act is imposed by law upon a corporation or an unincorporated association, any agent of the corporation or association having primary responsibility for the discharge of the duty is legally accountable for a reckless omission to perform the required act to the same extent as if the duty were imposed by law directly upon himself.

(c) When a person is convicted of an offense by reason of his legal accountability for the conduct of a corporation or an unincorporated association, he is subject to the sentence authorized by law when a natural person is convicted of an offense of the grade and the degree involved.

Chapter 6
UNITED STATES SENTENCING GUIDELINES

CHAPTER ONE — INTRODUCTION, AUTHORITY, AND GENERAL APPLICATION PRINCIPLES

PART A — INTRODUCTION AND AUTHORITY

Introductory Commentary

Subparts 1 and 2 of this Part provide an introduction to the Guidelines Manual describing the historical development and evolution of the federal sentencing guidelines. Subpart 1 sets forth the original introduction to the Guidelines Manual as it first appeared in 1987, with the inclusion of amendments made occasionally thereto between 1987 and 2000. The original introduction, as so amended, explained a number of policy decisions made by the United States Sentencing Commission ("Commission") when it promulgated the initial set of guidelines and therefore provides a useful reference for contextual and historical purposes. Subpart 2 further describes the evolution of the federal sentencing guidelines after the initial guidelines were promulgated.

Subpart 3 of this Part states the authority of the Commission to promulgate federal sentencing guidelines, policy statements, and commentary.

1. Original Introduction to the Guidelines Manual

The following provisions of this Subpart set forth the original introduction to this manual, effective November 1, 1987, and as amended through November 1, 2000:

1. Authority

The United States Sentencing Commission ("Commission") is an independent agency in the judicial branch composed of seven voting and two non-voting, ex officio members. Its principal purpose is to establish sentencing policies and practices for the federal criminal justice system that will assure the ends of justice by promulgating detailed guidelines prescribing the appropriate sentences for offenders convicted of federal crimes.

The guidelines and policy statements promulgated by the Commission are issued pursuant to Section 994(a) of Title 28, United States Code.

2. The Statutory Mission

The Sentencing Reform Act of 1984 (Title II of the Comprehensive Crime Control Act of 1984) provides for the development of guidelines that will further the basic purposes of criminal punishment: deterrence, incapacitation, just punishment, and rehabilitation. The Act delegates broad authority to the Commission to review and rationalize the federal sentencing process.

The Act contains detailed instructions as to how this determination should be made, the most important of which directs the Commission to create categories of offense behavior and offender characteristics. An offense behavior category might consist, for example, of "bank robbery/committed with a gun/$2500 taken." An offender characteristic category might be "offender with one prior conviction not resulting in imprisonment." The Commission is required to prescribe guideline ranges that specify an appropriate sentence for each class of convicted persons determined by coordinating the offense behavior categories with the offender characteristic categories. Where the guidelines call for imprisonment, the range must be narrow: the maximum of the range cannot exceed the minimum by more than the greater of 25 percent or six months. 28 U.S.C. § 994(b)(2).

Pursuant to the Act, the sentencing court must select a sentence from within the guideline range. If, however, a particular case presents atypical features, the Act allows the court to depart from the guidelines and sentence outside the prescribed range. In that case, the court must specify reasons for departure. 18 U.S.C. § 3553(b). If the court sentences within the guideline range, an appellate court may review the sentence to determine whether the guidelines were correctly applied. If the court departs from the guideline range, an appellate court may review the reasonableness of the departure. 18 U.S.C. § 3742. The Act also abolishes parole, and substantially reduces and restructures good behavior adjustments.

The Commission's initial guidelines were submitted to Congress on April 13, 1987. After the prescribed period of Congressional review, the guidelines took effect on November 1, 1987, and apply to all offenses committed on or after that date. The Commission has the authority to submit guideline amendments each year to Congress between the beginning of a regular Congressional session and May 1. Such amendments automatically take effect 180 days after submission unless a law is enacted to the contrary. 28 U.S.C. § 994(p).

The initial sentencing guidelines and policy statements were developed after extensive hearings, deliberation, and consideration of substantial public comment. The Commission emphasizes, however, that it views the guideline-writing process as evolutionary. It expects, and the governing statute anticipates, that continuing research, experience, and analysis will result in modifications and revisions to the guidelines through submission of amendments to Congress. To this end, the Commission is established as a permanent agency to monitor sentencing practices in the federal courts.

3. The Basic Approach (Policy Statement)

To understand the guidelines and their underlying rationale, it is important to focus on the three objectives that Congress sought to achieve in enacting the Sentencing Reform Act of 1984. The Act's basic objective was to enhance the ability of the criminal justice system to combat crime through an effective, fair sentencing system. To achieve this end, Congress first sought honesty in sentencing. It sought to avoid the confusion and implicit deception that arose out of the pre-guidelines sentencing system which required the court to impose an indeterminate sentence of imprisonment and empowered the parole commission to determine how much of the sentence an offender actually would serve in prison. This practice usually resulted in a substantial reduction in the effective length of the sentence imposed, with defendants often serving only about one-third of the sentence imposed by the court.

Second, Congress sought reasonable uniformity in sentencing by narrowing the wide disparity in sentences imposed for similar criminal offenses committed by similar offenders. Third, Congress sought proportionality in sentencing through a system that imposes appropriately different sentences for criminal conduct of differing severity.

Honesty is easy to achieve: the abolition of parole makes the sentence imposed by the court the sentence the offender will serve, less approximately fifteen percent for good behavior. There is a tension, however, between the mandate of uniformity and the mandate of proportionality. Simple uniformity — sentencing every offender to five years — destroys proportionality. Having only a few simple categories of crimes would make the guidelines uniform and easy to administer, but might lump together offenses that are different in important respects. For example, a single category for robbery that included armed and unarmed robberies, robberies with and without injuries, robberies of a few dollars and robberies of millions, would be far too broad.

A sentencing system tailored to fit every conceivable wrinkle of each case would quickly become unworkable and seriously compromise the certainty of punishment and its deterrent effect. For example: a bank robber with (or without) a gun, which the robber kept hidden (or brandished), might have frightened (or merely warned), injured seriously (or less seriously), tied up (or simply pushed) a guard, teller, or customer, at night (or at noon), in an effort to obtain money for other crimes (or for other purposes), in the company of a few (or many) other robbers, for the first (or fourth) time.

The list of potentially relevant features of criminal behavior is long; the fact that they can occur in multiple combinations means that the list of possible permutations of factors is virtually endless. The appropriate relationships among these different factors are exceedingly difficult to establish, for they are often context specific. Sentencing courts do not treat the occurrence of a simple bruise identically in all cases, irrespective of whether that bruise occurred in the context of a bank robbery or in the context of a breach of peace. This is so, in part, because the risk that such a harm will occur differs depending on the underlying offense with which it is connected; and also because, in part, the relationship between punishment and multiple harms is not simply additive. The relation varies depending on how much other harm has occurred. Thus, it would not be proper to assign points for each kind of harm and simply add them up, irrespective of context and total amounts.

The larger the number of subcategories of offense and offender characteristics included in the guidelines, the greater the complexity and the less workable the system. Moreover, complex combinations of offense and offender characteristics would apply and interact in unforeseen ways to unforeseen situations, thus failing to cure the unfairness of a simple, broad category system. Finally, and perhaps most importantly, probation officers and courts, in applying a complex system having numerous subcategories, would be required to make a host of decisions regarding whether the underlying facts were sufficient to bring the case within a particular subcategory. The greater the number of decisions required and the greater their complexity, the greater the risk that different courts would apply the guidelines differently to situations that, in fact, are similar, thereby reintroducing the very disparity that the guidelines were designed to reduce.

In view of the arguments, it would have been tempting to retreat to the simple, broad category approach and to grant courts the discretion to select the proper point along a broad sentencing range. Granting such broad discretion, however, would have risked correspondingly broad disparity in sentencing, for different courts may exercise their discretionary powers in different ways. Such an approach would have risked a return to the wide disparity that Congress established the Commission to reduce and would have been contrary to the Commission's mandate set forth in the Sentencing Reform Act of 1984.

In the end, there was no completely satisfying solution to this problem. The Commission had to balance the comparative virtues and vices of broad, simple categorization and detailed, complex subcategorization, and within the constraints established by that balance, minimize the discretionary powers of the sentencing court. Any system will, to a degree, enjoy the benefits and suffer from the drawbacks of each approach.

A philosophical problem arose when the Commission attempted to reconcile the differing perceptions of the purposes of criminal punishment. Most observers of the criminal law agree that the ultimate aim of the law itself, and of punishment in particular, is the control of crime. Beyond this point, however, the consensus seems to break down. Some argue that appropriate punishment should be defined primarily on the basis of the principle of "just deserts." Under this principle, punishment should be scaled to the offender's culpability and the resulting harms. Others argue that punishment should be imposed primarily on the basis of practical "crime control" considerations. This theory calls for sentences that most effectively lessen the likelihood of future crime, either by deterring others or incapacitating the defendant.

Adherents of each of these points of view urged the Commission to choose between them and accord one primacy over the other. As a practical matter, however, this choice was unnecessary because in most sentencing decisions the application of either philosophy will produce the same or similar results.

In its initial set of guidelines, the Commission sought to solve both the practical and philosophical problems of developing a coherent sentencing system by taking an empirical approach that used as a starting point data estimating pre-guidelines sentencing practice. It analyzed data drawn from 10,000 presentence investigations, the differing elements of various crimes as distinguished in substantive criminal statutes, the United States Parole Commission's guidelines and statistics, and data from other relevant sources in order to determine which distinctions were important in pre-guidelines practice. After consideration, the Commission accepted, modified, or rationalized these distinctions.

This empirical approach helped the Commission resolve its practical problem by defining a list of relevant distinctions that, although of considerable length, was short enough to create a manageable set of guidelines. Existing categories are relatively broad and omit distinctions that some may believe important, yet they include most of the major distinctions that statutes and data suggest made a significant difference in sentencing decisions. Relevant distinctions not reflected in the guidelines probably will occur rarely and sentencing courts may take such unusual cases into account by departing from the guidelines.

The Commission's empirical approach also helped resolve its philosophical dilemma. Those who adhere to a just deserts philosophy may concede that the lack of consensus might make it difficult to say exactly what punishment is deserved for a particular crime. Likewise, those who subscribe to a philosophy of crime control may acknowledge that the lack of sufficient data might make it difficult to determine exactly the punishment that will best prevent that crime. Both groups might therefore recognize the wisdom of looking to those distinctions that judges and legislators have, in fact, made over the course of time. These established distinctions are ones that the community believes, or has found over time, to be important from either a just deserts or crime control perspective.

The Commission did not simply copy estimates of pre-guidelines practice as revealed by the data, even though establishing offense values on this basis would help eliminate disparity because the data represent averages. Rather, it departed from the data at different points for various important reasons. Congressional statutes, for example, suggested or required departure, as in the case of the Anti-Drug Abuse Act of 1986 that imposed increased and mandatory minimum sentences. In addition, the data revealed inconsistencies in treatment, such as punishing economic crime less severely than other apparently equivalent behavior.

Despite these policy-oriented departures from pre-guidelines practice, the guidelines represent an approach that begins with, and builds upon, empirical data. The guidelines will not please those who wish the Commission to adopt a single philosophical theory and then work deductively to establish a simple and perfect set of categorizations and distinctions. The guidelines may prove acceptable, however, to those who seek more modest, incremental improvements in the status quo, who believe the best is often the enemy of the good, and who recognize that these guidelines are, as the Act contemplates, but the first step in an evolutionary process. After spending considerable time and resources exploring alternative approaches, the Commission developed these guidelines as a practical effort toward the achievement of a more honest, uniform, equitable, proportional, and therefore effective sentencing system.

4. The Guidelines' Resolution of Major Issues (Policy Statement)

The guideline-drafting process required the Commission to resolve a host of important policy questions typically involving rather evenly balanced sets of competing considerations. As an aid to understanding the guidelines, this introduction briefly discusses several of those issues; commentary in the guidelines explains others.

(a) Real Offense vs. Charge Offense Sentencing

One of the most important questions for the Commission to decide was whether to base sentences upon the actual conduct in which the defendant engaged regardless of the charges for which he was indicted or convicted ("real offense" sentencing), or upon the conduct that constitutes the elements of the offense for which the defendant was charged and of which he was convicted ("charge offense" sentencing). A bank robber, for example, might have used a gun, frightened bystanders, taken $50,000, injured a teller, refused to stop when ordered, and raced away damaging property during his escape. A pure real offense system would sentence on the basis of all identifiable conduct. A pure charge offense system would overlook some of the harms that did not constitute statutory elements of the offenses of which the defendant was convicted.

The Commission initially sought to develop a pure real offense system. After all, the pre-guidelines sentencing system was, in a sense, this type of system. The sentencing court and the parole commission took account of the conduct in which the defendant actually engaged, as determined in a presentence report, at the sentencing hearing, or before a parole commission hearing officer. The Commission's initial efforts in this direction, carried out in the spring and early summer of 1986, proved unproductive, mostly for practical reasons. To make such a system work, even to formalize and rationalize the status quo, would have required the Commission to decide precisely which harms to take into account, how to add them up, and what kinds of procedures the courts should use to determine the presence or absence of disputed factual elements. The Commission found no practical way to combine and account for the large number of diverse harms arising in different circumstances; nor did it find a practical way to reconcile the need for a fair adjudicatory procedure with the need for a speedy sentencing process given the potential existence of hosts of adjudicated "real harm" facts in many typical cases. The effort proposed as a solution to these problems required the use of, for example, quadratic roots and other mathematical operations that the Commission considered too complex to be workable. In the Commission's view, such a system risked return to wide disparity in sentencing practice.

In its initial set of guidelines submitted to Congress in April 1987, the Commission moved closer to a charge offense system. This system, however, does contain a significant number of real offense elements. For one thing, the hundreds of overlapping and duplicative statutory provisions that make up the federal criminal law forced the Commission to write guidelines that are descriptive of generic conduct rather than guidelines that track purely statutory language. For another, the guidelines take account of a number of important, commonly occurring real offense elements such as role in the offense, the presence of a gun, or the amount of money actually taken, through alternative base offense levels, specific offense characteristics, cross references, and adjustments.

The Commission recognized that a charge offense system has drawbacks of its own. One of the most important is the potential it affords prosecutors to influence sentences by increasing or decreasing the number of counts in an indictment. Of course, the defendant's actual conduct (that which the prosecutor can prove in court) imposes a natural limit upon the prosecutor's ability to increase a defendant's sentence. Moreover, the Commission has written its rules for the treatment of multicount convictions with an eye toward eliminating unfair treatment that might flow from count manipulation. For example, the guidelines treat a three-count indictment, each count of which charges sale of 100 grams of heroin or theft of $10,000, the same as a single-count indictment charging sale of 300 grams of heroin or theft of $30,000. Furthermore, a sentencing court may control any inappropriate manipulation of the indictment through use of its departure power. Finally, the Commission will closely monitor charging and plea agreement practices and will make appropriate adjustments should they become necessary.

(b) Departures

The sentencing statute permits a court to depart from a guideline-specified sentence only when it finds "an aggravating or mitigating circumstance of a kind, or to a degree, not adequately taken into consideration by the Sentencing Commission in formulating the guidelines that should result in a sentence different from that described." 18 U.S.C. § 3553(b). The Commission intends the sentencing courts to treat each guideline as carving out a "heartland," a set of typical cases embodying the conduct that each guideline describes. When a court finds an atypical case, one to which a particular guideline linguistically applies but where conduct significantly differs from the norm, the court may consider whether a departure is warranted. Section 5H1.10 (Race, Sex, National Origin, Creed, Religion, and Socio-Economic Status), § 5H1.12 (Lack of Guidance as a Youth and Similar Circumstances), the third sentence of § 5H1.4 (Physical Condition, Including Drug or Alcohol Dependence or Abuse), the last sentence of § 5K2.12 (Coercion and Duress), and § 5K2.19 (Post-Sentencing Rehabilitative Efforts) list several factors that the court cannot take into account as grounds for departure. With those specific exceptions, however, the Commission does not intend to limit the kinds of factors, whether or not mentioned anywhere else in the guidelines, that could constitute grounds for departure in an unusual case.

The Commission has adopted this departure policy for two reasons. First, it is difficult to prescribe a single set of guidelines that encompasses the vast range of human conduct potentially relevant to a sentencing decision. The Commission also recognizes that the initial set of guidelines need not do so. The Commission is a permanent body, empowered by law to write and rewrite guidelines, with progressive changes, over many years. By monitoring when courts depart from the guidelines and by analyzing their stated reasons for doing so and court decisions with references thereto, the Commission, over time, will be able to refine the guidelines to specify more precisely when departures should and should not be permitted.

Second, the Commission believes that despite the courts' legal freedom to depart from the guidelines, they will not do so very often. This is because the guidelines, offense by offense, seek to take account of those factors that the Commission's data indicate made a significant difference in pre-guidelines sentencing practice. Thus, for example, where the presence of physical injury made an important difference in pre-guidelines sentencing practice (as in the case of robbery or assault), the guidelines specifically include this factor to enhance the sentence. Where the guidelines do not specify an augmentation or diminution, this is generally because the sentencing data did not permit the Commission to conclude that the factor was empirically important in relation to the particular offense. Of course, an important factor (e.g., physical injury) may infrequently occur in connection with a particular crime (e.g., fraud). Such rare occurrences are precisely the type of events that the courts' departure powers were designed to cover — unusual cases outside the range of the more typical offenses for which the guidelines were designed.

It is important to note that the guidelines refer to two different kinds of departure. The first involves instances in which the guidelines provide specific guidance for departure by analogy or by other numerical or non-numerical suggestions. The Commission intends such suggestions as policy guidance for the courts. The Commission expects that most departures will reflect the suggestions and that the courts of appeals may prove more likely to find departures "unreasonable" where they fall outside suggested levels.

A second type of departure will remain unguided. It may rest upon grounds referred to in Chapter Five, Part K (Departures) or on grounds not mentioned in the guidelines. While Chapter Five, Part K lists factors that the Commission believes may constitute grounds for departure, the list is not exhaustive. The Commission recognizes that there may be other grounds for departure that are not mentioned; it also believes there may be cases in which a departure outside suggested levels is warranted. In its view, however, such cases will be highly infrequent.

(c) Plea Agreements

Nearly ninety percent of all federal criminal cases involve guilty pleas and many of these cases involve some form of plea agreement. Some commentators on early Commission guideline drafts urged the Commission not to attempt any major reforms of the plea agreement process on the grounds that any set of guidelines that threatened to change pre-guidelines practice radically also threatened to make the federal system unmanageable. Others argued that guidelines that failed to control and limit plea agreements would leave untouched a "loophole" large enough to undo the good that sentencing guidelines would bring.

The Commission decided not to make major changes in plea agreement practices in the initial guidelines, but rather to provide guidance by issuing general policy statements concerning the acceptance of plea agreements in Chapter Six, Part B (Plea Agreements). The rules set forth in Fed. R. Crim. P. 11(e) govern the acceptance or rejection of such agreements. The Commission will collect data on the courts' plea practices and will analyze this information to determine when and why the courts accept or reject plea agreements and whether plea agreement practices are undermining the intent of the Sentencing Reform Act. In light of this information and analysis, the Commission will seek to further regulate the plea agreement process as appropriate. Importantly, if the policy statements relating to plea agreements are followed, circumvention of the Sentencing Reform Act and the guidelines should not occur.

The Commission expects the guidelines to have a positive, rationalizing impact upon plea agreements for two reasons. First, the guidelines create a clear, definite expectation in respect to the sentence that a court will impose if a trial takes place. In the event a prosecutor and defense attorney explore the possibility of a negotiated plea, they will no longer work in the dark. This fact alone should help to reduce irrationality in respect to actual sentencing outcomes. Second, the guidelines create a norm to which courts will likely refer when they decide whether, under Rule 11(e), to accept or to reject a plea agreement or recommendation.

(d) Probation and Split Sentences

The statute provides that the guidelines are to "reflect the general appropriateness of imposing a sentence other than imprisonment in cases in which the defendant is a first offender who has not been convicted of a crime of violence or an otherwise serious offense . . . ." 28 U.S.C. § 994(j). Under pre-guidelines sentencing practice, courts sentenced to probation an inappropriately high percentage of offenders guilty of certain economic crimes, such as theft, tax evasion, antitrust offenses, insider trading, fraud, and embezzlement, that in the Commission's view are "serious."

The Commission's solution to this problem has been to write guidelines that classify as serious many offenses for which probation previously was frequently given and provide for at least a short period of imprisonment in such cases. The Commission concluded that the definite prospect of prison, even though the term may be short, will serve as a significant deterrent, particularly when compared with pre-guidelines practice where probation, not prison, was the norm.

More specifically, the guidelines work as follows in respect to a first offender. For offense levels one through eight, the sentencing court may elect to sentence the offender to probation (with or without confinement conditions) or to a prison term. For offense levels nine and ten, the court may substitute probation for a prison term, but the probation must include confinement conditions (community confinement, intermittent confinement, or home detention). For offense levels eleven and twelve, the court must impose at least one-half the minimum confinement sentence in the form of prison confinement, the remainder to be served on supervised release with a condition of community confinement or home detention. The Commission, of course, has not dealt with the single acts of aberrant behavior that still may justify probation at higher offense levels through departures.*

*Note: Although the Commission had not addressed "single acts of aberrant behavior" at the time the Introduction to the Guidelines Manual originally was written, it subsequently addressed the issue in Amendment 603, effective November 1, 2000. (See Supplement to Appendix C, amendment 603.)

(e) Multi-Count Convictions

The Commission, like several state sentencing commissions, has found it particularly difficult to develop guidelines for sentencing defendants convicted of multiple violations of law, each of which makes up a separate count in an indictment. The difficulty is that when a defendant engages in conduct that causes several harms, each additional harm, even if it increases the extent to which punishment is warranted, does not necessarily warrant a proportionate increase in punishment. A defendant who assaults others during a fight, for example, may warrant more punishment if he injures ten people than if he injures one, but his conduct does not necessarily warrant ten times the punishment. If it did, many of the simplest offenses, for reasons that are often fortuitous, would lead to sentences of life imprisonment — sentences that neither just deserts nor crime control theories of punishment would justify.

Several individual guidelines provide special instructions for increasing punishment when the conduct that is the subject of that count involves multiple occurrences or has caused several harms. The guidelines also provide general rules for aggravating punishment in light of multiple harms charged separately in separate counts. These rules may produce occasional anomalies, but normally they will permit an appropriate degree of aggravation of punishment for multiple offenses that are the subjects of separate counts.

These rules are set out in Chapter Three, Part D (Multiple Counts). They essentially provide: (1) when the conduct involves fungible items (e.g., separate drug transactions or thefts of money), the amounts are added and the guidelines apply to the total amount; (2) when nonfungible harms are involved, the offense level for the most serious count is increased (according to a diminishing scale) to reflect the existence of other counts of conviction. The guidelines have been written in order to minimize the possibility that an arbitrary casting of a single transaction into several counts will produce a longer sentence. In addition, the sentencing court will have adequate power to prevent such a result through departures.

(f) Regulatory Offenses

Regulatory statutes, though primarily civil in nature, sometimes contain criminal provisions in respect to particularly harmful activity. Such criminal provisions often describe not only substantive offenses, but also more technical, administratively-related offenses such as failure to keep accurate records or to provide requested information. These statutes pose two problems: first, which criminal regulatory provisions should the Commission initially consider, and second, how should it treat technical or administratively-related criminal violations?

In respect to the first problem, the Commission found that it could not comprehensively treat all regulatory violations in the initial set of guidelines. There are hundreds of such provisions scattered throughout the United States Code. To find all potential violations would involve examination of each individual federal regulation. Because of this practical difficulty, the Commission sought to determine, with the assistance of the Department of Justice and several regulatory agencies, which criminal regulatory offenses were particularly important in light of the need for enforcement of the general regulatory scheme. The Commission addressed these offenses in the initial guidelines.

In respect to the second problem, the Commission has developed a system for treating technical recordkeeping and reporting offenses that divides them into four categories. First, in the simplest of cases, the offender may have failed to fill out a form intentionally, but without knowledge or intent that substantive harm would likely follow. He might fail, for example, to keep an accurate record of toxic substance transport, but that failure may not lead, nor be likely to lead, to the release or improper handling of any toxic substance. Second, the same failure may be accompanied by a significant likelihood that substantive harm will occur; it may make a release of a toxic substance more likely. Third, the same failure may have led to substantive harm. Fourth, the failure may represent an effort to conceal a substantive harm that has occurred.

The structure of a typical guideline for a regulatory offense provides a low base offense level (e.g., 6) aimed at the first type of recordkeeping or reporting offense. Specific offense characteristics designed to reflect substantive harms that do occur in respect to some regulatory offenses, or that are likely to occur, increase the offense level. A specific offense characteristic also provides that a recordkeeping or reporting offense that conceals a substantive offense will have the same offense level as the substantive offense.

(g) Sentencing Ranges

In determining the appropriate sentencing ranges for each offense, the Commission estimated the average sentences served within each category under the pre-guidelines sentencing system. It also examined the sentences specified in federal statutes, in the parole guidelines, and in other relevant, analogous sources. The Commission's Supplementary Report on the Initial Sentencing Guidelines (1987) contains a comparison between estimates of pre-guidelines sentencing practice and sentences under the guidelines.

While the Commission has not considered itself bound by pre-guidelines sentencing practice, it has not attempted to develop an entirely new system of sentencing on the basis of theory alone. Guideline sentences, in many instances, will approximate average pre-guidelines practice and adherence to the guidelines will help to eliminate wide disparity. For example, where a high percentage of persons received probation under pre-guidelines practice, a guideline may include one or more specific offense characteristics in an effort to distinguish those types of defendants who received probation from those who received more severe sentences. In some instances, short sentences of incarceration for all offenders in a category have been substituted for a pre-guidelines sentencing practice of very wide variability in which some defendants received probation while others received several years in prison for the same offense. Moreover, inasmuch as those who pleaded guilty under pre-guidelines practice often received lesser sentences, the guidelines permit the court to impose lesser sentences on those defendants who accept responsibility for their misconduct. For defendants who provide substantial assistance to the government in the investigation or prosecution of others, a downward departure may be warranted.

The Commission has also examined its sentencing ranges in light of their likely impact upon prison population. Specific legislation, such as the Anti-Drug Abuse Act of 1986 and the career offender provisions of the Sentencing Reform Act of 1984 (28 U.S.C. § 994(h)), required the Commission to promulgate guidelines that will lead to substantial prison population increases. These increases will occur irrespective of the guidelines. The guidelines themselves, insofar as they reflect policy decisions made by the Commission (rather than legislated mandatory minimum or career offender sentences), are projected to lead to an increase in prison population that computer models, produced by the

Commission and the Bureau of Prisons in 1987, estimated at approximately 10 percent over a period of ten years.

(h) The Sentencing Table

The Commission has established a sentencing table that for technical and practical reasons contains 43 levels. Each level in the table prescribes ranges that overlap with the ranges in the preceding and succeeding levels. By overlapping the ranges, the table should discourage unnecessary litigation. Both prosecution and defense will realize that the difference between one level and another will not necessarily make a difference in the sentence that the court imposes. Thus, little purpose will be served in protracted litigation trying to determine, for example, whether $10,000 or $11,000 was obtained as a result of a fraud. At the same time, the levels work to increase a sentence proportionately. A change of six levels roughly doubles the sentence irrespective of the level at which one starts. The guidelines, in keeping with the statutory requirement that the maximum of any range cannot exceed the minimum by more than the greater of 25 percent or six months (28 U.S.C. § 994(b)(2)), permit courts to exercise the greatest permissible range of sentencing discretion. The table overlaps offense levels meaningfully, works proportionately, and at the same time preserves the maximum degree of allowable discretion for the court within each level.

Similarly, many of the individual guidelines refer to tables that correlate amounts of money with offense levels. These tables often have many rather than a few levels. Again, the reason is to minimize the likelihood of unnecessary litigation. If a money table were to make only a few distinctions, each distinction would become more important and litigation over which category an offender fell within would become more likely. Where a table has many small monetary distinctions, it minimizes the likelihood of litigation because the precise amount of money involved is of considerably less importance.

5. **A Concluding Note**

The Commission emphasizes that it drafted the initial guidelines with considerable caution. It examined the many hundreds of criminal statutes in the United States Code. It began with those that were the basis for a significant number of prosecutions and sought to place them in a rational order. It developed additional distinctions relevant to the application of these provisions and it applied sentencing ranges to each resulting category. In doing so, it relied upon pre-guidelines sentencing practice as revealed by its own statistical analyses based on summary reports of some 40,000 convictions, a sample of 10,000 augmented presentence reports, the parole guidelines, and policy judgments.

The Commission recognizes that some will criticize this approach as overly cautious, as representing too little a departure from pre-guidelines sentencing practice. Yet, it will cure wide disparity. The Commission is a permanent body that can amend the guidelines each year. Although the data available to it, like all data, are imperfect, experience with the guidelines will lead to additional information and provide a firm empirical basis for consideration of revisions.

Finally, the guidelines will apply to more than 90 percent of all felony and Class A misdemeanor cases in the federal courts. Because of time constraints and the nonexistence of statistical information, some offenses that occur infrequently are not considered in the guidelines. Their exclusion does not reflect any judgment regarding their seriousness and they will be addressed as the Commission refines the guidelines over time.

2. Continuing Evolution and Role of the Guidelines

The Sentencing Reform Act of 1984 changed the course of federal sentencing. Among other things, the Act created the United States Sentencing Commission as an independent agency in the Judicial Branch, and directed it to develop guidelines and policy statements for sentencing courts to use when sentencing offenders convicted of federal crimes. Moreover, it empowered the Commission with ongoing responsibilities to monitor the guidelines, submit to Congress appropriate modifications of the guidelines and recommended changes in criminal statutes, and establish education and research programs. The mandate rested on congressional awareness that sentencing is a dynamic field that requires continuing review by an expert body to revise sentencing policies, in light of application experience, as new criminal statutes are enacted, and as more is learned about what motivates and controls criminal behavior.

This statement finds resonance in a line of Supreme Court cases that, taken together, echo two themes. The first theme is that the guidelines are the product of a deliberative process that seeks to embody the purposes of sentencing set forth in the Sentencing Reform Act, and as such they continue to play an important role in the sentencing court's determination of an appropriate sentence in a particular case. The Supreme Court alluded to this in Mistretta v. United States, 488 U.S. 361 (1989), which upheld the constitutionality of both the federal sentencing guidelines and the Commission against nondelegation and separation of powers challenges. Therein the Court stated:

> Developing proportionate penalties for hundreds of different crimes by a virtually limitless array of offenders is precisely the sort of intricate, labor-intensive task for which delegation to an expert body is especially appropriate. Although Congress has delegated significant discretion to the Commission to draw judgments from its analysis of existing sentencing practice and alternative sentencing models, . . . [w]e have no doubt that in the hands of the Commission "the criteria which Congress has supplied are wholly adequate for carrying out the general policy and purpose" of the Act.

Id. at 379 (internal quotation marks and citations omitted).

The continuing importance of the guidelines in federal sentencing was further acknowledged by the Court in United States v. Booker, 543 U.S. 220 (2005), even as that case rendered the guidelines advisory in nature. In Booker, the Court held that the imposition of an enhanced sentence under the federal sentencing guidelines based on the sentencing judge's determination of a fact (other than a prior conviction) that was not found by the jury or admitted by the defendant violated the Sixth Amendment. The Court reasoned that an advisory guideline system, while lacking the mandatory features that Congress enacted, retains other features that help to further congressional objectives, including providing certainty and fairness in meeting the purposes of sentencing, avoiding unwarranted sentencing disparities, and maintaining sufficient flexibility to permit individualized sentences when warranted. The Court concluded that an advisory guideline system would "continue to move sentencing in Congress' preferred direction, helping to avoid excessive sentencing disparities while maintaining flexibility sufficient to individualize sentences where necessary." Id. at 264–65. An advisory guideline system continues to assure transparency by requiring that sentences be based on articulated reasons stated in open court that are subject to appellate review. An advisory guideline system also continues to promote certainty and predictability in sentencing, thereby enabling the parties to better anticipate the likely sentence based on the individualized facts of the case.

The continuing importance of the guidelines in the sentencing determination is predicated in large part on the Sentencing Reform Act's intent that, in promulgating guidelines, the Commission must take into account the purposes of sentencing as set forth in 18 U.S.C. § 3553(a). See 28 U.S.C. §§ 994(f), 991(b)(1). The Supreme Court reinforced this view in Rita v. United States, 551 U.S. 338 (2007), which held that a court of appeals may apply a presumption of reasonableness to a sentence imposed by a district court within a properly calculated guideline range without violating the Sixth Amendment. In Rita, the Court relied heavily on the complementary roles of the Commission and the sentencing court in federal sentencing, stating:

> [T]he presumption reflects the nature of the Guidelines-writing task that Congress set for the Commission and the manner in which the Commission carried out that task. In instructing both the sentencing judge and the Commission what to do, Congress referred to the basic sentencing objectives that the statute sets forth in 18 U.S.C. § 3553(a) . . . . The provision also tells the sentencing judge to "impose a sentence sufficient, but not greater than necessary, to comply with" the basic aims of sentencing as set out above. Congressional statutes then tell the Commission to write Guidelines that will carry out these same § 3553(a) objectives.

Id. at 347–48 (emphasis in original). The Court concluded that "[t]he upshot is that the sentencing statutes envision both the sentencing judge and the Commission as carrying out the same basic § 3553(a) objectives, the one, at retail, the other at wholesale[,]" id. at 348, and that the Commission's process for promulgating guidelines results in "a set of Guidelines that seek to embody the § 3553(a) considerations, both in principle and in practice." Id. at 350.

Consequently, district courts are required to properly calculate and consider the guidelines when sentencing, even in an advisory guideline system. See 18 U.S.C. § 3553(a)(4), (a)(5); Booker, 543 U.S. at 264 ("The district courts, while not bound to apply the Guidelines, must . . . take them into account when sentencing."); Rita, 551 U.S. at 351 (stating that a district court should begin all sentencing proceedings by correctly calculating the applicable Guidelines range); Gall v. United States, 552 U.S. 38, 49 (2007) ("As a matter of administration and to secure nationwide consistency, the Guidelines should be the starting point and the initial benchmark."). The district court, in determining the appropriate sentence in a particular case, therefore, must consider the properly calculated guideline range, the grounds for departure provided in the policy statements, and then the factors under 18 U.S.C. § 3553(a). See Rita, 551 U.S. at 351. The appellate court engages in a two-step process upon review. The appellate court "first ensure[s] that the district court committed no significant procedural error, such as failing to calculate (or improperly calculating) the Guidelines range . . . [and] then consider[s] the substantive reasonableness of the sentence imposed under an abuse-of-discretion standard[,] . . . tak[ing] into account the totality of the circumstances, including the extent of any variance from the Guidelines range." Gall, 552 U.S. at 51.

The second and related theme resonant in this line of Supreme Court cases is that, as contemplated by the Sentencing Reform Act, the guidelines are evolutionary in nature. They are the product of the Commission's fulfillment of its statutory duties to monitor federal sentencing law and practices, to seek public input on the operation of the guidelines, and to revise the guidelines accordingly. As the Court acknowledged in Rita:

> The Commission's work is ongoing. The statutes and the Guidelines themselves foresee continuous evolution helped by the sentencing courts and courts of appeals in that process. The sentencing courts, applying the Guidelines in individual cases may depart (either pursuant to the Guidelines or, since Booker, by imposing a non-Guidelines sentence). The judges will set forth their reasons. The Courts of Appeals will determine the reasonableness of the resulting sentence. The Commission will collect and examine the results. In doing so, it may obtain advice from prosecutors, defenders, law enforcement groups, civil liberties associations, experts in penology, and others. And it can revise the Guidelines accordingly.

Rita, 551 U.S. at 350; see also Booker, 543 U.S. at 264 ("[T]he Sentencing Commission remains in place, writing Guidelines, collecting information about actual district court sentencing decisions, undertaking research, and revising the Guidelines accordingly."); Gall, 552 U.S. at 46 ("[E]ven though the Guidelines are advisory rather than mandatory, they are, as we pointed out in Rita, the product of careful study based on extensive empirical evidence derived from the review of thousands of individual sentencing decisions.").

Provisions of the Sentencing Reform Act promote and facilitate this evolutionary process. For example, pursuant to 28 U.S.C. § 994(x), the Commission publishes guideline amendment proposals in the Federal Register and conducts hearings to solicit input on those proposals from experts and other members of the public. Pursuant to 28 U.S.C. § 994(o), the Commission periodically reviews and revises the guidelines in consideration of comments it receives from members of the federal criminal justice system, including the courts, probation officers, the Department of Justice, the Bureau of Prisons, defense attorneys and the federal public defenders, and in consideration of data it receives from sentencing courts and other sources. Statutory mechanisms such as these bolster the Commission's ability to take into account fully the purposes of sentencing set forth in 18 U.S.C. § 3553(a)(2) in its promulgation of the guidelines.

Congress retains authority to require certain sentencing practices and may exercise its authority through specific directives to the Commission with respect to the guidelines. As the Supreme Court noted in Kimbrough v. United States, 552 U.S. 85 (2007), "Congress has shown that it knows how to direct sentencing practices in express terms. For example, Congress has specifically required the Sentencing Commission to set Guideline sentences for serious recidivist offenders 'at or near' the statutory maximum." Id. at 103; 28 U.S.C. § 994(h).

As envisioned by Congress, implemented by the Commission, and reaffirmed by the Supreme Court, the guidelines are the product of a deliberative and dynamic process that seeks to embody within federal sentencing policy the purposes of sentencing set forth in the Sentencing Reform Act. As such, the guidelines continue to be a key component of federal sentencing and to play an important role in the sentencing court's determination of an appropriate sentence in any particular case.

§ 1A3.1. Authority

The guidelines, policy statements, and commentary set forth in this Guidelines Manual, including amendments thereto, are promulgated by the United States Sentencing Commission pursuant to:

(1) Section 994(a) of title 28, United States Code; and

(2) with respect to guidelines, policy statements, and commentary promulgated or amended pursuant to specific congressional directive, pursuant to the authority contained in that directive in addition to the authority under section 994(a) of title 28, United States Code.

PART B — GENERAL APPLICATION PRINCIPLES

§ 1B1.3. Relevant Conduct (Factors that Determine the Guideline Range)

(a) Chapters Two (Offense Conduct) and Three (Adjustments). Unless otherwise specified, (i) the base offense level where the guideline specifies more than one base offense level, (ii) specific offense characteristics and (iii) cross references in Chapter Two, and (iv) adjustments in Chapter Three, shall be determined on the basis of the following:

(1)

(A) all acts and omissions committed, aided, abetted, counseled, commanded, induced, procured, or willfully caused by the defendant; and

(B) in the case of a jointly undertaken criminal activity (a criminal plan, scheme, endeavor, or enterprise undertaken by the defendant in concert with others, whether or not charged as a conspiracy), all reasonably foreseeable acts and omissions of others in furtherance of the jointly undertaken criminal activity,

that occurred during the commission of the offense of conviction, in preparation for that offense, or in the course of attempting to avoid detection or responsibility for that offense;

(2) solely with respect to offenses of a character for which § 3D1.2(d) would

require grouping of multiple counts, all acts and omissions described in subdivisions (1)(A) and (1)(B) above that were part of the same course of conduct or common scheme or plan as the offense of conviction;

(3) all harm that resulted from the acts and omissions specified in subsections (a)(1) and (a)(2) above, and all harm that was the object of such acts and omissions; and

(4) any other information specified in the applicable guideline.

(b) Chapters Four (Criminal History and Criminal Livelihood) and Five (Determining the Sentence). Factors in Chapters Four and Five that establish the guideline range shall be determined on the basis of the conduct and information specified in the respective guidelines.

COMMENTARY

Application Notes:

1.) The principles and limits of sentencing accountability under this guideline are not always the same as the principles and limits of criminal liability. Under subsections (a)(1) and (a)(2), the focus is on the specific acts and omissions for which the defendant is to be held accountable in determining the applicable guideline range, rather than on whether the defendant is criminally liable for an offense as a principal, accomplice, or conspirator.

2.) A "jointly undertaken criminal activity" is a criminal plan, scheme, endeavor, or enterprise undertaken by the defendant in concert with others, whether or not charged as a conspiracy.

In the case of a jointly undertaken criminal activity, subsection (a)(1)(B) provides that a defendant is accountable for the conduct (acts and omissions) of others that was both:

(A) in furtherance of the jointly undertaken criminal activity; and

(B) reasonably foreseeable in connection with that criminal activity.

Because a count may be worded broadly and include the conduct of many participants over a period of time, the scope of the criminal activity jointly undertaken by the defendant (the "jointly undertaken criminal activity") is not necessarily the same as the scope of the entire conspiracy, and hence relevant conduct is not necessarily the same for every participant. In order to determine the defendant's accountability for the conduct of others under subsection (a)(1)(B), the court must first determine the scope of the criminal activity the particular defendant agreed to jointly undertake (i.e., the scope of the specific conduct and objectives embraced by the defendant's agreement). The conduct of others that was both in furtherance of, and reasonably foreseeable in connection with, the criminal activity jointly undertaken by the defendant is relevant conduct under this provision. The conduct of others that was not in furtherance of the criminal activity jointly undertaken by the defendant, or was not reasonably foreseeable in connection with that criminal activity, is not relevant conduct under this provision.

In determining the scope of the criminal activity that the particular defendant agreed to jointly undertake (i.e., the scope of the specific conduct and objectives embraced by the defendant's agreement), the court may consider any explicit agreement or implicit agreement fairly inferred from the conduct of the defendant and others.

Note that the criminal activity that the defendant agreed to jointly undertake, and the reasonably foreseeable conduct of others in furtherance of that criminal activity, are not necessarily identical. For example, two defendants agree to commit a robbery and, during the course of that robbery, the first defendant assaults and injures a victim. The second defendant is accountable for the assault and injury to the victim (even if the second defendant had not agreed to the assault and had cautioned the first defendant to be careful not to hurt anyone) because the assaultive conduct was in furtherance of the jointly undertaken criminal activity (the robbery) and was reasonably foreseeable in connection with that criminal activity (given the nature of the offense).

With respect to offenses involving contraband (including controlled substances), the defendant is accountable for all quantities of contraband with which he was directly involved and, in the case of a jointly undertaken criminal activity, all reasonably foreseeable quantities of contraband that were within the scope of the criminal activity that he jointly undertook.

The requirement of reasonable foreseeability applies only in respect to the conduct (i.e., acts and omissions) of others under subsection (a)(1)(B). It does not apply to conduct that the defendant personally undertakes, aids, abets, counsels, commands, induces, procures, or willfully causes; such conduct is addressed under subsection (a)(1)(A).

A defendant's relevant conduct does not include the conduct of members of a conspiracy prior to the defendant joining the conspiracy, even if the defendant knows of that conduct (e.g., in the case of a defendant who joins an ongoing drug distribution conspiracy knowing that it had been selling two kilograms of cocaine per week, the cocaine sold prior to the defendant joining the conspiracy is not included as relevant conduct in determining the defendant's offense level). The Commission does not foreclose the possibility that there may be some unusual set of circumstances in which the exclusion of such conduct may not adequately reflect the defendant's culpability; in such a case, an upward departure may be warranted.

Illustrations of Conduct for Which the Defendant is Accountable

(a) Acts and omissions aided or abetted by the defendant

(1) Defendant A is one of ten persons hired by Defendant B to off-load a ship containing marihuana. The off-loading of the ship is interrupted by law enforcement officers and one ton of marihuana is seized (the amount on the ship as well as the amount off-loaded). Defendant A and the other off-loaders are arrested and convicted of importation of marihuana. Regardless of the number of bales he personally unloaded, Defendant A is accountable for the entire one-ton quantity of marihuana. Defendant A aided and abetted the off-loading of the entire shipment of marihuana by directly participating in the

off-loading of that shipment (i.e., the specific objective of the criminal activity he joined was the off-loading of the entire shipment). Therefore, he is accountable for the entire shipment under subsection (a)(1)(A) without regard to the issue of reasonable foreseeability. This is conceptually similar to the case of a defendant who transports a suitcase knowing that it contains a controlled substance and, therefore, is accountable for the controlled substance in the suitcase regardless of his knowledge or lack of knowledge of the actual type or amount of that controlled substance.

In certain cases, a defendant may be accountable for particular conduct under more than one subsection of this guideline. As noted in the preceding paragraph, Defendant A is accountable for the entire one-ton shipment of marihuana under subsection (a)(1)(A). Defendant A also is accountable for the entire one-ton shipment of marihuana on the basis of subsection (a)(1)(B) (applying to a jointly undertaken criminal activity). Defendant A engaged in a jointly undertaken criminal activity (the scope of which was the importation of the shipment of marihuana). A finding that the one-ton quantity of marihuana was reasonably foreseeable is warranted from the nature of the undertaking itself (the importation of marihuana by ship typically involves very large quantities of marihuana). The specific circumstances of the case (the defendant was one of ten persons off-loading the marihuana in bales) also support this finding. In an actual case, of course, if a defendant's accountability for particular conduct is established under one provision of this guideline, it is not necessary to review alternative provisions under which such accountability might be established.

(b) Acts and omissions aided or abetted by the defendant; requirement that the conduct of others be in furtherance of the jointly undertaken criminal activity and reasonably foreseeable

(1) Defendant C is the getaway driver in an armed bank robbery in which $15,000 is taken and a teller is assaulted and injured. Defendant C is accountable for the money taken under subsection (a)(1)(A) because he aided and abetted the act of taking the money (the taking of money was the specific objective of the offense he joined). Defendant C is accountable for the injury to the teller under subsection (a)(1)(B) because the assault on the teller was in furtherance of the jointly undertaken criminal activity (the robbery) and was reasonably foreseeable in connection with that criminal activity (given the nature of the offense).

As noted earlier, a defendant may be accountable for particular conduct under more than one subsection. In this example, Defendant C also is accountable for the money taken on the basis of subsection (a)(1)(B) because the taking of money was in furtherance of the jointly undertaken criminal activity (the robbery) and was reasonably foreseeable (as noted, the taking of money was the specific objective of the jointly undertaken criminal activity).

(c) Requirement that the conduct of others be in furtherance of the jointly undertaken criminal activity and reasonably foreseeable; scope of the criminal activity

(1) Defendant D pays Defendant E a small amount to forge an endorsement

on an $800 stolen government check. Unknown to Defendant E, Defendant D then uses that check as a down payment in a scheme to fraudulently obtain $15,000 worth of merchandise. Defendant E is convicted of forging the $800 check and is accountable for the forgery of this check under subsection (a)(1)(A). Defendant E is not accountable for the $15,000 because the fraudulent scheme to obtain $15,000 was not in furtherance of the criminal activity he jointly undertook with Defendant D (i.e., the forgery of the $800 check).

(2) Defendants F and G, working together, design and execute a scheme to sell fraudulent stocks by telephone. Defendant F fraudulently obtains $20,000. Defendant G fraudulently obtains $35,000. Each is convicted of mail fraud. Defendants F and G each are accountable for the entire amount ($55,000). Each defendant is accountable for the amount he personally obtained under subsection (a)(1)(A). Each defendant is accountable for the amount obtained by his accomplice under subsection (a)(1)(B) because the conduct of each was in furtherance of the jointly undertaken criminal activity and was reasonably foreseeable in connection with that criminal activity.

(3) Defendants H and I engaged in an ongoing marihuana importation conspiracy in which Defendant J was hired only to help off-load a single shipment. Defendants H, I, and J are included in a single count charging conspiracy to import marihuana. Defendant J is accountable for the entire single shipment of marihuana he helped import under subsection (a)(1)(A) and any acts and omissions in furtherance of the importation of that shipment that were reasonably foreseeable (see the discussion in example (a)(1) above). He is not accountable for prior or subsequent shipments of marihuana imported by Defendants H or I because those acts were not in furtherance of his jointly undertaken criminal activity (the importation of the single shipment of marihuana).

(4) Defendant K is a wholesale distributor of child pornography. Defendant L is a retail-level dealer who purchases child pornography from Defendant K and resells it, but otherwise operates independently of Defendant K. Similarly, Defendant M is a retail-level dealer who purchases child pornography from Defendant K and resells it, but otherwise operates independently of Defendant K. Defendants L and M are aware of each other's criminal activity but operate independently. Defendant N is Defendant K's assistant who recruits customers for Defendant K and frequently supervises the deliveries to Defendant K's customers. Each defendant is convicted of a count charging conspiracy to distribute child pornography. Defendant K is accountable under subsection (a)(1)(A) for the entire quantity of child pornography sold to Defendants L and M. Defendant N also is accountable for the entire quantity sold to those defendants under subsection (a)(1)(B) because the entire quantity was within the scope of his jointly undertaken criminal activity and reasonably foreseeable. Defendant L is accountable under subsection (a)(1)(A) only for the quantity of child pornography that he purchased from Defendant K because the scope of his jointly undertaken criminal activity is limited to that amount. For the same reason, Defendant M is accountable under subsection (a)(1)(A)

only for the quantity of child pornography that he purchased from Defendant K.

(5) Defendant O knows about her boyfriend's ongoing drug-trafficking activity, but agrees to participate on only one occasion by making a delivery for him at his request when he was ill. Defendant O is accountable under subsection (a)(1)(A) for the drug quantity involved on that one occasion. Defendant O is not accountable for the other drug sales made by her boyfriend because those sales were not in furtherance of her jointly undertaken criminal activity (i.e., the one delivery).

(6) Defendant P is a street-level drug dealer who knows of other street-level drug dealers in the same geographic area who sell the same type of drug as he sells. Defendant P and the other dealers share a common source of supply, but otherwise operate independently. Defendant P is not accountable for the quantities of drugs sold by the other street-level drug dealers because he is not engaged in a jointly undertaken criminal activity with them. In contrast, Defendant Q, another street-level drug dealer, pools his resources and profits with four other street-level drug dealers. Defendant Q is engaged in a jointly undertaken criminal activity and, therefore, he is accountable under subsection (a)(1)(B) for the quantities of drugs sold by the four other dealers during the course of his joint undertaking with them because those sales were in furtherance of the jointly undertaken criminal activity and reasonably foreseeable in connection with that criminal activity.

(7) Defendant R recruits Defendant S to distribute 500 grams of cocaine. Defendant S knows that Defendant R is the prime figure in a conspiracy involved in importing much larger quantities of cocaine. As long as Defendant S's agreement and conduct is limited to the distribution of the 500 grams, Defendant S is accountable only for that 500 gram amount (under subsection (a)(1)(A)), rather than the much larger quantity imported by Defendant R.

(8) Defendants T, U, V, and W are hired by a supplier to backpack a quantity of marihuana across the border from Mexico into the United States. Defendants T, U, V, and W receive their individual shipments from the supplier at the same time and coordinate their importation efforts by walking across the border together for mutual assistance and protection. Each defendant is accountable for the aggregate quantity of marihuana transported by the four defendants. The four defendants engaged in a jointly undertaken criminal activity, the object of which was the importation of the four backpacks containing marihuana (subsection (a)(1)(B)), and aided and abetted each other's actions (subsection (a)(1)(A)) in carrying out the jointly undertaken criminal activity. In contrast, if Defendants T, U, V, and W were hired individually, transported their individual shipments at different times, and otherwise operated independently, each defendant would be accountable only for the quantity of marihuana he personally transported (subsection (a)(1)(A)). As this example illustrates, in cases involving contraband (including controlled substances), the scope of the jointly undertaken criminal activity (and thus the accountability of the defendant for the contraband that was the object of that jointly undertaken activity) may depend upon whether, in the particular

circumstances, the nature of the offense is more appropriately viewed as one jointly undertaken criminal activity or as a number of separate criminal activities.

3.) "Offenses of a character for which § 3D1.2(d) would require grouping of multiple counts," as used in subsection (a)(2), applies to offenses for which grouping of counts would be required under § 3D1.2(d) had the defendant been convicted of multiple counts. Application of this provision does not require the defendant, in fact, to have been convicted of multiple counts. For example, where the defendant engaged in three drug sales of 10, 15, and 20 grams of cocaine, as part of the same course of conduct or common scheme or plan, subsection (a)(2) provides that the total quantity of cocaine involved (45 grams) is to be used to determine the offense level even if the defendant is convicted of a single count charging only one of the sales. If the defendant is convicted of multiple counts for the above noted sales, the grouping rules of Chapter Three, Part D (Multiple Counts) provide that the counts are grouped together. Although Chapter Three, Part D (Multiple Counts) applies to multiple counts of conviction, it does not limit the scope of subsection (a)(2). Subsection (a)(2) merely incorporates by reference the types of offenses set forth in § 3D1.2(d); thus, as discussed above, multiple counts of conviction are not required for subsection (a)(2) to apply.

As noted above, subsection (a)(2) applies to offenses of a character for which § 3D1.2(d) would require grouping of multiple counts, had the defendant been convicted of multiple counts. For example, the defendant sells 30 grams of cocaine (a violation of 21 U.S.C. § 841) on one occasion and, as part of the same course of conduct or common scheme or plan, attempts to sell an additional 15 grams of cocaine (a violation of 21 U.S.C. § 846) on another occasion. The defendant is convicted of one count charging the completed sale of 30 grams of cocaine. The two offenses (sale of cocaine and attempted sale of cocaine), although covered by different statutory provisions, are of a character for which § 3D1.2(d) would require the grouping of counts, had the defendant been convicted of both counts. Therefore, subsection (a)(2) applies and the total amount of cocaine (45 grams) involved is used to determine the offense level.

4.) "Harm" includes bodily injury, monetary loss, property damage and any resulting harm.

5.) If the offense guideline includes creating a risk or danger of harm as a specific offense characteristic, whether that risk or danger was created is to be considered in determining the offense level. See, e.g., § 2K1.4 (Arson; Property Damage by Use of Explosives); § 2Q1.2 (Mishandling of Hazardous or Toxic Substances or Pesticides). If, however, the guideline refers only to harm sustained (e.g., § 2A2.2 (Aggravated Assault); § 2B3.1(Robbery)) or to actual, attempted or intended harm (e.g., § 2B1.1 (Theft, Property Destruction, and Fraud); § 2X1.1 (Attempt, Solicitation, or Conspiracy)), the risk created enters into the determination of the offense level only insofar as it is incorporated into the base offense level. Unless clearly indicated by the guidelines, harm that is merely risked is not to be treated as the equivalent of harm that occurred. In a case in which creation of risk is not adequately taken into account by the applicable offense guideline, an upward departure may be warranted.See generally § 1B1.4 (Information to be Used in Imposing Sentence); § 5K2.0 (Grounds for Departure). The extent to which harm that was attempted or intended enters into the determination of the offense level should be determined in accordance with § 2X1.1 (Attempt, Solicitation, or Conspiracy) and the applicable offense guideline.

6.) A particular guideline (in the base offense level or in a specific offense characteristic) may expressly direct that a particular factor be applied only if the defendant was convicted of a particular statute. For example, in § 2S1.1 (Laundering of Monetary Instruments; Engaging in Monetary Transactions in Property Derived from Unlawful Activity), subsection (b)(2)(B) applies if the defendant "was convicted under 18 U.S.C. § 1956". Unless such an express direction is included, conviction under the statute is not required. Thus, use of a statutory reference to describe a particular set of circumstances does not require a conviction under the referenced statute. An example of this usage is found in § 2A3.4(a)(2) ("if the offense involved conduct described in 18 U.S.C. § 2242").

Unless otherwise specified, an express direction to apply a particular factor only if the defendant was convicted of a particular statute includes the determination of the offense level where the defendant was convicted of conspiracy, attempt, solicitation, aiding or abetting, accessory after the fact, or misprision of felony in respect to that particular statute. For example, § 2S1.1(b)(2)(B) (which is applicable only if the defendant is convicted under 18 U.S.C. § 1956) would be applied in determining the offense level under § 2X3.1 (Accessory After the Fact) in a case in which the defendant was convicted of accessory after the fact to a violation of 18 U.S.C. § 1956 but would not be applied in a case in which the defendant is convicted of a conspiracy under 18 U.S.C. § 1956(h) and the sole object of that conspiracy was to commit an offense set forth in 18 U.S.C. § 1957. See Application Note 3(C) of § 2S1.1.

7.) In the case of a partially completed offense (e.g., an offense involving an attempted theft of $800,000 and a completed theft of $30,000), the offense level is to be determined in accordance with § 2X1.1 (Attempt, Solicitation, or Conspiracy) whether the conviction is for the substantive offense, the inchoate offense (attempt, solicitation, or conspiracy), or both. See Application Note 4 in the Commentary to § 2X1.1. Note, however, that Application Note 4 is not applicable where the offense level is determined under § 2X1.1(c)(1).

8.) For the purposes of subsection (a)(2), offense conduct associated with a sentence that was imposed prior to the acts or omissions constituting the instant federal offense (the offense of conviction) is not considered as part of the same course of conduct or common scheme or plan as the offense of conviction.

Examples: (1) The defendant was convicted for the sale of cocaine and sentenced to state prison. Immediately upon release from prison, he again sold cocaine to the same person, using the same accomplices and modus operandi. The instant federal offense (the offense of conviction) charges this latter sale. In this example, the offense conduct relevant to the state prison sentence is considered as prior criminal history, not as part of the same course of conduct or common scheme or plan as the offense of conviction. The prior state prison sentence is counted under Chapter Four (Criminal History and Criminal Livelihood). (2) The defendant engaged in two cocaine sales constituting part of the same course of conduct or common scheme or plan. Subsequently, he is arrested by state authorities for the first sale and by federal authorities for the second sale. He is convicted in state court for the first sale and sentenced to imprisonment; he is then convicted in federal court for the second sale. In this case, the cocaine sales are not separated by an intervening sentence. Therefore, under subsection (a)(2), the cocaine sale associated with the state conviction is considered as relevant conduct to the instant federal offense. The state prison sentence for that sale is not counted as a prior sentence; see § 4A1.2(a)(1).

Note, however, in certain cases, offense conduct associated with a previously imposed sentence may be expressly charged in the offense of conviction. Unless otherwise provided, such conduct will be considered relevant conduct under subsection (a)(1), not (a)(2).

9.) "Common scheme or plan" and "same course of conduct" are two closely related concepts.

(A) Common scheme or plan. For two or more offenses to constitute part of a common scheme or plan, they must be substantially connected to each other by at least one common factor, such as common victims, common accomplices, common purpose, or similar modus operandi. For example, the conduct of five defendants who together defrauded a group of investors by computer manipulations that unlawfully transferred funds over an eighteen-month period would qualify as a common scheme or plan on the basis of any of the above listed factors; i.e., the commonality of victims (the same investors were defrauded on an ongoing basis), commonality of offenders (the conduct constituted an ongoing conspiracy), commonality of purpose (to defraud the group of investors), or similarity of modus operandi (the same or similar computer manipulations were used to execute the scheme).

(B) Same course of conduct. Offenses that do not qualify as part of a common scheme or plan may nonetheless qualify as part of the same course of conduct if they are sufficiently connected or related to each other as to warrant the conclusion that they are part of a single episode, spree, or ongoing series of offenses. Factors that are appropriate to the determination of whether offenses are sufficiently connected or related to each other to be considered as part of the same course of conduct include the degree of similarity of the offenses, the regularity (repetitions) of the offenses, and the time interval between the offenses. When one of the above factors is absent, a stronger presence of at least one of the other factors is required. For example, where the conduct alleged to be relevant is relatively remote to the offense of conviction, a stronger showing of similarity or regularity is necessary to compensate for the absence of temporal proximity. The nature of the offenses may also be a relevant consideration (e.g., a defendant's failure to file tax returns in three consecutive years appropriately would be considered as part of the same course of conduct because such returns are only required at yearly intervals).

10.) In the case of solicitation, misprision, or accessory after the fact, the conduct for which the defendant is accountable includes all conduct relevant to determining the offense level for the underlying offense that was known, or reasonably should have been known, by the defendant.

Background: This section prescribes rules for determining the applicable guideline sentencing range, whereas § 1B1.4 (Information to be Used in Imposing Sentence) governs the range of information that the court may consider in adjudging sentence once the guideline sentencing range has been determined. Conduct that is not formally charged or is not an element of the offense of conviction may enter into the determination of the applicable guideline sentencing range. The range of information that may be considered at sentencing is broader than the range of information upon which the applicable sentencing range is determined.

Subsection (a) establishes a rule of construction by specifying, in the absence of more explicit instructions in the context of a specific guideline, the range of conduct that is relevant to determining the applicable offense level (except for the determination of the applicable offense guideline, which is governed by § 1B1.2(a)). No such rule of construction is necessary with respect to Chapters Four and Five because the guidelines in those Chapters are explicit as to the specific factors to be considered.

Subsection (a)(2) provides for consideration of a broader range of conduct with respect to one class of offenses, primarily certain property, tax, fraud and drug offenses for which the guidelines depend substantially on quantity, than with respect to other offenses such as assault, robbery and burglary. The distinction is made on the basis of § 3D1.2(d), which provides for grouping together (i.e., treating as a single count) all counts charging offenses of a type covered by this subsection. However, the applicability of subsection (a)(2) does not depend upon whether multiple counts are alleged. Thus, in an embezzlement case, for example, embezzled funds that may not be specified in any count of conviction are nonetheless included in determining the offense level if they were part of the same course of conduct or part of the same scheme or plan as the count of conviction. Similarly, in a drug distribution case, quantities and types of drugs not specified in the count of conviction are to be included in determining the offense level if they were part of the same course of conduct or part of a common scheme or plan as the count of conviction. On the other hand, in a robbery case in which the defendant robbed two banks, the amount of money taken in one robbery would not be taken into account in determining the guideline range for the other robbery, even if both robberies were part of a single course of conduct or the same scheme or plan. (This is true whether the defendant is convicted of one or both robberies.)

Subsections (a)(1) and (a)(2) adopt different rules because offenses of the character dealt with in subsection (a)(2) (i.e., to which § 3D1.2(d) applies) often involve a pattern of misconduct that cannot readily be broken into discrete, identifiable units that are meaningful for purposes of sentencing. For example, a pattern of embezzlement may consist of several acts of taking that cannot separately be identified, even though the overall conduct is clear. In addition, the distinctions that the law makes as to what constitutes separate counts or offenses often turn on technical elements that are not especially meaningful for purposes of sentencing. Thus, in a mail fraud case, the scheme is an element of the offense and each mailing may be the basis for a separate count; in an embezzlement case, each taking may provide a basis for a separate count. Another consideration is that in a pattern of small thefts, for example, it is important to take into account the full range of related conduct. Relying on the entire range of conduct, regardless of the number of counts that are alleged or on which a conviction is obtained, appears to be the most reasonable approach to writing workable guidelines for these offenses. Conversely, when § 3D1.2(d) does not apply, so that convictions on multiple counts are considered separately in determining the guideline sentencing range, the guidelines prohibit aggregation of quantities from other counts in order to prevent "double counting" of the conduct and harm from each count of conviction. Continuing offenses present similar practical problems. The reference to § 3D1.2(d), which provides for grouping of multiple counts arising out of a continuing offense when the offense guideline takes the continuing nature into account, also prevents double counting.

Subsection (a)(4) requires consideration of any other information specified in the applicable guideline. For example, § 2A1.4 (Involuntary Manslaughter) specifies consideration of the defendant's state of mind; § 2K1.4 (Arson; Property Damage By Use of Explosives) specifies consideration of the risk of harm created.

§ 1B1.6. Structure of the Guidelines

The guidelines are presented in numbered chapters divided into alphabetical parts. The parts are divided into subparts and individual guidelines. Each guideline is identified by three numbers and a letter corresponding to the chapter, part, subpart and individual guideline.

The first number is the chapter, the letter represents the part of the chapter, the second number is the subpart, and the final number is the guideline. Section 2B1.1, for example, is the first guideline in the first subpart in Part B of Chapter Two. Or, § 3A1.2 is the second guideline in the first subpart in Part A of Chapter Three. Policy statements are similarly identified.

To illustrate:

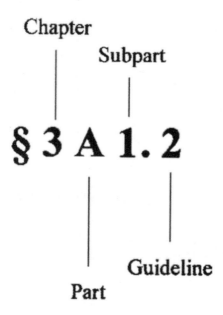

Chapter

Subpart

§ 3 A 1. 2

Guideline

Part

§ 1B1.7. Significance of Commentary

The Commentary that accompanies the guideline sections may serve a number of purposes. First, it may interpret the guideline or explain how it is to be applied. Failure to follow such commentary could constitute an incorrect application of the guidelines, subjecting the sentence to possible reversal on appeal. See 18 U.S.C. § 3742. Second, the commentary may suggest circumstances which, in the view of the Commission, may warrant departure from the guidelines. Such commentary is to be treated as the legal equivalent of a policy statement. Finally, the commentary may provide background information, including factors considered in promulgating the guideline or reasons underlying promulgation of the guideline. As with a policy statement, such commentary may provide guidance in assessing the reasonableness of any departure from the guidelines.

COMMENTARY

Portions of this document not labeled as guidelines or commentary also express the policy of the Commission or provide guidance as to the interpretation and application of the guidelines. These are to be construed as commentary and thus have the force of policy statements.

"[C]ommentary in the Guidelines Manual that interprets or explains a guideline is authoritative unless it violates the Constitution or a federal statute, or is inconsistent with, or a plainly erroneous reading of, that guideline." Stinson v. United States, 508 U.S. 36, 38 (1993).

CHAPTER TWO — OFFENSE CONDUCT

PART B — BASIC ECONOMIC OFFENSES

§ 2B1.1. **Larceny, Embezzlement, and Other Forms of Theft; Offenses Involving Stolen Property; Property Damage or Destruction; Fraud and Deceit; Forgery; Offenses Involving Altered or Counterfeit Instruments Other than Counterfeit Bearer Obligations of the United States**

(a) Base Offense Level:

(1) 7, if

(A) the defendant was convicted of an offense referenced to this guideline; and

(B) that offense of conviction has a statutory maximum term of imprisonment of 20 years or more; or

(2) 6, otherwise.

(b) Specific Offense Characteristics

(1) If the loss exceeded $5,000, increase the offense level as follows:

	Loss (Apply the Greatest)	Increase in Level
(A)	$5,000 or less	no increase
(B)	More than $5,000	add 2
(C)	More than $10,000	add 4
(D)	More than $30,000	add 6
(E)	More than $70,000	add 8
(F)	More than $120,000	add 10
(G)	More than $200,000	add 12
(H)	More than $400,000	add 14
(I)	More than $1,000,000	add 16
(J)	More than $2,500,000	add 18
(K)	More than $7,000,000	add 20
(L)	More than $20,000,000	add 22
(M)	More than $50,000,000	add 24
(N)	More than $100,000,000	add 26
(O)	More than $200,000,000	add 28
(P)	More than $400,000,000	add 30.

(2) (Apply the greatest) If the offense—

    (A)

        (i) involved 10 or more victims; or

        (ii) was committed through mass-marketing, increase by 2 levels;

    (B) involved 50 or more victims, increase by 4 levels; or

    (C) involved 250 or more victims, increase by 6 levels.

(3) If the offense involved a theft from the person of another, increase by 2 levels.

(4) If the offense involved receiving stolen property, and the defendant was a person in the business of receiving and selling stolen property, increase by 2 levels.

(5) If the offense involved theft of, damage to, destruction of, or trafficking in,

property from a national cemetery or veterans' memorial, increase by 2 levels.

(6) If

(A) the defendant was convicted of an offense under 18 U.S.C. § 1037; and

(B) the offense involved obtaining electronic mail addresses through improper means, increase by 2 levels.

(7) If

(A) the defendant was convicted of a Federal health care offense involving a Government health care program; and

(B) the loss under subsection (b)(1) to the Government health care program was

(i) more than $1,000,000, increase by 2 levels;

(ii) more than $7,000,000, increase by 3 levels; or

(iii) more than $20,000,000, increase by 4 levels.

(8) (Apply the greater) If—

(A) the offense involved conduct described in 18 U.S.C. § 670, increase by 2 levels; or

(B) the offense involved conduct described in 18 U.S.C. § 670, and the defendant was employed by, or was an agent of, an organization in the supply chain for the pre-retail medical product, increase by 4 levels.

(9) If the offense involved

(A) a misrepresentation that the defendant was acting on behalf of a charitable, educational, religious, or political organization, or a government agency;

(B) a misrepresentation or other fraudulent action during the course of a bankruptcy proceeding;

(C) a violation of any prior, specific judicial or administrative order, injunction, decree, or process not addressed elsewhere in the guidelines; or

(D) a misrepresentation to a consumer in connection with obtaining, providing, or furnishing financial assistance for an institution of higher education, increase by 2 levels. If the resulting offense level is less than level 10, increase to level 10.

(10) If

(A) the defendant relocated, or participated in relocating, a fraudulent scheme to another jurisdiction to evade law enforcement or regulatory officials;

(B) a substantial part of a fraudulent scheme was committed from outside the United States; or

(C) the offense otherwise involved sophisticated means, increase by 2 levels.

If the resulting offense level is less than level 12, increase to level 12.

(11) If

  (A) the possession or use of any

    (i) device-making equipment, or

    (ii) authentication feature;

  (B) the production or trafficking of any

    (i) unauthorized access device or counterfeit access device, or

    (ii) authentication feature; or

  (C)

    (i) the unauthorized transfer or use of any means of identification unlawfully to produce or obtain any other means of identification, or

    (ii) the possession of 5 or more means of identification that unlawfully were produced from, or obtained by the use of, another means of identification, increase by 2 levels. If the resulting offense level is less than level 12, increase to level 12.

(12) If the offense involved conduct described in 18 U.S.C. § 1040, increase by 2 levels. If the resulting offense level is less than level 12, increase to level 12.

(13) (Apply the greater) If the offense involved misappropriation of a trade secret and the defendant knew or intended—

  (A) that the trade secret would be transported or transmitted out of the United States, increase by 2 levels; or

  (B) that the offense would benefit a foreign government, foreign instrumentality, or foreign agent, increase by 4 levels.

If subparagraph (B) applies and the resulting offense level is less than level 14, increase to level 14.

(14) If the offense involved an organized scheme to steal or to receive stolen

  (A) vehicles or vehicle parts; or

  (B) goods or chattels that are part of a cargo shipment, increase by 2 levels. If the resulting offense level is less than level 14, increase to level 14.

(15) If the offense involved (A) the conscious or reckless risk of death or serious bodily injury; or (B) possession of a dangerous weapon (including a firearm) in connection with the offense, increase by 2 levels. If the resulting offense level is less than level 14, increase to level 14.

(16) (Apply the greater) If—

  (A) the defendant derived more than $1,000,000 in gross receipts from one or more financial institutions as a result of the offense, increase by 2 levels; or

  (B) the offense

(i) substantially jeopardized the safety and soundness of a financial institution;

(ii) substantially endangered the solvency or financial security of an organization that, at any time during the offense,

(I) was a publicly traded company; or

(II) had 1,000 or more employees; or (iii) substantially endangered the solvency or financial security of 100 or more victims, increase by 4 levels.

(C) The cumulative adjustments from application of both subsections (b)(2) and (b)(16)(B) shall not exceed 8 levels, except as provided in subdivision (D).

(D) If the resulting offense level determined under subdivision (A) or (B) is less than level 24, increase to level 24.

(17) If

(A) the defendant was convicted of an offense under 18 U.S.C. § 1030, and the offense involved an intent to obtain personal information, or

(B) the offense involved the unauthorized public dissemination of personal information, increase by 2 levels.

(18)

(A) (Apply the greatest) If the defendant was convicted of an offense under:

(i) 18 U.S.C. § 1030, and the offense involved a computer system used to maintain or operate a critical infrastructure, or used by or for a government entity in furtherance of the administration of justice, national defense, or national security, increase by 2 levels.

(ii) 18 U.S.C. § 1030(a)(5)(A), increase by 4 levels.

(iii) 18 U.S.C. § 1030, and the offense caused a substantial disruption of a critical infrastructure, increase by 6 levels.

(B) If subdivision (A)(iii) applies, and the offense level is less than level 24, increase to level 24.

(19) If the offense involved—

(A) a violation of securities law and, at the time of the offense, the defendant was

(i) an officer or a director of a publicly traded company;

(ii) a registered broker or dealer, or a person associated with a broker or dealer; or

(iii) an investment adviser, or a person associated with an investment adviser; or

(B) a violation of securities law and, at the time of the offense, the defendant was

(i) an officer or a director of a futures commission merchant or an introducing broker;

(ii) a commodities trading advisor; or

(iii) a commodity pool operator,

increase by 4 levels.

(c) Cross References

(1) If

(A) a firearm, destructive device, explosive material, or controlled substance was taken, or the taking of any such item was an object of the offense; or

(B) the stolen property received, transported, transferred, transmitted, or possessed was a firearm, destructive device, explosive material, or controlled substance, apply § 2D1.1 (Unlawful Manufacturing, Importing, Exporting, or Trafficking (Including Possession with Intent to Commit These Offenses); Attempt or Conspiracy), § 2D2.1 (Unlawful Possession; Attempt or Conspiracy), § 2K1.3 (Unlawful Receipt, Possession, or Transportation of Explosive Materials; Prohibited Transactions Involving Explosive Materials), or § 2K2.1 (Unlawful Receipt, Possession, or Transportation of Firearms or Ammunition; Prohibited Transactions Involving Firearms or Ammunition), as appropriate.

(2) If the offense involved arson, or property damage by use of explosives, apply § 2K1.4 (Arson; Property Damage by Use of Explosives), if the resulting offense level is greater than that determined above.

(3) If

(A) neither subdivision (1) nor (2) of this subsection applies;

(B) the defendant was convicted under a statute proscribing false, fictitious, or fraudulent statements or representations generally (e.g., 18 U.S.C. § 1001, § 1341, § 1342, or § 1343); and

(C) the conduct set forth in the count of conviction establishes an offense specifically covered by another guideline in Chapter Two (Offense Conduct), apply that other guideline.

(4) If the offense involved a cultural heritage resource or a paleontological resource, apply § 2B1.5 (Theft of, Damage to, or Destruction of, Cultural Heritage Resources or Paleontological Resources; Unlawful Sale, Purchase, Exchange, Transportation, or Receipt of Cultural Heritage Resources or Paleontological Resources), if the resulting offense level is greater than that determined above.

COMMENTARY

Statutory Provisions: 7 U.S.C. §§ 6, 6b, 6c, 6h, 6o, 13, 23; 15 U.S.C. §§ 50, 77e, 77q, 77x, 78j, 78ff, 80b-6, 1644, 6821; 18 U.S.C. §§ 38, 225, 285–289, 471–473, 500, 510, 553(a)(1), 641, 656, 657, 659, 662, 664, 1001–1008, 1010–1014, 1016–1022, 1025, 1026, 1028, 1029, 1030(a)(4)–(5), 1031, 1037, 1040, 1341–1344, 1348, 1350, 1361, 1363, 1369, 1702, 1703 (if vandalism or malicious mischief, including destruction of mail, is involved), 1708, 1831, 1832, 1992(a)(1), (a)(5), 2113(b), 2282A, 2282B, 2291, 2312–2317, 2332b(a)(1), 2701; 19 U.S.C. § 2401f; 29 U.S.C. § 501(c); 42 U.S.C. § 1011; 49 U.S.C. §§ 14915, 30170, 46317(a), 60123(b). For additional statutory provision(s), see Appendix A (Statutory Index).

Application Notes:

1. Definitions.— For purposes of this guideline:

"Cultural heritage resource" has the meaning given that term in Application Note 1 of the Commentary to § 2B1.5 (Theft of, Damage to, or Destruction of, Cultural Heritage Resources or Paleontological Resources; Unlawful Sale, Purchase, Exchange, Transportation, or Receipt of Cultural Heritage Resources or Paleontological Resources).

"Equity securities" has the meaning given that term in section 3(a)(11) of the Securities Exchange Act of 1934 (15 U.S.C. § 78c(a)(11)).

"Federal health care offense" has the meaning given that term in 18 U.S.C. § 24.

"Financial institution" includes any institution described in 18 U.S.C. § 20, § 656, § 657, § 1005, § 1006, § 1007, or § 1014; any state or foreign bank, trust company, credit union, insurance company, investment company, mutual fund, savings (building and loan) association, union or employee pension fund; any health, medical, or hospital insurance association; brokers and dealers registered, or required to be registered, with the Securities and Exchange Commission; futures commodity merchants and commodity pool operators registered, or required to be registered, with the Commodity Futures Trading Commission; and any similar entity, whether or not insured by the federal government. "Union or employee pension fund" and "any health, medical, or hospital insurance association," primarily include large pension funds that serve many persons (e.g., pension funds of large national and international organizations, unions, and corporations doing substantial interstate business), and associations that undertake to provide pension, disability, or other benefits (e.g., medical or hospitalization insurance) to large numbers of persons.

"Firearm" and "destructive device" have the meaning given those terms in the Commentary to § 1B1.1 (Application Instructions).

"Foreign instrumentality" and "foreign agent" have the meaning given those terms in 18 U.S.C. § 1839(1) and (2), respectively.

"Government health care program" means any plan or program that provides health benefits, whether directly, through insurance, or otherwise, which is funded directly, in whole or in part, by federal or state government. Examples of such programs are the Medicare program, the Medicaid program, and the CHIP program.

"Means of identification" has the meaning given that term in 18 U.S.C. § 1028(d)(7), except that such means of identification shall be of an actual (i.e., not fictitious) individual, other than the defendant or a person for whose conduct the defendant is accountable under § 1B1.3 (Relevant Conduct).

"National cemetery" means a cemetery

(A) established under section 2400 of title 38, United States Code; or

(B) under the jurisdiction of the Secretary of the Army, the Secretary of the Navy, the Secretary of the Air Force, or the Secretary of the Interior.

"Paleontological resource" has the meaning given that term in Application Note 1 of the Commentary to § 2B1.5 (Theft of, Damage to, or Destruction of, Cultural Heritage Resources or Paleontological Resources; Unlawful Sale, Purchase, Exchange, Transportation, or Receipt of Cultural Heritage Resources or Paleontological Resources).

"Personal information" means sensitive or private information involving an identifiable individual (including such information in the possession of a third party), including

(A) medical records;

(B) wills;

(C) diaries;

(D) private correspondence, including e-mail;

(E) financial records;

(F) photographs of a sensitive or private nature; or

(G) similar information.

"Pre-retail medical product" has the meaning given that term in 18 U.S.C. § 670(e).

"Publicly traded company" means an issuer (A) with a class of securities registered under section 12 of the Securities Exchange Act of 1934 (15 U.S.C. § 78l); or (B) that is required to file reports under section 15(d) of the Securities Exchange Act of 1934 (15 U.S.C. § 78o(d)). "Issuer" has the meaning given that term in section 3 of the Securities Exchange Act of 1934 (15 U.S.C. § 78c).

"Supply chain" has the meaning given that term in 18 U.S.C. § 670(e).

"Theft from the person of another" means theft, without the use of force, of property that was being held by another person or was within arms' reach. Examples include pick-pocketing and non-forcible purse-snatching, such as the theft of a purse from a shopping cart.

"Trade secret" has the meaning given that term in 18 U.S.C. § 1839(3).

"Veterans' memorial" means any structure, plaque, statue, or other monument described in 18 U.S.C. § 1369(a).

"Victim" means

(A) any person who sustained any part of the actual loss determined under subsection (b)(1); or

(B) any individual who sustained bodily injury as a result of the offense. "Person" includes individuals, corporations, companies, associations, firms, partnerships, societies, and joint stock companies.

2. Application of Subsection (a)(1).—

(A) "Referenced to this Guideline".— For purposes of subsection (a)(1), an offense is "referenced to this guideline" if

(i) this guideline is the applicable Chapter Two guideline determined under the provisions of § 1B1.2 (Applicable Guidelines) for the offense of conviction; or

(ii) in the case of a conviction for conspiracy, solicitation, or attempt to which § 2X1.1 (Attempt, Solicitation, or Conspiracy) applies, this guideline is the appropriate guideline for the offense the defendant was convicted of conspiring, soliciting, or attempting to commit.

(B) Definition of "Statutory Maximum Term of Imprisonment".— For purposes of this guideline, "statutory maximum term of imprisonment" means the maximum term of imprisonment authorized for the offense of conviction, including any increase in that maximum term under a statutory enhancement provision.

(C) Base Offense Level Determination for Cases Involving Multiple Counts.— In a case involving multiple counts sentenced under this guideline, the applicable base offense level is determined by the count of conviction that provides the highest statutory maximum term of imprisonment.

3. Loss Under Subsection (b)(1).— This application note applies to the determination of loss under subsection (b)(1).

(A) General Rule.— Subject to the exclusions in subdivision (D), loss is the greater of actual loss or intended loss.

(i) Actual Loss.— "Actual loss" means the reasonably foreseeable pecuniary harm that resulted from the offense.

(ii) Intended Loss.— "Intended loss"

(I) means the pecuniary harm that was intended to result from the offense; and

(II) includes intended pecuniary harm that would have been impossible or unlikely to occur (e.g., as in a government sting operation, or an insurance fraud in which the claim exceeded the insured value).

(iii) Pecuniary Harm.— "Pecuniary harm" means harm that is monetary or that otherwise is readily measurable in money. Accordingly, pecuniary harm does not include emotional distress, harm to reputation, or other non-economic harm.

(iv) Reasonably Foreseeable Pecuniary Harm.— For purposes of this guideline, "reasonably foreseeable pecuniary harm" means pecuniary harm that the defendant knew or, under the circumstances, reasonably should have known, was a potential result of the offense.

(v) Rules of Construction in Certain Cases.— In the cases described in subdivisions (I) through (III), reasonably foreseeable pecuniary harm shall be considered to include the pecuniary harm specified for those cases as follows:

(I) Product Substitution Cases.— In the case of a product substitution offense, the reasonably foreseeable pecuniary harm includes the reasonably foreseeable costs of making substitute transactions and handling or disposing of the product delivered, or of retrofitting the product so that it can be used for its intended purpose, and the reasonably foreseeable costs of rectifying the actual or potential disruption to the victim's business operations caused by the product substitution.

(II) Procurement Fraud Cases.— In the case of a procurement fraud, such as a fraud affecting a defense contract award, reasonably foreseeable pecuniary harm includes the reasonably foreseeable administrative costs to the government and other participants of repeating or correcting the procurement action affected, plus any increased costs to procure the product or service involved that was reasonably foreseeable.

(III) Offenses Under 18 U.S.C. § 1030.— In the case of an offense under 18 U.S.C. § 1030, actual loss includes the following pecuniary harm, regardless of whether such pecuniary harm was reasonably foreseeable: any reasonable cost to any victim, including the cost of responding to an offense, conducting a damage assessment, and restoring the data, program, system, or information to its condition prior to the offense, and any revenue lost, cost incurred, or other damages incurred because of interruption of service.

(B) Gain.— The court shall use the gain that resulted from the offense as an alternative measure of loss only if there is a loss but it reasonably cannot be determined.

(C) Estimation of Loss.— The court need only make a reasonable estimate of the loss. The sentencing judge is in a unique position to assess the evidence and estimate the loss based upon that evidence. For this reason, the court's loss determination is entitled to appropriate deference. See 18 U.S.C. § 3742(e) and (f).

The estimate of the loss shall be based on available information, taking into account, as appropriate and practicable under the circumstances, factors such as the following:

(i) The fair market value of the property unlawfully taken, copied, or destroyed; or, if the fair market value is impracticable to determine or inadequately measures the harm, the cost to the victim of replacing that property.

(ii) In the case of proprietary information (e.g., trade secrets), the cost of developing that information or the reduction in the value of that information that resulted from the offense.

(iii) The cost of repairs to damaged property.

(iv) The approximate number of victims multiplied by the average loss to each victim.

(v) The reduction that resulted from the offense in the value of equity securities or other corporate assets.

(vi) More general factors, such as the scope and duration of the offense and revenues generated by similar operations.

(D) Exclusions from Loss.— Loss shall not include the following:

(i) Interest of any kind, finance charges, late fees, penalties, amounts based on an agreed-upon return or rate of return, or other similar costs.

(ii) Costs to the government of, and costs incurred by victims primarily to aid the government in, the prosecution and criminal investigation of an offense.

(E) Credits Against Loss.— Loss shall be reduced by the following:

(i) The money returned, and the fair market value of the property returned and the services rendered, by the defendant or other persons acting jointly with the defendant, to the victim before the offense was detected. The time of detection of the offense is the earlier of

(I) the time the offense was discovered by a victim or government agency; or

(II) the time the defendant knew or reasonably should have known that the offense was detected or about to be detected by a victim or government agency.

(ii) In a case involving collateral pledged or otherwise provided by the defendant, the amount the victim has recovered at the time of sentencing from disposition of the collateral, or if the collateral has not been disposed of by that time, the fair market value of the collateral at the time of sentencing.

(iii) Notwithstanding clause (ii), in the case of a fraud involving a mortgage loan, if the collateral has not been disposed of by the time of sentencing, use the fair market value of the collateral as of the date on which the guilt of the defendant has been established, whether by guilty plea, trial, or plea of nolo contendere.

In such a case, there shall be a rebuttable presumption that the most recent tax assessment value of the collateral is a reasonable estimate of the fair market value. In determining whether the most recent tax assessment value is a reasonable estimate of the fair market value, the court may consider, among other factors, the recency of the tax assessment and the extent to which the jurisdiction's tax assessment practices reflect factors not relevant to fair market value.

(F) Special Rules.— Notwithstanding subdivision (A), the following special rules shall be used to assist in determining loss in the cases indicated:

(i) Stolen or Counterfeit Credit Cards and Access Devices; Purloined Numbers and Codes.— In a case involving any counterfeit access device or unauthorized access device, loss includes any unauthorized charges made with the counterfeit access device or unauthorized access device and shall be not less than $500 per access device. However, if the unauthorized access device is a means of telecommunications access that identifies a specific telecommunications instrument or telecommunications account (including an electronic serial number/mobile identification number (ESN/MIN) pair), and that means was only possessed, and not used, during the commission of the offense, loss shall be not less than $100 per unused means. For purposes of this subdivision, "counterfeit access device" and "unauthorized access device" have the meaning given those terms in Application Note 10(A).

(ii) Government Benefits.— In a case involving government benefits (e.g., grants, loans, entitlement program payments), loss shall be considered to be not less than the value of the benefits obtained by unintended recipients or diverted to unintended uses, as the case may be. For example, if the defendant was the intended recipient of food stamps having a value of $100 but fraudulently received food stamps having a value of $150, loss is $50.

(iii) Davis-Bacon Act Violations.— In a case involving a Davis-Bacon Act violation (i.e., a violation of 40 U.S.C. § 3142, criminally prosecuted under 18 U.S.C. § 1001), the value of the benefits shall be considered to be not less than the difference between the legally required wages and actual wages paid.

(iv) Ponzi and Other Fraudulent Investment Schemes.— In a case involving a fraudulent investment scheme, such as a Ponzi scheme, loss shall not be reduced by the money or the value of the property transferred to any individual investor in the scheme in excess of that investor's principal investment (i.e., the gain to an individual investor in the scheme shall not be used to offset the loss to another individual investor in the scheme).

(v) Certain Other Unlawful Misrepresentation Schemes.— In a case involving a scheme in which

(I) services were fraudulently rendered to the victim by persons falsely posing as licensed professionals;

(II) goods were falsely represented as approved by a governmental regulatory agency; or

(III) goods for which regulatory approval by a government agency was required but not obtained, or was obtained by fraud, loss shall include the amount paid for the property, services or goods transferred, rendered, or misrepresented, with no credit provided for the value of those items or services.

(vi) Value of Controlled Substances.— In a case involving controlled substances, loss is the estimated street value of the controlled substances.

(vii) Value of Cultural Heritage Resources or Paleontological Resources.— In a case involving a cultural heritage resource or paleontological resource, loss attributable to that resource shall be determined in accordance with the rules for determining the "value of the resource" set forth in Application Note 2 of the Commentary to § 2B1.5.

(viii) Federal Health Care Offenses Involving Government Health Care Programs.— In a case in which the defendant is convicted of a Federal health care offense involving a Government health care program, the aggregate dollar amount of fraudulent bills submitted to the Government health care program shall constitute prima facie evidence of the amount of the intended loss, i.e., is evidence sufficient to establish the amount of the intended loss, if not rebutted.

(ix) Fraudulent Inflation or Deflation in Value of Securities or Commodities.— In a case involving the fraudulent inflation or deflation in the value of a publicly traded security or commodity, there shall be a rebuttable presumption that the actual loss attributable to the change in value of the security or commodity is the amount determined by—

(I) calculating the difference between the average price of the security or commodity during the period that the fraud occurred and the average price of the security or commodity during the 90-day period after the fraud was disclosed to the market, and

(II) multiplying the difference in average price by the number of shares outstanding.

In determining whether the amount so determined is a reasonable estimate of the actual loss attributable to the change in value of the security or commodity, the court may consider, among other factors, the extent to which the amount so determined includes significant changes in value not resulting from the offense (e.g., changes caused by external market forces, such as changed economic circumstances, changed investor expectations, and new industry-specific or firm-specific facts, conditions, or events).

4. Application of Subsection (b)(2).—

(A) Definition.— For purposes of subsection (b)(2), "mass-marketing" means a plan, program, promotion, or campaign that is conducted through solicitation by telephone, mail, the Internet, or other means to induce a large number of persons to

(i) purchase goods or services;

(ii) participate in a contest or sweepstakes; or

(iii) invest for financial profit. "Mass-marketing" includes, for example, a telemarketing campaign that solicits a large number of individuals to purchase fraudulent life insurance policies.

(B) Applicability to Transmission of Multiple Commercial Electronic Mail Messages.— For purposes of subsection (b)(2), an offense under 18 U.S.C. § 1037, or any other offense involving conduct described in 18 U.S.C. § 1037, shall be considered to have been committed through mass-marketing. Accordingly, the defendant shall receive at least a two-level enhancement under subsection (b)(2) and may, depending on the facts of the case, receive a greater enhancement under such subsection, if the defendant was convicted under, or the offense involved conduct described in, 18 U.S.C. § 1037.

(C) Undelivered United States Mail.—

(i) In General.— In a case in which undelivered United States mail was taken, or the taking of such item was an object of the offense, or in a case in which the stolen property received, transported, transferred, transmitted, or possessed was undelivered United States mail, "victim" means

(I) any victim as defined in Application Note 1; or

(II) any person who was the intended recipient, or addressee, of the undelivered United States mail.

(ii) Special Rule.— A case described in subdivision (C)(i) of this note that involved—

(I) a United States Postal Service relay box, collection box, delivery vehicle, satchel, or cart, shall be considered to have involved at least 50 victims.

(II) a housing unit cluster box or any similar receptacle that contains multiple mailboxes, whether such receptacle is owned by the United States Postal Service or otherwise owned, shall, unless proven otherwise, be presumed to have involved the number of victims corresponding to the number of mailboxes in each cluster box or similar receptacle.

(iii) Definition.— "Undelivered United States mail" means mail that has not actually been received by the addressee or the addressee's agent (e.g., mail taken from the addressee's mail box).

(D) Vulnerable Victims.— If subsection (b)(2)(B) or (C) applies, an enhancement under § 3A1.1(b)(2) shall not apply.

(E) Cases Involving Means of Identification.— For purposes of subsection (b)(2), in a case involving means of identification "victim" means (i) any victim as defined in Application Note 1; or (ii) any individual whose means of identification was used unlawfully or without authority.

5. Enhancement for Business of Receiving and Selling Stolen Property under Subsection (b)(4).— For purposes of subsection (b)(4), the court shall consider the following non-exhaustive list of factors in determining whether the defendant was in the business of receiving and selling stolen property:

(A) The regularity and sophistication of the defendant's activities.

(B) The value and size of the inventory of stolen property maintained by the defendant.

(C) The extent to which the defendant's activities encouraged or facilitated other crimes.

(D) The defendant's past activities involving stolen property.

6. Application of Subsection (b)(6).— For purposes of subsection (b)(6), "improper means" includes the unauthorized harvesting of electronic mail

addresses of users of a website, proprietary service, or other online public forum.

7. Application of Subsection (b)(8)(B).— If subsection (b)(8)(B) applies, do not apply an adjustment under § 3B1.3 (Abuse of Position of Trust or Use of Special Skill).

8. Application of Subsection (b)(9).—

(A) In General.— The adjustments in subsection (b)(9) are alternative rather than cumulative. If, in a particular case, however, more than one of the enumerated factors applied, an upward departure may be warranted.

(B) Misrepresentations Regarding Charitable and Other Institutions.— Subsection (b)(9)(A) applies in any case in which the defendant represented that the defendant was acting to obtain a benefit on behalf of a charitable, educational, religious, or political organization, or a government agency (regardless of whether the defendant actually was associated with the organization or government agency) when, in fact, the defendant intended to divert all or part of that benefit (e.g., for the defendant's personal gain). Subsection (b)(9)(A) applies, for example, to the following:

(i) A defendant who solicited contributions for a non-existent famine relief organization.

(ii) A defendant who solicited donations from church members by falsely claiming to be a fundraiser for a religiously affiliated school.

(iii) A defendant, chief of a local fire department, who conducted a public fundraiser representing that the purpose of the fundraiser was to procure sufficient funds for a new fire engine when, in fact, the defendant intended to divert some of the funds for the defendant's personal benefit.

(C) Fraud in Contravention of Prior Judicial Order.— Subsection (b)(9)(C) provides an enhancement if the defendant commits a fraud in contravention of a prior, official judicial or administrative warning, in the form of an order, injunction, decree, or process, to take or not to take a specified action. A defendant who does not comply with such a prior, official judicial or administrative warning demonstrates aggravated criminal intent and deserves additional punishment. If it is established that an entity the defendant controlled was a party to the prior proceeding that resulted in the official judicial or administrative action, and the defendant had knowledge of that prior decree or order, this enhancement applies even if the defendant was not a specifically named party in that prior case. For example, a defendant whose business previously was enjoined from selling a dangerous product, but who nonetheless engaged in fraudulent conduct to sell the product, is subject to this enhancement. This enhancement does not apply if the same conduct resulted in an enhancement pursuant to a provision found elsewhere in the guidelines (e.g., a violation of a condition of release addressed in § 3C1.3 (Commission of Offense While on Release) or a violation of probation addressed in § 4A1.1 (Criminal History Category)).

(D) College Scholarship Fraud.— For purposes of subsection (b)(9)(D):

"Financial assistance" means any scholarship, grant, loan, tuition, discount, award, or other financial assistance for the purpose of financing an education.

"Institution of higher education" has the meaning given that term in section 101 of the Higher Education Act of 1954 (20 U.S.C. § 1001).

(E) Non-Applicability of Chapter Three Adjustments.—

(i) Subsection (b)(9)(A).— If the conduct that forms the basis for an enhancement under subsection (b)(9)(A) is the only conduct that forms the basis for an adjustment under § 3B1.3 (Abuse of Position of Trust or Use of Special Skill), do not apply that adjustment under § 3B1.3.

(ii) Subsection (b)(9)(B) and (C).— If the conduct that forms the basis for an enhancement under subsection (b)(9)(B) or (C) is the only conduct that forms the basis for an adjustment under § 3C1.1 (Obstructing or Impeding the Administration of Justice), do not apply that adjustment under § 3C1.1.

9. Sophisticated Means Enhancement under Subsection (b)(10).—

(A) Definition of United States.— For purposes of subsection (b)(10)(B), "United States" means each of the 50 states, the District of Columbia, the Commonwealth of Puerto Rico, the United States Virgin Islands, Guam, the Northern Mariana Islands, and American Samoa.

(B) Sophisticated Means Enhancement.— For purposes of subsection (b)(10)(C), "sophisticated means" means especially complex or especially intricate offense conduct pertaining to the execution or concealment of an offense. For example, in a telemarketing scheme, locating the main office of the scheme in one jurisdiction but locating soliciting operations in another jurisdiction ordinarily indicates sophisticated means.Conduct such as hiding assets or transactions, or both, through the use of fictitious entities, corporate shells, or offshore financial accounts also ordinarily indicates sophisticated means.

(C) Non-Applicability of Chapter Three Adjustment.— If the conduct that forms the basis for an enhancement under subsection (b)(10) is the only conduct that forms the basis for an adjustment under § 3C1.1, do not apply that adjustment under § 3C1.1.

10. Application of Subsection (b)(11).—

(A) Definitions.— For purposes of subsection (b)(11):

"Authentication feature" has the meaning given that term in 18 U.S.C. § 1028(d)(1).

"Counterfeit access device"

(i) has the meaning given that term in 18 U.S.C. § 1029(e)(2); and

(ii) includes a telecommunications instrument that has been modified or altered to obtain unauthorized use of telecommunications service.

"Device-making equipment"

(i) has the meaning given that term in 18 U.S.C. § 1029(e)(6); and

(ii) includes

(I) any hardware or software that has been configured as described in 18 U.S.C. § 1029(a)(9); and

(II) a scanning receiver referred to in 18 U.S.C. § 1029(a)(8). "Scanning receiver" has the meaning given that term in 18 U.S.C. § 1029(e)(8).

"Produce" includes manufacture, design, alter, authenticate, duplicate, or assemble. "Production" includes manufacture, design, alteration, authentication, duplication, or assembly.

"Telecommunications service" has the meaning given that term in 18 U.S.C. § 1029(e)(9).

"Unauthorized access device" has the meaning given that term in 18 U.S.C. § 1029(e)(3).

(B) Authentication Features and Identification Documents.— Offenses involving authentication features, identification documents, false identification documents, and means of identification, in violation of 18 U.S.C. § 1028, also are covered by this guideline. If the primary purpose of the offense, under 18 U.S.C. § 1028, was to violate, or assist another to violate, the law pertaining to naturalization, citizenship, or legal resident status, apply § 2L2.1 (Trafficking in a Document Relating to Naturalization) or § 2L2.2 (Fraudulently Acquiring Documents Relating to Naturalization), as appropriate, rather than this guideline.

(C) Application of Subsection (b)(11)(C)(i).—

(i) In General.— Subsection (b)(11)(C)(i) applies in a case in which a means of identification of an individual other than the defendant (or a person for whose conduct the defendant is accountable under § 1B1.3 (Relevant Conduct)) is used without that individual's authorization unlawfully to produce or obtain another means of identification.

(ii) Examples.— Examples of conduct to which subsection (b)(11)(C)(i) applies are as follows:

(I) A defendant obtains an individual's name and social security number from a source (e.g., from a piece of mail taken from the individual's mailbox) and obtains a bank loan in that individual's name. In this example, the account number of the bank loan is the other means of identification that has been obtained unlawfully.

(II) A defendant obtains an individual's name and address from a source (e.g., from a driver's license in a stolen wallet) and applies for, obtains, and subsequently uses a credit card in that individual's name. In this example, the credit card is the other means of identification that has been obtained unlawfully.

(iii) Non-Applicability of Subsection (b)(11)(C)(i).— Examples of conduct to which subsection (b)(11)(C)(i) does not apply are as follows:

(I) A defendant uses a credit card from a stolen wallet only to make a purchase. In such a case, the defendant has not used the stolen credit card to obtain another means of identification.

(II) A defendant forges another individual's signature to cash a stolen check. Forging another individual's signature is not producing another means of identification.

(D) Application of Subsection (b)(11)(C)(ii).— Subsection (b)(11)(C)(ii) applies in any case in which the offense involved the possession of 5 or more means of identification that unlawfully were produced or obtained, regardless of the number of individuals in whose name (or other identifying information) the means of identification were so produced or so obtained.

11. Application of Subsection (b)(14).— Subsection (b)(14) provides a minimum offense level in the case of an ongoing, sophisticated operation (e.g., an auto theft ring or "chop shop") to steal or to receive stolen

(A) vehicles or vehicle parts; or

(B) goods or chattels that are part of a cargo shipment. For purposes of this subsection, "vehicle" means motor vehicle, vessel, or aircraft. A "cargo shipment" includes cargo transported on a railroad car, bus, steamboat, vessel, or airplane.

12. Gross Receipts Enhancement under Subsection (b)(16)(A).—

(A) In General.— For purposes of subsection (b)(16)(A), the defendant shall be considered to have derived more than $1,000,000 in gross receipts if the gross receipts to the defendant individually, rather than to all participants, exceeded $1,000,000.

(B) Definition.— "Gross receipts from the offense" includes all property, real or personal, tangible or intangible, which is obtained directly or indirectly as a result of such offense. See 18 U.S.C. § 982(a)(4).

13. Application of Subsection (b)(16)(B).—

(A) Application of Subsection (b)(16)(B)(i).— The following is a non-exhaustive list of factors that the court shall consider in determining whether, as a result of the offense, the safety and soundness of a financial institution was substantially jeopardized:

(i) The financial institution became insolvent.

(ii) The financial institution substantially reduced benefits to pensioners or insureds.

(iii) The financial institution was unable on demand to refund fully any deposit, payment, or investment.

(iv) The financial institution was so depleted of its assets as to be forced to merge with another institution in order to continue active operations.

(v) One or more of the criteria in clauses (i) through (iv) was likely to result from the offense but did not result from the offense because of federal government intervention, such as a "bailout".

(B) Application of Subsection (b)(16)(B)(ii).—

(i) Definition.— For purposes of this subsection, "organization" has the meaning given that term in Application Note 1 of § 8A1.1 (Applicability of Chapter Eight).

(ii) In General.— The following is a non-exhaustive list of factors that the court shall consider in determining whether, as a result of the offense, the solvency or financial security of an organization that was a publicly traded company or that had more than 1,000 employees was substantially endangered:

(I) The organization became insolvent or suffered a substantial reduction in the value of its assets.

(II) The organization filed for bankruptcy under Chapters 7, 11, or 13 of the Bankruptcy Code (title 11, United States Code).

(III) The organization suffered a substantial reduction in the value of its equity securities or the value of its employee retirement accounts.

(IV) The organization substantially reduced its workforce.

(V) The organization substantially reduced its employee pension benefits.

(VI) The liquidity of the equity securities of a publicly traded company was substantially endangered. For example, the company was delisted from its primary listing exchange, or trading of the company's securities was halted for more than one full trading day.

(VII) One or more of the criteria in subclauses (I) through (VI) was likely to result from the offense but did not result from the offense because of federal government intervention, such as a "bailout".

14. Application of Subsection (b)(18).—

(A) Definitions.— For purposes of subsection (b)(18):

"Critical infrastructure" means systems and assets vital to national defense, national security, economic security, public health or safety, or any combination of those matters. A critical infrastructure may be publicly or privately owned. Examples of critical infrastructures include gas and oil production, storage, and delivery systems, water supply systems, telecommunications networks, electrical power delivery systems, financing and banking systems, emergency services (including medical, police, fire, and rescue services), transportation systems and services (including highways, mass transit, airlines, and airports), and government operations that provide essential services to the public.

"Government entity" has the meaning given that term in 18 U.S.C. § 1030(e)(9).

(B) Subsection (b)(18)(A)(iii).— If the same conduct that forms the basis for an enhancement under subsection (b)(18)(A)(iii) is the only conduct that forms the basis for an enhancement under subsection (b)(16)(B), do not apply the enhancement under subsection (b)(16)(B).

15. Application of Subsection (b)(19).—

    (A) Definitions.— For purposes of subsection (b)(19):

"Commodities law" means

    (i) the Commodity Exchange Act (7 U.S.C. § 1 etseq.) and 18 U.S.C. § 1348; and

    (ii) includes the rules, regulations, and orders issued by the Commodity Futures Trading Commission.

"Commodity pool operator" has the meaning given that term in section 1a(11) of the Commodity Exchange Act (7 U.S.C. § 1a(11)).

"Commodity trading advisor" has the meaning given that term in section 1a(12) of the Commodity Exchange Act (7 U.S.C. § 1a(12)).

"Futures commission merchant" has the meaning given that term in section 1a(28) of the Commodity Exchange Act (7 U.S.C. § 1a(28)).

"Introducing broker" has the meaning given that term in section 1a(31) of the Commodity Exchange Act (7 U.S.C. § 1a(31)).

"Investment adviser" has the meaning given that term in section 202(a)(11) of the Investment Advisers Act of 1940 (15 U.S.C. § 80b-2(a)(11)).

"Person associated with a broker or dealer" has the meaning given that term in section 3(a)(18) of the Securities Exchange Act of 1934 (15 U.S.C. § 78c(a)(18)).

"Person associated with an investment adviser" has the meaning given that term in section 202(a)(17) of the Investment Advisers Act of 1940 (15 U.S.C. § 80b-2(a)(17)).

"Registered broker or dealer" has the meaning given that term in section 3(a)(48) of the Securities Exchange Act of 1934 (15 U.S.C. § 78c(a)(48)).

"Securities law"

    (i) means 18 U.S.C. §§ 1348, 1350, and the provisions of law referred to in section 3(a)(47) of the Securities Exchange Act of 1934 (15 U.S.C. § 78c(a)(47)); and

    (ii) includes the rules, regulations, and orders issued by the Securities and Exchange Commission pursuant to the provisions of law referred to in such section.

    (B) In General.— A conviction under a securities law or commodities law is not required in order for subsection (b)(19) to apply. This subsection would apply in the case of a defendant convicted under a general fraud statute if the defendant's conduct violated a securities law or commodities law. For example, this subsection would apply if an officer of a publicly traded company violated regulations issued by the Securities and Exchange Commission by fraudulently influencing an independent audit of the company's financial statements for the purposes of rendering such financial statements materially misleading, even if the officer is convicted only of wire fraud.

(C) Nonapplicability of § 3B1.3 (Abuse of Position of Trust or Use of Special Skill).— If subsection (b)(18) applies, do not apply § 3B1.3.

16. Cross Reference in Subsection (c)(3).— Subsection (c)(3) provides a cross reference to another guideline in Chapter Two (Offense Conduct) in cases in which the defendant is convicted of a general fraud statute, and the count of conviction establishes an offense involving fraudulent conduct that is more aptly covered by another guideline. Sometimes, offenses involving fraudulent statements are prosecuted under 18 U.S.C. § 1001, or a similarly general statute, although the offense involves fraudulent conduct that is also covered by a more specific statute. Examples include false entries regarding currency transactions, for which § 2S1.3 (Structuring Transactions to Evade Reporting Requirements) likely would be more apt, and false statements to a customs officer, for which § 2T3.1 (Evading Import Duties or Restrictions (Smuggling); Receiving or Trafficking in Smuggled Property) likely would be more apt. In certain other cases, the mail or wire fraud statutes, or other relatively broad statutes, are used primarily as jurisdictional bases for the prosecution of other offenses. For example, a state employee who improperly influenced the award of a contract and used the mails to commit the offense may be prosecuted under 18 U.S.C. § 1341 for fraud involving the deprivation of the intangible right of honest services. Such a case would be more aptly sentenced pursuant to § 2C1.1 (Offering, Giving, Soliciting, or Receiving a Bribe; Extortion Under Color of Official Right; Fraud involving the Deprivation of the Intangible Right to Honest Services of Public Officials; Conspiracy to Defraud by Interference with Governmental Functions).

17. Continuing Financial Crimes Enterprise.— If the defendant is convicted under 18 U.S.C. § 225 (relating to a continuing financial crimes enterprise), the offense level is that applicable to the underlying series of offenses comprising the "continuing financial crimes enterprise".

18. Partially Completed Offenses.— In the case of a partially completed offense (e.g., an offense involving a completed theft or fraud that is part of a larger, attempted theft or fraud), the offense level is to be determined in accordance with the provisions of § 2X1.1 (Attempt, Solicitation, or Conspiracy) whether the conviction is for the substantive offense, the inchoate offense (attempt, solicitation, or conspiracy), or both. See Application Note 4 of the Commentary to § 2X1.1.

19. Multiple-Count Indictments.— Some fraudulent schemes may result in multiple-count indictments, depending on the technical elements of the offense. The cumulative loss produced by a common scheme or course of conduct should be used in determining the offense level, regardless of the number of counts of conviction. See Chapter Three, Part D (Multiple Counts).

20. Departure Considerations.—

(A) Upward Departure Considerations.— There may be cases in which the offense level determined under this guideline substantially understates the seriousness of the offense. In such cases, an upward departure may be warranted. The following is a non-exhaustive list of factors that the court may consider in determining whether an upward departure is warranted:

(i) A primary objective of the offense was an aggravating, non-monetary objective. For example, a primary objective of the offense was to inflict emotional harm.

(ii) The offense caused or risked substantial non-monetary harm. For example, the offense caused physical harm, psychological harm, or severe emotional trauma, or resulted in a substantial invasion of a privacy interest (through, for example, the theft of personal information such as medical, educational, or financial records). An upward departure would be warranted, for example, in an 18 U.S.C. § 1030 offense involving damage to a protected computer, if, as a result of that offense, death resulted. An upward departure also would be warranted, for example, in a case involving animal enterprise terrorism under 18 U.S.C. § 43, if, in the course of the offense, serious bodily injury or death resulted, or substantial scientific research or information were destroyed. Similarly, an upward departure would be warranted in a case involving conduct described in 18 U.S.C. § 670 if the offense resulted in serious bodily injury or death, including serious bodily injury or death resulting from the use of the pre-retail medical product.

(iii) The offense involved a substantial amount of interest of any kind, finance charges, late fees, penalties, amounts based on an agreed-upon return or rate of return, or other similar costs, not included in the determination of loss for purposes of subsection (b)(1).

(iv) The offense created a risk of substantial loss beyond the loss determined for purposes of subsection (b)(1), such as a risk of a significant disruption of a national financial market.

(v) In a case involving stolen information from a "protected computer", as defined in 18 U.S.C. § 1030(e)(2), the defendant sought the stolen information to further a broader criminal purpose.

(vi) In a case involving access devices or unlawfully produced or unlawfully obtained means of identification:

(I) The offense caused substantial harm to the victim's reputation or credit record, or the victim suffered a substantial inconvenience related to repairing the victim's reputation or a damaged credit record.

(II) An individual whose means of identification the defendant used to obtain unlawful means of identification is erroneously arrested or denied a job because an arrest record has been made in that individual's name.

(III) The defendant produced or obtained numerous means of identification with respect to one individual and essentially assumed that individual's identity.

(B) Upward Departure for Debilitating Impact on a Critical Infrastructure.— An upward departure would be warranted in a case in which subsection (b)(18)(A)(iii) applies and the disruption to the critical infrastructure(s) is so substantial as to have a debilitating impact on national security, national economic security, national public health or safety, or any combination of those matters.

(C) Downward Departure Consideration.— There may be cases in which the offense level determined under this guideline substantially overstates the seriousness of the offense. In such cases, a downward departure may be warranted.

For example, a securities fraud involving a fraudulent statement made publicly to the market may produce an aggregate loss amount that is substantial but diffuse, with relatively small loss amounts suffered by a relatively large number of victims. In such a case, the loss table in subsection (b)(1) and the victims table in subsection (b)(2) may combine to produce an offense level that substantially overstates the seriousness of the offense. If so, a downward departure may be warranted.

(D) Downward Departure for Major Disaster or Emergency Victims.— If

(i) the minimum offense level of level 12 in subsection (b)(12) applies;

(ii) the defendant sustained damage, loss, hardship, or suffering caused by a major disaster or an emergency as those terms are defined in 42 U.S.C. § 5122; and

(iii) the benefits received illegally were only an extension or overpayment of benefits received legitimately, a downward departure may be warranted.

Background: This guideline covers offenses involving theft, stolen property, property damage or destruction, fraud, forgery, and counterfeiting (other than offenses involving altered or counterfeit bearer obligations of the United States).

Because federal fraud statutes often are broadly written, a single pattern of offense conduct usually can be prosecuted under several code sections, as a result of which the offense of conviction may be somewhat arbitrary. Furthermore, most fraud statutes cover a broad range of conduct with extreme variation in severity. The specific offense characteristics and cross references contained in this guideline are designed with these considerations in mind.

The Commission has determined that, ordinarily, the sentences of defendants convicted of federal offenses should reflect the nature and magnitude of the loss caused or intended by their crimes. Accordingly, along with other relevant factors under the guidelines, loss serves as a measure of the seriousness of the offense and the defendant's relative culpability and is a principal factor in determining the offense level under this guideline.

Theft from the person of another, such as pickpocketing or non-forcible purse-snatching, receives an enhanced sentence because of the increased risk of physical injury. This guideline does not include an enhancement for thefts from the person by means of force or fear; such crimes are robberies and are covered under § 2B3.1 (Robbery).

A minimum offense level of level 14 is provided for offenses involving an organized scheme to steal vehicles or vehicle parts. Typically, the scope of such activity is substantial, but the value of the property may be particularly difficult to ascertain in individual cases because the stolen property is rapidly resold or otherwise disposed of in the course of the offense. Therefore, the specific offense characteristic of "organized scheme" is used as an alternative to "loss" in setting a minimum offense level.

Use of false pretenses involving charitable causes and government agencies enhances the sentences of defendants who take advantage of victims' trust in government or law enforcement agencies or the generosity and charitable motives of victims. Taking advantage of a victim's self-interest does not mitigate the seriousness of fraudulent conduct; rather, defendants who exploit victims' charitable impulses or trust in government create particular social harm. In a similar vein, a defendant who has been subject to civil or administrative proceedings for the same or similar fraudulent conduct demonstrates aggravated criminal intent and is deserving of additional punishment for not conforming with the requirements of judicial process or orders issued by federal, state, or local administrative agencies.

Offenses that involve the use of financial transactions or financial accounts outside the United States in an effort to conceal illicit profits and criminal conduct involve a particularly high level of sophistication and complexity. These offenses are difficult to detect and require costly investigations and prosecutions. Diplomatic processes often must be used to secure testimony and evidence beyond the jurisdiction of United States courts. Consequently, a minimum offense level of level 12 is provided for these offenses.

Subsection (b)(5) implements the instruction to the Commission in section 2 of Public Law 105-101 and the directive to the Commission in section 3 of Public Law 110-384.

Subsection (b)(7) implements the directive to the Commission in section 10606 of Public Law 111-148.

Subsection (b)(8) implements the directive to the Commission in section 7 of Public Law 112-186.

Subsection (b)(9)(D) implements, in a broader form, the directive in section 3 of the College Scholarship Fraud Prevention Act of 2000, Public Law 106-420.

Subsection (b)(10) implements, in a broader form, the instruction to the Commission in section 6(c)(2) of Public Law 105-184.

Subsections (b)(11)(A)(i) and (B)(i) implement the instruction to the Commission in section 4 of the Wireless Telephone Protection Act, Public Law 105-172.

Subsection (b)(11)(C) implements the directive to the Commission in section 4 of the Identity Theft and Assumption Deterrence Act of 1998, Public Law 105-318. This subsection focuses principally on an aggravated form of identity theft known as "affirmative identity theft" or "breeding", in which a defendant uses another individual's name, social security number, or some other form of identification (the "means of identification") to "breed" (i.e., produce or obtain) new or additional forms of identification. Because 18 U.S.C. § 1028(d) broadly defines "means of identification", the new or additional forms of identification can include items such as a driver's license, a credit card, or a bank loan. This subsection provides a minimum offense level of level 12, in part because of the seriousness of the offense. The minimum offense level accounts for the fact that the means of identification that were "bred" (i.e., produced or obtained) often are within the defendant's exclusive control, making it difficult for the individual victim to detect that the victim's identity has been "stolen." Generally, the victim does not become aware of the offense until certain harms have already occurred (e.g., a damaged credit rating or an inability to obtain a loan). The minimum offense level also accounts for the non-monetary harm associated with these types of offenses, much of which may be difficult or impossible to quantify (e.g., harm to the individual's reputation or credit rating, inconvenience, and other difficulties resulting from the offense). The legislative history of the Identity Theft and Assumption Deterrence Act of 1998 indicates that Congress was especially concerned with providing increased punishment for this type of harm.

Subsection (b)(12) implements the directive in section 5 of Public Law 110-179.

Subsection (b)(13) implements the directive in section 3 of Public Law 112-269.

Subsection (b)(15)(B) implements, in a broader form, the instruction to the Commission in section 110512 of Public Law 103-322.

Subsection (b)(16)(A) implements, in a broader form, the instruction to the Commission in section 2507 of Public Law 101-647.

Subsection (b)(16)(B)(i) implements, in a broader form, the instruction to the Commission in section 961(m) ofPublic Law 101-73.

Subsection (b)(17) implements the directive in section 209 of Public Law 110-326.

Subsection (b)(18) implements the directive in section 225(b) of Public Law 107-296. The minimum offense level of level 24 provided in subsection (b)(18)(B) for an offense that resulted in a substantial disruption of a critical infrastructure reflects the serious impact such an offense could have on national security, national economic security, national public health or safety, or a combination of any of these matters.

§ 2B1.4.   Insider Trading

(a) Base Offense Level: 8

(b) Specific Offense Characteristics

(1) If the gain resulting from the offense exceeded $5,000, increase by the number of levels from the table in § 2B1.1 (Theft, Property Destruction, and Fraud) corresponding to that amount.

(2) If the offense involved an organized scheme to engage in insider trading and the offense level determined above is less than level 14, increase to level 14.

CREDIT(S)

(Effective November 1, 2001; amended effective November 1, 2010; November 1, 2012.)

COMMENTARY

Statutory Provisions: 15 U.S.C. 78j and 17 CFR 240.10b-5. For additional statutory provisions(s), see Appendix A (Statutory Index).

Application Notes:

1. *Application of Subsection (b)(2).—* For purposes of subsection (b)(2), an "organized scheme to engage in insider trading" means a scheme to engage in insider trading that involves considered, calculated, systematic, or repeated efforts to obtain and trade on inside information, as distinguished from fortuitous or opportunistic instances of insider trading.

The following is a non-exhaustive list of factors that the court may consider in determining whether the offense involved an organized scheme to engage in insider trading:

(A) The number of transactions;

(B) The dollar value of the transactions;

(C) The number of securities involved;

(D) The duration of the offense;

(E) The number of participants in the scheme (although such a scheme may exist even in the absence of more than one participant);

(F) The efforts undertaken to obtain material, nonpublic information;

(G) The number of instances in which material, nonpublic information was obtained; and

(H) The efforts undertaken to conceal the offense.

2. *Application of § 3B1.3.—* Section 3B1.3 (Abuse of Position of Trust or Use of Special Skill) should be applied if the defendant occupied and abused a position of special trust. Examples might include a corporate president or an attorney who misused information regarding a planned but unannounced takeover attempt. It typically would not apply to an ordinary "tippee".

Furthermore, § 3B1.3 should be applied if the defendant's employment in a position that involved regular participation or professional assistance in creating, issuing, buying, selling, or trading securities or commodities was used to facilitate significantly the commission or concealment of the offense. It would apply, for example, to a hedge fund professional who regularly participates in securities transactions or to a lawyer who regularly provides professional assistance in securities transactions, if the defendant's employment in such a position was used to facilitate significantly the commission or concealment of the offense. It ordinarily would not apply to a position such as a clerical worker in an investment firm, because such a position ordinarily does not involve special skill. See § 3B1.3, comment. (n. 4).

Background: This guideline applies to certain violations of Rule 10b-5 that are commonly referred to as "inside trading". Insider trading is treated essentially as a sophisticated fraud. Because the victims and their losses are difficult if not impossible to identify, the gain, i.e., the total increase in value realized through trading in securities by the defendant and persons acting in concert with the defendant or to whom the defendant provide inside information, is employed instead of the victims' losses.

Certain other offenses, e.g., 7 U.S.C. 13(e), that involve misuse of inside information for personal gain also appropriately may be covered by this guideline.

Subsection (b)(2) implements the directive to the Commission in section 1079A(a)(1)(A) of Public Law 111-203.

PART C —   OFFENSES INVOLVING PUBLIC OFFICIALS

§ 2C1.1.   Offering, Giving, Soliciting, or Receiving a Bribe; Extortion Under Color of Official Right; Fraud Involving the Deprivation of the Intangible Right to Honest Services of Public Officials; Conspiracy to Defraud by Interference with Governmental Functions

(a) Base Offense Level:

(1) 14, if the defendant was a public official; or

(2) 12, otherwise.

(b) Specific Offense Characteristics

(1) If the offense involved more than one bribe or extortion, increase by 2 levels.

(2) If the value of the payment, the benefit received or to be received in return for the payment, the value of anything obtained or to be obtained by a public official or others acting with a public official, or the loss to the government from the offense, whichever is greatest, exceeded $5,000, increase by the number of levels from the table in § 2B1.1 (Theft, Property Destruction, and Fraud) corresponding to that amount.

(3) If the offense involved an elected public official or any public official in a high-level decision-making or sensitive position, increase by 4 levels. If the resulting offense level is less than level 18, increase to level 18.

(4) If the defendant was a public official who facilitated

(A) entry into the United States for a person, a vehicle, or cargo;

(B) the obtaining of a passport or a document relating to naturalization, citizenship, legal entry, or legal resident status; or

(C) the obtaining of a government identification document, increase by 2 levels.

(c) Cross References

(1) If the offense was committed for the purpose of facilitating the commission of another criminal offense, apply the offense guideline applicable to a conspiracy to commit that other offense, if the resulting offense level is greater than that determined above.

(2) If the offense was committed for the purpose of concealing, or obstructing justice in respect to, another criminal offense, apply § 2X3.1 (Accessory After the Fact) or § 2J1.2 (Obstruction of Justice), as appropriate, in respect to that other offense, if the resulting offense level is greater than that determined above.

(3) If the offense involved a threat of physical injury or property destruction, apply § 2B3.2 (Extortion by Force or Threat of Injury or Serious Damage), if the resulting offense level is greater than that determined above.

(d) Special Instruction for Fines — Organizations

(1) In lieu of the pecuniary loss under subsection (a)(3) of § 8C2.4 (Base Fine), use the greatest of:

(A) the value of the unlawful payment;

(B) the value of the benefit received or to be received in return for the unlawful payment; or

(C) the consequential damages resulting from the unlawful payment.

COMMENTARY

Statutory Provisions: 15 U.S.C. §§ 78dd-1, 78dd-2, 78dd-3; 18 U.S.C. §§ 201(b)(1), (2), 226, 227, 371 (if conspiracy to defraud by interference with governmental functions), 872, 1341 (if the scheme or artifice to defraud was to deprive another of the intangible right of honest services of a public official), 1342 (if the scheme or artifice to defraud was to deprive another of the intangible right of honest services of a public official), 1343 (if the scheme or artifice to defraud was to deprive another of the intangible right of honest services of a public official), 1951. For additional statutory provision(s), see Appendix A (Statutory Index).

Application Notes:

1. Definitions.— For purposes of this guideline:

"Government identification document" means a document made or issued by or under the authority of the United States Government, a State, or a political subdivision of a State, which, when completed with information concerning a particular individual, is of a type intended or commonly accepted for the purpose of identification of individuals.

"Payment" means anything of value. A payment need not be monetary.

"Public official" shall be construed broadly and includes the following:

(A) "Public official" as defined in 18 U.S.C. § 201(a)(1).

(B) A member of a state or local legislature. "State" means a State of the United States, and any commonwealth, territory, or possession of the United States.

(C) An officer or employee or person acting for or on behalf of a state or local government, or any department, agency, or branch of government thereof, in any official function, under or by authority of such department, agency, or branch of government, or a juror in a state or local trial.

(D) Any person who has been selected to be a person described in subdivisions (A), (B), or (C), either before or after such person has qualified.

(E) An individual who, although not otherwise covered by subdivisions (A) through (D):

(i) is in a position of public trust with official responsibility for carrying out a government program or policy;

(ii) acts under color of law or official right; or

(iii) participates so substantially in government operations as to possess de facto authority to make governmental decisions (e.g., which may include a leader of a state or local political party who acts in the manner described in this subdivision).

2. More than One Bribe or Extortion.— Subsection (b)(1) provides an adjustment for offenses involving more than one incident of either bribery or extortion. Related payments that, in essence, constitute a single incident of bribery or extortion (e.g., a number of installment payments for a single action) are to be treated as a single bribe or extortion, even if charged in separate counts.

In a case involving more than one incident of bribery or extortion, the applicable amounts under subsection (b)(2) (i.e., the greatest of the value of the payment, the benefit received or to be received, the value of anything obtained or to be obtained by a public official or others acting with a public official, or the loss to the government) are determined separately for each incident and then added together.

3. Application of Subsection (b)(2).— "Loss", for purposes of subsection (b)(2), shall be determined in accordance with Application Note 3 of the Commentary to § 2B1.1 (Theft, Property Destruction, and Fraud). The value of "the benefit received or to be received" means the net value of such benefit. Examples: (A) A government employee, in return for a $500 bribe, reduces the price of a piece of surplus property offered for sale by the government from $10,000 to $2,000; the value of the benefit received is $8,000. (B) A $150,000 contract on which $20,000 profit was made was awarded in return for a bribe; the value of the benefit received is $20,000. Do not deduct the value of the bribe itself in computing the value of the benefit received or to be received. In the preceding examples, therefore, the value of the benefit received would be the same regardless of the value of the bribe.

4. Application of Subsection (b)(3).—

(A) Definition.— "High-level decision-making or sensitive position" means a position characterized by a direct authority to make decisions for, or on behalf of, a government department, agency, or other government entity, or by a substantial influence over the decision-making process.

(B) Examples.— Examples of a public official in a high-level decision-making position include a prosecuting attorney, a judge, an agency administrator, and any other public official with a similar level of authority. Examples of a public official who holds a sensitive position include a juror, a law enforcement officer, an election official, and any other similarly situated individual.

5. Application of Subsection (c).— For the purposes of determining whether to

apply the cross references in this section, the "resulting offense level" means the final offense level (i.e., the offense level determined by taking into account both the Chapter Two offense level and any applicable adjustments from Chapter Three, Parts A–D). See § 1B1.5(d); Application Note 2 of the Commentary to § 1B1.5 (Interpretation of References to Other Offense Guidelines).

6. Inapplicability of § 3B1.3.— Do not apply § 3B1.3 (Abuse of Position of Trust or Use of Special Skill).

7. Upward Departure Provisions.— In some cases the monetary value of the unlawful payment may not be known or may not adequately reflect the seriousness of the offense. For example, a small payment may be made in exchange for the falsification of inspection records for a shipment of defective parachutes or the destruction of evidence in a major narcotics case. In part, this issue is addressed by the enhancements in § 2C1.1(b)(2) and (c)(1), (2), and (3). However, in cases in which the seriousness of the offense is still not adequately reflected, an upward departure is warranted. See Chapter Five, Part K (Departures).

In a case in which the court finds that the defendant's conduct was part of a systematic or pervasive corruption of a governmental function, process, or office that may cause loss of public confidence in government, an upward departure may be warranted. See § 5K2.7 (Disruption of Governmental Function).

Background: This section applies to a person who offers or gives a bribe for a corrupt purpose, such as inducing a public official to participate in a fraud or to influence such individual's official actions, or to a public official who solicits or accepts such a bribe.

The object and nature of a bribe may vary widely from case to case. In some cases, the object may be commercial advantage (e.g., preferential treatment in the award of a government contract). In others, the object may be issuance of a license to which the recipient is not entitled. In still others, the object may be the obstruction of justice. Consequently, a guideline for the offense must be designed to cover diverse situations.

In determining the net value of the benefit received or to be received, the value of the bribe is not deducted from the gross value of such benefit; the harm is the same regardless of value of the bribe paid to receive the benefit. In a case in which the value of the bribe exceeds the value of the benefit, or in which the value of the benefit cannot be determined, the value of the bribe is used because it is likely that the payer of such a bribe expected something in return that would be worth more than the value of the bribe. Moreover, for deterrence purposes, the punishment should be commensurate with the gain to the payer or the recipient of the bribe, whichever is greater.

Under § 2C1.1(b)(3), if the payment was for the purpose of influencing an official act by certain officials, the offense level is increased by 4 levels.

Under § 2C1.1(c)(1), if the payment was to facilitate the commission of another criminal offense, the guideline applicable to a conspiracy to commit that other offense will apply if the result is greater than that determined above. For example, if a bribe was given to a law enforcement officer to allow the smuggling of a quantity of cocaine, the guideline for conspiracy to import cocaine would be applied if it resulted in a greater offense level.

Under § 2C1.1(c)(2), if the payment was to conceal another criminal offense or obstruct justice in respect to another criminal offense, the guideline from § 2X3.1 (Accessory After the Fact) or § 2J1.2 (Obstruction of Justice), as appropriate, will apply if the result is greater than that determined above. For example, if a bribe was given for the purpose of concealing the offense of espionage, the guideline for accessory after the fact to espionage would be applied.

Under § 2C1.1(c)(3), if the offense involved forcible extortion, the guideline from § 2B3.2 (Extortion by Force or Threat of Injury or Serious Damage) will apply if the result is greater than that determined above.

Section 2C1.1 also applies to offenses under 15 U.S.C. §§ 78dd-1, 78dd-2, and 78dd-3. Such offenses generally involve a payment to a foreign public official, candidate for public office, or agent or intermediary, with the intent to influence an official act or decision of a foreign government or political party. Typically, a case prosecuted under these provisions will involve an intent to influence governmental action.

Section 2C1.1 also applies to fraud involving the deprivation of the intangible right to honest services of government officials under 18 U.S.C. §§ 1341–1343 and conspiracy to defraud by interference with governmental functions under 18 U.S.C. § 371. Such fraud offenses typically involve an improper use of government influence that harms the operation of government in a manner similar to bribery offenses.

Offenses involving attempted bribery are frequently not completed because the offense is reported to authorities or an individual involved in the offense is acting in an undercover capacity. Failure to complete the offense does not lessen the defendant's culpability in attempting to use public position for personal gain. Therefore, solicitations and attempts are treated as equivalent to the underlying offense.

§ 2C1.2. Offering, Giving, Soliciting, or Receiving a Gratuity

(a) Base Offense Level:

(1) 11, if the defendant was a public official; or

(2) 9, otherwise.

(b) Specific Offense Characteristics

(1) If the offense involved more than one gratuity, increase by 2 levels.

(2) If the value of the gratuity exceeded $5,000, increase by the number of levels from the table in § 2B1.1 (Theft, Property Destruction, and Fraud) corresponding to that amount.

(3) If the offense involved an elected public official or any public official in a high-level decision-making or sensitive position, increase by 4 levels. If the resulting offense level is less than level 15, increase to level 15.

(4) If the defendant was a public official who facilitated

(A) entry into the United States for a person, a vehicle, or cargo;

(B) the obtaining of a passport or a document relating to naturalization, citizenship, legal entry, or legal resident status; or

(C) the obtaining of a government identification document, increase by 2 levels.

(c) Special Instruction for Fines — Organizations

(1) In lieu of the pecuniary loss under subsection (a)(3) of § 8C2.4 (Base Fine), use the value of the unlawful payment.

COMMENTARY

Statutory Provisions: 18 U.S.C. §§ 201(c)(1), 212–214, 217. For additional statutory provision(s), see Appendix A (Statutory Index).

Application Notes:

1. Definitions.— For purposes of this guideline:

"Government identification document" means a document made or issued by or under the authority of the United States Government, a State, or a political subdivision of a State, which, when completed with information concerning a particular individual, is of a type intended or commonly accepted for the purpose of identification of individuals.

"Public official" shall be construed broadly and includes the following:

(A) "Public official" as defined in 18 U.S.C. § 201(a)(1).

(B) A member of a state or local legislature. "State" means a State of the United States, and any commonwealth, territory, or possession of the United States.

(C) An officer or employee or person acting for or on behalf of a state or local government, or any department, agency, or branch of government thereof, in any official function, under or by authority of such department, agency, or branch of government, or a juror.

(D) Any person who has been selected to be a person described in subdivisions (A), (B), or (C), either before or after such person has qualified.

(E) An individual who, although not otherwise covered by subdivisions (A) through (D):

(i) is in a position of public trust with official responsibility for carrying out a government program or policy;

(ii) acts under color of law or official right; or

(iii) participates so substantially in government operations as to possess de facto authority to make governmental decisions (e.g., which may include a leader of a state or local political party who acts in the manner described in this subdivision).

2. Application of Subsection (b)(1).— Related payments that, in essence, constitute a single gratuity (e.g., separate payments for airfare and hotel for a single vacation trip) are to be treated as a single gratuity, even if charged in separate counts.

3. Application of Subsection (b)(3).—

(A) Definition.— "High-level decision-making or sensitive position" means a position characterized by a direct authority to make decisions for, or on behalf of, a government department, agency, or other government entity, or by a substantial influence over the decision-making process.

(B) Examples.— Examples of a public official in a high-level decision-making position include a prosecuting attorney, a judge, an agency administrator, a law enforcement officer, and any other public official with a similar level of authority. Examples of a public official who holds a sensitive position include a juror, a law enforcement officer, an election official, and any other similarly situated individual.

4. Inapplicability of § 3B1.3.— Do not apply the adjustment in § 3B1.3 (Abuse of Position of Trust or Use of Special Skill).

Background: This section applies to the offering, giving, soliciting, or receiving of a gratuity to a public official in respect to an official act. It also applies in cases involving

(1) the offer to, or acceptance by, a bank examiner of a loan or gratuity;

(2) the offer or receipt of anything of value for procuring a loan or discount of commercial bank paper from a Federal Reserve Bank; and

(3) the acceptance of a fee or other consideration by a federal employee for adjusting or cancelling a farm debt.

PART J — OFFENSES INVOLVING THE ADMINISTRATION OF JUSTICE

§ 2J1.2. Obstruction of Justice

(a) Base Offense Level: 14

(b) Specific Offense Characteristics

(1) (Apply the greatest):

(A) If the

(i) defendant was convicted under 18 U.S.C. § 1001; and

(ii) statutory maximum term of eight years' imprisonment applies because the matter relates to sex offenses under 18 U.S.C. § 1591 or chapters 109A, 109B, 110, or 117 of title 18, United States Code, increase by 4 levels.

(B) If the offense involved causing or threatening to cause physical injury to a person, or property damage, in order to obstruct the administration of justice, increase by 8 levels.

(C) If the (i) defendant was convicted under 18 U.S.C. § 1001 or § 1505; and (ii) statutory maximum term of eight years' imprisonment applies because the matter relates to international terrorism or domestic terrorism, increase by 12 levels.

(2) If the offense resulted in substantial interference with the administration of justice, increase by 3 levels.

(3) If the offense

(A) involved the destruction, alteration, or fabrication of a substantial number of records, documents, or tangible objects;

(B) involved the selection of any essential or especially probative record, document, or tangible object, to destroy or alter; or

(C) was otherwise extensive in scope, planning, or preparation, increase by 2 levels.

(c) Cross Reference

(1) If the offense involved obstructing the investigation or prosecution of a criminal offense, apply § 2X3.1 (Accessory After the Fact) in respect to that criminal offense, if the resulting offense level is greater than that determined above.

COMMENTARY

Statutory Provisions: 18 U.S.C. §§ 1001 (when the statutory maximum term of eight years' imprisonment applies because the matter relates to international terrorism or domestic terrorism, or to sex offenses under 18 U.S.C. § 1591 or chapters 109A, 109B, 110, or 117 of title 18, United States Code), 1503, 1505–1513, 1516, 1519. For additional statutory provision(s), see Appendix A (Statutory Index).

Application Notes:

1. Definitions.— For purposes of this guideline:

"Domestic terrorism" has the meaning given that term in 18 U.S.C. § 2331(5).

"International terrorism" has the meaning given that term in 18 U.S.C. § 2331(1).

"Records, documents, or tangible objects" includes

(A) records, documents, or tangible objects that are stored on, or that are, magnetic, optical, digital, other electronic, or other storage mediums or devices; and

(B) wire or electronic communications.

"Substantial interference with the administration of justice" includes a premature or improper termination of a felony investigation; an indictment, verdict, or any judicial determination based upon perjury, false testimony, or other false evidence; or the unnecessary expenditure of substantial governmental or court resources.

2. Chapter Three Adjustments.—

(A) Inapplicability of § 3C1.1.— For offenses covered under this section, § 3C1.1 (Obstructing or Impeding the Administration of Justice) does not apply, unless the defendant obstructed the investigation, prosecution, or sentencing of the obstruction of justice count.

(B) Interaction with Terrorism Adjustment.— If § 3A1.4 (Terrorism) applies, do not apply subsection (b)(1)(C).

3. Convictions for the Underlying Offense.— In the event that the defendant is convicted of an offense sentenced under this section as well as for the underlying offense (i.e., the offense that is the object of the obstruction), see the Commentary to Chapter Three, Part C (Obstruction and Related Adjustments), and to § 3D1.2(c) (Groups of Closely Related Counts).

4. Upward Departure Considerations.— If a weapon was used, or bodily injury or significant property damage resulted, an upward departure may be warranted. See Chapter Five, Part K (Departures). In a case involving an act of extreme violence (for example, retaliating against a government witness by throwing acid in the witness's face) or a particularly serious sex offense, an upward departure would be warranted.

5. Subsection (b)(1)(B).— The inclusion of "property damage" under subsection (b)(1)(B) is designed to address cases in which property damage is caused or threatened as a means of intimidation or retaliation (e.g., to intimidate a witness from, or retaliate against a witness for, testifying). Subsection (b)(1)(B) is not intended to apply, for example, where the offense consisted of destroying a ledger containing an incriminating entry.

Background: This section addresses offenses involving the obstruction of justice generally prosecuted under the above-referenced statutory provisions. Numerous offenses of varying seriousness may constitute obstruction of justice: using threats or force to intimidate or influence a juror or federal officer; obstructing a civil or administrative proceeding; stealing or altering court records; unlawfully intercepting grand jury deliberations; obstructing a criminal investigation; obstructing a state or local investigation of illegal gambling; using intimidation or force to influence testimony, alter evidence, evade legal process, or obstruct the communication of a judge or law enforcement officer; or causing a witness bodily injury or property damage in retaliation for providing testimony, information or evidence in a federal proceeding. The conduct that gives rise to the violation may, therefore, range from a mere threat to an act of extreme violence.

The specific offense characteristics reflect the more serious forms of obstruction. Because the conduct covered by this guideline is frequently part of an effort to avoid punishment for an offense that the defendant has committed or to assist another person to escape punishment for an offense, a cross reference to § 2X3.1 (Accessory After the Fact) is provided. Use of this cross reference will provide an enhanced offense level when the obstruction is in respect to a particularly serious offense, whether such offense was committed by the defendant or another person.

§ 2J1.3. Perjury or Subornation of Perjury; Bribery of Witness

(a) Base Offense Level: 14

(b) Specific Offense Characteristics

(1) If the offense involved causing or threatening to cause physical injury to a person, or property damage, in order to suborn perjury, increase by 8 levels.

(2) If the perjury, subornation of perjury, or witness bribery resulted in substantial interference with the administration of justice, increase by 3 levels.

(c) Cross Reference

(1) If the offense involved perjury, subornation of perjury, or witness bribery in respect to a criminal offense, apply § 2X3.1 (Accessory After the Fact) in respect to that criminal offense, if the resulting offense level is greater than that determined above.

(d) Special Instruction

(1) In the case of counts of perjury or subornation of perjury arising from testimony given, or to be given, in separate proceedings, do not group the counts together under § 3D1.2 (Groups of Closely Related Counts).

COMMENTARY

Statutory Provisions: 18 U.S.C. §§ 201(b)(3), (4), 1621–1623. For additional statutory provision(s), see Appendix A (Statutory Index).

Application Notes:

1. "Substantial interference with the administration of justice" includes a premature or improper termination of a felony investigation; an indictment, verdict, or any judicial determination based upon perjury, false testimony, or other false evidence; or the unnecessary expenditure of substantial governmental or court resources.

2. For offenses covered under this section, § 3C1.1 (Obstructing or Impeding the Administration of Justice) does not apply, unless the defendant obstructed the investigation or trial of the perjury count.

3. In the event that the defendant is convicted under this section as well as for the underlying offense (i.e., the offense with respect to which he committed perjury, subornation of perjury, or witness bribery), see the Commentary to Chapter Three, Part C (Obstruction and Related Adjustments), and to § 3D1.2(c) (Groups of Closely Related Counts).

4. If a weapon was used, or bodily injury or significant property damage resulted, an upward departure may be warranted. See Chapter Five, Part K (Departures).

5. "Separate proceedings," as used in subsection (d)(1), includes different proceedings in the same case or matter (e.g., a grand jury proceeding and a trial, or a trial and retrial), and proceedings in separate cases or matters (e.g., separate

trials of codefendants), but does not include multiple grand jury proceedings in the same case.

Background: This section applies to perjury, subornation of perjury, and witness bribery, generally prosecuted under the referenced statutes. The guidelines provide a higher penalty for perjury than the pre-guidelines practice estimate of ten months imprisonment. The Commission believes that perjury should be treated similarly to obstruction of justice. Therefore, the same considerations for enhancing a sentence are applied in the specific offense characteristics, and an alternative reference to the guideline for accessory after the fact is made.

PART S — MONEY LAUNDERING AND MONETARY TRANSACTION REPORTING

§ 2S1.1. Laundering of Monetary Instruments; Engaging in Monetary Transactions in Property Derived from Unlawful Activity

(a) Base Offense Level:

(1) The offense level for the underlying offense from which the laundered funds were derived, if

(A) the defendant committed the underlying offense (or would be accountable for the underlying offense under subsection (a)(1)(A) of § 1B1.3 (Relevant Conduct)); and

(B) the offense level for that offense can be determined; or

(2) 8 plus the number of offense levels from the table in § 2B1.1 (Theft, Property Destruction, and Fraud) corresponding to the value of the laundered funds, otherwise.

(b) Specific Offense Characteristics

(1) If

(A) subsection (a)(2) applies; and

(B) the defendant knew or believed that any of the laundered funds were the proceeds of, or were intended to promote

(i) an offense involving the manufacture, importation, or distribution of a controlled substance or a listed chemical;

(ii) a crime of violence; or

(iii) an offense involving firearms, explosives, national security, or the sexual exploitation of a minor, increase by 6 levels.

(2) (Apply the Greatest):

(A) If the defendant was convicted under 18 U.S.C. § 1957, increase by 1 level.

(B) If the defendant was convicted under 18 U.S.C. § 1956, increase by 2 levels.

(A) If

(i) subsection (a)(2) applies; and

(ii) the defendant was in the business of laundering funds, increase by 4 levels.

(3) If

(A) subsection (b)(2)(B) applies;

(B) the offense involved sophisticated laundering, increase by 2 levels.

COMMENTARY

Statutory Provisions: 18 U.S.C. §§ 1956, 1957, 1960 (but only with respect to unlicensed money transmitting businesses as defined in 18 U.S.C. § 1960(b)(1)(C)). For additional statutory provision(s), see Appendix A (Statutory Index).

Application Notes:

1. Definitions.— For purposes of this guideline:

"Crime of violence" has the meaning given that term in subsection (a)(1) of § 4B1.2 (Definitions of Terms Used in Section 4B1.1).

"Criminally derived funds" means any funds derived, or represented by a law enforcement officer, or by another person at the direction or approval of an authorized Federal official, to be derived from conduct constituting a criminal offense.

"Laundered funds" means the property, funds, or monetary instrument involved in the transaction, financial transaction, monetary transaction, transportation, transfer, or transmission in violation of 18 U.S.C. § 1956 or § 1957.

"Laundering funds" means making a transaction, financial transaction, monetary transaction, or transmission, or transporting or transferring property, funds, or a monetary instrument in violation of 18 U.S.C. § 1956 or § 1957.

"Sexual exploitation of a minor" means an offense involving

(A) promoting prostitution by a minor;

(B) sexually exploiting a minor by production of sexually explicit visual or printed material;

(C) distribution of material involving the sexual exploitation of a minor, or possession of material involving the sexual exploitation of a minor with intent to distribute; or

(D) aggravated sexual abuse, sexual abuse, or abusive sexual contact involving a minor.

"Minor" means an individual under the age of 18 years.

2. Application of Subsection (a)(1).—

(A) Multiple Underlying Offenses.— In cases in which subsection (a)(1) applies and there is more than one underlying offense, the offense level for the underlying offense is to be determined under the procedures set forth in Application Note 3 of the Commentary to § 1B1.5 (Interpretation of References to Other Offense Guidelines).

(B) Defendants Accountable for Underlying Offense.— In order for subsection (a)(1) to apply, the defendant must have committed the underlying offense or be accountable for the underlying offense under § 1B1.3(a)(1)(A). The fact that the defendant was involved in laundering criminally derived funds after the commission of the underlying offense, without additional involvement in the underlying offense, does not establish that the defendant committed, aided, abetted, counseled, commanded, induced, procured, or willfully caused the underlying offense.

(C) Application of Chapter Three Adjustments.— Notwithstanding § 1B1.5(c), in cases in which subsection (a)(1) applies, application of any Chapter Three adjustment shall be determined based on the offense covered by this guideline (i.e., the laundering of criminally derived funds) and not on the underlying offense from which the laundered funds were derived.

3. Application of Subsection (a)(2)—

(A) In General.— Subsection (a)(2) applies to any case in which

(i) the defendant did not commit the underlying offense; or

(ii) the defendant committed the underlying offense (or would be accountable for the underlying offense under § 1B1.3(a)(1)(A)), but the offense level for the underlying offense is impossible or impracticable to determine.

(B) Commingled Funds.— In a case in which a transaction, financial transaction, monetary transaction, transportation, transfer, or transmission results in the commingling of legitimately derived funds with criminally derived funds, the value of the laundered funds, for purposes of subsection (a)(2), is the amount of the criminally derived funds, not the total amount of the commingled funds, if the defendant provides sufficient information to determine the amount of criminally derived funds without unduly complicating or prolonging the sentencing process. If the amount of the criminally derived funds is difficult or impracticable to determine, the value of the laundered funds, for purposes of subsection (a)(2), is the total amount of the commingled funds.

(C) Non-Applicability of Enhancement.— Subsection (b)(2)(B) shall not apply if the defendant was convicted of a conspiracy under 18 U.S.C. § 1956(h) and the sole object of that conspiracy was to commit an offense set forth in 18 U.S.C. § 1957.

4. Enhancement for Business of Laundering Funds.—

(A) In General.— The court shall consider the totality of the circumstances to determine whether a defendant who did not commit the underlying offense was in the business of laundering funds, for purposes of subsection (b)(2)(C).

(B) Factors to Consider.— The following is a non-exhaustive list of factors that may indicate the defendant was in the business of laundering funds for purposes of subsection (b)(2)(C):

(i) The defendant regularly engaged in laundering funds.

(ii) The defendant engaged in laundering funds during an extended period of time.

(iii) The defendant engaged in laundering funds from multiple sources.

(iv) The defendant generated a substantial amount of revenue in return for laundering funds.

(v) At the time the defendant committed the instant offense, the defendant had one or more prior convictions for an offense under 18 U.S.C. § 1956 or § 1957, or under 31 U.S.C. § 5313, § 5314, § 5316, § 5324 or § 5326, or any similar offense under state law, or an attempt or conspiracy to commit any such federal or state offense. A conviction taken into account under subsection (b)(2)(C) is not excluded from consideration of whether that conviction receives criminal history points pursuant to Chapter Four, Part A (Criminal History).

(vi) During the course of an undercover government investigation, the defendant made statements that the defendant engaged in any of the conduct described in subdivisions (i) through (iv).

5.

(A) Sophisticated Laundering under Subsection (b)(3).— For purposes of subsection (b)(3), "sophisticated laundering" means complex or intricate offense conduct pertaining to the execution or concealment of the 18 U.S.C. § 1956 offense.

Sophisticated laundering typically involves the use of—

(i) fictitious entities;

(ii) shell corporations;

(iii) two or more levels (i.e., layering) of transactions, transportation, transfers, or transmissions, involving criminally derived funds that were intended to appear legitimate; or

(iv) offshore financial accounts.

(A) Non-Applicability of Enhancement.— If subsection (b)(3) applies, and the conduct that forms the basis for an enhancement under the guideline applicable to the underlying offense is the only conduct that forms the basis for application of subsection (b)(3) of this guideline, do not apply subsection (b)(3) of this guideline.

6. Grouping of Multiple Counts.— In a case in which the defendant is convicted of a count of laundering funds and a count for the underlying offense from which the laundered funds were derived, the counts shall be grouped pursuant to subsection (c) of § 3D1.2 (Groups of Closely-Related Counts).

§ 2S1.3.   Structuring Transactions to Evade Reporting Requirements; Failure to Report Cash or Monetary Transactions; Failure to File Currency and Monetary Instrument Report; Knowingly Filing False Reports; Bulk Cash Smuggling; Establishing or Maintaining Prohibited Accounts

(a) Base Offense Level:

(1) 8, if the defendant was convicted under 31 U.S.C. § 5318 or § 5318A; or

(2) 6 plus the number of offense levels from the table in § 2B1.1 (Theft, Property Destruction, and Fraud) corresponding to the value of the funds, if subsection (a)(1) does not apply.

(b) Specific Offense Characteristics

(1) If

(A) the defendant knew or believed that the funds were proceeds of unlawful activity, or were intended to promote unlawful activity; or

(B) the offense involved bulk cash smuggling, increase by 2 levels.

(2) If the defendant

(A) was convicted of an offense under subchapter II of chapter 53 of title 31, United States Code; and

(B) committed the offense as part of a pattern of unlawful activity involving more than $100,000 in a 12-month period, increase by 2 levels.

(3) If

(A) subsection (a)(2) applies and subsections (b)(1) and (b)(2) do not apply;

(B) the defendant did not act with reckless disregard of the source of the funds;

(C) the funds were the proceeds of lawful activity; and

(D) the funds were to be used for a lawful purpose, decrease the offense level to level 6.

(c) Cross Reference

(1) If the offense was committed for the purposes of violating the Internal Revenue laws, apply the most appropriate guideline from Chapter Two, Part T (Offenses Involving Taxation) if the resulting offense level is greater than that determined above.

COMMENTARY

Statutory Provisions: 18 U.S.C. § 1960 (but only with respect to unlicensed money transmitting businesses as defined in 18 U.S.C. § 1960(b)(1)(A) and (B)); 26 U.S.C. §§ 7203 (if a violation based upon 26 U.S.C. § 6050I), 7206 (if a violation based upon 26 U.S.C. § 6050I); 31 U.S.C. §§ 5313, 5314, 5316, 5318, 5318A(b), 5322, 5324, 5326, 5331, 5332. For additional statutory provision(s), see Appendix A (Statutory Index).

Application Notes:

1. Definition of "Value of the Funds".— For purposes of this guideline, "value of the funds" means the amount of the funds involved in the structuring or reporting conduct. The relevant statutes require monetary reporting without regard to whether the funds were lawfully or unlawfully obtained.

2. Bulk Cash Smuggling.— For purposes of subsection (b)(1)(B), "bulk cash smuggling" means

(A) knowingly concealing, with the intent to evade a currency reporting requirement under 31 U.S.C. § 5316, more than $10,000 in currency or other monetary instruments; and

(B) transporting or transferring (or attempting to transport or transfer) such currency or monetary instruments into or outside of the United States. "United States" has the meaning given that term in Application Note 1 of the Commentary to § 2B5.1 (Offenses Involving Counterfeit Bearer Obligations of the United States).

3. Enhancement for Pattern of Unlawful Activity.— For purposes of subsection (b)(2), "pattern of unlawful activity" means at least two separate occasions of unlawful activity involving a total amount of more than $100,000 in a 12-month period, without regard to whether any such occasion occurred during the course of the offense or resulted in a conviction for the conduct that occurred on that occasion.

Background: Some of the offenses covered by this guideline relate to records and reports of certain transactions involving currency and monetary instruments. These reports include Currency Transaction Reports, Currency and Monetary Instrument Reports, Reports of Foreign Bank and Financial Accounts, and Reports of Cash Payments Over $10,000 Received in a Trade or Business.

This guideline also covers offenses under 31 U.S.C. §§ 5318 and 5318A, pertaining to records, reporting and identification requirements, prohibited accounts involving certain foreign jurisdictions, foreign institutions, and foreign banks, and other types of transactions and types of accounts.

PART X — OTHER OFFENSES

§ 2X1.1. Attempt, Solicitation, or Conspiracy (Not Covered by a Specific Offense Guideline)

(a) Base Offense Level: The base offense level from the guideline for the substantive offense, plus any adjustments from such guideline for any intended offense conduct that can be established with reasonable certainty.

(b) Specific Offense Characteristics

(1) If an attempt, decrease by 3 levels, unless the defendant completed all the acts the defendant believed necessary for successful completion of the substantive offense or the circumstances demonstrate that the defendant was about to complete all such acts but for apprehension or interruption by some similar event beyond the defendant's control.

(2) If a conspiracy, decrease by 3 levels, unless the defendant or a co-conspirator completed all the acts the conspirators believed necessary on their part for the successful completion of the substantive offense or the circumstances demonstrate that the conspirators were about to complete all such acts but for apprehension or interruption by some similar event beyond their control.

(3)

(A) If a solicitation, decrease by 3 levels unless the person solicited to commit or aid the substantive offense completed all the acts he believed necessary for successful completion of the substantive offense or the circumstances demonstrate that the person was about to complete all such acts but for apprehension or interruption by some similar event beyond such person's control.

(B) If the statute treats solicitation of the substantive offense identically with the substantive offense, do not apply subdivision (A) above; i.e., the offense level for solicitation is the same as that for the substantive offense.

(c) Cross Reference

(1) When an attempt, solicitation, or conspiracy is expressly covered by another offense guideline section, apply that guideline section.

(d) Special Instruction

(1) Subsection (b) shall not apply to:

(A) Any of the following offenses, if such offense involved, or was intended to promote, a federal crime of terrorism as defined in 18 U.S.C. § 2332b(g)(5): 18 U.S.C. § 81; 18 U.S.C. § 930(c); 18 U.S.C. § 1362; 18 U.S.C. § 1363; 18 U.S.C. § 1992(a)(1)–(a)(7), (a)(9), (a)(10); 18 U.S.C. § 2339A; 18 U.S.C. § 2340A; 49 U.S.C. § 46504; 49 U.S.C. § 46505; and 49 U.S.C. § 60123(b).

(B) Any of the following offenses: 18 U.S.C. § 32; and 18 U.S.C. § 2332a.

COMMENTARY

Statutory Provisions: 18 U.S.C. §§ 371, 372, 2271, 2282A, 2282B. For additional statutory provision(s), see Appendix A (Statutory Index).

Application Notes:

1. Certain attempts, conspiracies, and solicitations are expressly covered by other offense guidelines.

Offense guidelines that expressly cover attempts include:

§§ 2A2.1, 2A3.1, 2A3.2, 2A3.3, 2A3.4, 2A4.2, 2A5.1;

§§ 2C1.1, 2C1.2;

§§ 2D1.1, 2D1.2, 2D1.5, 2D1.6, 2D1.7, 2D1.8, 2D1.9, 2D1.10, 2D1.11, 2D1.12, 2D1.13, 2D2.1, 2D2.2, 2D3.1, 2D3.2;

§ 2E5.1;

§ 2M6.1;

§ 2N1.1;

§ 2Q1.4.

Offense guidelines that expressly cover conspiracies include:

§ 2A1.5;

§§ 2D1.1, 2D1.2, 2D1.5, 2D1.6, 2D1.7, 2D1.8, 2D1.9, 2D1.10, 2D1.11, 2D1.12, 2D1.13, 2D2.1, 2D2.2, 2D3.1, 2D3.2;

§ 2H1.1;

§ 2M6.1;

§ 2T1.9.

Offense guidelines that expressly cover solicitations include:

§ 2A1.5;

§§ 2C1.1, 2C1.2;

§ 2E5.1.

2. "Substantive offense," as used in this guideline, means the offense that the defendant was convicted of soliciting, attempting, or conspiring to commit. Under § 2X1.1(a), the base offense level will be the same as that for the substantive offense. But the only specific offense characteristics from the guideline for the substantive offense that apply are those that are determined to have been specifically intended or actually occurred. Speculative specific offense characteristics will not be applied. For example, if two defendants are arrested during the conspiratorial stage of planning an armed bank robbery, the offense level ordinarily would not include aggravating factors regarding possible injury to others, hostage taking, discharge of a weapon, or obtaining a large sum of money, because such factors would be speculative. The offense level would simply reflect the level applicable to robbery of a financial institution, with the enhancement for possession of a weapon. If it was established that the defendants actually intended to physically restrain the teller, the specific offense characteristic for physical restraint would be added. In an attempted theft, the value of the items that the defendant attempted to steal would be considered.

3. If the substantive offense is not covered by a specific guideline, see § 2X5.1 (Other Offenses).

4. In certain cases, the participants may have completed (or have been about to complete but for apprehension or interruption) all of the acts necessary for the successful completion of part, but not all, of the intended offense. In such cases, the offense level for the count (or group of closely related multiple counts) is whichever of the following is greater: the offense level for the intended offense minus 3 levels (under § 2X1.1(b)(1), (b)(2), or (b)(3)(A)), or the offense level for the part of the offense for which the necessary acts were completed (or about to be completed but for apprehension or interruption). For example, where the intended offense was the theft of $800,000 but the participants completed (or were about to complete) only the acts necessary to steal $30,000, the offense level is the offense level for the theft of $800,000 minus 3 levels, or the offense level for the theft of $30,000, whichever is greater.

In the case of multiple counts that are not closely related counts, whether the 3-level reduction under § 2X1.1(b)(1), (b)(2), or (b)(3)(A) applies is determined separately for each count.

Background: In most prosecutions for conspiracies or attempts, the substantive offense was substantially completed or was interrupted or prevented on the verge of completion by the intercession of law enforcement authorities or the victim. In such cases, no reduction of the offense level is warranted. Sometimes, however, the arrest occurs well before the defendant or any coconspirator has completed the acts necessary for the substantive offense. Under such circumstances, a reduction of 3 levels is provided under § 2X1.1(b)(1) or (2).

§ 2X2.1. Aiding and abetting

The offense level is the same level as that for the underlying offense.

COMMENTARY

Statutory Provisions: 18 U.S.C. §§ 2, 2284, 2339, 2339A, 2339C(a)(1)(A).

Application Note:

1. Definition.— For purposes of this guideline, "underlying offense" means the offense the defendant is convicted of aiding or abetting, or in the case of a violation of 18 U.S.C. § 2339A or § 2339C(a)(1)(A), "underlying offense" means the offense the defendant is convicted of having materially supported or provided or collected funds for, prior to or during its commission.

Background: A defendant convicted of aiding and abetting is punishable as a principal. 18 U.S.C. § 2. This section provides that aiding and abetting the commission of an offense has the same offense level as the underlying offense. An adjustment for a mitigating role (§ 3B1.2) may be applicable.

§ 2X3.1. Accessory After the Fact

(a) Base Offense Level:

(1) 6 levels lower than the offense level for the underlying offense, except as provided in subdivisions (2) and (3).

(2) The base offense level under this guideline shall be not less than level 4.

(3)

(A) The base offense level under this guideline shall be not more than level 30, except as provided in subdivision (B).

(B) In any case in which the conduct is limited to harboring a fugitive, other than a case described in subdivision (C), the base offense level under this guideline shall be not more than level 20.

(C) The limitation in subdivision (B) shall not apply in any case in which

(i) the defendant is convicted under 18 U.S.C. § 2339 or § 2339A; or

(ii) the conduct involved harboring a person who committed any offense listed in18 U.S.C. § 2339 or § 2339A or who committed any offense involving or intending to promote a federal crime of terrorism, as defined in 18 U.S.C. § 2332b(g)(5). In such a case, the base offense level under this guideline shall be not more than level 30, as provided in subdivision (A).

COMMENTARY

Statutory Provisions: 18 U.S.C. §§ 3, 757, 1071, 1072, 2284, 2339, 2339A, 2339C(c)(2)(A), (c)(2)(B) (but only with respect to funds known or intended to have been provided or collected in violation of 18 U.S.C. § 2339C(a)(1)(A)).

Application Notes:

1. Definition.— For purposes of this guideline, "underlying offense" means the offense as to which the defendant is convicted of being an accessory, or in the case of a violation of 18 U.S.C. § 2339A, "underlying offense" means the offense the defendant is convicted of having materially supported after its commission (i.e., in connection with the concealment of or an escape from that offense), or in the case of a violation of 18 U.S.C. § 2339C(c)(2)(A), "underlying offense" means the violation of 18 U.S.C. § 2339B with respect to which the material support or resources were concealed or disguised. Apply the base offense level plus any applicable specific offense characteristics that were known, or reasonably should have been known, by the defendant; see Application Note 10 of the Commentary to § 1B1.3 (Relevant Conduct).

2. Application of Mitigating Role Adjustment.— The adjustment from § 3B1.2 (Mitigating Role) normally would not apply because an adjustment for reduced culpability is incorporated in the base offense level.

CHAPTER THREE — ADJUSTMENTS

PART B — ROLE IN THE OFFENSE

§ 3B1.1. Aggravating Role

Based on the defendant's role in the offense, increase the offense level as follows:

(a) If the defendant was an organizer or leader of a criminal activity that involved five or more participants or was otherwise extensive, increase by 4 levels.

(b) If the defendant was a manager or supervisor (but not an organizer or leader) and the criminal activity involved five or more participants or was otherwise extensive, increase by 3 levels.

(c) If the defendant was an organizer, leader, manager, or supervisor in any criminal activity other than described in (a) or (b), increase by 2 levels.

COMMENTARY

Application Notes:

1. A "participant" is a person who is criminally responsible for the commission of the offense, but need not have been convicted. A person who is not criminally responsible for the commission of the offense (e.g., an undercover law enforcement officer) is not a participant.

2. To qualify for an adjustment under this section, the defendant must have been the organizer, leader, manager, or supervisor of one or more other participants. An upward departure may be warranted, however, in the case of a defendant who did not organize, lead, manage, or supervise another participant, but who nevertheless exercised management responsibility over the property, assets, or activities of a criminal organization.

3. In assessing whether an organization is "otherwise extensive," all persons involved during the course of the entire offense are to be considered. Thus, a fraud that involved only three participants but used the unknowing services of many outsiders could be considered extensive.

4. In distinguishing a leadership and organizational role from one of mere management or supervision, titles such as "kingpin" or "boss" are not controlling. Factors the court should consider include the exercise of decision making authority, the nature of participation in the commission of the offense, the recruitment of accomplices, the claimed right to a larger share of the fruits of the crime, the degree of participation in planning or organizing the offense, the nature and scope of the illegal activity, and the degree of control and authority exercised over others. There can, of course, be more than one person who qualifies as a leader or organizer of a criminal association or conspiracy. This adjustment does not apply to a defendant who merely suggests committing the offense.

Background: This section provides a range of adjustments to increase the offense level based upon the size of a criminal organization (i.e., the number of participants in the offense) and the degree to which the defendant was responsible for committing the offense. This adjustment is included primarily because of concerns about relative responsibility. However, it is also likely that persons who exercise a supervisory or managerial role in the commission of an offense tend to profit more from it and present a greater danger to the public and/or are more likely to recidivate. The Commission's intent is that this adjustment should increase with both the size of the organization and the degree of the defendant's responsibility.

In relatively small criminal enterprises that are not otherwise to be considered as extensive in scope or in planning or preparation, the distinction between organization and leadership, and that of management or supervision, is of less significance than in larger enterprises that tend to have clearly delineated divisions of responsibility. This is reflected in the inclusiveness of § 3B1.1(c).

§ 3B1.3. Abuse of Position of Trust or Use of Special Skill

If the defendant abused a position of public or private trust, or used a special skill, in a manner that significantly facilitated the commission or concealment of the offense, increase by 2 levels. This adjustment may not be employed if an abuse of trust or skill is included in the base offense level or specific offense characteristic. If this adjustment is based upon an abuse of a position of trust, it may be employed in addition to an adjustment under § 3B1.1 (Aggravating Role); if this adjustment is based solely on the use of a special skill, it may not be employed in addition to an adjustment under § 3B1.1 (Aggravating Role).

COMMENTARY

Application Notes:

1. Definition of "Public or Private Trust".— "Public or private trust" refers to a position of public or private trust characterized by professional or managerial discretion (i.e., substantial discretionary judgment that is ordinarily given considerable deference). Persons holding such positions ordinarily are subject to significantly less supervision than employees whose responsibilities are primarily non-discretionary in nature. For this adjustment to apply, the position of public or private trust must have contributed in some significant way to facilitating the commission or concealment of the offense (e.g., by making the detection of the offense or the defendant's responsibility for the offense more difficult). This adjustment, for example, applies in the case of an embezzlement of a client's funds by an attorney serving as a guardian, a bank executive's fraudulent loan scheme, or the criminal sexual abuse of a patient by a physician under the guise of an examination. This adjustment does not apply in the case of an embezzlement or theft by an ordinary bank teller or hotel clerk because such positions are not characterized by the above-described factors.

2. Application of Adjustment in Certain Circumstances.— Notwithstanding Application Note 1, or any other provision of this guideline, an adjustment under this guideline shall apply to the following:

   (A) An employee of the United States Postal Service who engages in the theft or destruction of undelivered United States mail.

(B) A defendant who exceeds or abuses the authority of his or her position in order to obtain, transfer, or issue unlawfully, or use without authority, any means of identification. "Means of identification" has the meaning given that term in 18 U.S.C. § 1028(d)(7). The following are examples to which this subdivision would apply:

(i) an employee of a state motor vehicle department who exceeds or abuses the authority of his or her position by knowingly issuing a driver's license based on false, incomplete, or misleading information;

(ii) a hospital orderly who exceeds or abuses the authority of his or her position by obtaining or misusing patient identification information from a patient chart; and

(iii) a volunteer at a charitable organization who exceeds or abuses the authority of his or her position by obtaining or misusing identification information from a donor's file.

3. This adjustment also applies in a case in which the defendant provides sufficient indicia to the victim that the defendant legitimately holds a position of private or public trust when, in fact, the defendant does not. For example, the adjustment applies in the case of a defendant who (A) perpetrates a financial fraud by leading an investor to believe the defendant is a legitimate investment broker; or (B) perpetrates a fraud by representing falsely to a patient or employer that the defendant is a licensed physician. In making the misrepresentation, the defendant assumes a position of trust, relative to the victim, that provides the defendant with the same opportunity to commit a difficult-to-detect crime that the defendant would have had if the position were held legitimately.

4. "Special skill" refers to a skill not possessed by members of the general public and usually requiring substantial education, training or licensing. Examples would include pilots, lawyers, doctors, accountants, chemists, and demolition experts.

5. The following additional illustrations of an abuse of a position of trust pertain to theft or embezzlement from employee pension or welfare benefit plans or labor unions:

(A) If the offense involved theft or embezzlement from an employee pension or welfare benefit plan and the defendant was a fiduciary of the benefit plan, an adjustment under this section for abuse of a position of trust will apply. "Fiduciary of the benefit plan" is defined in 29 U.S.C. § 1002(21)(A) to mean a person who exercises any discretionary authority or control in respect to the management of such plan or exercises authority or control in respect to management or disposition of its assets, or who renders investment advice for a fee or other direct or indirect compensation with respect to any moneys or other property of such plan, or has any authority or responsibility to do so, or who has any discretionary authority or responsibility in the administration of such plan.

(B) If the offense involved theft or embezzlement from a labor union and the defendant was a union officer or occupied a position of trust in the union (as set forth in 29 U.S.C. § 501(a)), an adjustment under this section for an abuse of a position of trust will apply.

Background: This adjustment applies to persons who abuse their positions of trust or their special skills to facilitate significantly the commission or concealment of a crime. The adjustment also applies to persons who provide sufficient indicia to the victim that they legitimately hold a position of public or private trust when, in fact, they do not. Such persons generally are viewed as more culpable.

PART C — OBSTRUCTION AND RELATED ADJUSTMENTS

§ 3C1.1.　Obstructing or Impeding the Administration of Justice

If

(A) the defendant willfully obstructed or impeded, or attempted to obstruct or impede, the administration of justice with respect to the investigation, prosecution, or sentencing of the instant offense of conviction, and

(B) the obstructive conduct related to

(i) the defendant's offense of conviction and any relevant conduct; or

(ii) a closely related offense, increase the offense level by 2 levels.

COMMENTARY

Application Notes:

1. In General.— This adjustment applies if the defendant's obstructive conduct

(A) occurred with respect to the investigation, prosecution, or sentencing of the defendant's instant offense of conviction, and

(B) related to

(i) the defendant's offense of conviction and any relevant conduct; or

(ii) an otherwise closely related case, such as that of a co-defendant.

Obstructive conduct that occurred prior to the start of the investigation of the instant offense of conviction may be covered by this guideline if the conduct was purposefully calculated, and likely, to thwart the investigation or prosecution of the offense of conviction.

2. Limitations on Applicability of Adjustment.— This provision is not intended to punish a defendant for the exercise of a constitutional right. A defendant's denial of guilt (other than a denial of guilt under oath that constitutes perjury), refusal to admit guilt or provide information to a probation officer, or refusal to enter a plea of guilty is not a basis for application of this provision. In applying this provision in respect to alleged false testimony or statements by the defendant, the court should be cognizant that inaccurate testimony or statements sometimes may result from confusion, mistake, or faulty memory and, thus, not all inaccurate testimony or statements necessarily reflect a willful attempt to obstruct justice.

3. Covered Conduct Generally.— Obstructive conduct can vary widely in nature, degree of planning, and seriousness. Application Note 4 sets forth examples of the types of conduct to which this adjustment is intended to apply. Application Note 5 sets forth examples of less serious forms of conduct to which this enhancement is not intended to apply, but that ordinarily can appropriately be sanctioned by the determination of the particular sentence within the otherwise applicable guideline range. Although the conduct to which this adjustment applies is not subject to precise definition, comparison of the examples set forth in Application Notes 4 and 5 should assist the court in determining whether application of this adjustment is warranted in a particular case.

4. Examples of Covered Conduct.— The following is a non-exhaustive list of examples of the types of conduct to which this adjustment applies:

(A) threatening, intimidating, or otherwise unlawfully influencing a co-defendant, witness, or juror, directly or indirectly, or attempting to do so;

(B) committing, suborning, or attempting to suborn perjury, including during the course of a civil proceeding if such perjury pertains to conduct that forms the basis of the offense of conviction;

(C) producing or attempting to produce a false, altered, or counterfeit document or record during an official investigation or judicial proceeding;

(D) destroying or concealing or directing or procuring another person to destroy or conceal evidence that is material to an official investigation or judicial proceeding (e.g., shredding a document or destroying ledgers upon learning that an official investigation has commenced or is about to commence), or attempting to do so; however, if such conduct occurred contemporaneously with arrest (e.g., attempting to swallow or throw away a controlled substance), it shall not, standing alone, be sufficient to warrant an adjustment for obstruction unless it resulted in a material hindrance to the official investigation or prosecution of the instant offense or the sentencing of the offender;

(E) escaping or attempting to escape from custody before trial or sentencing; or willfully failing to appear, as ordered, for a judicial proceeding;

(F) providing materially false information to a judge or magistrate judge;

(G) providing a materially false statement to a law enforcement officer that significantly obstructed or impeded the official investigation or prosecution of the instant offense;

(H) providing materially false information to a probation officer in respect to a presentence or other investigation for the court;

(I) other conduct prohibited by obstruction of justice provisions under Title 18, United States Code (e.g., 18 U.S.C. §§ 1510, 1511);

(J) failing to comply with a restraining order or injunction issued pursuant to 21 U.S.C. § 853(e) or with an order to repatriate property issued pursuant to 21 U.S.C. § 853(p);

(K) threatening the victim of the offense in an attempt to prevent the victim from reporting the conduct constituting the offense of conviction.

This adjustment also applies to any other obstructive conduct in respect to the official investigation, prosecution, or sentencing of the instant offense where there is a separate count of conviction for such conduct.

5. Examples of Conduct Ordinarily Not Covered.— Some types of conduct ordinarily do not warrant application of this adjustment but may warrant a greater sentence within the otherwise applicable guideline range or affect the determination of whether other guideline adjustments apply (e.g., § 3E1.1 (Acceptance of Responsibility)). However, if the defendant is convicted of a separate count for such conduct, this adjustment will apply and increase the offense level for the underlying offense (i.e., the offense with respect to which the obstructive conduct occurred). See Application Note 8, below.

The following is a non-exhaustive list of examples of the types of conduct to which this application note applies:

(A) providing a false name or identification document at arrest, except where such conduct actually resulted in a significant hindrance to the investigation or prosecution of the instant offense;

(B) making false statements, not under oath, to law enforcement officers, unless Application Note 4(G) above applies;

(C) providing incomplete or misleading information, not amounting to a material falsehood, in respect to a presentence investigation;

(D) avoiding or fleeing from arrest (see, however, § 3C1.2 (Reckless Endangerment During Flight));

(E) lying to a probation or pretrial services officer about defendant's drug use while on pretrial release, although such conduct may be a factor in determining whether to reduce the defendant's sentence under § 3E1.1 (Acceptance of Responsibility).

6. "Material" Evidence Defined.— "Material" evidence, fact, statement, or information, as used in this section, means evidence, fact, statement, or information that, if believed, would tend to influence or affect the issue under determination.

7. Inapplicability of Adjustment in Certain Circumstances.— If the defendant is convicted of an offense covered by § 2J1.1 (Contempt), § 2J1.2 (Obstruction of Justice), § 2J1.3 (Perjury or Subornation of Perjury; Bribery of Witness), § 2J1.5 (Failure to Appear by Material Witness), § 2J1.6 (Failure to Appear by Defendant), § 2J1.9 (Payment to Witness), § 2X3.1 (Accessory After the Fact), or § 2X4.1 (Misprision of Felony), this adjustment is not to be applied to the offense level for that offense except if a significant further obstruction occurred during the investigation, prosecution, or sentencing of the obstruction offense itself (e.g., if the defendant threatened a witness during the course of the prosecution for the obstruction offense).

Similarly, if the defendant receives an enhancement under § 2D1.1(b)(15)(D), do not apply this adjustment.

8. Grouping Under § 3D1.2(c).— If the defendant is convicted both of an obstruction offense (e.g., 18 U.S.C. § 3146 (Penalty for failure to appear); 18 U.S.C. § 1621 (Perjury generally)) and an underlying offense (the offense with respect to which the obstructive conduct occurred), the count for the obstruction offense will be grouped with the count for the underlying offense under subsection (c) of § 3D1.2 (Groups of Closely Related Counts). The offense level for that group of closely related counts will be the offense level for the underlying offense increased by the 2-level adjustment specified by this section, or the offense level for the obstruction offense, whichever is greater.

9. Accountability for § 1B1.3(a)(1)(A) Conduct.— Under this section, the defendant is accountable for the defendant's own conduct and for conduct that the defendant aided or abetted, counseled, commanded, induced, procured, or willfully caused.

PART D — MULTIPLE COUNTS

§ 3D1.1. Procedure for Determining Offense Level on Multiple Counts

(a) When a defendant has been convicted of more than one count, the court shall:

(1) Group the counts resulting in conviction into distinct Groups of Closely Related Counts ("Groups") by applying the rules specified in § 3D1.2.

(2) Determine the offense level applicable to each Group by applying the rules specified in § 3D1.3.

(3) Determine the combined offense level applicable to all Groups taken together by applying the rules specified in § 3D1.4.

(b) Exclude from the application of §§ 3D1.2–3D1.5 the following:

(1) Any count for which the statute

(A) specifies a term of imprisonment to be imposed; and

(B) requires that such term of imprisonment be imposed to run consecutively to any other term of imprisonment. Sentences for such counts are governed by the provisions of § 5G1.2(a).

(2) Any count of conviction under 18 U.S.C. § 1028A. See Application Note 2(B) of the Commentary to § 5G1.2 (Sentencing on Multiple Counts of Conviction) for guidance on how sentences for multiple counts of conviction under 18 U.S.C. § 1028A should be imposed.

COMMENTARY

Application Notes:

1. In General.— For purposes of sentencing multiple counts of conviction, counts can be

(A) contained in the same indictment or information; or

(B) contained in different indictments or informations for which sentences are to be imposed at the same time or in a consolidated proceeding.

2. Subsection (b)(1) applies if a statute

(A) specifies a term of imprisonment to be imposed; and

(B) requires that such term of imprisonment be imposed to run consecutively to any other term of imprisonment. See, e.g., 18 U.S.C. § 924(c) (requiring mandatory minimum terms of imprisonment, based on the conduct involved, to run consecutively). The multiple count rules set out under this Part do not apply to a count of conviction covered by subsection (b). However, a count covered by subsection (b)(1) may affect the offense level determination for other counts. For example, a defendant is convicted of one count of bank robbery (18 U.S.C. § 2113), and one count of use of a firearm in the commission of a crime of violence (18 U.S.C. § 924(c)). The two counts are not grouped together pursuant to this guideline, and, to avoid unwarranted double counting, the offense level for the bank robbery count under § 2B3.1 (Robbery) is computed without application of the enhancement for weapon possession or use as otherwise required by subsection (b)(2) of that guideline. Pursuant to 18 U.S.C. § 924(c), the mandatory minimum five-year sentence on the weapon-use count runs consecutively to the guideline sentence imposed on the bank robbery count. See § 5G1.2(a).

Unless specifically instructed, subsection (b)(1) does not apply when imposing a sentence under a statute that requires the imposition of a consecutive term of imprisonment only if a term of imprisonment is imposed (i.e., the statute does not otherwise require a term of imprisonment to be imposed). See, e.g., 18 U.S.C. § 3146 (Penalty for failure to appear); 18 U.S.C. § 924(a)(4) (regarding penalty for 18 U.S.C. § 922(q) (possession or discharge of a firearm in a school zone)); 18 U.S.C. § 1791(c) (penalty for providing or possessing a controlled substance in prison). Accordingly, the multiple count rules set out under this Part do apply to a count of conviction under this type of statute.

Background: This section outlines the procedure to be used for determining the combined offense level. After any adjustments from Chapter 3, Part E (Acceptance of Responsibility) and Chapter 4, Part B (Career Offenders and Criminal Livelihood) are made, this combined offense level is used to determine the guideline sentence range. Chapter Five (Determining the Sentence) discusses how to determine the sentence from the (combined) offense level; § 5G1.2 deals specifically with determining the sentence of imprisonment when convictions on multiple counts are involved. References in Chapter Five (Determining the Sentence) to the "offense level" should be treated as referring to the combined offense level after all subsequent adjustments have been made.

§ 3D1.2. Groups of Closely Related Counts

All counts involving substantially the same harm shall be grouped together into a single Group. Counts involve substantially the same harm within the meaning of this rule:

(a) When counts involve the same victim and the same act or transaction.

(b) When counts involve the same victim and two or more acts or transactions connected by a common criminal objective or constituting part of a common scheme or plan.

(c) When one of the counts embodies conduct that is treated as a specific offense characteristic in, or other adjustment to, the guideline applicable to another of the counts.

(d) When the offense level is determined largely on the basis of the total amount of harm or loss, the quantity of a substance involved, or some other measure of aggregate harm, or if the offense behavior is ongoing or continuous in nature and the offense guideline is written to cover such behavior.

Offenses covered by the following guidelines are to be grouped under this subsection:

§ 2A3.5;

§§ 2B1.1, 2B1.4, 2B1.5, 2B4.1, 2B5.1, 2B5.3, 2B6.1;

§§ 2C1.1, 2C1.2, 2C1.8;

§§ 2D1.1, 2D1.2, 2D1.5, 2D1.11, 2D1.13;

§§ 2E4.1, 2E5.1;

§§ 2G2.2, 2G3.1;

§ 2K2.1;

§§ 2L1.1, 2L2.1;

§ 2N3.1;

§ 2Q2.1;

§ 2R1.1;

§§ 2S1.1, 2S1.3;

§§ 2T1.1, 2T1.4, 2T1.6, 2T1.7, 2T1.9, 2T2.1, 2T3.1.

Specifically excluded from the operation of this subsection are:

all offenses in Chapter Two, Part A (except § 2A3.5);

§§ 2B2.1, 2B2.3, 2B3.1, 2B3.2, 2B3.3;

§ 2C1.5;

§§ 2D2.1, 2D2.2, 2D2.3;

§§ 2E1.3, 2E1.4, 2E2.1;

§§ 2G1.1, 2G2.1;

§§ 2H1.1, 2H2.1, 2H4.1;

§§ 2L2.2, 2L2.5;

§§ 2M2.1, 2M2.3, 2M3.1, 2M3.2, 2M3.3, 2M3.4, 2M3.5, 2M3.9;

§§ 2P1.1, 2P1.2, 2P1.3;

§ 2X6.1.

For multiple counts of offenses that are not listed, grouping under this subsection may or may not be appropriate; a case-by-case determination must be made based upon the facts of the case and the applicable guidelines (including specific offense characteristics and other adjustments) used to determine the offense level.

Exclusion of an offense from grouping under this subsection does not necessarily preclude grouping under another subsection.

COMMENTARY

Application Notes:

1. Subsections (a)–(d) set forth circumstances in which counts are to be grouped together into a single Group. Counts are to be grouped together into a single Group if any one or more of the subsections provide for such grouping. Counts for which the statute

(A) specifies a term of imprisonment to be imposed; and

(B) requires that such term of imprisonment be imposed to run consecutively to any other term of imprisonment are excepted from application of the multiple count rules. See § 3D1.1(b)(1); id., comment. (n.1).

2. The term "victim" is not intended to include indirect or secondary victims. Generally, there will be one person who is directly and most seriously affected by the offense and is therefore identifiable as the victim. For offenses in which there are no identifiable victims (e.g., drug or immigration offenses, where society at large is the victim), the "victim" for purposes of subsections (a) and (b) is the societal interest that is harmed. In such cases, the counts are grouped together when the societal interests that are harmed are closely related. Where one count, for example, involves unlawfully entering the United States and the other involves possession of fraudulent evidence of citizenship, the counts are grouped together because the societal interests harmed (the interests protected by laws governing immigration) are closely related. In contrast, where one count involves the sale of controlled substances and the other involves an immigration law violation, the counts are not grouped together because different societal interests are harmed. Ambiguities should be resolved in accordance with the purpose of this section as stated in the lead paragraph, i.e., to identify and group "counts involving substantially the same harm."

3. Under subsection (a), counts are to be grouped together when they represent essentially a single injury or are part of a single criminal episode or transaction involving the same victim.

When one count charges an attempt to commit an offense and the other charges the commission of that offense, or when one count charges an offense based on a general prohibition and the other charges violation of a specific prohibition encompassed in the general prohibition, the counts will be grouped together under subsection (a).

Examples: (1) The defendant is convicted of forging and uttering the same check. The counts are to be grouped together. (2) The defendant is convicted of kidnapping and assaulting the victim during the course of the kidnapping. The counts are to be grouped together. (3) The defendant is convicted of bid rigging (an antitrust offense) and of mail fraud for signing and mailing a false statement that the bid was competitive. The counts are to be grouped together. (4) The defendant is convicted of two counts of assault on a federal officer for shooting at the same officer twice while attempting to prevent apprehension as part of a single criminal episode. The counts are to be grouped together. (5) The defendant is convicted of three counts of unlawfully bringing aliens into the United States, all counts arising out of a single incident. The three counts are to be grouped together. But: (6) The defendant is convicted of two counts of assault on a federal officer for shooting at the officer on two separate days. The counts are not to be grouped together.

4. Subsection (b) provides that counts that are part of a single course of conduct with a single criminal objective and represent essentially one composite harm to the same victim are to be grouped together, even if they constitute legally distinct offenses occurring at different times. This provision does not authorize the grouping of offenses that cannot be considered to represent essentially one composite harm (e.g., robbery of the same victim on different occasions involves multiple, separate instances of fear and risk of harm, not one composite harm).

When one count charges a conspiracy or solicitation and the other charges a substantive offense that was the sole object of the conspiracy or solicitation, the counts will be grouped together under subsection (b).

Examples: (1) The defendant is convicted of one count of conspiracy to commit extortion and one count of extortion for the offense he conspired to commit. The counts are to be grouped together. (2) The defendant is convicted of two counts of mail fraud and one count of wire fraud, each in furtherance of a single fraudulent scheme. The counts are to be grouped together, even if the mailings and telephone call occurred on different days. (3) The defendant is convicted of one count of auto theft and one count of altering the vehicle identification number of the car he stole. The counts are to be grouped together. (4) The defendant is convicted of two counts of distributing a controlled substance, each count involving a separate sale of 10 grams of cocaine that is part of a common scheme or plan. In addition, a finding is made that there are two other sales, also part of the common scheme or plan, each involving 10 grams of cocaine. The total amount of all four sales (40 grams of cocaine) will be used to determine the offense level for each count under § 1B1.3(a)(2). The two counts will then be grouped together under either this subsection or subsection (d) to avoid double counting. But: (5) The defendant is convicted of two counts of rape for raping the same person on different days. The counts are not to be grouped together.

5. Subsection (c) provides that when conduct that represents a separate count, e.g., bodily injury or obstruction of justice, is also a specific offense characteristic in or other adjustment to another count, the count represented by that conduct is to be grouped with the count to which it constitutes an aggravating factor. This provision prevents "double counting" of offense behavior. Of course, this rule applies only if the offenses are closely related. It is not, for example, the intent of this rule that (assuming they could be joined together) a bank robbery on one occasion and an assault resulting in bodily injury on another occasion be grouped together. The bodily injury (the harm from the assault) would not be a specific

offense characteristic to the robbery and would represent a different harm. On the other hand, use of a firearm in a bank robbery and unlawful possession of that firearm are sufficiently related to warrant grouping of counts under this subsection. Frequently, this provision will overlap subsection (a), at least with respect to specific offense characteristics. However, a count such as obstruction of justice, which represents a Chapter Three adjustment and involves a different harm or societal interest than the underlying offense, is covered by subsection (c) even though it is not covered by subsection (a).

Sometimes there may be several counts, each of which could be treated as an aggravating factor to another more serious count, but the guideline for the more serious count provides an adjustment for only one occurrence of that factor. In such cases, only the count representing the most serious of those factors is to be grouped with the other count. For example, if in a robbery of a credit union on a military base the defendant is also convicted of assaulting two employees, one of whom is injured seriously, the assault with serious bodily injury would be grouped with the robbery count, while the remaining assault conviction would be treated separately.

A cross reference to another offense guideline does not constitute "a specific offense characteristic . . . or other adjustment" within the meaning of subsection (c). For example, the guideline for bribery of a public official contains a cross reference to the guideline for a conspiracy to commit the offense that the bribe was to facilitate. Nonetheless, if the defendant were convicted of one count of securities fraud and one count of bribing a public official to facilitate the fraud, the two counts would not be grouped together by virtue of the cross reference. If, however, the bribe was given for the purpose of hampering a criminal investigation into the offense, it would constitute obstruction and under § 3C1.1 would result in a 2-level enhancement to the offense level for the fraud. Under the latter circumstances, the counts would be grouped together.

6. Subsection (d) likely will be used with the greatest frequency. It provides that most property crimes (except robbery, burglary, extortion and the like), drug offenses, firearms offenses, and other crimes where the guidelines are based primarily on quantity or contemplate continuing behavior are to be grouped together. The list of instances in which this subsection should be applied is not exhaustive. Note, however, that certain guidelines are specifically excluded from the operation of subsection (d).

A conspiracy, attempt, or solicitation to commit an offense is covered under subsection (d) if the offense that is the object of the conspiracy, attempt, or solicitation is covered under subsection (d).

Counts involving offenses to which different offense guidelines apply are grouped together under subsection (d) if the offenses are of the same general type and otherwise meet the criteria for grouping under this subsection. In such cases, the offense guideline that results in the highest offense level is used; see § 3D1.3(b). The "same general type" of offense is to be construed broadly.

Examples: (1) The defendant is convicted of five counts of embezzling money from a bank. The five counts are to be grouped together. (2) The defendant is convicted of two counts of theft of social security checks and three counts of theft from the mail, each from a different victim. All five counts are to be grouped together. (3) The defendant is convicted of five counts of mail fraud and ten counts of wire fraud. Although the counts arise from various schemes, each involves a monetary objective. All fifteen counts are to be grouped together. (4) The defendant is convicted of three counts of unlicensed dealing in firearms. All three counts are to be grouped together. (5) The defendant is convicted of one count of selling heroin, one count of selling PCP, and one count of selling cocaine. The counts are to be grouped together. The Commentary to § 2D1.1 provides rules for combining (adding) quantities of different drugs to determine a single combined offense level. (6) The defendant is convicted of three counts of tax evasion. The counts are to be grouped together. (7) The defendant is convicted of three counts of discharging toxic substances from a single facility. The counts are to be grouped together. (8) The defendant is convicted on two counts of check forgery and one count of uttering the first of the forged checks. All three counts are to be grouped together. Note, however, that the uttering count is first grouped with the first forgery count under subsection (a) of this guideline, so that the monetary amount of that check counts only once when the rule in § 3D1.3(b) is applied. But: (9) The defendant is convicted of three counts of bank robbery. The counts are not to be grouped together, nor are the amounts of money involved to be added.

7. A single case may result in application of several of the rules in this section. Thus, for example, example (8) in the discussion of subsection (d) involves an application of § 3D1.2(a) followed by an application of § 3D1.2(d). Note also that a Group may consist of a single count; conversely, all counts may form a single Group.

8. A defendant may be convicted of conspiring to commit several substantive offenses and also of committing one or more of the substantive offenses. In such cases, treat the conspiracy count as if it were several counts, each charging conspiracy to commit one of the substantive offenses. See § 1B1.2(d) and accompanying commentary. Then apply the ordinary grouping rules to determine the combined offense level based upon the substantive counts of which the defendant is convicted and the various acts cited by the conspiracy count that would constitute behavior of a substantive nature. Example: The defendant is convicted of two counts: conspiring to commit offenses A, B, and C, and committing offense A. Treat this as if the defendant was convicted of (1) committing offense A; (2) conspiracy to commit offense A; (3) conspiracy to commit offense B; and (4) conspiracy to commit offense C. Count (1) and count (2) are grouped together under § 3D1.2(b). Group the remaining counts, including the various acts cited by the conspiracy count that would constitute behavior of a substantive nature, according to the rules in this section.

Background: Ordinarily, the first step in determining the combined offense level in a case involving multiple counts is to identify those counts that are sufficiently related to be placed in the same Group of Closely Related Counts ("Group"). This section specifies four situations in which counts are to be grouped together. Although it appears last for conceptual reasons, subsection (d) probably will be used most frequently.

A primary consideration in this section is whether the offenses involve different victims. For example, a defendant may stab three prison guards in a single escape attempt. Some would argue that all counts arising out of a single transaction or occurrence should be grouped together even when there are distinct victims. Although such a proposal was considered, it was rejected because it probably would require departure in many cases in order to capture adequately the criminal behavior. Cases involving injury to distinct victims are sufficiently comparable, whether or not the injuries are inflicted in distinct transactions, so that each such count should be treated separately rather than grouped together. Counts involving different victims (or societal harms in the case of "victimless" crimes) are grouped together only as provided in subsection (c) or (d).

Even if counts involve a single victim, the decision as to whether to group them together may not always be clear cut. For example, how contemporaneous must two assaults on the same victim be in order to warrant grouping together as constituting a single transaction or occurrence? Existing case law may provide some guidance as to what constitutes distinct offenses, but such decisions often turn on the technical language of the statute and cannot be controlling. In interpreting this Part and resolving ambiguities, the court should look to the underlying policy of this Part as stated in the Introductory Commentary.

§ 3D1.3. Offense Level Applicable to Each Group of Closely Related Counts

Determine the offense level applicable to each of the Groups as follows:

(a) In the case of counts grouped together pursuant to § 3D1.2(a)–(c), the offense level applicable to a Group is the offense level, determined in accordance with Chapter Two and Parts A, B, and C of Chapter Three, for the most serious of the counts comprising the Group, i.e., the highest offense level of the counts in the Group.

(b) In the case of counts grouped together pursuant to § 3D1.2(d), the offense level applicable to a Group is the offense level corresponding to the aggregated quantity, determined in accordance with Chapter Two and Parts A, B and C of Chapter Three. When the counts involve offenses of the same general type to which different guidelines apply, apply the offense guideline that produces the highest offense level.

COMMENTARY

Application Notes:

1. The "offense level" for a count refers to the offense level from Chapter Two after all adjustments from Parts A, B, and C of Chapter Three.

2. When counts are grouped pursuant to § 3D1.2(a)–(c), the highest offense level of the counts in the group is used. Ordinarily, it is necessary to determine the offense level for each of the counts in a Group in order to ensure that the highest is correctly identified. Sometimes, it will be clear that one count in the Group cannot have a higher offense level than another, as with a count for an attempt or conspiracy to commit the completed offense. The formal determination of the offense level for such a count may be unnecessary.

3. When counts are grouped pursuant to § 3D1.2(d), the offense guideline

applicable to the aggregate behavior is used. If the counts in the Group are covered by different guidelines, use the guideline that produces the highest offense level. Determine whether the specific offense characteristics or adjustments from Chapter Three, Parts A, B, and C apply based upon the combined offense behavior taken as a whole. Note that guidelines for similar property offenses have been coordinated to produce identical offense levels, at least when substantial property losses are involved. However, when small sums are involved the differing specific offense characteristics that require increasing the offense level to a certain minimum may affect the outcome.

4. Sometimes the rule specified in this section may not result in incremental punishment for additional criminal acts because of the grouping rules. For example, if the defendant commits forcible criminal sexual abuse (rape), aggravated assault, and robbery, all against the same victim on a single occasion, all of the counts are grouped together under § 3D1.2. The aggravated assault will increase the guideline range for the rape. The robbery, however, will not. This is because the offense guideline for rape (§ 2A3.1) includes the most common aggravating factors, including injury, that data showed to be significant in actual practice. The additional factor of property loss ordinarily can be taken into account adequately within the guideline range for rape, which is fairly wide. However, an exceptionally large property loss in the course of the rape would provide grounds for an upward departure. See § 5K2.5 (Property Damage or Loss).

Background: This section provides rules for determining the offense level associated with each Group of Closely Related Counts. Summary examples of the application of these rules are provided at the end of the Commentary to this Part.

§ 3D1.4.   Determining the Combined Offense Level

The combined offense level is determined by taking the offense level applicable to the Group with the highest offense level and increasing that offense level by the amount indicated in the following table:

Number of Units	Increase in Offense Level
1	none
1 1/2	add 1 level
2	add 2 levels
2 1/2–3	add 3 levels
3 1/2–5	add 4 levels
More than 5	add 5 levels.

In determining the number of Units for purposes of this section:

(a) Count as one Unit the Group with the highest offense level. Count one additional Unit for each Group that is equally serious or from 1 to 4 levels less serious.

(b) Count as one-half Unit any Group that is 5 to 8 levels less serious than the Group with the highest offense level.

(c) Disregard any Group that is 9 or more levels less serious than the Group with the highest offense level. Such Groups will not increase the applicable offense level but may provide a reason for sentencing at the higher end of the sentencing range for the applicable offense level.

COMMENTARY

Application Notes:

1. Application of the rules in §§ 3D1.2 and 3D1.3 may produce a single Group of Closely Related Counts. In such cases, the combined offense level is the level corresponding to the Group determined in accordance with § 3D1.3.

2. The procedure for calculating the combined offense level when there is more than one Group of Closely Related Counts is as follows: First, identify the offense level applicable to the most serious Group; assign it one Unit. Next, determine the number of Units that the remaining Groups represent. Finally, increase the offense level for the most serious Group by the number of levels indicated in the table corresponding to the total number of Units.

Background: When Groups are of roughly comparable seriousness, each Group will represent one Unit. When the most serious Group carries an offense level substantially higher than that applicable to the other Groups, however, counting the lesser Groups fully for purposes of the table could add excessive punishment, possibly even more than those offenses would carry if prosecuted separately. To avoid this anomalous result and produce declining marginal punishment, Groups 9 or more levels less serious than the most serious Group should not be counted for purposes of the table, and that Groups 5 to 8 levels less serious should be treated as equal to one-half of a Group. Thus, if the most serious Group is at offense level 15 and if two other Groups are at level 10, there would be a total of two Units for purposes of the table (one plus one-half plus one-half) and the combined offense level would be 17. Inasmuch as the maximum increase provided in the guideline is 5 levels, departure would be warranted in the unusual case where the additional offenses resulted in a total of significantly more than 5 Units.

In unusual circumstances, the approach adopted in this section could produce adjustments for the additional counts that are inadequate or excessive. If there are several groups and the most serious offense is considerably more serious than all of the others, there will be no increase in the offense level resulting from the additional counts. Ordinarily, the court will have latitude to impose added punishment by sentencing toward the upper end of the range authorized for the most serious offense. Situations in which there will be inadequate scope for ensuring appropriate additional punishment for the additional crimes are likely to be unusual and can be handled by departure from the guidelines. Conversely, it is possible that if there are several minor offenses that are not grouped together, application of the rules in this Part could result in an excessive increase in the sentence range. Again, such situations should be infrequent and can be handled through departure. An alternative method for ensuring more precise adjustments would have been to determine the appropriate offense level adjustment through a more complicated mathematical formula; that approach was not adopted because of its complexity.

§ 3D1.5. Determining the Total Punishment

Use the combined offense level to determine the appropriate sentence in accordance with the provisions of Chapter Five.

COMMENTARY

This section refers the court to Chapter Five (Determining the Sentence) in order to determine the total punishment to be imposed based upon the combined offense level. The combined offense level is subject to adjustments from Chapter Three, Part E (Acceptance of Responsibility) and Chapter Four, Part B (Career Offenders and Criminal Livelihood).

Historical Note: Effective November 1, 1987.

Illustrations of the Operation of the Multiple-Count Rules

The following examples, drawn from presentence reports in the Commission's files, illustrate the operation of the guidelines for multiple counts. The examples are discussed summarily; a more thorough, step-by-step approach is recommended until the user is thoroughly familiar with the guidelines.

1. Defendant A was convicted on four counts, each charging robbery of a different bank. Each would represent a distinct Group. § 3D1.2. In each of the first three robberies, the offense level was 22 (20 plus a 2-level increase because a financial institution was robbed) (§ 2B3.1(b)). In the fourth robbery $12,000 was taken and a firearm was displayed; the offense level was therefore 28. As the first three counts are 6 levels lower than the fourth, each of the first three represents one-half unit for purposes of § 3D1.4. Altogether there are 2 1/2 Units, and the offense level for the most serious (28) is therefore increased by 3 levels under the table. The combined offense level is 31.

2. Defendant C was convicted on four counts: (1) distribution of 230 grams of cocaine; (2) distribution of 150 grams of cocaine; (3) distribution of 75 grams of heroin; (4) offering a DEA agent $20,000 to avoid prosecution. The combined offense level for drug offenses is determined by the total quantity of drugs, converted to marihuana equivalents (using the Drug Equivalency Tables in the Commentary to § 2D1.1 (Unlawful Manufacturing, Importing, Exporting, or Trafficking)). The first count translates into 46 kilograms of marihuana; the second count translates into 30 kilograms of marihuana; and the third count translates into 75 kilograms of marihuana. The total is 151 kilograms of marihuana. Under § 2D1.1, the combined offense level for the drug offenses is 24. In addition, because of the attempted bribe of the DEA agent, this offense level is increased by 2 levels to 26 under § 3C1.1 (Obstructing or Impeding the Administration of Justice). Because the conduct constituting the bribery offense is accounted for by § 3C1.1, it becomes part of the same Group as the drug offenses pursuant to § 3D1.2(c). The combined offense level is 26 pursuant to § 3D1.3(a), because the offense level for bribery (22) is less than the offense level for the drug offenses (26).

3. Defendant D was convicted of four counts arising out of a scheme pursuant to which the defendant received kickbacks from subcontractors. The counts were as follows: (1) The defendant received $27,000 from subcontractor A relating to

contract X (Mail Fraud). (2) The defendant received $12,000 from subcontractor A relating to contract X (Commercial Bribery). (3) The defendant received $15,000 from subcontractor A relating to contract Y (Mail Fraud). (4) The defendant received $20,000 from subcontractor B relating to contract Z (Commercial Bribery). The mail fraud counts are covered by § 2B1.1 (Theft, Property Destruction, and Fraud). The bribery counts are covered by § 2B4.1 (Bribery in Procurement of Bank Loan and Other Commercial Bribery), which treats the offense as a sophisticated fraud. The total money involved is $74,000, which results in an offense level of 16 under either § 2B1.1 (assuming the application of the "sophisticated means" enhancement in § 2B1.1(b)(10)) or § 2B4.1. Since these two guidelines produce identical offense levels, the combined offense level is 16.

PART E — ACCEPTANCE OF RESPONSIBILITY

§ 3E1.1. Acceptance of responsibility

(a) If the defendant clearly demonstrates acceptance of responsibility for his offense, decrease the offense level by 2 levels.

(b) If the defendant qualifies for a decrease under subsection (a), the offense level determined prior to the operation of subsection (a) is level 16 or greater, and upon motion of the government stating that the defendant has assisted authorities in the investigation or prosecution of his own misconduct by timely notifying authorities of his intention to enter a plea of guilty, thereby permitting the government to avoid preparing for trial and permitting the government and the court to allocate their resources efficiently, decrease the offense level by 1 additional level.

COMMENTARY

Application Notes:

1. In determining whether a defendant qualifies under subsection (a), appropriate considerations include, but are not limited to, the following:

   (A) truthfully admitting the conduct comprising the offense(s) of conviction, and truthfully admitting or not falsely denying any additional relevant conduct for which the defendant is accountable under § 1B1.3 (Relevant Conduct). Note that a defendant is not required to volunteer, or affirmatively admit, relevant conduct beyond the offense of conviction in order to obtain a reduction under subsection (a). A defendant may remain silent in respect to relevant conduct beyond the offense of conviction without affecting his ability to obtain a reduction under this subsection. However, a defendant who falsely denies, or frivolously contests, relevant conduct that the court determines to be true has acted in a manner inconsistent with acceptance of responsibility;

   (B) voluntary termination or withdrawal from criminal conduct or associations;

   (C) voluntary payment of restitution prior to adjudication of guilt;

   (D) voluntary surrender to authorities promptly after commission of the offense;

(E) voluntary assistance to authorities in the recovery of the fruits and instrumentalities of the offense;

(F) voluntary resignation from the office or position held during the commission of the offense;

(G) post-offense rehabilitative efforts (e.g., counseling or drug treatment); and

(H) the timeliness of the defendant's conduct in manifesting the acceptance of responsibility.

2. This adjustment is not intended to apply to a defendant who puts the government to its burden of proof at trial by denying the essential factual elements of guilt, is convicted, and only then admits guilt and expresses remorse. Conviction by trial, however, does not automatically preclude a defendant from consideration for such a reduction. In rare situations a defendant may clearly demonstrate an acceptance of responsibility for his criminal conduct even though he exercises his constitutional right to a trial. This may occur, for example, where a defendant goes to trial to assert and preserve issues that do not relate to factual guilt (e.g., to make a constitutional challenge to a statute or a challenge to the applicability of a statute to his conduct). In each such instance, however, a determination that a defendant has accepted responsibility will be based primarily upon pre-trial statements and conduct.

3. Entry of a plea of guilty prior to the commencement of trial combined with truthfully admitting the conduct comprising the offense of conviction, and truthfully admitting or not falsely denying any additional relevant conduct for which he is accountable under § 1B1.3 (Relevant Conduct) (see Application Note 1(A)), will constitute significant evidence of acceptance of responsibility for the purposes of subsection (a). However, this evidence may be outweighed by conduct of the defendant that is inconsistent with such acceptance of responsibility. A defendant who enters a guilty plea is not entitled to an adjustment under this section as a matter of right.

4. Conduct resulting in an enhancement under § 3C1.1 (Obstructing or Impeding the Administration of Justice) ordinarily indicates that the defendant has not accepted responsibility for his criminal conduct. There may, however, be extraordinary cases in which adjustments under both §§ 3C1.1 and 3E1.1 may apply.

5. The sentencing judge is in a unique position to evaluate a defendant's acceptance of responsibility. For this reason, the determination of the sentencing judge is entitled to great deference on review.

6. Subsection (a) provides a 2-level decrease in offense level. Subsection (b) provides an additional 1-level decrease in offense level for a defendant at offense level 16 or greater prior to the operation of subsection (a) who both qualifies for a decrease under subsection (a) and who has assisted authorities in the investigation or prosecution of his own misconduct by taking the steps set forth in subsection (b). The timeliness of the defendant's acceptance of responsibility is a consideration under both subsections, and is context specific. In general, the

conduct qualifying for a decrease in offense level under subsection (b) will occur particularly early in the case. For example, to qualify under subsection (b), the defendant must have notified authorities of his intention to enter a plea of guilty at a sufficiently early point in the process so that the government may avoid preparing for trial and the court may schedule its calendar efficiently.

Because the Government is in the best position to determine whether the defendant has assisted authorities in a manner that avoids preparing for trial, an adjustment under subsection (b) may only be granted upon a formal motion by the Government at the time of sentencing. See section 401(g)(2)(B) of Public Law 108-21. The government should not withhold such a motion based on interests not identified in § 3E1.1, such as whether the defendant agrees to waive his or her right to appeal.

If the government files such a motion, and the court in deciding whether to grant the motion also determines that the defendant has assisted authorities in the investigation or prosecution of his own misconduct by timely notifying authorities of his intention to enter a plea of guilty, thereby permitting the government to avoid preparing for trial and permitting the government and the court to allocate their resources efficiently, the court should grant the motion.

Background: The reduction of offense level provided by this section recognizes legitimate societal interests. For several reasons, a defendant who clearly demonstrates acceptance of responsibility for his offense by taking, in a timely fashion, the actions listed above (or some equivalent action) is appropriately given a lower offense level than a defendant who has not demonstrated acceptance of responsibility.

Subsection (a) provides a 2-level decrease in offense level. Subsection (b) provides an additional 1-level decrease for a defendant at offense level 16 or greater prior to operation of subsection (a) who both qualifies for a decrease under subsection (a) and has assisted authorities in the investigation or prosecution of his own misconduct by taking the steps specified in subsection (b). Such a defendant has accepted responsibility in a way that ensures the certainty of his just punishment in a timely manner, thereby appropriately meriting an additional reduction. Subsection (b) does not apply, however, to a defendant whose offense level is level 15 or lower prior to application of subsection (a). At offense level 15 or lower, the reduction in the guideline range provided by a 2-level decrease in offense level under subsection (a) (which is a greater proportional reduction in the guideline range than at higher offense levels due to the structure of the Sentencing Table) is adequate for the court to take into account the factors set forth in subsection (b) within the applicable guideline range. Section 401(g) of Public Law 108-21 directly amended subsection (b), Application Note 6 (including adding the first sentence of the second paragraph of that application note), and the Background Commentary, effective April 30, 2003.

CHAPTER FOUR — CRIMINAL HISTORY AND CRIMINAL LIVELIHOOD

PART A — CRIMINAL HISTORY

§ 4A1.1. Criminal History Category

The total points from subsections (a) through (e) determine the criminal history category in the Sentencing Table in Chapter Five, Part A.

(a) Add 3 points for each prior sentence of imprisonment exceeding one year and one month.

(b) Add 2 points for each prior sentence of imprisonment of at least sixty days not counted in (a).

(c) Add 1 point for each prior sentence not counted in (a) or (b), up to a total of 4 points for this subsection.

(d) Add 2 points if the defendant committed the instant offense while under any criminal justice sentence, including probation, parole, supervised release, imprisonment, work release, or escape status.

(e) Add 1 point for each prior sentence resulting from a conviction of a crime of violence that did not receive any points under (a), (b), or (c) above because such sentence was counted as a single sentence, up to a total of 3points for this subsection.

COMMENTARY

The total criminal history points from § 4A1.1 determine the criminal history category (I–VI) in the Sentencing Table in Chapter Five, Part A. The definitions and instructions in § 4A1.2 govern the computation of the criminal history points. Therefore, §§ 4A1.1 and 4A1.2 must be read together. The following notes highlight the interaction of §§ 4A1.1 and 4A1.2.

Application Notes:

1. § 4A1.1(a). Three points are added for each prior sentence of imprisonment exceeding one year and one month. There is no limit to the number of points that may be counted under this subsection. The term "prior sentence" is defined at § 4A1.2(a). The term "sentence of imprisonment" is defined at § 4A1.2(b). Where a prior sentence of imprisonment resulted from a revocation of probation, parole, or a similar form of release, see § 4A1.2(k).

Certain prior sentences are not counted or are counted only under certain conditions:

A sentence imposed more than fifteen years prior to the defendant's commencement of the instant offense is not counted unless the defendant's incarceration extended into this fifteen-year period. See § 4A1.2(e).

A sentence imposed for an offense committed prior to the defendant's eighteenth birthday is counted under this subsection only if it resulted from an adult conviction. See § 4A1.2(d).

A sentence for a foreign conviction, a conviction that has been expunged, or an invalid conviction is not counted. See § 4A1.2(h) and (j) and the Commentary to § 4A1.2.

2. § 4A1.1(b). Two points are added for each prior sentence of imprisonment of at least sixty days not counted in § 4A1.1(a). There is no limit to the number of points that may be counted under this subsection. The term "prior sentence" is defined at § 4A1.2(a). The term "sentence of imprisonment" is defined at § 4A1.2(b). Where a prior sentence of imprisonment resulted from a revocation of probation, parole, or a similar form of release, see § 4A1.2(k).

Certain prior sentences are not counted or are counted only under certain conditions:

A sentence imposed more than ten years prior to the defendant's commencement of the instant offense is not counted. See § 4A1.2(e).

An adult or juvenile sentence imposed for an offense committed prior to the defendant's eighteenth birthday is counted only if confinement resulting from such sentence extended into the five-year period preceding the defendant's commencement of the instant offense. See § 4A1.2(d).

Sentences for certain specified non-felony offenses are never counted. See § 4A1.2(c)(2).

A sentence for a foreign conviction or a tribal court conviction, an expunged conviction, or an invalid conviction is not counted. See § 4A1.2(h), (i), (j), and the Commentary to § 4A1.2.

A military sentence is counted only if imposed by a general or special court-martial. See § 4A1.2(g).

3. § 4A1.1(c). One point is added for each prior sentence not counted under § 4A1.1(a) or (b). A maximum of four points may be counted under this subsection. The term "prior sentence" is defined at § 4A1.2(a).

Certain prior sentences are not counted or are counted only under certain conditions:

A sentence imposed more than ten years prior to the defendant's commencement of the instant offense is not counted. See § 4A1.2(e).

An adult or juvenile sentence imposed for an offense committed prior to the defendant's eighteenth birthday is counted only if imposed within five years of the defendant's commencement of the current offense. See § 4A1.2(d).

Sentences for certain specified non-felony offenses are counted only if they meet certain requirements. See § 4A1.2(c)(1).

Sentences for certain specified non-felony offenses are never counted. See § 4A1.2(c)(2).

A diversionary disposition is counted only where there is a finding or admission of guilt in a judicial proceeding. See § 4A1.2(f).

A sentence for a foreign conviction, a tribal court conviction, an expunged conviction, or an invalid conviction, is not counted. See § 4A1.2(h), (i), (j), and the Commentary to § 4A1.2.

A military sentence is counted only if imposed by a general or special court-martial. See § 4A1.2(g).

4. § 4A1.1(d). Two points are added if the defendant committed any part of the instant offense (i.e., any relevant conduct) while under any criminal justice sentence, including probation, parole, supervised release, imprisonment, work release, or escape status. Failure to report for service of a sentence of imprisonment is to be treated as an escape from such sentence. See § 4A1.2(n). For the purposes of this subsection, a "criminal justice sentence" means a sentence countable under § 4A1.2 (Definitions and Instructions for Computing Criminal History) having a custodial or supervisory component, although active supervision is not required for this subsection to apply. For example, a term of unsupervised probation would be included; but a sentence to pay a fine, by itself, would not be included. A defendant who commits the instant offense while a violation warrant from a prior sentence is outstanding (e.g., a probation, parole, or supervised release violation warrant) shall be deemed to be under a criminal justice sentence for the purposes of this provision if that sentence is otherwise countable, even if that sentence would have expired absent such warrant. See § 4A1.2(m).

5. § 4A1.1(e). In a case in which the defendant received two or more prior sentences as a result of convictions for crimes of violence that are counted as a single sentence (see § 4A1.2(a)(2)), one point is added under § 4A1.1(e) for each such sentence that did not result in any additional points under § 4A1.1(a), (b), or (c). A total of up to 3 points may be added under § 4A1.1(e).

For purposes of this guideline, "crime of violence" has the meaning given that term in § 4B1.2(a). See § 4A1.2(p).

For example, a defendant's criminal history includes two robbery convictions for offenses committed on different occasions. The sentences for these offenses were imposed on the same day and are counted as a single prior sentence. See § 4A1.2(a)(2). If the defendant received a five-year sentence of imprisonment for one robbery and a four-year sentence of imprisonment for the other robbery (consecutively or concurrently), a total of 3 points is added under § 4A1.1(a). An additional point is added under § 4A1.1(e) because the second sentence did not result in any additional point(s) (under § 4A1.1(a), (b), or (c)). In contrast, if the defendant received a one-year sentence of imprisonment for one robbery and a nine-month consecutive sentence of imprisonment for the other robbery, a total of 3 points also is added under § 4A1.1(a) (a one-year sentence of imprisonment and a consecutive nine-month sentence of imprisonment are treated as a combined one-year-nine-month sentence of imprisonment). But no additional point is added under § 4A1.1(e) because the sentence for the second robbery already resulted in an additional point under § 4A1.1(a). Without the second sentence, the defendant would only have received two points under § 4A1.1(b) for the one-year sentence of imprisonment.

Background: Prior convictions may represent convictions in the federal system, fifty state systems, the District of Columbia, territories, and foreign, tribal, and military courts. There are jurisdictional variations in offense definitions, sentencing structures, and manner of sentence pronouncement. To minimize problems with imperfect measures of past crime seriousness, criminal history categories are based on the maximum term imposed in previous sentences rather than on other measures, such as whether the conviction was designated a felony or misdemeanor. In recognition of the imperfection of this measure however, § 4A1.3 authorizes the court to depart from the otherwise applicable criminal history category in certain circumstances.

Subsections (a), (b), and (c) of § 4A1.1 distinguish confinement sentences longer than one year and one month, shorter confinement sentences of at least sixty days, and all other sentences, such as confinement sentences of less than sixty days, probation, fines, and residency in a halfway house.

Section 4A1.1(d) adds two points if the defendant was under a criminal justice sentence during any part of the instant offense.

§ 4A1.3.   Departures Based on Inadequacy of Criminal History Category (Policy Statement)

(a) Upward Departures.—

(1) Standard for Upward Departure.— If reliable information indicates that the defendant's criminal history category substantially under-represents the seriousness of the defendant's criminal history or the likelihood that the defendant will commit other crimes, an upward departure may be warranted.

(2) Types of information Forming the Basis for Upward Departure.— The information described in subsection (a) may include information concerning the following:

(A) Prior sentence(s) not used in computing the criminal history category (e.g., sentences for foreign and tribal offenses).

(B) Prior sentence(s) of substantially more than one year imposed as a result of independent crimes committed on different occasions.

(C) Prior similar misconduct established by a civil adjudication or by a failure to comply with an administrative order.

(D) Whether the defendant was pending trial or sentencing on another charge at the time of the instant offense.

(E) Prior similar adult criminal conduct not resulting in a criminal conviction.

(3) Prohibition.— A prior arrest record itself shall not be considered for purposes of an upward departure under this policy statement.

(4) Determination of Extent of Upward Departure.—

(A) In General.— Except as provided in subdivision (B), the court shall determine the extent of a departure under this subsection by using, as a reference, the criminal history category applicable to defendants whose criminal history or likelihood to recidivate most closely resembles that of the defendant's.

(B) Upward Departures From Category VI.— In a case in which the court determines that the extent and nature of the defendant's criminal history, taken together, are sufficient to warrant an upward departure from Criminal History Category VI, the court should structure the departure by moving incrementally down the sentencing table to the next higher offense level in Criminal History Category VI until it finds a guideline range appropriate to the case.

(b) Downward Departures.—

(1) Standard for Downward Departure.— If reliable information indicates that the defendant's criminal history category substantially overrepresents the seriousness of the defendant's criminal history or the likelihood that the defendant will commit other crimes, a downward departure may be warranted.

(2) Prohibitions.—

(A) Criminal History Cateogry I.— A departure below the lower limit of the applicable guideline range for Criminal History Category I is prohibited.

(B) Armed Career Criminal And Repeat and Dangerous Sex Offender.— A downward departure under this subsection is prohibited for

(i) an armed career criminal within the meaning of § 4B1.4 (Armed Career Criminal); and

(ii) a repeat and dangerous sex offender against minors within the meaning of § 4B1.5 (Repeat and Dangerous Sex Offender Against Minors).

(3) Limitations.—

(A) Limitation on Extent of Downward Departure For Career Offender.— The extent of a downward departure under this subsection for a career offender within the meaning of § 4B1.1 (Career Offender) may not exceed one criminal history category.

(B) Limitation of Applicability on § 5C1.2 in Event of Downward Departure of Category I.— A defendant whose criminal history category is Category I after receipt of a downward departure under this subsection does not meet the criterion of subsection (a)(1) of § 5C1.2 (Limitation on Applicability of Statutory Maximum Sentences in Certain Cases) if, before receipt of the downward departure, the defendant had more than one criminal history point under § 4A1.1 (Criminal History Category).

(c) Written Specification of Basis for Departure.— In departing from the otherwise applicable criminal history category under this policy statement, the court shall specify in writing the following:

(1) In the case of an upward departure, the specific reasons why the applicable criminal history category substantially under-represents the seriousness of the defendant's criminal history or the likelihood that the defendant will commit other crimes.

(2) In the case of a downward departure, the specific reasons why the applicable criminal history category substantially over-represents the seriousness of the defendant's criminal history or the likelihood that the defendant will

commit other crimes.

COMMENTARY

Application Notes:

1. Definitions.— For purposes of this policy statement, the terms "depart", "departure", "downward departure", and "upward departure" have the meaning given those terms in Application Note 1 of the Commentary to § 1B1.1 (Application Instructions).

2. Upward Departures.—

(A) Examples.— An upward departure from the defendant's criminal history category may be warranted based on any of the following circumstances:

(i) A previous foreign sentence for a serious offense.

(ii) Receipt of a prior consolidated sentence of ten years for a series of serious assaults.

(iii) A similar instance of large scale fraudulent misconduct established by an adjudication in a Securities and Exchange Commission enforcement proceeding.

(iv) Commission of the instant offense while on bail or pretrial release for another serious offense.

(B) Upward Departures from Criminal History Category VI.— In the case of an egregious, serious criminal record in which even the guideline range for Criminal History Category VI is not adequate to reflect the seriousness of the defendant's criminal history, a departure above the guideline range for a defendant with Criminal History Category VI may be warranted. In determining whether an upward departure from Criminal History Category VI is warranted, the court should consider that the nature of the prior offenses rather than simply their number is often more indicative of the seriousness of the defendant's criminal record. For example, a defendant with five prior sentences for very large-scale fraud offenses may have 15 criminal history points, within the range of points typical for Criminal History Category VI, yet have a substantially more serious criminal history overall because of the nature of the prior offenses.

3. Downward Departures.— A downward departure from the defendant's criminal history category may be warranted if, for example, the defendant had two minor misdemeanor convictions close to ten years prior to the instant offense and no other evidence of prior criminal behavior in the intervening period. A departure below the lower limit of the applicable guideline range for Criminal History Category I is prohibited under subsection (b)(2)(B), due to the fact that the lower limit of the guideline range for Criminal History Category I is set for a first offender with the lowest risk of recidivism.

Background: This policy statement recognizes that the criminal history score is unlikely to take into account all the variations in the seriousness of criminal history that may occur. For example, a defendant with an extensive record of serious, assaultive conduct who had received what might now be considered extremely lenient treatment in the past might have the same criminal history category as a defendant who had a record of less serious conduct. Yet, the first defendant's criminal history clearly may be more serious. This may be particularly true in the case of younger defendants (e.g., defendants in their early twenties or younger) who are more likely to have received repeated lenient treatment, yet who may actually pose a greater risk of serious recidivism than older defendants. This policy statement authorizes the consideration of a departure from the guidelines in the limited circumstances where reliable information indicates that the criminal history category does not adequately reflect the seriousness of the defendant's criminal history or likelihood of recidivism, and provides guidance for the consideration of such departures.

CHAPTER FIVE — DETERMINING THE SENTENCE

PART B — PROBATION

§ 5B1.1.   Imposition of a Term of Probation

(a) Subject to the statutory restrictions in subsection (b) below, a sentence of probation is authorized if:

(1) the applicable guideline range is in Zone A of the Sentencing Table; or

(2) the applicable guideline range is in Zone B of the Sentencing Table and the court imposes a condition or combination of conditions requiring intermittent confinement, community confinement, or home detention as provided in subsection (c)(3) of § 5C1.1 (Imposition of a Term of Imprisonment).

(b) A sentence of probation may not be imposed in the event:

(1) the offense of conviction is a Class A or B felony, 18 U.S.C. § 3561(a)(1);

(2) the offense of conviction expressly precludes probation as a sentence, 18 U.S.C. § 3561(a)(2);

(3) the defendant is sentenced at the same time to a sentence of imprisonment for the same or a different offense, 18 U.S.C. § 3561(a)(3).

COMMENTARY

Application Notes:

1. Except where prohibited by statute or by the guideline applicable to the offense in Chapter Two, the guidelines authorize, but do not require, a sentence of probation in the following circumstances:

(A) Where the applicable guideline range is in Zone A of the Sentencing Table (i.e., the minimum term of imprisonment specified in the applicable guideline range is zero months). In such cases, a condition requiring a period of community confinement, home detention, or intermittent confinement may be imposed but is not required.

(B) Where the applicable guideline range is in Zone B of the Sentencing Table (i.e., the minimum term of imprisonment specified in the applicable guideline range is at least one but not more than nine months). In such cases, the court may impose probation only if it imposes a condition or combination of conditions requiring a period of community confinement, home detention, or intermittent confinement sufficient to satisfy the minimum term of imprisonment specified in the guideline range. For example, where the offense level is 7 and the criminal history category is II, the guideline range from the Sentencing Table is 2–8 months. In such a case, the court may impose a sentence of probation only if it imposes a condition or conditions requiring at least two months of community confinement, home detention, or intermittent confinement, or a combination of community confinement, home detention, and intermittent confinement totaling at least two months.

2. Where the applicable guideline range is in Zone C or D of the Sentencing Table (i.e., the minimum term of imprisonment specified in the applicable guideline range is ten months or more), the guidelines do not authorize a sentence of probation. See § 5C1.1 (Imposition of a Term of Imprisonment).

Background: This section provides for the imposition of a sentence of probation. The court may sentence a defendant to a term of probation in any case unless

(1) prohibited by statute, or

(2) where a term of imprisonment is required under § 5C1.1 (Imposition of a Term of Imprisonment).

Under 18 U.S.C. § 3561(a)(3), the imposition of a sentence of probation is prohibited where the defendant is sentenced at the same time to a sentence of imprisonment for the same or a different offense. Although this provision has effectively abolished the use of "split sentences" imposable pursuant to the former 18 U.S.C. § 3651, the drafters of the Sentencing Reform Act noted that the functional equivalent of the split sentence could be "achieved by a more direct and logically consistent route" by providing that a defendant serve a term of imprisonment followed by a period of supervised release. (S. Rep. No. 225, 98th Cong., 1st Sess. 89 (1983)). Section 5B1.1(a)(2) provides a transition between the circumstances under which a "straight" probationary term is authorized and those where probation is prohibited.

PART C — IMPRISONMENT

§ 5C1.1. Imposition of a Term of Imprisonment

(a) A sentence conforms with the guidelines for imprisonment if it is within the minimum and maximum terms of the applicable guideline range.

(b) If the applicable guideline range is in Zone A of the Sentencing Table, a sentence of imprisonment is not required, unless the applicable guideline in Chapter Two expressly requires such a term.

(c) If the applicable guideline range is in Zone B of the Sentencing Table, the minimum term may be satisfied by—

(1) a sentence of imprisonment; or

(2) a sentence of imprisonment that includes a term of supervised release with a condition that substitutes community confinement or home detention according to the schedule in subsection (e), provided that at least one month is satisfied by imprisonment; or

(3) a sentence of probation that includes a condition or combination of conditions that substitute intermittent confinement, community confinement, or home detention for imprisonment according to the schedule in subsection (e).

(d) If the applicable guideline range is in Zone C of the Sentencing Table, the minimum term may be satisfied by—

(1) a sentence of imprisonment; or

(2) a sentence of imprisonment that includes a term of supervised release with a condition that substitutes community confinement or home detention according

to the schedule in subsection (e), provided that at least one-half of the minimum term is satisfied by imprisonment.

(e) Schedule of Substitute Punishments:

(1) One day of intermittent confinement in prison or jail for one day of imprisonment (each 24 hours of confinement is credited as one day of intermittent confinement, provided, however, that one day shall be credited for any calendar day during which the defendant is employed in the community and confined during all remaining hours);

(2) One day of community confinement (residence in a community treatment center, halfway house, or similar residential facility) for one day of imprisonment;

(3) One day of home detention for one day of imprisonment.

(f) If the applicable guideline range is in Zone D of the Sentencing Table, the minimum term shall be satisfied by a sentence of imprisonment.

COMMENTARY

Application Notes:

1. Subsection (a) provides that a sentence conforms with the guidelines for imprisonment if it is within the minimum and maximum terms of the applicable guideline range specified in the Sentencing Table in Part A of this Chapter. For example, if the defendant has an Offense Level of 20 and a Criminal History Category of I, the applicable guideline range is 33–41 months of imprisonment. Therefore, a sentence of imprisonment of at least thirty-three months, but not more than forty-one months, is within the applicable guideline range.

2. Subsection (b) provides that where the applicable guideline range is in Zone A of the Sentencing Table (i.e., the minimum term of imprisonment specified in the applicable guideline range is zero months), the court is not required to impose a sentence of imprisonment unless a sentence of imprisonment or its equivalent is specifically required by the guideline applicable to the offense. Where imprisonment is not required, the court, for example, may impose a sentence of probation. In some cases, a fine appropriately may be imposed as the sole sanction.

3. Subsection (c) provides that where the applicable guideline range is in Zone B of the Sentencing Table (i.e., the minimum term of imprisonment specified in the applicable guideline range is at least one but not more than nine months), the court has three options:

(A) It may impose a sentence of imprisonment.

(B) It may impose a sentence of probation provided that it includes a condition of probation requiring a period of intermittent confinement, community confinement, or home detention, or combination of intermittent confinement, community confinement, and home detention, sufficient to satisfy the minimum period of imprisonment specified in the guideline range. For example, where the guideline range is 4–10 months, a sentence of probation with a condition requiring at least four months of intermittent confinement, community confinement, or home detention would satisfy the minimum term of imprisonment specified in the guideline range.

(C) Or, it may impose a sentence of imprisonment that includes a term of supervised release with a condition that requires community confinement or home detention. In such case, at least one month must be satisfied by actual imprisonment and the remainder of the minimum term specified in the guideline range must be satisfied by community confinement or home detention. For example, where the guideline range is 4–10 months, a sentence of imprisonment of one month followed by a term of supervised release with a condition requiring three months of community confinement or home detention would satisfy the minimum term of imprisonment specified in the guideline range.

The preceding examples illustrate sentences that satisfy the minimum term of imprisonment required by the guideline range. The court, of course, may impose a sentence at a higher point within the applicable guideline range. For example, where the guideline range is 4–10 months, both a sentence of probation with a condition requiring six months of community confinement or home detention (under subsection (c)(3)) and a sentence of two months imprisonment followed by a term of supervised release with a condition requiring four months of community confinement or home detention (under subsection (c)(2)) would be within the guideline range.

4. Subsection (d) provides that where the applicable guideline range is in Zone C of the Sentencing Table (i.e., the minimum term specified in the applicable guideline range is ten or twelve months), the court has two options:

(A) It may impose a sentence of imprisonment.

(B) Or, it may impose a sentence of imprisonment that includes a term of supervised release with a condition requiring community confinement or home detention. In such case, at least one-half of the minimum term specified in the guideline range must be satisfied by imprisonment, and the remainder of the minimum term specified in the guideline range must be satisfied by community confinement or home detention. For example, where the guideline range is 10–16 months, a sentence of five months imprisonment followed by a term of supervised release with a condition requiring five months community confinement or home detention would satisfy the minimum term of imprisonment required by the guideline range.

The preceding example illustrates a sentence that satisfies the minimum term of imprisonment required by the guideline range. The court, of course, may impose a sentence at a higher point within the guideline range. For example, where the guideline range is 10–16 months, both a sentence of five months imprisonment followed by a term of supervised release with a condition requiring six months of community confinement or home detention (under subsection (d)), and a sentence of ten months imprisonment followed by a term of supervised release with a condition requiring four months of community confinement or home detention (also under subsection (d)) would be within the guideline range.

5. Subsection (e) sets forth a schedule of imprisonment substitutes.

6. There may be cases in which a departure from the sentencing options authorized for Zone C of the Sentencing Table (under which at least half the minimum term must be satisfied by imprisonment) to the sentencing options authorized for Zone B of the Sentencing Table (under which all or most of the minimum term may be satisfied by intermittent confinement, community confinement, or home detention instead of imprisonment) is appropriate to accomplish a specific treatment purpose. Such a departure should be considered only in cases where the court finds that

(A) the defendant is an abuser of narcotics, other controlled substances, or alcohol, or suffers from a significant mental illness, and

(B) the defendant's criminality is related to the treatment problem to be addressed.

In determining whether such a departure is appropriate, the court should consider, among other things,

(1) the likelihood that completion of the treatment program will successfully address the treatment problem, thereby reducing the risk to the public from further crimes of the defendant, and

(2) whether imposition of less imprisonment than required by Zone C will increase the risk to the public from further crimes of the defendant.

Examples: The following examples both assume the applicable guideline range is 12–18 months and the court departs in accordance with this application note. Under Zone C rules, the defendant must be sentenced to at least six months imprisonment. (1) The defendant is a nonviolent drug offender in Criminal History Category I and probation is not prohibited by statute. The court departs downward to impose a sentence of probation, with twelve months of intermittent confinement, community confinement, or home detention and participation in a substance abuse treatment program as conditions of probation. (2) The defendant is convicted of a Class A or B felony, so probation is prohibited by statute (see § 5B1.1(b)). The court departs downward to impose a sentence of one month imprisonment, with eleven months in community confinement or home detention and participation in a substance abuse treatment program as conditions of supervised release.

7. The use of substitutes for imprisonment as provided in subsections (c) and (d) is not recommended for most defendants with a criminal history category of III or above.

8. In a case in which community confinement in a residential treatment program is imposed to accomplish a specific treatment purpose, the court should consider the effectiveness of the residential treatment program.

9. Subsection (f) provides that, where the applicable guideline range is in Zone D of the Sentencing Table (i.e., the minimum term of imprisonment specified in the applicable guideline range is 15 months or more), the minimum term must be satisfied by a sentence of imprisonment without the use of any of the imprisonment substitutes in subsection (e).

PART E — RESTITUTION, FINES, ASSESSMENTS, FORFEITURES

§ 5E1.4. Forfeiture

Forfeiture is to be imposed upon a convicted defendant as provided by statute.

COMMENTARY

Background: Forfeiture provisions exist in various statutes. For example, 18 U.S.C. § 3554 requires the court imposing a sentence under 18 U.S.C. § 1962 (proscribing the use of the proceeds of racketeering activities in the operation of an enterprise engaged in interstate commerce) or Titles II and III of the Comprehensive Drug Abuse Prevention and Control Act of 1970 (proscribing the manufacture and distribution of controlled substances) to order the forfeiture of property in accordance with 18 U.S.C. § 1963 and 21 U.S.C. § 853, respectively. Those provisions require the automatic forfeiture of certain property upon conviction of their respective underlying offenses.

In addition, the provisions of 18 U.S.C. §§ 3681–3682 authorizes the court, in certain circumstances, to order the forfeiture of a violent criminal's proceeds from the depiction of his crime in a book, movie, or other medium. Those sections authorize the deposit of proceeds in an escrow account in the Crime Victims Fund of the United States Treasury. The money is to remain available in the account for five years to satisfy claims brought against the defendant by the victim(s) of his offenses. At the end of the five-year period, the court may require that any proceeds remaining in the account be released from escrow and paid into the Fund. 18 U.S.C. § 3681(c)(2).

PART K — DEPARTURES

§ 5K1.1. Substantial Assistance to Authorities (Policy Statements)

Upon motion of the government stating that the defendant has provided substantial assistance in the investigation or prosecution of another person who has committed an offense, the court may depart from the guidelines.

(a) The appropriate reduction shall be determined by the court for reasons stated that may include, but are not limited to, consideration of the following:

(1) the court's evaluation of the significance and usefulness of the defendant's assistance, taking into consideration the government's evaluation of the assistance rendered;

(2) the truthfulness, completeness, and reliability of any information or testimony provided by the defendant;

(3) the nature and extent of the defendant's assistance;

(4) any injury suffered, or any danger or risk of injury to the defendant or his family resulting from his assistance;

(5) the timeliness of the defendant's assistance.

COMMENTARY

Application Notes:

1. Under circumstances set forth in 18 U.S.C. § 3553(e) and 28 U.S.C. § 994(n), as amended, substantial assistance in the investigation or prosecution of another person who has committed an offense may justify a sentence below a statutorily required minimum sentence.

2. The sentencing reduction for assistance to authorities shall be considered independently of any reduction for acceptance of responsibility. Substantial assistance is directed to the investigation and prosecution of criminal activities by persons other than the defendant, while acceptance of responsibility is directed to the defendant's affirmative recognition of responsibility for his own conduct.

3. Substantial weight should be given to the government's evaluation of the extent of the defendant's assistance, particularly where the extent and value of the assistance are difficult to ascertain.

Background: A defendant's assistance to authorities in the investigation of criminal activities has been recognized in practice and by statute as a mitigating sentencing factor. The nature, extent, and significance of assistance can involve a broad spectrum of conduct that must be evaluated by the court on an individual basis. Latitude is, therefore, afforded the sentencing judge to reduce a sentence based upon variable relevant factors, including those listed above. The sentencing judge must, however, state the reasons for reducing a sentence under this section. 18 U.S.C. § 3553(c). The court may elect to provide its reasons to the defendant in camera and in writing under seal for the safety of the defendant or to avoid disclosure of an ongoing investigation.

§ 5K1.2.   Refusal to Assist (Policy Statement)

A defendant's refusal to assist authorities in the investigation of other persons may not be considered as an aggravating sentencing factor.

§ 5K2.0.   Grounds for Departure (Policy Statement)

(a) Upward Departures in General and Downward Departures in Criminal Cases Other Than Child Crimes and Sexual Offenses.—

(1) In General.— The sentencing court may depart from the applicable guideline range if—

(A) in the case of offenses other than child crimes and sexual offenses, the court finds, pursuant to 18 U.S.C. § 3553(b)(1), that there exists an aggravating or mitigating circumstance; or

(B) in the case of child crimes and sexual offenses, the court finds, pursuant to 18 U.S.C. § 3553(b)(2)(A)(i), that there exists an aggravating circumstance, of a kind, or to a degree, not adequately taken into consideration by the Sentencing Commission in formulating the guidelines that, in order to advance the objectives set forth in 18 U.S.C. § 3553(a)(2), should result in a sentence different from that described.

(2) Departures Based on Circumstances of a Kind not Adequately Taken into Consideration.—

(A) Identified Circumstances.— This subpart (Chapter Five, Part K, Subpart 2 (Other Grounds for Departure)) identifies some of the circumstances that the Commission may have not adequately taken into consideration in determining the applicable guideline range (e.g., as a specific offense characteristic or other adjustment). If any such circumstance is present in the case and has not adequately been taken into consideration in determining the applicable guideline range, a departure consistent with 18 U.S.C. § 3553(b) and the provisions of this subpart may be warranted.

(B) Unidentified Circumstances.— A departure may be warranted in the exceptional case in which there is present a circumstance that the Commission has not identified in the guidelines but that nevertheless is relevant to determining the appropriate sentence.

(3) Departures Based on Circumstances Present to a Degree not Adequately Taken into Consideration.— A departure may be warranted in an exceptional case, even though the circumstance that forms the basis for the departure is taken into consideration in determining the guideline range, if the court determines that such circumstance is present in the offense to a degree substantially in excess of, or substantially below, that which ordinarily is involved in that kind of offense.

(4) Departures Based on not Ordinarily Relevant Offender Characteristics and Other Circumstances.— An offender characteristic or other circumstance identified in Chapter Five, Part H (Offender Characteristics) or elsewhere in the guidelines as not ordinarily relevant in determining whether a departure is warranted may be relevant to this determination only if such offender characteristic or other circumstance is present to an exceptional degree.

(b) Downward Departures in Child Crimes and Sexual Offenses.— Under 18 U.S.C. § 3553(b)(2)(A)(ii), the sentencing court may impose a sentence below the range established by the applicable guidelines only if the court finds that there exists a mitigating circumstance of a kind, or to a degree, that—

(1) has been affirmatively and specifically identified as a permissible ground of downward departure in the sentencing guidelines or policy statements issued under section 994(a) of title 28, United States Code, taking account of any amendments to such sentencing guidelines or policy statements by act of Congress;

(2) has not adequately been taken into consideration by the Sentencing Commission in formulating the guidelines; and

(3) should result in a sentence different from that described.

The grounds enumerated in this Part K of Chapter Five are the sole grounds that have been affirmatively and specifically identified as a permissible ground of downward departure in these sentencing guidelines and policy statements. Thus, notwithstanding any other reference to authority to depart downward elsewhere in this Sentencing Manual, a ground of downward departure has not been affirmatively and specifically identified as a permissible ground of downward departure within the meaning of section 3553(b)(2) unless it is expressly enumerated in this Part K as a ground upon which a downward departure may be granted.

(c) Limitation on Departures Based on Multiple Circumstances.— The court may depart from the applicable guideline range based on a combination of two or more offender characteristics or other circumstances, none of which independently is sufficient to provide a basis for departure, only if—

(1) such offender characteristics or other circumstances, taken together, make the case an exceptional one; and

(2) each such offender characteristic or other circumstance is—

(A) present to a substantial degree; and

(B) identified in the guidelines as a permissible ground for departure, even if such offender characteristic or other circumstance is not ordinarily relevant to a determination of whether a departure is warranted.

(d) Prohibited Departures.— Notwithstanding subsections (a) and (b) of this policy statement, or any other provision in the guidelines, the court may not depart from the applicable guideline range based on any of the following circumstances:

(1) Any circumstance specifically prohibited as a ground for departure in §§ 5H1.10 (Race, Sex, National Origin, Creed, Religion, and Socio-Economic Status), 5H1.12 (Lack of Guidance as a Youth and Similar Circumstances), the last sentence of 5H1.4 (Physical Condition, Including Drug or Alcohol Dependence or Abuse; Gambling Addiction), and the last sentence of 5K2.12 (Coercion and Duress).

(2) The defendant's acceptance of responsibility for the offense, which may be taken into account only under § 3E1.1 (Acceptance of Responsibility).

(3) The defendant's aggravating or mitigating role in the offense, which may be taken into account only under § 3B1.1 (Aggravating Role) or § 3B1.2 (Mitigating Role), respectively.

(4) The defendant's decision, in and of itself, to plead guilty to the offense or to enter a plea agreement with respect to the offense (i.e., a departure may not be based merely on the fact that the defendant decided to plead guilty or to enter into a plea agreement, but a departure may be based on justifiable, non-prohibited reasons as part of a sentence that is recommended, or agreed to, in the plea agreement and accepted by the court. See § 6B1.2 (Standards for Acceptance of Plea Agreement).

(5) The defendant's fulfillment of restitution obligations only to the extent required by law including the guidelines (i.e., a departure may not be based on unexceptional efforts to remedy the harm caused by the offense).

(6) Any other circumstance specifically prohibited as a ground for departure in the guidelines.

(e) Requirement of Specific Written Reasons for Departure.— If the court departs from the applicable guideline range, it shall state, pursuant to 18 U.S.C. § 3553(c), its specific reasons for departure in open court at the time of sentencing and, with limited exception in the case of statements received in camera, shall state those reasons with specificity in the statement of reasons form.

COMMENTARY

Application Notes:

1. Definitions.— For purposes of this policy statement:

"Circumstance" includes, as appropriate, an offender characteristic or any other offense factor.

"Depart", "departure", "downward departure", and "upward departure" have the meaning given those terms in Application Note 1 of the Commentary to § 1B1.1 (Application Instructions).

2. Scope of this Policy Statement.—

(A) Departures Covered by this Policy Statement.— This policy statement covers departures from the applicable guideline range based on offense characteristics or offender characteristics of a kind, or to a degree, not adequately taken into consideration in determining that range. See 18 U.S.C. § 3553(b).

Subsection (a) of this policy statement applies to upward departures in all cases covered by the guidelines and to downward departures in all such cases except for downward departures in child crimes and sexual offenses.

Subsection (b) of this policy statement applies only to downward departures in child crimes and sexual offenses.

(B) Departures Covered by Other Guidelines.— This policy statement does not cover the following departures, which are addressed elsewhere in the guidelines:

(i) departures based on the defendant's criminal history (see Chapter Four (Criminal History and Criminal Livelihood), particularly § 4A1.3 (Departures Based on Inadequacy of Criminal History Category));

(ii) departures based on the defendant's substantial assistance to the authorities (see § 5K1.1 (Substantial Assistance to Authorities)); and

(iii) departures based on early disposition programs (see § 5K3.1 (Early Disposition Programs)).

3. Kinds and Expected Frequency of Departures under Subsection (a).— As set forth in subsection (a), there generally are two kinds of departures from the guidelines based on offense characteristics and/or offender characteristics: (A) departures based on circumstances of a kind not adequately taken into consideration in the guidelines; and (B) departures based on circumstances that are present to a degree not adequately taken into consideration in the guidelines.

(A) Departures Based on Circumstances of a Kind Not Adequately Taken into Account in Guidelines.— Subsection (a)(2) authorizes the court to depart if there exists an aggravating or a mitigating circumstance in a case under 18 U.S.C. § 3553(b)(1), or an aggravating circumstance in a case under 18 U.S.C. § 3553(b)(2)(A)(i), of a kind not adequately taken into consideration in the guidelines.

(i) Identified Circumstances.— This subpart (Chapter Five, Part K, Subpart 2) identifies several circumstances that the Commission may have not adequately taken into consideration in setting the offense level for certain cases. Offense guidelines in Chapter Two (Offense Conduct) and adjustments in Chapter Three (Adjustments) sometimes identify circumstances the Commission may have not adequately taken into consideration in setting the offense level for offenses covered by those guidelines. If the offense guideline in Chapter Two or an adjustment in Chapter Three does not adequately take that circumstance into consideration in setting the offense level for the offense, and only to the extent not adequately taken into consideration, a departure based on that circumstance may be warranted.

(ii) Unidentified Circumstances.— A case may involve circumstances, in addition to those identified by the guidelines, that have not adequately been taken into consideration by the Commission, and the presence of any such circumstance may warrant departure from the guidelines in that case. However, inasmuch as the Commission has continued to monitor and refine the guidelines since their inception to take into consideration relevant circumstances in sentencing, it is expected that departures based on such unidentified circumstances will occur rarely and only in exceptional cases.

(B) Departures Based on Circumstances Present to a Degree Not Adequately Taken into Consideration in Guidelines.—

(i) In General.— Subsection (a)(3) authorizes the court to depart if there exists an aggravating or a mitigating circumstance in a case under 18 U.S.C. § 3553(b)(1), or an aggravating circumstance in a case under 18 U.S.C. § 3553(b)(2)(A)(i), to a degree not adequately taken into consideration in the guidelines. However, inasmuch as the Commission has continued to monitor and refine the guidelines since their inception to determine the most appropriate weight to be accorded the mitigating and aggravating circumstances specified in the guidelines, it is expected that departures based on the weight accorded to any such circumstance will occur rarely and only in exceptional cases.

(ii) Examples.— As set forth in subsection (a)(3), if the applicable offense guideline and adjustments take into consideration a circumstance identified in this subpart, departure is warranted only if the circumstance is present to a degree substantially in excess of that which ordinarily is involved in the offense. Accordingly, a departure pursuant to § 5K2.7 for the disruption of a governmental function would have to be substantial to warrant departure from the guidelines when the applicable offense guideline is bribery or obstruction of justice. When the guideline covering the mailing of injurious articles is applicable, however, and the offense caused disruption of a governmental function, departure from the applicable guideline range more readily would be appropriate. Similarly, physical injury would not warrant departure from the guidelines when the robbery offense guideline is applicable because the robbery guideline includes a specific adjustment based on the extent of any injury. However, because the robbery guideline does not deal with injury to more than one victim, departure may be warranted if several persons were injured.

(C) Departures Based on Circumstances Identified as Not Ordinarily Relevant.— Because certain circumstances are specified in the guidelines as not ordinarily relevant to sentencing (see, e.g., Chapter Five, Part H (Specific Offender Characteristics)), a departure based on any one of such circumstances should occur only in exceptional cases, and only if the circumstance is present in the case to an exceptional degree. If two or more of such circumstances each is present in the case to a substantial degree, however, and taken together make the case an exceptional one, the court may consider whether a departure would be warranted pursuant to subsection (c). Departures based on a combination of not ordinarily relevant circumstances that are present to a substantial degree should occur extremely rarely and only in exceptional cases.

In addition, as required by subsection (e), each circumstance forming the basis for a departure described in this subdivision shall be stated with specificity in the statement of reasons form.

4. Downward Departures in Child Crimes and Sexual Offenses.—

(A) Definition.— For purposes of this policy statement, the term "child crimes and sexual offenses" means offenses under any of the following: 18 U.S.C. § 1201 (involving a minor victim), 18 U.S.C. § 1591, or chapter 71, 109A, 110, or 117 of title 18, United States Code.

(B) Standard for Departure.—

(i) Requirement of Affirmative and Specific Identification of Departure Ground.— The standard for a downward departure in child crimes and sexual offenses differs from the standard for other departures under this policy statement in that it includes a requirement, set forth in 18 U.S.C. § 3553(b)(2)(A)(ii)(I) and subsection (b)(1) of this guideline, that any mitigating circumstance that forms the basis for such a downward departure be affirmatively and specifically identified as a ground for downward departure in this part (i.e., Chapter Five, Part K).

(ii) Application of Subsection (b)(2).— The commentary in Application Note 3 of this policy statement, except for the commentary in Application Note 3(A)(ii) relating to unidentified circumstances, shall apply to the court's determination of whether a case meets the requirement, set forth in subsection 18 U.S.C. § 3553(b)(2)(A)(ii)(II) and subsection (b)(2) of this policy statement, that the mitigating circumstance forming the basis for a downward departure in child crimes and sexual offenses be of kind, or to a degree, not adequately taken into consideration by the Commission.

5. Departures Based on Plea Agreements.— Subsection (d)(4) prohibits a

downward departure based only on the defendant's decision, in and of itself, to plead guilty to the offense or to enter a plea agreement with respect to the offense. Even though a departure may not be based merely on the fact that the defendant agreed to plead guilty or enter a plea agreement, a departure may be based on justifiable, non-prohibited reasons for departure as part of a sentence that is recommended, or agreed to, in the plea agreement and accepted by the court. See § 6B1.2 (Standards for Acceptance of Plea Agreements). In cases in which the court departs based on such reasons as set forth in the plea agreement, the court must state the reasons for departure with specificity in the statement of reasons form, as required by subsection (e).

Background: This policy statement sets forth the standards for departing from the applicable guideline range based on offense and offender characteristics of a kind, or to a degree, not adequately considered by the Commission. Circumstances the Commission has determined are not ordinarily relevant to determining whether a departure is warranted or are prohibited as bases for departure are addressed in Chapter Five, Part H (Offender Characteristics) and in this policy statement. Other departures, such as those based on the defendant's criminal history, the defendant's substantial assistance to authorities, and early disposition programs, are addressed elsewhere in the guidelines.

As acknowledged by Congress in the Sentencing Reform Act and by the Commission when the first set of guidelines was promulgated, "it is difficult to prescribe a single set of guidelines that encompasses the vast range of human conduct potentially relevant to a sentencing decision." (See Chapter One, Part A). Departures, therefore, perform an integral function in the sentencing guideline system. Departures permit courts to impose an appropriate sentence in the exceptional case in which mechanical application of the guidelines would fail to achieve the statutory purposes and goals of sentencing. Departures also help maintain "sufficient flexibility to permit individualized sentences when warranted by mitigating or aggravating factors not taken into account in the establishment of general sentencing practices." 28 U.S.C. § 991(b)(1)(B). By monitoring when courts depart from the guidelines and by analyzing their stated reasons for doing so, along with appellate cases reviewing these departures, the Commission can further refine the guidelines to specify more precisely when departures should and should not be permitted.

As reaffirmed in the Prosecutorial Remedies and Other Tools to end the Exploitation of Children Today Act of 2003 (the "PROTECT Act", Public Law 108-21), circumstances warranting departure should be rare. Departures were never intended to permit sentencing courts to substitute their policy judgments for those of Congress and the Sentencing Commission. Departure in such circumstances would produce unwarranted sentencing disparity, which the Sentencing Reform Act was designed to avoid.

In order for appellate courts to fulfill their statutory duties under 18 U.S.C. § 3742 and for the Commission to fulfill its ongoing responsibility to refine the guidelines in light of information it receives on departures, it is essential that sentencing courts state with specificity the reasons for departure, as required by the PROTECT Act.

This policy statement, including its commentary, was substantially revised, effective October 27, 2003, in response to directives contained in the PROTECT Act, particularly the directive in section 401(m) of that Act to—

"(1) review the grounds of downward departure that are authorized by the sentencing guidelines, policy statements, and official commentary of the Sentencing Commission; and

"(2) promulgate, pursuant to section 994 of title 28, United States Code—

(A) appropriate amendments to the sentencing guidelines, policy statements, and official commentary to ensure that the incidence of downward departures is substantially reduced;

(B) a policy statement authorizing a departure pursuant to an early disposition program; and

(C) any other conforming amendments to the sentencing guidelines, policy statements, and official commentary of the Sentencing Commission necessitated by the Act, including a revision of . . . section 5K2.0"

The substantial revision of this policy statement in response to the PROTECT Act was intended to refine the standards applicable to departures while giving due regard for concepts, such as the "heartland", that have evolved in departure jurisprudence over time.

Section 401(b)(1) of the PROTECT Act directly amended this policy statement to add subsection (b), effective April 30, 2003.

"USSG Chapters 6 and 7 intentionally omitted"

CHAPTER EIGHT — SENTENCING OF ORGANIZATIONS

PART A — GENERAL APPLICATION PRINCIPLES

§ 8A1.1. Applicability of Chapter Eight

This chapter applies to the sentencing of all organizations for felony and Class A misdemeanor offenses.

COMMENTARY

Application Notes:

1. "Organization" means "a person other than an individual." 18 U.S.C. § 18. The term includes corporations, partnerships, associations, joint-stock companies, unions, trusts, pension funds, unincorporated organizations, governments and political subdivisions thereof, and non-profit organizations.

2. The fine guidelines in §§ 8C2.2 through 8C2.9 apply only to specified types of offenses. The other provisions of this chapter apply to the sentencing of all organizations for all felony and Class A misdemeanor offenses. For example, the restitution and probation provisions in Parts B and D of this chapter apply to the sentencing of an organization, even if the fine guidelines in §§ 8C2.2 through 8C2.9 do not apply.

§ 8A1.2. Application Instructions — Organizations

(a) Determine from Part B, Subpart 1 (Remedying Harm from Criminal Conduct) the sentencing requirements and options relating to restitution, remedial orders, community service, and notice to victims.

(b) Determine from Part C (Fines) the sentencing requirements and options relating to fines:

(1) If the organization operated primarily for a criminal purpose or primarily by criminal means, apply § 8C1.1 (Determining the Fine — Criminal Purpose Organizations).

(2) Otherwise, apply § 8C2.1 (Applicability of Fine Guidelines) to identify the counts for which the provisions of §§ 8C2.2 through 8C2.9 apply. For such counts:

(A) Refer to § 8C2.2 (Preliminary Determination of Inability to Pay Fine) to determine whether an abbreviated determination of the guideline fine range may be warranted.

(B) Apply § 8C2.3 (Offense Level) to determine the offense level from Chapter Two (Offense Conduct) and Chapter Three, Part D (Multiple Counts).

(C) Apply § 8C2.4 (Base Fine) to determine the base fine.

(D) Apply § 8C2.5 (Culpability Score) to determine the culpability score. To determine whether the organization had an effective compliance and ethics program for purposes of § 8C2.5(f), apply § 8B2.1 (Effective Compliance and Ethics Program).

(E) Apply § 8C2.6 (Minimum and Maximum Multipliers) to determine the minimum and maximum multipliers corresponding to the culpability score.

(F) Apply § 8C2.7 (Guideline Fine Range — Organizations) to determine the minimum and maximum of the guideline fine range.

(G) Refer to § 8C2.8 (Determining the Fine Within the Range) to determine the amount of the fine within the applicable guideline range.

(H) Apply § 8C2.9 (Disgorgement) to determine whether an increase to the fine is required.

For any count or counts not covered under § 8C2.1 (Applicability of Fine Guidelines), apply § 8C2.10 (Determining the Fine for Other Counts).

(3) Apply the provisions relating to the implementation of the sentence of a fine in Part C, Subpart 3 (Implementing the Sentence of a Fine).

(4) For grounds for departure from the applicable guideline fine range, refer to Part C, Subpart 4 (Departures from the Guideline Fine Range).

(c) Determine from Part D (Organizational Probation) the sentencing requirements and options relating to probation.

(d) Determine from Part E (Special Assessments, Forfeitures, and Costs) the sentencing requirements relating to special assessments, forfeitures, and costs.

COMMENTARY

Application Notes:

1. Determinations under this chapter are to be based upon the facts and information specified in the applicable guideline. Determinations that reference other chapters are to be made under the standards applicable to determinations under those chapters.

2. The definitions in the Commentary to § 1B1.1 (Application Instructions) and the guidelines and commentary in §§ 1B1.2 through 1B1.8 apply to determinations under this chapter unless otherwise specified. The adjustments in Chapter Three, Parts A (Victim-Related Adjustments), B (Role in the Offense), C (Obstruction and Related Adjustments), and E (Acceptance of Responsibility) do not apply. The provisions of Chapter Six (Sentencing Procedures, Plea Agreements, and Crime Victims' Rights) apply to proceedings in which the defendant is an organization. Guidelines and policy statements not referenced in this chapter, directly or indirectly, do not apply when the defendant is an organization; e.g., the policy statements in Chapter Seven (Violations of Probation and Supervised Release) do not apply to organizations.

3. The following are definitions of terms used frequently in this chapter:

(A) "Offense" means the offense of conviction and all relevant conduct under § 1B1.3 (Relevant Conduct) unless a different meaning is specified or is otherwise clear from the context. The term "instant" is used in connection with "offense," "federal offense," or "offense of conviction," as the case may be, to distinguish the violation for which the defendant is being sentenced from a prior or subsequent offense, or from an offense before another court (e.g., an offense before a state court involving the same underlying conduct).

(B) "High-level personnel of the organization" means individuals who have substantial control over the organization or who have a substantial role in the making of policy within the organization. The term includes: a director; an executive officer; an individual in charge of a major business or functional unit of the organization, such as sales, administration, or finance; and an individual with a substantial ownership interest. "High-level personnel of a unit of the organization" is defined in the Commentary to § 8C2.5 (Culpability Score).

(C) "Substantial authority personnel" means individuals who within the scope of their authority exercise a substantial measure of discretion in acting on behalf of an organization. The term includes high-level personnel of the organization, individuals who exercise substantial supervisory authority (e.g., a plant manager, a sales manager), and any other individuals who, although not a part of an organization's management, nevertheless exercise substantial discretion when acting within the scope of their authority (e.g., an individual with authority in an organization to negotiate or set price levels or an individual authorized to negotiate or approve significant contracts). Whether an individual falls within this category must be determined on a case-by-case basis.

(D) "Agent" means any individual, including a director, an officer, an employee, or an independent contractor, authorized to act on behalf of the organization.

(E) An individual "condoned" an offense if the individual knew of the offense and did not take reasonable steps to prevent or terminate the offense.

(F) "Similar misconduct" means prior conduct that is similar in nature to the conduct underlying the instant offense, without regard to whether or not such conduct violated the same statutory provision. For example, prior Medicare fraud would be misconduct similar to an instant offense involving another type of fraud.

(G) "Prior criminal adjudication" means conviction by trial, plea of guilty (including an Alford plea), or plea of nolo contendere.

(H) "Pecuniary gain" is derived from 18 U.S.C. § 3571(d) and means the additional before-tax profit to the defendant resulting from the relevant conduct of the offense. Gain can result from either additional revenue or cost savings. For example, an offense involving odometer tampering can produce additional revenue. In such a case, the pecuniary gain is the additional revenue received because the automobiles appeared to have less mileage, i.e., the difference between the price received or expected for the automobiles with the apparent mileage and the fair market value of the automobiles with the actual mileage. An offense involving defense procurement fraud related to defective product testing can produce pecuniary gain resulting from cost savings. In such a case, the pecuniary gain is the amount saved because the product was not tested in the required manner.

(I) "Pecuniary loss" is derived from 18 U.S.C. § 3571(d) and is equivalent to the term "loss" as used in Chapter Two (Offense Conduct). See Commentary to § 2B1.1 (Theft, Property Destruction, and Fraud), and definitions of "tax loss" in Chapter Two, Part T (Offenses Involving Taxation).

(J) An individual was "willfully ignorant of the offense" if the individual did not investigate the possible occurrence of unlawful conduct despite knowledge of circumstances that would lead a reasonable person to investigate whether unlawful conduct had occurred.

PART B — REMEDYING HARM FROM CRIMINAL CONDUCT, AND EFFECTIVE COMPLIANCE AND ETHICS PROGRAM

§ 8B2.1. Effective Compliance and Ethics Program

(a) To have an effective compliance and ethics program, for purposes of subsection (f) of § 8C2.5 (Culpability Score) and subsection (b)(1) of § 8D1.4 (Recommended Conditions of Probation — Organizations), an organization shall—

(1) exercise due diligence to prevent and detect criminal conduct; and

(2) otherwise promote an organizational culture that encourages ethical conduct and a commitment to compliance with the law.

Such compliance and ethics program shall be reasonably designed, implemented, and enforced so that the program is generally effective in preventing and detecting criminal conduct. The failure to prevent or detect the instant offense does not necessarily mean that the program is not generally effective in preventing and detecting criminal conduct.

(b) Due diligence and the promotion of an organizational culture that encourages ethical conduct and a commitment to compliance with the law within the meaning of subsection (a) minimally require the following:

(1) The organization shall establish standards and procedures to prevent and detect criminal conduct.

(2)

(A) The organization's governing authority shall be knowledgeable about the content and operation of the compliance and ethics program and shall exercise reasonable oversight with respect to the implementation and effectiveness of the compliance and ethics program.

(B) High-level personnel of the organization shall ensure that the organization has an effective compliance and ethics program, as described in this guideline. Specific individual(s) within high-level personnel shall be assigned overall responsibility for the compliance and ethics program.

(C) Specific individual(s) within the organization shall be delegated day-to-day operational responsibility for the compliance and ethics program. Individual(s) with operational responsibility shall report periodically to high-level personnel and, as appropriate, to the governing authority, or an appropriate subgroup of the governing authority, on the effectiveness of the compliance and ethics program. To carry out such operational responsibility, such individual(s) shall be given adequate resources, appropriate authority, and direct access to the governing authority or an appropriate subgroup of the governing authority.

(3) The organization shall use reasonable efforts not to include within the substantial authority personnel of the organization any individual whom the organization knew, or should have known through the exercise of due diligence, has engaged in illegal activities or other conduct inconsistent with an effective compliance and ethics program.

(4)

(A) The organization shall take reasonable steps to communicate periodically and in a practical manner its standards and procedures, and other aspects of the compliance and ethics program, to the individuals referred to in subparagraph (B) by conducting effective training programs and otherwise disseminating information appropriate to such individuals' respective roles and responsibilities.

(B) The individuals referred to in subparagraph (A) are the members of the governing authority, high-level personnel, substantial authority personnel, the organization's employees, and, as appropriate, the organization's agents.

(5) The organization shall take reasonable steps—

(A) to ensure that the organization's compliance and ethics program is followed, including monitoring and auditing to detect criminal conduct;

(B) to evaluate periodically the effectiveness of the organization's compliance and ethics program; and

(C) to have and publicize a system, which may include mechanisms that allow for anonymity or confidentiality, whereby the organization's employees and agents may report or seek guidance regarding potential or actual criminal conduct without fear of retaliation.

(6) The organization's compliance and ethics program shall be promoted and enforced consistently throughout the organization through

(A) appropriate incentives to perform in accordance with the compliance and ethics program; and

(B) appropriate disciplinary measures for engaging in criminal conduct and for failing to take reasonable steps to prevent or detect criminal conduct.

(7) After criminal conduct has been detected, the organization shall take reasonable steps to respond appropriately to the criminal conduct and to prevent further similar criminal conduct, including making any necessary modifications to the organization's compliance and ethics program.

(c) In implementing subsection (b), the organization shall periodically assess the risk of criminal conduct and shall take appropriate steps to design, implement, or modify each requirement set forth in subsection (b) to reduce the risk of criminal conduct identified through this process.

COMMENTARY

Application Notes:

1. Definitions.— For purposes of this guideline:

"Compliance and ethics program" means a program designed to prevent and detect criminal conduct.

"Governing authority" means the

(A) the Board of Directors; or

(B) if the organization does not have a Board of Directors, the highest-level governing body of the organization.

"High-level personnel of the organization" and "substantial authority personnel" have the meaning given those terms in the Commentary to § 8A1.2 (Application Instructions — Organizations).

"Standards and procedures" means standards of conduct and internal controls that are reasonably capable of reducing the likelihood of criminal conduct.

2. Factors to Consider in Meeting Requirements of this Guideline.—

(A) In General.— Each of the requirements set forth in this guideline shall be met by an organization; however, in determining what specific actions are necessary to meet those requirements, factors that shall be considered include:

(i) applicable industry practice or the standards called for by any applicable governmental regulation;

(ii) the size of the organization; and

(iii) similar misconduct.

(B) Applicable Governmental Regulation and Industry Practice.— An organization's failure to incorporate and follow applicable industry practice or the standards called for by any applicable governmental regulation weighs against a finding of an effective compliance and ethics program.

(C) The Size of the Organization.—

(i) In General.— The formality and scope of actions that an organization shall take to meet the requirements of this guideline, including the necessary features of the organization's standards and procedures, depend on the size of the organization.

(ii) Large Organizations.— A large organization generally shall devote more formal operations and greater resources in meeting the requirements of this guideline than shall a small organization. As appropriate, a large organization should encourage small organizations (especially those that have, or seek to have, a business relationship with the large organization) to implement effective compliance and ethics programs.

(iii) Small Organizations.— In meeting the requirements of this guideline, small organizations shall demonstrate the same degree of commitment to ethical conduct and compliance with the law as large organizations. However, a small organization may meet the requirements of this guideline with less formality and fewer resources than would be expected of large organizations. In appropriate circumstances, reliance on existing resources and simple systems can demonstrate a degree of commitment that, for a large organization, would only be demonstrated through more formally planned and implemented systems.

Examples of the informality and use of fewer resources with which a small organization may meet the requirements of this guideline include the following:

(I) the governing authority's discharge of its responsibility for oversight of the compliance and ethics program by directly managing the organization's compliance and ethics efforts;

(II) training employees through informal staff meetings, and monitoring through regular "walk-arounds" or continuous observation while managing the organization;

(III) using available personnel, rather than employing separate staff, to carry out the compliance and ethics program; and

(IV) modeling its own compliance and ethics program on existing, well-regarded compliance and ethics programs and best practices of other similar organizations.

(D) Recurrence of Similar Misconduct.— Recurrence of similar misconduct creates doubt regarding whether the organization took reasonable steps to meet the requirements of this guideline. For purposes of this subparagraph, "similar misconduct" has the meaning given that term in the Commentary to § 8A1.2 (Application Instructions — Organizations).

3. Application of Subsection (b)(2).— High-level personnel and substantial authority personnel of the organization shall be knowledgeable about the content and operation of the compliance and ethics program, shall perform their assigned duties consistent with the exercise of due diligence, and shall promote an organizational culture that encourages ethical conduct and a commitment to compliance with the law.

If the specific individual(s) assigned overall responsibility for the compliance and ethics program does not have day-to-day operational responsibility for the program, then the individual(s) with day-to-day operational responsibility for the program typically should, no less than annually, give the governing authority or an appropriate subgroup thereof information on the implementation and effectiveness of the compliance and ethics program.

4. Application of Subsection (b)(3).—

(A) Consistency with Other Law.— Nothing in subsection (b)(3) is intended to require conduct inconsistent with any Federal, State, or local law, including any law governing employment or hiring practices.

(B) Implementation.— In implementing subsection (b)(3), the organization shall hire and promote individuals so as to ensure that all individuals within the high-level personnel and substantial authority personnel of the organization will perform their assigned duties in a manner consistent with the exercise of due diligence and the promotion of an organizational culture that encourages ethical conduct and a commitment to compliance with the law under subsection (a). With respect to the hiring or promotion of such individuals, an organization shall consider the relatedness of the individual's illegal activities and other misconduct (i.e., other conduct inconsistent with an effective compliance and ethics program) to the specific responsibilities the individual is anticipated to be assigned and other factors such as:

(i) the recency of the individual's illegal activities and other misconduct; and

(ii) whether the individual has engaged in other such illegal activities and other such misconduct.

5. Application of Subsection (b)(6).— Adequate discipline of individuals responsible for an offense is a necessary component of enforcement; however, the form of discipline that will be appropriate will be case specific.

6. Application of Subsection (b)(7).— Subsection (b)(7) has two aspects.

First, the organization should respond appropriately to the criminal conduct. The organization should take reasonable steps, as warranted under the circumstances, to remedy the harm resulting from the criminal conduct. These steps may include, where appropriate, providing restitution to identifiable victims, as well as other forms of remediation. Other reasonable steps to respond appropriately to the criminal conduct may include self-reporting and cooperation with authorities.

Second, the organization should act appropriately to prevent further similar criminal conduct, including assessing the compliance and ethics program and making modifications necessary to ensure the program is effective. The steps taken should be consistent with subsections (b)(5) and (c) and may include the use of an outside professional advisor to ensure adequate assessment and implementation of any modifications.

7. Application of Subsection (c).— To meet the requirements of subsection (c), an organization shall:

(A) Assess periodically the risk that criminal conduct will occur, including assessing the following:

(i) The nature and seriousness of such criminal conduct.

(ii) The likelihood that certain criminal conduct may occur because of the nature of the organization's business. If, because of the nature of an organization's business, there is a substantial risk that certain types of criminal conduct may occur, the organization shall take reasonable steps to prevent and detect that type of criminal conduct. For example, an organization that, due to the nature of its business, employs sales personnel who have flexibility to set prices shall establish standards and procedures designed to prevent and detect price-fixing. An organization that, due to the nature of its business, employs sales personnel who have flexibility to represent the material characteristics of a product shall establish standards and procedures designed to prevent and detect fraud.

(iii) The prior history of the organization. The prior history of an organization may indicate types of criminal conduct that it shall take actions to prevent and detect.

(B) Prioritize periodically, as appropriate, the actions taken pursuant to any requirement set forth in subsection (b), in order to focus on preventing and detecting the criminal conduct identified under subparagraph (A) of this note as most serious, and most likely, to occur.

(C) Modify, as appropriate, the actions taken pursuant to any requirement set forth in subsection (b) to reduce the risk of criminal conduct identified under subparagraph (A) of this note as most serious, and most likely, to occur.

Background: This section sets forth the requirements for an effective compliance and ethics program. This section responds to section 805(a)(5) of the Sarbanes-Oxley Act of 2002, Public Law 107-204, which directed the Commission to review and amend, as appropriate, the guidelines and related policy statements to ensure that the guidelines that apply to organizations in this chapter "are sufficient to deter and punish organizational criminal misconduct."

The requirements set forth in this guideline are intended to achieve reasonable prevention and detection of criminal conduct for which the organization would be vicariously liable. The prior diligence of an organization in seeking to prevent and detect criminal conduct has a direct bearing on the appropriate penalties and probation terms for the organization if it is convicted and sentenced for a criminal offense.

PART C — FINES

§ 8C1.1. Determining the Fine — Criminal Purpose Organizations

If, upon consideration of the nature and circumstances of the offense and the history and characteristics of the organization, the court determines that the organization operated primarily for a criminal purpose or primarily by criminal means, the fine shall be set at an amount (subject to the statutory maximum) sufficient to divest the organization of all its net assets. When this section applies, Subpart 2 (Determining the Fine — Other Organizations) and § 8C3.4 (Fines Paid by Owners of Closely Held Organizations) do not apply.

COMMENTARY

Application Note:

1. "Net assets," as used in this section, means the assets remaining after payment of all legitimate claims against assets by known innocent bona fide creditors.

Background: This guideline addresses the case in which the court, based upon an examination of the nature and circumstances of the offense and the history and characteristics of the organization, determines that the organization was operated primarily for a criminal purpose (e.g., a front for a scheme that was designed to commit fraud; an organization established to participate in the illegal manufacture, importation, or distribution of a controlled substance) or operated primarily by criminal means (e.g., a hazardous waste disposal business that had no legitimate means of disposing of hazardous waste). In such a case, the fine shall be set at an amount sufficient to remove all of the organization's net assets. If the extent of the assets of the organization is unknown, the maximum fine authorized by statute should be imposed, absent innocent bona fide creditors.

§ 8C2.1. Applicability of Fine Guidelines

The provisions of §§ 8C2.2 through 8C2.9 apply to each count for which the applicable guideline offense level is determined under:

(a) §§ 2B1.1, 2B1.4, 2B2.3, 2B4.1, 2B5.3, 2B6.1; §§ 2C1.1, 2C1.2, 2C1.6;

§§ 2E3.1, 2E4.1, 2E5.1, 2E5.3;

§ 2G3.1;

§§ 2K1.1, 2K2.1;

§ 2L1.1;

§ 2N3.1;

§ 2R1.1;

§§ 2S1.1, 2S1.3;

§§ 2T1.1, 2T1.4, 2T1.6, 2T1.7, 2T1.8, 2T1.9, 2T2.1, 2T2.2, 2T3.1; or

§§ 2D1.7, 2D3.1, 2D3.2;

(b) §§ 2E1.1, 2X1.1, 2X2.1, 2X3.1, 2X4.1, with respect to cases in which the offense level for the underlying offense is determined under one of the guideline sections listed in subsection (a) above.

COMMENTARY

Application Notes:

1. If the Chapter Two offense guideline for a count is listed in subsection (a) or (b) above, and the applicable guideline results in the determination of the offense level by use of one of the listed guidelines, apply the provisions of §§ 8C2.2 through 8C2.9 to that count. For example, §§ 8C2.2 through 8C2.9 apply to an offense under § 2K2.1 (an offense guideline listed in subsection (a)), unless the cross reference in that guideline requires the offense level to be determined under an offense guideline section not listed in subsection (a).

2. If the Chapter Two offense guideline for a count is not listed in subsection (a) or (b) above, but the applicable guideline results in the determination of the offense level by use of a listed guideline, apply the provisions of §§ 8C2.2 through 8C2.9 to that count. For example, where the conduct set forth in a count of conviction ordinarily referenced to § 2N2.1 (an offense guideline not listed in

subsection (a)) establishes § 2B1.1 (Theft, Property Destruction, and Fraud) as the applicable offense guideline (an offense guideline listed in subsection (a)), §§ 8C2.2 through 8C2.9 would apply because the actual offense level is determined under § 2B1.1 (Theft, Property Destruction, and Fraud).

Background: The fine guidelines of this subpart apply only to offenses covered by the guideline sections set forth in subsection (a) above. For example, the provisions of §§ 8C2.2 through 8C2.9 do not apply to counts for which the applicable guideline offense level is determined under Chapter Two, Part Q (Offenses Involving the Environment). For such cases, § 8C2.10 (Determining the Fine for Other Counts) is applicable.

§ 8C2.3. Offense Level

(a) For each count covered by § 8C2.1 (Applicability of Fine Guidelines), use the applicable Chapter Two guideline to determine the base offense level and apply, in the order listed, any appropriate adjustments contained in that guideline.

(b) Where there is more than one such count, apply Chapter Three, Part D (Multiple Counts) to determine the combined offense level.

COMMENTARY

Application Notes:

1. In determining the offense level under this section, "defendant," as used in Chapter Two, includes any agent of the organization for whose conduct the organization is criminally responsible.

2. In determining the offense level under this section, apply the provisions of §§ 1B1.2 through 1B1.8. Do not apply the adjustments in Chapter Three, Parts A (Victim-Related Adjustments), B (Role in the Offense), C (Obstruction and Related Adjustments), and E (Acceptance of Responsibility).

§ 8C2.4. Base Fine

(a) The base fine is the greatest of:

(1) the amount from the table in subsection (d) below corresponding to the offense level determined under § 8C2.3 (Offense Level); or

(2) the pecuniary gain to the organization from the offense; or

(3) the pecuniary loss from the offense caused by the organization, to the extent the loss was caused intentionally, knowingly, or recklessly.

(b) Provided, that if the applicable offense guideline in Chapter Two includes a special instruction for organizational fines, that special instruction shall be applied, as appropriate.

(c) Provided, further, that to the extent the calculation of either pecuniary gain or pecuniary loss would unduly complicate or prolong the sentencing process, that amount, i.e., gain or loss as appropriate, shall not be used for the determination of the base fine.

(d) Offense Level Fine Table

Offense Level	Amount
6 or less	$ 5,000
7	7,500
8	10,000
9	15,000
10	20,000
11	30,000
12	40,000
13	60,000
14	85,000
15	125,000
16	175,000
17	250,000
18	350,000
19	500,000
20	650,000
21	910,000
22	1,200,000
23	1,600,000
24	2,100,000
25	2,800,000
26	3,700,000
27	4,800,000
28	6,300,000
29	8,100,000
30	10,500,000
31	13,500,000
32	17,500,000
33	22,000,000
34	28,500,000
35	36,000,000
36	45,500,000
37	57,500,000
38 or more	72,500,000

COMMENTARY

Application Notes:

1. "Pecuniary gain," "pecuniary loss," and "offense" are defined in the Commentary to § 8A1.2 (Application Instructions — Organizations). Note that subsections (a)(2) and (a)(3) contain certain limitations as to the use of pecuniary gain and pecuniary loss in determining the base fine. Under subsection (a)(2), the pecuniary gain used to determine the base fine is the pecuniary gain to the organization from the offense. Under subsection (a)(3), the pecuniary loss used to determine the base fine is the pecuniary loss from the offense caused by the organization, to the extent that such loss was caused intentionally, knowingly, or recklessly.

2. Under 18 U.S.C. § 3571(d), the court is not required to calculate pecuniary loss or pecuniary gain to the extent that determination of loss or gain would unduly complicate or prolong the sentencing process. Nevertheless, the court may need to approximate loss in order to calculate offense levels under Chapter Two. See Commentary to § 2B1.1 (Theft, Property Destruction, and Fraud). If loss is approximated for purposes of determining the applicable offense level, the court should use that approximation as the starting point for calculating pecuniary loss under this section.

3. In a case of an attempted offense or a conspiracy to commit an offense, pecuniary loss and pecuniary gain are to be determined in accordance with the principles stated in § 2X1.1 (Attempt, Solicitation, or Conspiracy).

4. In a case involving multiple participants (i.e., multiple organizations, or the organization and individual(s) unassociated with the organization), the applicable offense level is to be determined without regard to apportionment of the gain from or loss caused by the offense. See § 1B1.3 (Relevant Conduct). However, if the base fine is determined under subsections (a)(2) or (a)(3), the court may, as appropriate, apportion gain or loss considering the defendant's relative culpability and other pertinent factors. Note also that under § 2R1.1(d)(1), the volume of commerce, which is used in determining a proxy for loss under § 8C2.4(a)(3), is limited to the volume of commerce attributable to the defendant.

5. Special instructions regarding the determination of the base fine are contained in §§ 2B4.1 (Bribery in Procurement of Bank Loan and Other Commercial Bribery); 2C1.1 (Offering, Giving, Soliciting, or Receiving a Bribe; Extortion Under Color of Official Right; Fraud Involving the Deprivation of the Intangible Right to Honest Services of Public Officials; Conspiracy to Defraud by Interference with Governmental Functions); 2C1.2 (Offering, Giving, Soliciting, or Receiving a Gratuity); 2E5.1 (Offering, Accepting, or Soliciting a Bribe or Gratuity Affecting the Operation of an Employee Welfare or Pension Benefit Plan; Prohibited Payments or Lending of Money by Employer or Agent to Employees, Representatives, or Labor Organizations); and 2R1.1 (Bid-Rigging, Price-Fixing or Market-Allocation Agreements Among Competitors).

Background: Under this section, the base fine is determined in one of three ways:

(1) by the amount, based on the offense level, from the table in subsection (d);

(2) by the pecuniary gain to the organization from the offense; and

(3) by the pecuniary loss caused by the organization, to the extent that such loss was caused intentionally, knowingly, or recklessly.

In certain cases, special instructions for determining the loss or offense level amount apply. As a general rule, the base fine measures the seriousness of the offense. The determinants of the base fine are selected so that, in conjunction with the multipliers derived from the culpability score in § 8C2.5 (Culpability Score), they will result in guideline fine ranges appropriate to deter organizational criminal conduct and to provide incentives for organizations to maintain internal mechanisms for preventing, detecting, and reporting criminal conduct. In order to deter organizations from seeking to obtain financial reward through criminal conduct, this section provides that, when greatest, pecuniary gain to the organization is used to determine the base fine. In order to ensure that organizations will seek to prevent losses intentionally, knowingly, or recklessly caused by their agents, this section provides that, when greatest, pecuniary loss is used to determine the base fine in such circumstances. Chapter Two provides special instructions for fines that include specific rules for determining the base fine in connection with certain types of offenses in which the calculation of loss or gain is difficult, e.g., price-fixing. For these offenses, the special instructions tailor the base fine to circumstances that occur in connection with such offenses and that generally relate to the magnitude of loss or gain resulting from such offenses.

§ 8C2.5. Culpability Score

(a) Start with 5 points and apply subsections (b) through (g) below.

(b) Involvement in or Tolerance of Criminal Activity

If more than one applies, use the greatest:

(1)

(A) the organization had 5,000 or more employees and

(i) an individual within high-level personnel of the organization participated in, condoned, or was willfully ignorant of the offense; or

(ii) tolerance of the offense by substantial authority personnel was pervasive throughout the organization; or

(B) the unit of the organization within which the offense was committed had 5,000 or more employees and

(i) an individual within high-level personnel of the unit participated in, condoned, or was willfully ignorant of the offense; or

(ii) tolerance of the offense by substantial authority personnel was pervasive throughout such unit,

add 5 points; or

(2) If—

(A) the organization had 1,000 or more employees and

(i) an individual within high-level personnel of the organization participated in, condoned, or was willfully ignorant of the offense; or

(ii) tolerance of the offense by substantial authority personnel was pervasive throughout the organization; or

(B) the unit of the organization within which the offense was committed had 1,000 or more employees and

(i) an individual within high-level personnel of the unit participated in, condoned, or was willfully ignorant of the offense; or

(ii) tolerance of the offense by substantial authority personnel was pervasive throughout such unit,

add 4 points; or

(3) If—

(A) the organization had 200 or more employees and

(i) an individual within high-level personnel of the organization participated in, condoned, or was willfully ignorant of the offense; or

(ii) tolerance of the offense by substantial authority personnel was pervasive throughout the organization; or

(B) the unit of the organization within which the offense was committed had 200 or more employees and

(i) an individual within high-level personnel of the unit participated in, condoned, or was willfully ignorant of the offense; or

(ii) tolerance of the offense by substantial authority personnel was pervasive throughout such unit,

add 3 points; or

(4) If the organization had 50 or more employees and an individual within substantial authority personnel participated in, condoned, or was willfully ignorant of the offense, add 2 points; or

(5) If the organization had 10 or more employees and an individual within substantial authority personnel participated in, condoned, or was willfully ignorant of the offense, add 1 point.

(c) Prior History

If more than one applies, use the greater:

(1) If the organization (or separately managed line of business) committed any part of the instant offense less than 10 years after

(A) a criminal adjudication based on similar misconduct; or

(B) civil or administrative adjudication(s) based on two or more separate instances of similar misconduct, add 1 point; or

(2) If the organization (or separately managed line of business) committed any

part of the instant offense less than 5 years after

(A) a criminal adjudication based on similar misconduct; or

(B) civil or administrative adjudication(s) based on two or more separate instances of similar misconduct, add 2 points.

(d) Violation of an Order

If more than one applies, use the greater:

(1)

(A) If the commission of the instant offense violated a judicial order or injunction, other than a violation of a condition of probation; or

(B) if the organization (or separately managed line of business) violated a condition of probation by engaging in similar misconduct, i.e., misconduct similar to that for which it was placed on probation, add 2 points; or

(2) If the commission of the instant offense violated a condition of probation, add 1 point.

(e) Obstruction of Justice

If the organization willfully obstructed or impeded, attempted to obstruct or impede, or aided, abetted, or encouraged obstruction of justice during the investigation, prosecution, or sentencing of the instant offense, or, with knowledge thereof, failed to take reasonable steps to prevent such obstruction or impedance or attempted obstruction or impedance, add 3 points.

(f) Effective Compliance and Ethics Program

(1) If the offense occurred even though the organization had in place at the time of the offense an effective compliance and ethics program, as provided in § 8B2.1 (Effective Compliance and Ethics Program), subtract 3 points.

(2) Subsection (f)(1) shall not apply if, after becoming aware of an offense, the organization unreasonably delayed reporting the offense to appropriate governmental authorities.

(3)

(A) Except as provided in subparagraphs (B) and (C), subsection (f)(1) shall not apply if an individual within high-level personnel of the organization, a person within high-level personnel of the unit of the organization within which the offense was committed where the unit had 200 or more employees, or an individual described in § 8B2.1(b)(2)(B) or (C), participated in, condoned, or was willfully ignorant of the offense.

(B) There is a rebuttable presumption, for purposes of subsection (f)(1), that the organization did not have an effective compliance and ethics program if an individual—

(i) within high-level personnel of a small organization; or

(ii) within substantial authority personnel, but not within high-level personnel, of any organization, participated in, condoned, or was willfully ignorant of, the offense.

(C) Subparagraphs (A) and (B) shall not apply if—

(i) the individual or individuals with operational responsibility for the compliance and ethics program (see § 8B2.1(b)(2)(C)) have direct reporting obligations to the governing authority or an appropriate subgroup thereof (e.g., an audit committee of the board of directors);

(ii) the compliance and ethics program detected the offense before discovery outside the organization or before such discovery was reasonably likely;

(iii) the organization promptly reported the offense to appropriate governmental authorities; and

(iv) no individual with operational responsibility for the compliance and ethics program participated in, condoned, or was willfully ignorant of the offense.

(g) Self-Reporting, Cooperation, and Acceptance of Responsibility

If more than one applies, use the greatest:

(1) If the organization

(A) prior to an imminent threat of disclosure or government investigation; and

(B) within a reasonably prompt time after becoming aware of the offense, reported the offense to appropriate governmental authorities, fully cooperated in the investigation, and clearly demonstrated recognition and affirmative acceptance of responsibility for its criminal conduct, subtract 5 points; or

(2) If the organization fully cooperated in the investigation and clearly demonstrated recognition and affirmative acceptance of responsibility for its criminal conduct, subtract 2 points; or

(3) If the organization clearly demonstrated recognition and affirmative acceptance of responsibility for its criminal conduct, subtract 1 point.

COMMENTARY

Application Notes:

1. Definitions.— For purposes of this guideline, "condoned", "prior criminal adjudication", "similar misconduct", "substantial authority personnel", and "willfully ignorant of the offense" have the meaning given those terms in Application Note 3 of the Commentary to § 8A1.2 (Application Instructions — Organizations).

"Small Organization", for purposes of subsection (f)(3), means an organization that, at the time of the instant offense, had fewer than 200 employees.

2. For purposes of subsection (b), "unit of the organization" means any reasonably distinct operational component of the organization. For example, a

large organization may have several large units such as divisions or subsidiaries, as well as many smaller units such as specialized manufacturing, marketing, or accounting operations within these larger units. For purposes of this definition, all of these types of units are encompassed within the term "unit of the organization."

3. "High-level personnel of the organization" is defined in the Commentary to § 8A1.2 (Application Instructions — Organizations). With respect to a unit with 200 or more employees, "high-level personnel of a unit of the organization" means agents within the unit who set the policy for or control that unit. For example, if the managing agent of a unit with 200 employees participated in an offense, three points would be added under subsection (b)(3); if that organization had 1,000 employees and the managing agent of the unit with 200 employees were also within high-level personnel of the organization in its entirety, four points (rather than three) would be added under subsection (b)(2).

4. Pervasiveness under subsection (b) will be case specific and depend on the number, and degree of responsibility, of individuals within substantial authority personnel who participated in, condoned, or were willfully ignorant of the offense. Fewer individuals need to be involved for a finding of pervasiveness if those individuals exercised a relatively high degree of authority. Pervasiveness can occur either within an organization as a whole or within a unit of an organization. For example, if an offense were committed in an organization with 1,000 employees but the tolerance of the offense was pervasive only within a unit of the organization with 200 employees (and no high-level personnel of the organization participated in, condoned, or was willfully ignorant of the offense), three points would be added under subsection (b)(3). If, in the same organization, tolerance of the offense was pervasive throughout the organization as a whole, or an individual within high-level personnel of the organization participated in the offense, four points (rather than three) would be added under subsection (b)(2).

5. A "separately managed line of business," as used in subsections (c) and (d), is a subpart of a for-profit organization that has its own management, has a high degree of autonomy from higher managerial authority, and maintains its own separate books of account. Corporate subsidiaries and divisions frequently are separately managed lines of business. Under subsection (c), in determining the prior history of an organization with separately managed lines of business, only the prior conduct or criminal record of the separately managed line of business involved in the instant offense is to be used. Under subsection (d), in the context of an organization with separately managed lines of business, in making the determination whether a violation of a condition of probation involved engaging in similar misconduct, only the prior misconduct of the separately managed line of business involved in the instant offense is to be considered.

6. Under subsection (c), in determining the prior history of an organization or separately managed line of business, the conduct of the underlying economic entity shall be considered without regard to its legal structure or ownership. For example, if two companies merged and became separate divisions and separately managed lines of business within the merged company, each division would retain the prior history of its predecessor company. If a company reorganized and

became a new legal entity, the new company would retain the prior history of the predecessor company. In contrast, if one company purchased the physical assets but not the ongoing business of another company, the prior history of the company selling the physical assets would not be transferred to the company purchasing the assets. However, if an organization is acquired by another organization in response to solicitations by appropriate federal government officials, the prior history of the acquired organization shall not be attributed to the acquiring organization.

7. Under subsections (c)(1)(B) and (c)(2)(B), the civil or administrative adjudication(s) must have occurred within the specified period (ten or five years) of the instant offense.

8. Adjust the culpability score for the factors listed in subsection (e) whether or not the offense guideline incorporates that factor, or that factor is inherent in the offense.

9. Subsection (e) applies where the obstruction is committed on behalf of the organization; it does not apply where an individual or individuals have attempted to conceal their misconduct from the organization. The Commentary to § 3C1.1 (Obstructing or Impeding the Administration of Justice) provides guidance regarding the types of conduct that constitute obstruction.

10. Subsection (f)(2) contemplates that the organization will be allowed a reasonable period of time to conduct an internal investigation. In addition, no reporting is required by subsection (f)(2) or (f)(3)(C)(iii) if the organization reasonably concluded, based on the information then available, that no offense had been committed.

11. For purposes of subsection (f)(3)(C)(i), an individual has "direct reporting obligations" to the governing authority or an appropriate subgroup thereof if the individual has express authority to communicate personally to the governing authority or appropriate subgroup thereof (A) promptly on any matter involving criminal conduct or potential criminal conduct, and (B) no less than annually on the implementation and effectiveness of the compliance and ethics program.

12. "Appropriate governmental authorities," as used in subsections (f) and (g)(1), means the federal or state law enforcement, regulatory, or program officials having jurisdiction over such matter. To qualify for a reduction under subsection (g)(1), the report to appropriate governmental authorities must be made under the direction of the organization.

13. To qualify for a reduction under subsection (g)(1) or (g)(2), cooperation must be both timely and thorough. To be timely, the cooperation must begin essentially at the same time as the organization is officially notified of a criminal investigation. To be thorough, the cooperation should include the disclosure of all pertinent information known by the organization. A prime test of whether the organization has disclosed all pertinent information is whether the information is sufficient for law enforcement personnel to identify the nature and extent of the offense and the individual(s) responsible for the criminal conduct. However, the cooperation to be measured is the cooperation of the organization itself, not the cooperation of individuals within the organization. If, because of the lack of

cooperation of particular individual(s), neither the organization nor law enforcement personnel are able to identify the culpable individual(s) within the organization despite the organization's efforts to cooperate fully, the organization may still be given credit for full cooperation.

14. Entry of a plea of guilty prior to the commencement of trial combined with truthful admission of involvement in the offense and related conduct ordinarily will constitute significant evidence of affirmative acceptance of responsibility under subsection (g), unless outweighed by conduct of the organization that is inconsistent with such acceptance of responsibility. This adjustment is not intended to apply to an organization that puts the government to its burden of proof at trial by denying the essential factual elements of guilt, is convicted, and only then admits guilt and expresses remorse. Conviction by trial, however, does not automatically preclude an organization from consideration for such a reduction. In rare situations, an organization may clearly demonstrate an acceptance of responsibility for its criminal conduct even though it exercises its constitutional right to a trial. This may occur, for example, where an organization goes to trial to assert and preserve issues that do not relate to factual guilt (e.g., to make a constitutional challenge to a statute or a challenge to the applicability of a statute to its conduct). In each such instance, however, a determination that an organization has accepted responsibility will be based primarily upon pretrial statements and conduct.

15. In making a determination with respect to subsection (g), the court may determine that the chief executive officer or highest ranking employee of an organization should appear at sentencing in order to signify that the organization has clearly demonstrated recognition and affirmative acceptance of responsibility.

Background: The increased culpability scores under subsection (b) are based on three interrelated principles. First, an organization is more culpable when individuals who manage the organization or who have substantial discretion in acting for the organization participate in, condone, or are willfully ignorant of criminal conduct. Second, as organizations become larger and their managements become more professional, participation in, condonation of, or willful ignorance of criminal conduct by such management is increasingly a breach of trust or abuse of position. Third, as organizations increase in size, the risk of criminal conduct beyond that reflected in the instant offense also increases whenever management's tolerance of that offense is pervasive. Because of the continuum of sizes of organizations and professionalization of management, subsection (b) gradually increases the culpability score based upon the size of the organization and the level and extent of the substantial authority personnel involvement.

§ 8C2.6. Minimum and Maximum Multipliers

Using the culpability score from § 8C2.5 (Culpability Score) and applying any applicable special instruction for fines in Chapter Two, determine the applicable minimum and maximum fine multipliers from the table below.

Culpability Score	Minimum Multiplier	Maximum Multiplier
10 or more	2.00	4.00
9	1.80	3.60
8	1.60	3.20
7	1.40	2.80
6	1.20	2.40
5	1.00	2.00
4	0.80	1.60
3	0.60	1.20
2	0.40	0.80
1	0.20	0.40
0 or less	0.05	0.20.

COMMENTARY

Application Note:

1. A special instruction for fines in § 2R1.1 (Bid-Rigging, Price-Fixing or Market-Allocation Agreements Among Competitors) sets a floor for minimum and maximum multipliers in cases covered by that guideline.

§ 8C2.7. Guideline Fine Range — Organizations

(a) The minimum of the guideline fine range is determined by multiplying the base fine determined under § 8C2.4 (Base Fine) by the applicable minimum multiplier determined under § 8C2.6 (Minimum and Maximum Multipliers).

(b) The maximum of the guideline fine range is determined by multiplying the base fine determined under § 8C2.4 (Base Fine) by the applicable maximum multiplier determined under § 8C2.6 (Minimum and Maximum Multipliers).

§ 8C2.8. Determining the Fine Within the Range (Policy Statement)

(a) In determining the amount of the fine within the applicable guideline range, the court should consider:

(1) the need for the sentence to reflect the seriousness of the offense, promote respect for the law, provide just punishment, afford adequate deterrence, and protect the public from further crimes of the organization;

(2) the organization's role in the offense;

(3) any collateral consequences of conviction, including civil obligations arising from the organization's conduct;

(4) any nonpecuniary loss caused or threatened by the offense;

(5) whether the offense involved a vulnerable victim;

(6) any prior criminal record of an individual within high-level personnel of the organization or high-level personnel of a unit of the organization who participated in, condoned, or was willfully ignorant of the criminal conduct;

(7) any prior civil or criminal misconduct by the organization other than that counted under § 8C2.5(c);

(8) any culpability score under § 8C2.5 (Culpability Score) higher than 10 or lower than 0;

(9) partial but incomplete satisfaction of the conditions for one or more of the mitigating or aggravating factors set forth in § 8C2.5 (Culpability Score);

(10) any factor listed in 18 U.S.C. § 3572(a); and

(11) whether the organization failed to have, at the time of the instant offense, an effective compliance and ethics program within the meaning of § 8B2.1 (Effective Compliance and Ethics Program).

(b) In addition, the court may consider the relative importance of any factor used to determine the range, including the pecuniary loss caused by the offense, the pecuniary gain from the offense, any specific offense characteristic used to determine the offense level, and any aggravating or mitigating factor used to determine the culpability score.

COMMENTARY

Application Notes:

1. Subsection (a)(2) provides that the court, in setting the fine within the guideline fine range, should consider the organization's role in the offense. This consideration is particularly appropriate if the guideline fine range does not take the organization's role in the offense into account. For example, the guideline fine range in an antitrust case does not take into consideration whether the organization was an organizer or leader of the conspiracy. A higher fine within the guideline fine range ordinarily will be appropriate for an organization that takes a leading role in such an offense.

2. Subsection (a)(3) provides that the court, in setting the fine within the guideline fine range, should consider any collateral consequences of conviction, including civil obligations arising from the organization's conduct. As a general rule, collateral consequences that merely make victims whole provide no basis for reducing the fine within the guideline range. If criminal and civil sanctions are unlikely to make victims whole, this may provide a basis for a higher fine within the guideline fine range. If punitive collateral sanctions have been or will be imposed on the organization, this may provide a basis for a lower fine within the guideline fine range.

3. Subsection (a)(4) provides that the court, in setting the fine within the guideline fine range, should consider any nonpecuniary loss caused or threatened by the offense. To the extent that nonpecuniary loss caused or threatened (e.g., loss of or threat to human life; psychological injury; threat to national security) by the offense is not adequately considered in setting the guideline fine range,

this factor provides a basis for a higher fine within the range. This factor is more likely to be applicable where the guideline fine range is determined by pecuniary loss or gain, rather than by offense level, because the Chapter Two offense levels frequently take actual or threatened nonpecuniary loss into account.

4. Subsection (a)(6) provides that the court, in setting the fine within the guideline fine range, should consider any prior criminal record of an individual within high-level personnel of the organization or within high-level personnel of a unit of the organization. Since an individual within high-level personnel either exercises substantial control over the organization or a unit of the organization or has a substantial role in the making of policy within the organization or a unit of the organization, any prior criminal misconduct of such an individual may be relevant to the determination of the appropriate fine for the organization.

5. Subsection (a)(7) provides that the court, in setting the fine within the guideline fine range, should consider any prior civil or criminal misconduct by the organization other than that counted under § 8C2.5(c). The civil and criminal misconduct counted under § 8C2.5(c) increases the guideline fine range. Civil or criminal misconduct other than that counted under § 8C2.5(c) may provide a basis for a higher fine within the range. In a case involving a pattern of illegality, an upward departure may be warranted.

6. Subsection (a)(8) provides that the court, in setting the fine within the guideline fine range, should consider any culpability score higher than ten or lower than zero. As the culpability score increases above ten, this may provide a basis for a higher fine within the range. Similarly, as the culpability score decreases below zero, this may provide a basis for a lower fine within the range.

7. Under subsection (b), the court, in determining the fine within the range, may consider any factor that it considered in determining the range. This allows for courts to differentiate between cases that have the same offense level but differ in seriousness (e.g., two fraud cases at offense level 12, one resulting in a loss of $21,000, the other $40,000). Similarly, this allows for courts to differentiate between two cases that have the same aggravating factors, but in which those factors vary in their intensity (e.g., two cases with upward adjustments to the culpability score under § 8C2.5(c)(2) (prior criminal adjudications within 5 years of the commencement of the instant offense, one involving a single conviction, the other involving two or more convictions).

Background: Subsection (a) includes factors that the court is required to consider under 18 U.S.C. §§ 3553(a) and 3572(a) as well as additional factors that the Commission has determined may be relevant in a particular case. A number of factors required for consideration under 18 U.S.C. § 3572(a) (e.g., pecuniary loss, the size of the organization) are used under the fine guidelines in this subpart to determine the fine range, and therefore are not specifically set out again in subsection (a) of this guideline. In unusual cases, factors listed in this section may provide a basis for departure.

§ 8C2.9. Disgorgement

The court shall add to the fine determined under § 8C2.8 (Determining the Fine Within the Range) any gain to the organization from the offense that has not and will not be paid as restitution or by way of other remedial measures.

COMMENTARY

Application Note:

1. This section is designed to ensure that the amount of any gain that has not and will not be taken from the organization for remedial purposes will be added to the fine. This section typically will apply in cases in which the organization has received gain from an offense but restitution or remedial efforts will not be required because the offense did not result in harm to identifiable victims, e.g., money laundering, obscenity, and regulatory reporting offenses. Money spent or to be spent to remedy the adverse effects of the offense, e.g., the cost to retrofit defective products, should be considered as disgorged gain. If the cost of remedial efforts made or to be made by the organization equals or exceeds the gain from the offense, this section will not apply.

PART D — ORGANIZATIONAL PROBATION

§ 8D1.1. Imposition of Probation — Organizations

(a) The court shall order a term of probation:

(1) if such sentence is necessary to secure payment of restitution (§ 8B1.1), enforce a remedial order (§ 8B1.2), or ensure completion of community service (§ 8B1.3);

(2) if the organization is sentenced to pay a monetary penalty (e.g., restitution, fine, or special assessment), the penalty is not paid in full at the time of sentencing, and restrictions are necessary to safeguard the organization's ability to make payments;

(3) if, at the time of sentencing,

(A) the organization

(i) has 50 or more employees, or

(ii) was otherwise required under law to have an effective compliance and ethics program; and

(B) the organization does not have such a program;

(4) if the organization within five years prior to sentencing engaged in similar misconduct, as determined by a prior criminal adjudication, and any part of the misconduct underlying the instant offense occurred after that adjudication;

(5) if an individual within high-level personnel of the organization or the unit of the organization within which the instant offense was committed participated in the misconduct underlying the instant offense and that individual within five years prior to sentencing engaged in similar misconduct, as determined by a prior criminal adjudication, and any part of the misconduct underlying the instant offense occurred after that adjudication;

(6) if such sentence is necessary to ensure that changes are made within the

organization to reduce the likelihood of future criminal conduct;

(7) if the sentence imposed upon the organization does not include a fine; or

(8) if necessary to accomplish one or more of the purposes of sentencing set forth in 18 U.S.C. § 3553(a)(2).

COMMENTARY

Background: Under 18 U.S.C. § 3561(a), an organization may be sentenced to a term of probation. Under 18 U.S.C. § 3551(c), imposition of a term of probation is required if the sentence imposed upon the organization does not include a fine.

§ 8D1.2. Term of Probation — Organizations

(a) When a sentence of probation is imposed—

(1) In the case of a felony, the term of probation shall be at least one year but not more than five years.

(2) In any other case, the term of probation shall be not more than five years.

COMMENTARY

Application Note:

1. Within the limits set by the guidelines, the term of probation should be sufficient, but not more than necessary, to accomplish the court's specific objectives in imposing the term of probation. The terms of probation set forth in this section are those provided in 18 U.S.C. § 3561(c).

§ 8D1.3. Conditions of Probation — Organizations

(a) Pursuant to 18 U.S.C. § 3563(a)(1), any sentence of probation shall include the condition that the organization not commit another federal, state, or local crime during the term of probation.

(b) Pursuant to 18 U.S.C. § 3563(a)(2), if a sentence of probation is imposed for a felony, the court shall impose as a condition of probation at least one of the following:

(1) restitution or

(2) community service, unless the court has imposed a fine, or unless the court finds on the record that extraordinary circumstances exist that would make such condition plainly unreasonable, in which event the court shall impose one or more other conditions set forth in18 U.S.C. § 3563(b).

(c) The court may impose other conditions that

(1) are reasonably related to the nature and circumstances of the offense or the history and characteristics of the organization; and

(2) involve only such deprivations of liberty or property as are necessary to effect the purposes of sentencing.

§ 8D1.4. Recommended Conditions of Probation — Organizations (Policy Statement)

(a) The court may order the organization, at its expense and in the format and media specified by the court, to publicize the nature of the offense committed, the fact of conviction, the nature of the punishment imposed, and the steps that will be taken to prevent the recurrence of similar offenses.

(b) If probation is imposed under § 8D1.1, the following conditions may be appropriate:

(1) The organization shall develop and submit to the court an effective compliance and ethics program consistent with § 8B2.1 (Effective Compliance and Ethics Program). The organization shall include in its submission a schedule for implementation of the compliance and ethics program.

(2) Upon approval by the court of a program referred to in paragraph (1), the organization shall notify its employees and shareholders of its criminal behavior and its program referred to in paragraph (1). Such notice shall be in a form prescribed by the court.

(3) The organization shall make periodic submissions to the court or probation officer, at intervals specified by the court,

(A) reporting on the organization's financial condition and results of business operations, and accounting for the disposition of all funds received, and

(B) reporting on the organization's progress in implementing the program referred to in paragraph (1). Among other things, reports under subparagraph (B) shall disclose any criminal prosecution, civil litigation, or administrative proceeding commenced against the organization, or any investigation or formal inquiry by governmental authorities of which the organization learned since its last report.

(4) The organization shall notify the court or probation officer immediately upon learning of

(A) any material adverse change in its business or financial condition or prospects, or

(B) the commencement of any bankruptcy proceeding, major civil litigation, criminal prosecution, or administrative proceeding against the organization, or any investigation or formal inquiry by governmental authorities regarding the organization.

(5) The organization shall submit to:

(A) a reasonable number of regular or unannounced examinations of its books and records at appropriate business premises by the probation officer or experts engaged by the court; and

(B) interrogation of knowledgeable individuals within the organization. Compensation to and costs of any experts engaged by the court shall be paid by the organization.

(6) The organization shall make periodic payments, as specified by the court, in the following priority:

(A) restitution;

(B) fine; and

(C) any other monetary sanction.

COMMENTARY

Application Note:

1. In determining the conditions to be imposed when probation is ordered under § 8D1.1, the court should consider the views of any governmental regulatory body that oversees conduct of the organization relating to the instant offense. To assess the efficacy of a compliance and ethics program submitted by the organization, the court may employ appropriate experts who shall be afforded access to all material possessed by the organization that is necessary for a comprehensive assessment of the proposed program. The court should approve any program that appears reasonably calculated to prevent and detect criminal conduct, as long as it is consistent with § 8B2.1 (Effective Compliance and Ethics Program), and any applicable statutory and regulatory requirements.

Periodic reports submitted in accordance with subsection (b)(3) should be provided to any governmental regulatory body that oversees conduct of the organization relating to the instant offense.

SENTENCING TABLE

The Sentencing Table used to determine the guideline range follows:

Criminal History Category (Criminal History Points)

	Offense Level	I (0 or 1)	II (2 or 3)	III (4, 5, 6)	IV (7, 8, 9)	V (10, 11, 12)	VI (13 or more)
Zone A	1	0–6	0–6	0–6	0–6	0–6	0–6
	2	0–6	0–6	0–6	0–6	0–6	1–7
	3	0–6	0–6	0–6	0–6	2–8	3–9
	4	0–6	0–6	0–6	2–8	4–10	6–12
	5	0–6	0–6	1–7	4–10	6–12	9–15
	6	0–6	1–7	2–8	6–12	9–15	12–18
	7	0–6	2–8	4–10	8–14	12–18	15–21
	8	0–6	4–10	6–12	10–16	15–21	18–24
Zone B	9	4–10	6–12	8–14	12–18	18–24	21–27
	10	6–12	8–14	10–16	15–21	21–27	24–30
Zone C	11	8–14	10–16	12–18	18–24	24–30	27–33
	12	10–16	12–18	15–21	21–27	27–33	30–37
Zone D	13	40165	15–21	18–24	24–30	30–37	33–41
	14	15–21	18–24	21–27	27–33	33–41	37–46
	15	18–24	21–27	24–30	30–37	37–46	41–51
	16	21–27	24–30	27–33	33–41	41–51	46–57
	17	24–30	27–33	30–37	37–46	46–57	51–63
	18	27–33	30–37	33–41	41–51	51–63	57–71
	19	30–37	33–41	37–46	46–57	57–71	63–78
	20	33–41	37–46	41–51	51–63	63–78	70–87
	21	37–46	41–51	46–57	57–71	70–87	77–96
	22	41–51	46–57	51–63	63–78	77–96	84–105
	23	46–57	51–63	57–71	70–87	84–105	92–115
	24	51–63	57–71	63–78	77–96	92–115	100–125
	25	57–71	63–78	70–87	84–105	100–125	110–137
	26	63–78	70–87	78–97	92–115	110–137	120–150
	27	70–87	78–97	87–108	100–125	120–150	130–162
	28	78–97	87–108	97–121	110–137	130–162	140–175
	29	87–108	97–121	108–135	121–151	140–175	151–188
	30	97–121	108–135	121–151	135–168	151–188	168–210
	31	108–135	121–151	135–168	151–188	168–210	188–235
	32	121–151	135–168	151–188	168–210	188–235	210–262
	33	135–168	151–188	168–210	188–235	210–262	235–293
	34	151–188	168–210	188–235	210–262	235–293	262–327
	35	168–210	188–235	210–262	235–293	262–327	292–365
	36	188–235	210–262	235–293	262–327	292–365	324–405
	37	210–262	235–293	262–327	292–365	324–405	360–life
	38	235–293	262–327	292–365	324–405	360–life	360–life
	39	262–327	292–365	324–405	360–life	360–life	360–life
	40	292–365	324–405	360–life	360–life	360–life	360–life
	41	324–405	360–life	360–life	360–life	360–life	360–life
	42	360–life	360–life	360–life	360–life	360–life	360–life
	43	life	life	life	life	life	life

Chapter 7
UNITED STATES SENTENCING GUIDELINES INDIVIDUAL WORKSHEETS

Worksheet A (Offense Level)

Defendant _____ District/Office _____

Docket Number (Year-Sequence-Defendant No.) ____ - ____ ____ ____ ____ - ____

Count Number(s) _____ U.S. Code Title & Section _____ : _____

_____ : _____

Guidelines Manual Edition Used: 20___ *(NOTE: worksheets keyed to the Manual effective November 1, 2010)*

Instructions:

For each count of conviction (or stipulated offense), complete a separate Worksheet A. Exception: Use only a single Worksheet A where the offense level for a group of closely related counts is based primarily on aggregate value or quantity (see §3D1.2(d)) or where a count of conspiracy, solicitation, or attempt is grouped with a substantive count that was the sole object of the conspiracy, solicitation, or attempt (see §3D1.2(a) and (b)).

1. **Offense Level** (See Chapter Two)

Enter the applicable base offense level and any specific offense characteristics from Chapter Two and explain the bases for these determinations. Enter the sum in the box provided.

Guideline	Description	Level
_____	_____	____
_____	_____	____
_____	_____	____
_____	_____	____
_____	_____	____
_____	_____	____

Sum [ ]

2. **Victim-Related Adjustments** (See Chapter Three, Part A)

Enter the applicable section and adjustment. If more than one section is applicable, list each section and enter the combined adjustment. If no adjustment is applicable enter "0." $_____ [ ]

3. **Role in the Offense Adjustments** (See Chapter Three, Part B)

Enter the applicable section and adjustment. If more than one section is applicable, list each section and enter the combined adjustment. If the adjustment reduces the offense level, enter a minus (-) sign in front of the adjustment. If no adjustment is applicable, enter "0." $_____ [ ]

4. **Obstruction Adjustments** (See Chapter Three, Part C)

Enter the applicable section and adjustment. If more than one section is applicable, list each section and enter the combined adjustment. If no adjustment is applicable, enter "0." $_____ [ ]

5. **Adjusted Offense Level**

Enter the sum of Items 1-4. If this worksheet does not cover all counts of conviction or stipulated offenses, complete Worksheet B. Otherwise, enter this result on Worksheet D, Item 1. [ ]

[ ] *Check if the defendant is convicted of a single count. In such case, Worksheet B need not be completed.*

[ ] *If the defendant has no criminal history, enter criminal history "I" here and on Item 4, Worksheet D. In such case, Worksheet C need not be completed.*

U.S. Sentencing Commission
November 22, 2010
H:\oesp\TRAINING\Worksheets\Worksheets-November2010.wpd

Worksheet B
(Multiple Counts or Stipulation to Additional Offenses)

Defendant _____   Docket Number _____

Instructions

Step 1: Determine if any of the counts group. (Note: All, some, or none of the counts may group. Some of the counts may have already been grouped in the application under Worksheet A, specifically, (1) counts grouped under §3D1.2(d), or (2) a count charging conspiracy, solicitation, or attempt that is grouped with the substantive count of conviction (see §3D1.2(a)). Explain the reasons for grouping:

_____

_____

_____

Step 2: Using the box(es) provided below, for each group of closely related counts, enter the highest adjusted offense level from the various "A" Worksheets (Item 5) that comprise the group (see §3D1.3). (Note: A "group" may consist of a single count that has not grouped with any other count. In those instances, the offense level for the group will be the adjusted offense level for the single count.)

Step 3: Enter the number of units to be assigned to each group (see §3D1.4) as follows:

- One unit (1) for the group of closely related counts with the highest offense level
- An additional unit (1) for each group that is equally serious or 1 to 4 levels less serious
- An additional half unit (1/2) for each group that is 5 to 8 levels less serious
- No increase in units for groups that are 9 or more levels less serious

1. **Adjusted Offense Level for the First Group of Closely Related Counts**
    Count number(s):_____   ☐ _____ (unit)

2. **Adjusted Offense Level for the Second Group of Closely Related Counts**
    Count number(s):_____   ☐ _____ (unit)

3. **Adjusted Offense Level for the Third Group of Closely Related Counts**
    Count number(s):_____   ☐ _____ (unit)

4. **Adjusted Offense Level for the Fourth Group of Closely Related Counts**
    Count number(s):_____   ☐ _____ (unit)

5. **Adjusted Offense Level for the Fifth Group of Closely Related Counts**
    Count number(s):_____   ☐ _____ (unit)

6. **Total Units**   _____
                                                       (total units)

7. **Increase in Offense Level Based on Total Units (See §3D1.4)**

    | 1 unit: | no increase | 2 1/2 - 3 units: | add 3 levels | ☐
    | 1 1/2 units: | add 1 level | 3 1/2 - 5 units: | add 4 levels |
    | 2 units: | add 2 levels | More than 5 units: | add 5 levels |

8. **Highest of the Adjusted Offense Levels from Items 1-5 Above**   ☐

9. **Combined Adjusted Offense Level (See §3D1.4)**   ☐
    Enter the sum of Items 7 and 8 here and on Worksheet D, Item 1.

Worksheet C (Criminal History)

Defendant _____ Docket Number _____

Enter the Date Defendant Commenced Participation in Instant Offense (Earliest Date of Relevant Conduct)_____

1. 3 Points for each prior ADULT sentence of imprisonment EXCEEDING ONE YEAR AND ONE MONTH imposed within 15 YEARS of the defendant's commencement of the instant offense OR resulting in incarceration during any part of that 15-YEAR period. (See §§4A1.1(a) and 4A1.2.)

2. 2 Points for each prior sentence of imprisonment of AT LEAST 60 DAYS resulting from an offense committed ON OR AFTER the defendant's 18th birthday not counted under §4A1.1(a) imposed within 10 YEARS of the instant offense; and

    2 Points for each prior sentence of imprisonment of AT LEAST 60 DAYS resulting from an offense committed BEFORE the defendant's 18th birthday not counted under §4A1.1(a) from which the defendant was released from confinement within 5 YEARS of the instant offense. (See §§4A1.1(b) and 4A1.2.)

3. 1 Point for each prior sentence resulting from an offense committed ON OR AFTER the defendant's 18th birthday not counted under §4A1.1(a) or §4A1.1(b) imposed within 10 YEARS of the instant offense; and

    1 Point for each prior sentence resulting from an offense committed BEFORE the defendant's 18th birthday not counted under §4A1.1(a) or §4A1.1(b) imposed within 5 YEARS of the instant offense. (See §§4A1.1(c) and 4A1.2.)

    NOTE: A maximum sum of 4 Points may be given for the prior sentences in Item 3.

Date of Imposition	Offense	Sentence	Release Date**	Guideline Section	Criminal History Pts.

*   Indicate with an asterisk those offenses where defendant was sentenced as a juvenile.

** A release date is required in only two instances:

    a. When a sentence covered under §4A1.1(a) was imposed more than 15 years prior to the commencement of the instant offense but release from incarceration occurred within such 15-year period;

    b. When a sentence counted under §4A1.1(b) was imposed for an offense committed prior to age 18 and more than 5 years prior to the commencement of the instant offense, but release from incarceration occurred within such 5-year period; and

4. Sum of Criminal History Points for prior sentences under §§4A1.1(a), 4A1.1(b), and 4A1.1(c) (Items 1,2,3). ☐

U.S. Sentencing Commission
November 22, 2010
H:\oesp\TRAINING\Worksheets\Worksheets-November2010.wpd

Worksheet C   Page 2

Defendant _____   Docket Number _____

5. <u>2 Points</u> if the defendant committed the instant offense while <u>under any criminal justice sentence</u> (e.g., probation, parole, supervised release, imprisonment, work release, escape status). (<u>See</u> §§4A1.1(d) and 4A1.2.) List the type of control and identify the sentence from which control resulted. Otherwise, enter <u>0 Points</u>.

6. <u>1 Point</u> for each prior sentence resulting from a conviction of a crime of violence that did not receive any points under §4A1.1(a), (b), or (c) because such sentence was counted as a single sentence which also included another sentence resulting from a conviction for a crime of violence. (<u>See</u> §§4A1.1(e) and 4A1.2.) Identify the crimes of violence and briefly explain why the cases are considered a single sentence. Otherwise, enter <u>0</u> Points.

_____

_____

_____

_____

_____

_____

_____

_____

_____

7. **Total Criminal History Points** (Sum of Items 4-6)

8. **Criminal History Category** (Enter here and on Worksheet D, Item 4)

Total Points	Criminal History Category
0-1	I
2-3	II
4-6	III
7-9	IV
10-12	V
13 or more	VI

Worksheet D (Guideline Worksheet)

Defendant _____   District _____

Docket Number _____

1. **Adjusted Offense Level** (From Worksheet A or B)
   If Worksheet B is required, enter the result from Worksheet B, Item 9.
   Otherwise, enter the result from Worksheet A, Item 5.

2. **Acceptance of Responsibility** (See Chapter Three, Part E)
   Enter the applicable reduction of 2 or 3 levels. If no adjustment is
   applicable, enter "0".

3. **Offense Level Total** (Item 1 less Item 2)

4. **Criminal History Category** (From Worksheet C)
   Enter the result from Worksheet C, Item 8.

5. **Terrorism/Career Offender/Criminal Livelihood/Armed
   Career Criminal/Repeat and Dangerous Sex Offender**
   (see Chapter Three, Part A, and Chapter Four, Part B)

   a. Offense Level Total

      If the provision for Career Offender (§4B1.1), Criminal
      Livelihood (§4B1.3), Armed Career Criminal (§4B1.4), or
      Repeat and Dangerous Sex Offender (§4B1.5) results in an
      offense level total higher than Item 3, enter the offense level
      total. Otherwise, enter "N/A."

   b. Criminal History Category

      If the provision for Terrorism (§3A1.4), Career Offender
      (§4B1.1), Armed Career Criminal (§4B1.4), or Repeat and
      Dangerous Sex Offender (§4B1.5) results in a criminal history
      category higher than Item 4, enter the applicable criminal history
      category. Otherwise, enter "N/A."

6. **Guideline Range from Sentencing Table**
   Enter the applicable guideline range from Chapter Five, Part A.   Months

7. **Restricted Guideline Range** (See Chapter Five, Part G)
   If the statutorily authorized maximum sentence or the statutorily
   required minimum sentence restricts the guideline range (Item 6) (see
   §§5G1.1 and 5G1.2), enter either the restricted guideline range or any   Months
   statutory maximum or minimum penalty that would modify the
   guideline range. Otherwise, enter "N/A."

   ☐ Check this box if §5C1.2 (Limitation on Applicability of Statutory Minimum Penalties in Certain Cases) is applicable.

8. **Undischarged Term of Imprisonment** (See §5G1.3)

   ☐ If the defendant is subject to an undischarged term of imprisonment, check this box and list the
      undischarged term(s) below.

   _____

   _____

Worksheet D   Page 2

Defendant _____   Docket Number _____

9. **Sentencing Options** (Check the applicable box that corresponds to the Guideline Range entered in Item 6 or Item 7,
    if applicable.)
    (See Chapter Five, Sentencing Table)

    ☐   Zone A If checked, the following options are available (see §5B1.1):

        •   Fine (See §5E1.2(a))

        •   "Straight" Probation

        •   Imprisonment

    ☐   Zone B If checked, the minimum term may be satisfied by:

        •   Imprisonment

        •   Imprisonment of at least one month plus supervised release with a condition that substitutes
            community confinement or home detention for imprisonment (see §5C1.1(c)(2))

        •   Probation with a condition that substitutes intermittent confinement, community confinement,
            or home detention for imprisonment (see §5B1.1(a)(2) and §5C1.1(c)(3))

    ☐   Zone C If checked, the minimum term may be satisfied by:

        •   Imprisonment

        •   Imprisonment of at least one-half of the minimum term plus supervised release with a condition that
            substitutes community confinement or home detention for imprisonment (see §5C1.1(d)(2))

    ☐   Zone D If checked, the minimum term shall be satisfied by a sentence of imprisonment (see §5C1.1(f))

10. **Length of Term of Probation** (See §5B1.2)

    If probation is imposed, the guideline for the length of such term of probation is: (Check applicable box)

    ☐   At least one year, but not more than five years if the offense level total is 6 or more

    ☐   No more than three years if the offense level total is 5 or less

11. **Conditions of Probation** (See §5B1.3)

    List any mandatory conditions ((a)(1)-(10)), standard conditions ((c)(1)-(14)), and any other special conditions that may be applicable:

    _____

    _____

    _____

    _____

    _____

    _____

    _____

    _____

Worksheet D

Page 3

Defendant _____   Docket Number _____

12. Supervised Release (See §§5D1.1 and 5D1.2)

a. A term of supervised release is: (Check applicable box)

☐ Required because a term of imprisonment of more than one year is to be imposed or if required by statute

☐ Authorized but not required because a term of imprisonment of one year or less is to be imposed

b. Length of Term (Guideline Range of Supervised Release): (Check applicable box)

☐ Class A or B Felony: Three to Five Year Term

☐ Class C or D Felony: Two to Three Year Term

☐ Class E Felony or Class A Misdemeanor: One Year Term

c. Restricted Guideline Range of Supervision Release

☐ If a statutorily required term of supervised release impacts the guideline range, check this box and enter the required term. _____

13. Conditions of Supervised Release (See §5D1.3)
List any mandatory conditions ((a)(1)-(8)), standard conditions ((c)(1)-(15)), and any other special conditions that may be applicable: _____
_____

14. Restitution (See §5E1.1)

a. If restitution is applicable, enter the amount. Otherwise enter "N/A" and the reason:_____
_____

b. Enter whether restitution is statutorily mandatory or discretionary: _____
_____

c. Enter whether restitution is by an order of restitution or solely as a condition of supervision. Enter the authorizing statute:
_____

15. Fines (Guideline Range of Fines for Individual Defendants) (See §5E1.2)

		Minimum	Maximum
a.	Special fine provisions		

☐ Check box if any of the counts of conviction is for a statute with a special fine provision. (This does not include the general fine provisions of 18 USC § 3571(b)(2), (d))

Enter the sum of statutory maximum fines for all such counts $_____

b. Fine Table (§5E1.2(c)(3))
Enter the minimum and maximum fines $_____ $_____

c. Guideline Range of Fines $_____ $_____
(determined by the minimum of the fine table (Item 15(b))
and the greater maximum above (Item 15(a) or 15(b)))

d. Ability to Pay

☐ Check this box if the defendant does not have an ability to pay.

Worksheet D

Page 4

Defendant _____ Docket Number _____

16. **Special Assessments** (See §5E1.3)

Enter the total amount of special assessments required for all counts of conviction:

- $25 for each misdemeanor count of conviction

- Not less than $100 for each felony count of conviction

$_____

17. **Additional Factors**

List any additional applicable guidelines, policy statements, and statutory provisions. Also list any applicable aggravating and mitigating factors that may warrant a sentence at a particular point either within or outside the applicable guideline range. Attach additional sheets as necessary.

_____

_____

_____

_____

_____

_____

_____

_____

_____

_____

_____

_____

_____

_____

_____

_____

_____

_____

_____

_____

Completed by _____ Date _____

U.S. Sentencing Commission
November 22, 2010
H:\oesp\TRAINING\Worksheets\Worksheets-November2010.wpd

Chapter 8
UNITED STATES SENTENCING GUIDELINES
ORGANIZATIONAL WORKSHEETS

Organizational Worksheet A
(Offense Level)

Defendant _____ Docket Number _____

Docket Number (Year-Sequence-Defendant No.) _____ - _____ - _____

Count Number(s) _____ U.S. Code Title & Section _____ : _____

_____ : _____

Guidelines Manual Edition Used: 20 __ (NOTE: worksheets keyed to the Manual effective November 1, 2001)

Instructions:
For each count of conviction (or stipulated offense listed at §8C2.1, complete a separate Worksheet A. Exceptions: Use only a single Worsheet A where the offense level for a group of closely related counts is based primarily on aggrregate value or quantity (See §3D1.2(d)) or where a count of conspiracy, solicitation, or attempt is grouped with a substantive count that was the sole object of the conspiracy, solicitation, or attempt (See §3D1.2(a) and (b)).

For counts of conviction (or stipulated offenses) not listed at §8C2.1, skip to Worksheet D, Item 1.

1. **Offense Level** (See §8C2.3).

    Enter the applicable base offense level and any specific offense characteristics from Chapter Two and explain the bases for these determinations. Enter the sum, the adjusted offense level, in the box provided below.

Guideline	Description	Level
_____	_____	_____
_____	_____	_____
_____	_____	_____

    If this worksheet does not cover all counts of conviction or stipulated offenses listed at §8C2.1, complete Worksheet B. Otherwise, enter this sum on Worksheet C, Item 1.

    Sum [   ]

    (Adjusted Offense Level)

    Notes: _____

    _____

    Note: Chapter Three Parts A, B, C and E, **do not** apply to organizational defendants.

[   ] Check if the defendant is convicted of a single count. In such case, Worksheet B need not be completed.

U.S. Sentencing Commission
December 17, 2001

Organizational Worksheet B
(Multiple Counts or Stipulation to Additional Offenses)

Defendant _____   Docket Number _____

Instructions

Step 1: Determine if any of the counts group. (Note: All, some, or none of the counts may group. Some of the counts may have already been grouped in the application under Worksheet A, specifically, (1) counts grouped under §3D1.2(d), or (2) a count charging conspiracy, solicitation, or attempt that is grouped with the substantive count of conviction (see §3D1.2(a)). Explain the reasons for grouping:

_____

_____

Step 2: Using the box(es) provided below, for each group of closely related counts, enter the highest adjusted offense level from the various "A" Worksheets (Worksheet A, Item 1) that comprise the group (see §3D1.3). (Note: A "group" may consist of a single count that has not grouped with any other count. In those instances, the offense level for the group will be the adjusted offense level for the single count.)

Step 3: Enter the number of units to be assigned to each group (see §3D1.4) as follows:

- One unit (1) for the group of closely related counts with the highest offense level
- An additional unit (1) for each group that is equally serious or 1 to 4 levels less serious
- An additional half unit (1/2) for each group that is 5 to 8 levels less serious
- No increase in units for groups that are 9 or more levels less serious

1. **Adjusted Offense Level for the First Group of Closely Related Counts**
   Count number(s):_____ ☐ ____(unit)

2. **Adjusted Offense Level for the Second Group of Closely Related Counts**
   Count number(s):_____ ☐ ____(unit)

3. **Adjusted Offense Level for the Third Group of Closely Related Counts**
   Count number(s):_____ ☐ ____(unit)

4. **Adjusted Offense Level for the Fourth Group of Closely Related Counts**
   Count number(s):_____ ☐ ____(unit)

5. **Adjusted Offense Level for the Fifth Group of Closely Related Counts**
   Count number(s):_____ ☐ ____(unit)

6. **Total Units** _____ (Total units)

7. **Increase in Offense Level Based on Total Units** (See §3D1.4)
1 unit:	no increase	2 1/2 - 3 units:	add 3 levels
1 1/2 units:	add 1 level	3 1/2 - 5 units:	add 4 levels
2 units:	add 2 levels	More than 5 units:	add 5 levels
   ☐

8. **Highest of the Adjusted Offense Levels from Items 1-5 Above** ☐

9. **Combined Adjusted Offense Level** (See §3D1.4)
   Enter the sum of Items 7 and 8 here and on Worksheet C, Item 1. ☐

U.S. Sentencing Commission
December 17, 2001

Organizational Worksheet C
(Base Fine, Culpability Score and Fine Range)

Defendant _____ Docket Number _____

1. **Offense Level Total**

   If Worksheet B is required, enter the combined adjusted offense level from
   Worksheet B, Item 9. Otherwise, enter the sum (the adjusted offense level) from
   Worksheet A, Item 1.

2. **Base Fine** (See §8C2.4(d))

   (a) Enter the amount from the Offense Level Fine Table (See §8C2.4(d))
   corresponding to the offense level total in Item 1 above. $_____

   (b) Enter the pecuniary gain to the organization (See §8C2.4(a)(2)). $_____

   (c) Enter the pecuniary loss caused by the organization to the extent the loss
   was caused intentionally, knowingly, or recklessly (See §8C2.4(a)(3)).
   Note: the following Chapter Two guidelines have special instructions
   regarding the determination of pecuniary loss: §§2B4.1, 2C1.1, 2C1.2,
   2E5.1, 2E5.6, and 2R1.1. $_____

   (d) Enter the amount from Item (a), (b), or (c) above, whichever is greatest. $_____

3. **Culpability Score (See §8C2.5)**

   (a) Start with five points and apply (b) through (g) below.

   (See §8C2.5(a)) | 5 |

   (b) Involvement/Tolerance (See §8C2.5(b))

   Enter the specific subdivision and points applicable. If more
   than one subdivision is applicable, use the greatest. If no
   adjustment is applicable, enter "0". $_____

   (c) Prior History (See §8C2.5(c))

   Enter the specific subdivision and points applicable. If both
   subdivision are applicable, use the greater. If no adjustment
   is applicable, enter "0". $_____

   Enter the earliest date of relevant conduct for the instant offense: _____

U.S. Sentencing Commission
December 17, 2001

Organizational Worksheet C, Page Two

Defendant _____   Docket Number _____

(d) Violation of an Order (<u>See</u> §8C2.5(d))

Enter the specific subdivision and points applicable. If both
subdivisions are applicable, use the greater. If no adjustment is
applicable, enter "0". $_____ [____]

(e) Obstruction of Justice (<u>See</u> §8C2.5(e))   [____]

If no adjustment is applicable, enter "0". $_____

(f) Effective Program to Prevent and Detect Violations of Law
(<u>See</u> §8C2.5(f))
If no adjustment is applicable, enter "0". $_____ [____]

(g) Self-Reporting, Cooperation, and Acceptance of Responsibility
(<u>See</u> §8C2.5(g))

Enter the specific subdivision and points applicable. If more than one
subdivision is applicable, use the greatest. If no adjustment is
applicable, enter "0". $_____ [____]

4. **Total Culpability Score**

Enter the total of Items 3(a) through 3(g).   _____

5. **Minimum and Maximum Multipliers** (<u>See</u> §8C2.6)

Enter the minimum and the maximum multipliers from the table at §8C2.6
corresponding to the total culpability score in Item 4 above.
<u>Note:</u> If the applicable Chapter Two guideline is §2R1.1, neither the minimum nor the
maximum multiplier shall be less than 0.75. (<u>See</u> §2R1.1(d)(2)).

(a) Minimum Multiplier   _____

(b) Maximum Multiplier   _____

Organizational Worksheet C, Page Three

Defendant _____   Docket Number _____

6.   **Fine Range** (See §8C2.7)

    (a)   Multiply the base fine (Item 2(d) above) by the minimum multiplier
            (Item 5(a) above) to establish the minimum of the fine range. Enter
            the result here and at Worksheet D, Item 4(a).

                                     Minimum of fine range $_____

    (b)   Multiply the base fine (Item 2(d) above) by the maximum multiplier
            (Item 5(b) above) to establish the maximum of the fine range. Enter
            the result here and at Worksheet D, Item 4(a).

                                    Maximum of fine range $_____

7.   **Disgorgement** (See §8C2.9)

Skip this item if any pending or anticipated civil or administrative proceeding is
expected to deprive the defendant of its gain from the offense.

    (a)   Enter the amount of pecuniary gain to the defendant from Item 2(b) above $_____

    (b)   Enter the amount of restitution already made and
            remedial costs already incurred. $_____

    (c)   Enter the amount of restitution and other remedial
            costs to be ordered by the court.
            (See §§8B1.1 and 8B1.2.) $_____

    (d)   Add Items (b) and (c) and enter the sum.

    (e)   Subtract the sum of restitution and remedial costs (Item (d))
            from the amount of pecuniary gain to the defendant (Item (a)) to
            determine undisgorged gain. Enter the result here and at Worksheet
            D, Item 4(b). Note: If the amount of undisgorged gain is less than zero, enter
            zero. $_____

U.S. Sentencing Commission
December 17, 2001

Organizational Worksheet D
(Guideline Worksheet)

Defendant _____   Docket Number _____

<u>Note</u>: Unless otherwise specified, all items on Worksheet D are applicable to **all** counts of conviction.

1. **Restitution** (<u>See</u> §8B1.1)

    a. If restitution is applicable, enter the amount. Otherwise enter "N/A" and the reason:

    _____

    b. Enter whether restitution is statutorily mandatory or discretionary:

    _____

    c. Enter whether restitution is by an order of restitution or solely as a condition of supervision. Enter the authorizing statute: _____

2. **Remedial Orders** (<u>See</u> §8B1.2), **Community Service** (<u>See</u> §8B1.3), **Order of Notice to Victims** (<u>See</u> §8B1.4)

    List if applicable. Otherwise enter "N/A".

    _____

    _____

3. **Criminal Purpose Organization** (<u>See</u> §8C1.1)

    If a preliminary determination indicates that the organization operated primarily for a criminal purpose or primarily by criminal means, enter the amount of the organization's net assets. This amount shall be the fine (subject to the statutory maximum) for all counts of conviction. $_____

4. **Guideline Range** (<u>Only</u> for counts listed under §8C2.1)

    (a) Enter the fine range from Worksheet C, Item 6 $_____ to $_____

    (b) Disgorgement (<u>See</u> §8C2.9)

    Enter the result from the Worksheet C, Item 7(e). The court shall add to the fine determined under §8C2.1 (Determining the Fine Within the Range) any undisgorged gain to the organization from the offense. $_____

5. **Counts Not Listed Under §8C2.1** (<u>See</u> §8C2.10)

    Enter the counts not listed under §8C2.1 and the statutory maximum fine for each count. The court may impose an additional fine for these counts.

    _____

    _____

U.S. Sentencing Commission
December 17, 2001

Organizational Worksheet D, Page Two
(Guideline Worksheet)

Defendant _____   Docket Number _____

6.   **Fine Offset** (See §8C3.4)

Multiply the total fines imposed upon individuals who each own at least
five percent (5%) interest in the organization by those individuals' total percentage
interest in the organization, and enter the result. The court **may** reduce the
fine imposed on a closely held organization by an amount not to exceed the fine
offset. $_____

7.   **Imposition of a Sentence of Probation** (See §8D1.1.)

(a) Probation is required if any of the following apply. Check the applicable boxes(es).

☐   (1) Probation is necessary as a mechanism to secure payment of restitution (§8B1.1), enforce a
         remedial order (§8B1.2), or ensure completion of community service (§8B1.3).

☐   (2) Any monetary penalty imposed (i.e., restitution, fine, or special assessment) is not paid in
         full at the time of sentencing and restrictions appear necessary to safeguard the defendant's
         ability to make payments.

☐   (3) At the time of sentencing the organization has 50 or more employees and does not have an
         effective program to prevent and detect violations of law.

☐   (4) Within the last five years prior to sentencing, the organization has engaged in similar
         misconduct, as determined by a prior criminal adjudication, and any part of the misconduct
         underlying the instant offense occurred after that adjudication.

☐   (5) An individual within high-level personnel of the organization or the unit of the organization
         within which the instant offense was committed participated in the misconduct underlying
         the instant offense; and that individual within five years prior to sentencing engaged in
         similar misconduct, as determined by a prior criminal adjudication; and any part of the
         misconduct underlying the instant offense occurred after that adjudication.

☐   (6) Probation is necessary to ensure that changes are made within the organization to reduce the
         likelihood of future criminal conduct.

☐   (7) The sentence imposed upon the organization does not include a fine.

☐   (8) Probation is necessary to accomplish one or more of the purposes of sentencing set forth in
         18 U.S.C. § 3553(a)(2). State purpose(s): _____

         _____

         _____

U.S. Sentencing Commission
December 17, 2001

Organizational Worksheet D, Page Three
(Guideline Worksheet)

Defendant _____ Docket Number _____

(b) Length of Term of Probation (See §8D1.2)
If probation is imposed, the guideline for the length of such term of probation is:
(Check the applicable box)

☐ (1) At least one year, but not more than five years if the offense is a felony

☐ (2) No more than five years if the offense is a Class A misdemeanor

(c) Conditions of Probation (See §§8D1.3 and 8D1.4)
List any mandatory conditions (§8D1.3), recommended conditions (§8D1.4), and any other
special conditions that may be applicable. _____

_____

_____

8. **Special Assessments** (See §8E1.1)

Enter the total amount of special assessments required for all counts of conviction. $ _____

9. **Additional Factors**

List any additional applicable guidelines, policy statements, and statutory provisions. Also list any
applicable aggravating and mitigating factors that may warrant a sentence at a particular point either
within or outside the applicable guideline range. Attach additional sheets as necessary.

_____

_____

_____

_____

_____

_____

_____

_____

_____

_____

_____

_____

Completed by _____ Date _____

U.S. Sentencing Commission
December 17, 2001